The Designation of the Individual

Expressive Usage in Biblical Narrative

Contributions to Biblical Exegesis and Theology

1. J.A. Loader, A Tale of Two Cities. Sodom and Gomorrah in the Old Testament, Early Jewish and Early Christian Traditions, Kampen, 1990.
2. P.W. van der Horst, Ancient Jewish Epitaphs. An Introductory Survey of a Millenium of Jewish Funerary Epigraphy (300 BCE-700 CE), Kampen, 1991.
3. E. Talstra, Solomon's Prayer. Synchrony and Diachrony in the Composition of 1 Kings 8, 14-61, Kampen, 1993.
4. R. Stahl, Von Weltengagement zur Weltüberwindung. Theologische Positionen im Danielbuch, Kampen, 1994.
5. J.N. Bremmer & F. García Martínez (eds.), Sacred History & Sacred Texts in Early Judaism. A Symposium in Honour of A.S. van der Woude, Kampen, 1992.
6. K. Larkin, The Eschatology of Second Zechariah. A Study of the Formation of a Mantological Wisdom Anthology, Kampen, 1994.
7. B. Aland & J. Delobel (eds.), New Testament Textual Criticism, Exegesis and Early Church History. A Discussion of Methods, Kampen, 1994.
8. P.W. van der Horst, Hellenism — Judaism — Christianity. Essays on their Interaction, Kampen, 1994.
9. C. Houtman, Der Pentateuch. Die Geschichte seiner Erforschung neben einer Auswertung, Kampen, 1994.
10. J. Van Seters, The Life of Moses. The Yahwist as Historian in Exodus-Numbers, Kampen / Louisville, KE, 1994.
11. Tj. Baarda, Essays on the Diatessaron, Kampen, 1994.
12. G.J. Steyn, Septuagint Quotations in the Context of the Petrine and Pauline Speeches of the Acta Apostolorum, Kampen, 1995.
13. D.V. Edelman (ed.), The Triumph of Elohim. From Yahwisms to Judaisms, Kampen, 1995.
14. E.J. Revell, The Designation of the Individual. Expressive Usage in Biblical Narrative, Kampen, 1996.

E.J. Revell

The Designation of the Individual
Expressive Usage in Biblical Narrative

Pharos

Kok Pharos Publishing House
Kampen – The Netherlands

CIP-GEGEVENS KONINKLIJKE BIBLIOTHEEK, DEN HAAG

© 1996, Kok Pharos Publishing House,
P.O. Box 5016, 8260 GA Kampen, The Netherlands
Lay-out by Peterjan van der Wal
Cover Design by Karel van Laar
ISBN 90 390 0161 8
ISSN 0926-6097
NUGI 632

Table of Contents

V DEFERENCE AND DISTANCE

VI THE INTERLOCUTORS

VII CONCLUSION

INDICES

Acknowledgements

The bibliography provided here is selected; it lists the studies most useful to this book, but does not exhaust its debt to the publications of others. I have also received much help through personal contacts, for which I offer my thanks here. I owe much to the help of my colleagues, particularly to Paul E. Dion's wide knowledge of the Ancient Near East and the literature on it. W. Randall Garr and Cynthia Miller offered valuable suggestions for reading in the area of pragmatics and sociolinguistics. The contribution of some who were students when I was working on the book was also important. Vince de Caen earnestly strove to instruct me on theoretical matters. Studies of various facets of the biblical text by Ahouva Shulman, Adina Levin, Marc Saunders, and Karljürgen Feuerherm provided useful information, as did the activities of Paul Sodtke and Laren Kurtz as research assistants. I am grateful to all. The project was supported by grants from the Social Sciences and Humanities Research Council of Canada, and from the Northrop Frye Centre at Victoria College in the University of Toronto. I am much obliged to these bodies for their help.

Acknowledgements

I INTRODUCTORY

Introduction

1.1 The Study

1.1.1 This study describes and analyzes the way individual characters are referred to or addressed in the biblical narratives. Much attention has been given, over the years, to the structure and meaning of personal names. However, other words or phrases are also used for reference or address, but there has been little study of their use, or of its relationship to the use of names. Nevertheless, critics do cite such matters from time to time in support of their views. It has, for instance, been argued that the designation of the prophet Elijah as "man of God" in 1K 17:18 supports the view that the later part of this chapter derives from a source different from that of the earlier, where he is referred to as "Elijah". Another critic draws meaning from the fact that, although Bathsheba marries King David in 2S 11:27, she is not referred to as his wife until 2S 12:24 (cf. 2S 12:15). Both arguments are reasonable within the rather narrow context in which they are made, but such arguments tend to be presented as self-evident, despite the very different assumptions which underlie them. This study was initiated with the intention of providing a comprehensive description of the use of designations — the names or other words or phrases used to represent the biblical characters in reference or address — against which such arguments might be evaluated.

1.1.2 As the study progressed, it became apparent that the use of designations often follows consistent patterns. This is something of a surprise in material frequently seen as put together from sources which can be recognized by their contrasting features, and as characterized by numerous errors in transmission. Nevertheless, further analysis does not refute the suggestion that the use of different designations for the same character is a matter of choice, not of chance. The extent to which the usage is patterned justifies approaching this aspect of the biblical narrative with the expectations which would be brought to the study of the spoken language of the

members of a living culture. The description is consequently based
on the assumption that the usage studied is self-consistent, and that
variation is deliberate and is likely to carry meaning. It is presented
with the intention of justifying this assumption, and therefore with
sufficient detail to allow the assumption to be evaluated. The biblical materials used are presented in English, since it is hoped that
interest in the study will not be limited to Hebrew specialists. The
translations represent my own understanding of the text, since
other translations are readily available. They are generally "literal",
in an attempt to give some idea of the Hebrew wording. The Hebrew is provided as a control.[1]

1.2 The Corpus: Delimitation and Basic Assumptions

1.2.1 The study is based on the books of Judges, Samuel, and Kings.
The poetical passages in Ju 5:2-30, 1S 2:1-10, 2S 1:18-27, 22:1-23:7,
are excluded, since poetical usage differs somewhat from that of
prose. The text so defined, referred to as "the corpus", provides an
adequate but not excessive body of more or less homogeneous
material rich in designations of individual characters. It was felt that
the material in the book of Joshua, which includes few characters
treated as individuals, would increase the bulk of the material,
without adding commensurably to the information to be obtained
from it. Consequently it was not included in the corpus, even
though this might have been expected on other grounds. The Book
of Ruth contains much material of interest within a small compass,
so its inclusion was also considered. Its usage in respect of the items
studied is very similar to that of the corpus, but this is too narrow
a basis on which to argue for the close relationship to the other
books desirable as a basis for a study of this sort.[2] The inclusion of

---

[1]   The Hebrew quoted represents the *qere* reading where one occurs, not the
ketiv, unless the difference between them is relevant to the point illustrated. Problems of translation are treated similarly; problematic words are translated traditionally, and not discussed, unless the problem affects the point at issue.

[2]   The opening words of the Book of Ruth assign the events described to the
period covered by the Book of Judges. The form of language used is "early biblical
Hebrew", as is that of the corpus, and also of much of the Pentateuch and Latter
Prophets. There is no firm basis for a more precise dating, a point underlined by
the difference of opinion recorded in Joüon, 1953:13, between that scholar and the
directorate of the École biblique. See also Sasson, 1979:240.

other material from the Book of Jeremiah, or the Books of Chronicles, was also considered, but it seemed best to restrict the study to material which has some claim to homogeneity, at least in its later development, as part of what is often seen as the "Deuteronomistic History". Other materials, both biblical and epigraphic, have been referred to, but only the designations in this corpus have been analyzed exhaustively.

1.2.2 The view governing the study, that the language of the corpus is as self-consistent as would be expected of an author today, requires a synchronic approach. The study is based on the masoretic text as we know it. The assumption that the usage of this text is self-consistent is made explicit by treating it as the work of a "narrator" who intentionally produced it in the form studied. The use of third person masculine singular pronouns to refer to this narrator is not intended to exclude the possibility that the text is the product of a woman or of a group. It is merely, like the term "narrator" itself, a convenient way to express the assumption that the language of the text is self-consistent. The topic of the study is the narrator's use of "designations". This term is understood here as including any noun or nominal structure used to address or refer to an individual which could be replaced by a pronoun, and, of course, pronouns themselves. A term in predicative or other descriptive use, which could not be replaced by a pronoun, is not included in the description unless the same term is used in ways which fit the definition.

1.2.3 The assumption that the language of the corpus is self-consistent is, of course, only a heuristic stance. It is reasonable to accept that variation or inconsistency could originate in the use of different sources, or could result from error in transmission. It is equally reasonable to claim, however, that it is rarely possible to recognize, with any certainty, cases where either phenomenon has been the cause of variation. Technical matters which support this view are mentioned in §1.8. Here, the claim can be defended on a general basis. It is extremely difficult for a critic or editor to show that an apparent error of fact in the authoritative text of a narrative was not intended by the author, even in the case of a modern novel.[3] The same must apply to an ancient work. A phenomenon like the use of "man of God" in place of "Elijah" may appear as a glaring inconsistency from one point of view, but may be easily explicable from another.

1.2.4 In the same way, the expectations which give rise to the assumption that some Hebrew form is in error are inevitably influenced by the linguistic experience and cultural background of the scholar. This may lead to the general stigmatization of a form as an error, even though it does not conflict with the usage of biblical Hebrew. The use of a feminine verb in Ju 16:19 where Delilah "called for the man and *she* cut" (ותקרא לאיש ותגלח) Samson's hair is an example. The verb is commonly changed to masculine, even though the use of a subject which represents the authority for an action, not the actor, is common enough in Hebrew, as in 1S 22:21, where the statement that "Saul killed the priests of the Lord" represents the fact that Saul ordered Doeg to do this (1S 22:18). The assumption that the verb "cut" should be masculine in Ju 16:19 may or may not be correct. The only way to evaluate it is to determine the commonness of the "subject as authority" phenomenon, and the range of its use.[4] This requires a description of usage as it actually is, based on the assumption that even apparent inconsistency may have a purpose. The same applies to other features of usage. It is thus a methodological requirement that the usage of the text be treated as self-consistent.

---

[3]   John Worthen discusses the controversy over whether an editor is justified in correcting such apparent error in the *Times Literary Supplement* for January 7th., 1994:11-12. Particular cases are discussed in Suzanne Lewis' notes 108, 222, in *A Dark Night's Work and other Stories by Elizabeth Gaskell*, ed. by Suzanne Lewis, (World Classics), Oxford: Oxford University Press, 1992.

[4]   It is, of course, familiar in English, where it is commonly used of a person who "built" an important building (or "had it built"), but not of one who arranged for another to cut a person's hair. A study of the range of its use would provide interesting sociological information.

1.3 Structure, Use, and "Meaning"

1.3.1 The views of language and its meaning on which this study is based are generally derived from standard works in pragmatics, sociolinguistics, and related areas.[5] However, the study is directed to students of the Hebrew Bible, not to linguists. It is simply a work of description, intended to show that certain features of biblical Hebrew are significant in a way that has not been formerly noticed. Words are generally used in a common sense (according to the New Shorter Oxford English Dictionary). Others, unless derived from an article cited in connection with their use, are used in accordance with Crystal, 1991. The few exceptions — words used in a technical way peculiar to this study — are explained where introduced, and can be traced through the index. The following paragraphs are intended to explain or justify, in general terms, the procedure followed in the study.

1.3.2 Studies of the structure of Hebrew tend to suggest a close relationship between structure and meaning, i.e. between form and content. A particular structure is seen as having a particular function, which constitutes its meaning. Studies of the way language is used would accept this as generally correct, but not as absolutely so. It is certainly true that a statement is usually presented by a clause of "declarative" or "statement form". A speaker may, however, choose to use a question form ("Didn't he do it" instead of "He did it"), and manipulate the context to make sure that it is understood as a statement. The relationship between a grammatical structure and its meaning is not necessarily closer than that between a lexical form and its content. A speaker or writer almost always has available, at any level of language, a choice of means for the expression of any particular thought. His intention is not necessarily evident from the form or structure used. The context in which it is used must also be taken into consideration, as with the question form used to present a statement. The importance of context is generally recognized. It "plays a crucial role in allowing syntax to be an efficient processing device" (Givón, 1983:16). Siewierska (1988: 263)

---

[5]   Those found most stimulating were Brown and Levinson, 1987, Mühlhäusler and Harré, 1990, and Parkinson, 1985.

lists "pragmatic factors" as one of the seven categories of information important to the understanding of word order. The understanding of Hebrew is likely to be improved by the attempt to
determine the relation between usage and its context.

1.3.3 Expository prose, concerned with clarity of presentation, is
unlikely to show any great variety in the sentence forms used for
any given function. Narrative prose is likely to take greater advan-
tage of the possibilities offered by the language for the dramatic
presentation of a story. Even greater use of these possibilities is likely to be made in speech, for the expression of the speaker's feelings.
An example occurs in Abner's speech in 2S 3:8. His question "Am
I a dog's head belonging to Judah?" (הראש כלב אנכי אשר ליהודה) is
clearly not a request for information; he does not even wait for a
reply. The context shows that it presents a protest such as "I am
not a dog's head..." or "You are treating me like a dog's head..."
Presumably Abner chooses a question form for this purpose because
the unusual use will draw the addressee's attention to the clause,
and encourage him to concentrate on that, rather than on others in
the speech. He thus ensures that the clause has a greater impact
than would be provided by the statement forms suggested above as
its meaning. The choice of a particular designation may similarly
reflect a speaker's attitude to what he is saying. Such choice is called
here "expressive" since it expresses the attitude of the speaker.

1.4 Expressive Choice

1.4.1 The importance of choice for the meaning of a designation is
illustrated by Abner's use of the term "dog's head" to designate
himself in 2S 3:8. It gives the speech a note of emotion which
would be lacking if he had chosen, for instance, "man" (איש) in its
place. This much can scarcely be denied, but it is not easy to evaluate the usage more precisely. In terms of translation, the meaning of
the term "dog's head" would be the term most likely to be used by
an English speaker in making a similar protest in an equivalent
socio-political situation. That is, the meaning is derived from the
context: the relationship of speaker to addressee, the fact of the protest, and the background to it, rather than from the lexical content
of the words. The context is also important for the determination
of the meaning in terms of Hebrew, but the main component of

that meaning is determined by the fact that the term "dog's head" was chosen, rather than one of the others which might have been used in such a protest. If Abner had a choice of two terms, "man" and "dog's head", the emotional content of the choice can only be stated in terms of "low" or "high". If he had a choice of a greater number of terms, the range covered by any one is correspondingly narrowed, and the emotional content of his choice can be more accurately determined.[6]

1.4.2 A good illustration of the value of choice of designation in relation to context is provided by the binary choice available in the second person pronoun used to designate an individual in French. The form *tu* is typically used in address to children and close adult friends, the form *vous* to other adults, even family members in some cases. If *vous* is used to a friend where *tu* has been the norm, the effect is not to express politeness, as does the standard use of *vous*, but to deny the existence of the friendship. The speaker's attitude to the addressee is clearly expressed by the choice of *vous*, in contrast to the established convention. A probable example of a similarly expressive choice in Hebrew occurs in Michal's scornful speech to her husband, King David, in 2S 6:20: "How noble today is the king of Israel, who exposed himself today to his ministers' maidservants" (מה נכבד היום מלך ישראל אשר נגלה היום לעיני אמהות עבדיו). Where a subject addresses or refers to King David, or either of the other kings of the divided monarchy, using the title alone as a designation, the form used is "the king" (המלך) (see §§6.8.1, 6.9.1). The title in the form "king of Israel" (מלך ישראל) is used for these kings in speech, but it is typically used by foreigners.

1.4.3 Michal is, then, using the "wrong" form for her situation, and it is reasonable to suggest that, like a French speaker using "vous" to an old friend, she is using it to present a message. The specific

---

6 Lexical value is similarly affected. "The house of PN" refers specifically to people where PN designates a king, and "the house of the king" (בית המלך) is used to refer to the building in which he lives (see §6.6.1). Where a title is not available as an alternative designation to the name, "the house of PN" is used to refer to the building, as well as to people, as in "the house of Micah" (בית מיכה) in Ju 18:22.

content of the message is debatable, but it can be classed as irony.[7] She uses the title to represent the ideal which David has failed, in her opinion, to live up to. The term "irony" can equally be applied to David's use of the same title in addressing King Saul in 1S 26:20: "The king of Israel has come out to search for a flea", and in the similar use in 1S 24:15. The term representing the ideal is contrasted with the far from ideal conduct described in the clause. As these examples show, the "meaning" of the term chosen — the value of the choice, the extent to which it is "expressive" — is determined by the situation in which the term is used, the range of terms available for use in that situation, and the extent to which the term chosen is consistent with the usage expected in that situation, or is unexpected. Earlier studies of the phenomena considered here, as Lande, 1949, typically do not give adequate attention to this range of factors.

1.5 Marked and Unmarked Usage

1.5.1 Where a particular context has been established, the use of the designation expected in it may be described as "unmarked", "default" or "standard" usage; the use of an unexpected form is "marked" or "exceptional" usage.[8] Such terminology cannot be used where no one form is dominant in a context. Where the terminology is applicable, the use simplifies description, as in the case of the form of title used for a king of the united monarchy. In the context of use by a subject, only the marked examples, the use of a title including the name of the state, need be discussed. The unmarked usage occurs wherever irony is not intended. Analysis of the situations in which it occurs can add nothing to this statement. It is sometimes said that, in a situation of this sort, the unmarked usage carries no meaning, being simply the default form, used where the speaker has no particular implications to convey. The use of the

---

[7] The specific content of such messages is equally debatable in spoken language. The classic study of such usage (Brown and Gilman, 1960), sees the usage in terms of a single contrast. Others have condemned this as obscuring the versatility of the usage. See Mühlhäusler and Harré, 1990:150-155.

[8] Mühlhäusler and Harré 1990:150-155, provides an example of the use of the terms "unmarked" and "marked" used with this value in the analysis of pronominal designations.

unmarked form does, however, show that this is the case. It thus confirms that the established relationship between speaker and addressee is unchanged, that the expected situation obtains.

1.5.2 The terms "marked" and "unmarked" apply to the use of the form in a particular context, not to the form itself. A designation may be marked in one context, unmarked in another, as may any grammatical feature (see §16.5.2). The lexical content of a designation may form part of the motivation of its use, but this is not necessarily the case, particularly where the use is marked. Just as the use of *vous* to an old friend in French only represents a denial of the situation recognized by the use of *tu*, so Michal's use of "king of Israel" in place of "the king" in address to David shows basically that the expected situation does not obtain, so the address is not to be taken at face value as the speech of a subject. "Israel" is added to the title to show this, rather than to inform the addressee of the state ruled by the king mentioned. Thus a designation may have quite different values in marked and unmarked use. The unmarked use of a title such as "the king" may recognize the status of the person designated, and so have a positive value. The marked use may be ironic, representing the ideal against which his incompetence is contrasted, and thus essentially negative.

1.5.3 It may be asked whether the choice between two designations which may be used in significant opposition is always deliberate and meaningful. The answer must be that designations do not differ from other words and phrases in this respect. Terms may contrast clearly in one aspect of their meaning, but not in another. One may say that "A house is not a home", contrasting the terms, but it is difficult to argue that there is much significance in the choice of "house" or "home" in stating one's destination. Thus the significance of the choice of one term from a contrasting pair may be considerable in some situations, but negligible in others. The general assumption made in this study is that all choice is deliberate, the assumption typically made about the choice of any word by a modern writer. The interpretation of the reason for the choice is necessarily subjective, whether a text is of ancient or of modern origin. The problem is complicated by the fact that, in spoken language, the basis for expressive choice is not always clear, even to those generally familiar with the language and culture in question.[9] However, such difficulties do not provide a reason for abandoning the attempt. The choosing of forms of expression intended to enhance the impact of a communication must be a characteristic of speakers and writers of any period.

1.6 Speech and Narration

1.6.1 The basic work of the study is, then, to determine the situational contexts in which each term is used, and the range of terms which may be used in the same context. The decision as to which contexts are or are not "the same" is thus of major importance. The first distinction to be made is that between speech, quoting the words which characters in the narrative are shown as uttering, and narration, describing these characters and the events in which they are concerned. These two types of language reflect different conventions to some extent, and so must be treated as providing different contexts. Speech is generally introduced by some form of the root אמר, and this objective guide has been followed to the extent of treating written and other indirect communication so introduced (as in 1K 21:9) as the "speech" of the originator. However, a form of אמר is occasionally used where what follows differs in form from the original words of the speaker, and occasionally does not appear before direct speech, so the decision as to whether material should be classed as "speech" or not is sometimes based on other features.[10]

---

[9]   For example, one servant gives a letter to another with the words "pour votre maître", but the recipient, reporting to his master, states that the words were "pour ton maître" (A. Dumas, *Les Trois Mousquetaires*, chapter xxx; vol. I, pp. 346-7 in the "nouvelle édition", Paris: Michel Lévy frères, 1860). An explanation of the shift in number could easily be suggested, but the adequate support of such a suggestion would need considerable knowledge of usage both in the days of the author and in the days he depicts.

[10] The words after "saying" (לאמר) in 2S 15:8 and 1K 1:51 do not seem to be direct speech, see §§8.3n, 24.2.7n. See also §6.9.2, and the discussion of "semi-indirect" speech in Goldenberg 1991:81-83. Introductions which do not use אמר are discussed in Meier 1992:91-94 with reference to "direct discourse" which has a slightly more restrictive definition than "speech".

1.6.2 Material classified as "narration" is spoken of as representing the usage of the narrator. Speech is spoken of as the usage of the character represented as speaking. This *naiveté* — both speech and narration are the product of the narrator — is justified by evidence that, in some cases at least, the speech of a character was intended to represent what would be expected from that character in that situation, and so may reflect attitudes different from those of the narrator (see §7.3). It is assumed that this was generally the case, that the common approach to the material as a record of the speech and actions of particular individuals is consistent with the narrator's intention. Nevertheless, it does occasionally appear that a character has been provided with words reflecting the narrator's point of view, not that to be expected from the individual in question. Possible cases occur in 1K 21:4 (see §4.12.1), 2S 11:11 (see §6.8.3), and Ju 11:19 (see §11.5.3), 1K 14:2 (see §13.2.2n).

1.7 The Classification of Context

1.7.1 The attempt to classify the context in which a designation is used requires the selection, for the framework of the description, of those few features which appear to condition the choice of designation in the widest range of cases, from among the many which might affect the usage. Some of those chosen can be identified simply by objective observation, as can the subject of a clause, the choice of which conditions the choice of designation for an individual who is object or goal of the action of that clause. The relative status of speaker and addressee, which may condition the speaker's choice of designations, can be assessed on a reasonably objective basis, see §2.5. A speaker's choice of designation may also be conditioned by the nature and purpose of the speech. This can often be adequately determined simply by classification of the clause as marked by a modal verb, or an interrogative particle, or as "other", i.e. as a modal, interrogative, or declarative clause. This generally indicates that the clause presents a request, question, or statement, but form does not necessarily determine function, as noted in §1.3.2.[11]

---

[11] I have used the term "request" instead of the usual "command", as an important proportion of the clauses with imperative verbs which have to be considered in this study occur in speech by a subordinate to a superior. This term is also better suited to the functional class as a whole, which includes many clauses which

Classification of the function of a speech can occasionally be made on other objective grounds, as the use of a form of the verb "to command" (צוה) in the introduction, which marks a speech as a "request". In most cases, however, the decision that a clause does not have the function suggested by its form is based on an interpretation of the context.[12]

1.7.2 Another aspect of "intention" which is even less amenable to objective assessment is the relative importance, to the speaker or the narrator, of the material presented. The term used here for this factor is "immediacy". Material which is a serious concern for the speaker or narrator, material central to the message which he wishes to convey, is "immediate". Material which is of little concern, which provides detail ancillary, not central, to the intended message, is "non-immediate".[13] In spoken language, a speaker can indicate that words or larger structures are immediate, of particular importance to the communication, by variation in prosodic features, such as tempo, pitch or loudness. Variation in other features, such as word order, may also be used, and particular grammatical structures may be chosen for the same purpose. Some features of this sort have been recognized in Hebrew. Unfortunately for the present purpose, studies of these have usually concentrated on the basic task of exploring structure and its unmarked use. Little has been said

---

do not have imperative verbs. The problem has, of course, been noted by others (see the discussion of the term "mand" in Lyons, 1977, 1:130), but no better term seems to be in general use.

[12] This is also essentially the case in spoken language, although there an addressee is likely to have a better appreciation of the signals provided in the context than is possible for a scholar in the case of an ancient language.

[13] In the neat phrasing of Hopper and Thompson (1980:280), the contrast is between "the material which supplies the main points of the discourse" and "that part of a discourse which does not immediately and crucially contribute to a speaker's goal, but which merely assists, amplifies, or comments on it". The terms "foreground" and "background" are used there. In the study of biblical Hebrew, these terms generally refer to features of the use of clause structures characteristic of narrative prose. This is referred to here as "grammatical" foreground or background. The terms "immediacy" and "non-immediacy" or "distance" are used here for the more general phenomenon to avoid confusion.

about marked uses.[14] The features treated in these studies, the use of the different types of clauses, and variations in their word order, are often of interest here. However, other features are more frequently cited as reflecting the relative importance of material, as showing that it is immediate or is not so.

1.7.3 The view taken here is that, where information is "immediate for" or "central to the concerns of" a speaker, or the narrator, particular features can be used to "draw attention to it", and so ensure that the addressee concentrates on it. It is thus "given prominence", "highlighted", or "foregrounded". Some features may be chosen to mark information as "non-immediate", "distanced" or "background", but this is less common. The concerns of the speaker are determined from the interpretation of the speech in its context. Those of the narrator, are determined from interpretation of the narrative context, and of the narrator's purpose in presenting the story. In this context, the term "the narrator's focus" is used, following the view that the narrator tends to present the narrative as if with a camera, concentrating on one actor or one scene at a time (see Berlin, 1983:44-46). An actor on whom the narrator's focus is concentrated in a passage is called the "thematic actor" in that passage. It would be relatively easy to formulate largely objective guidelines for the recognition of a thematic actor, although this is not attempted here. The objective determination of the narrator's focus would be more difficult, but, as used here, the term is rarely likely to be controversial.[15]

---

[14]   The studies of greatest value to the present topic are Lode, 1984, 1989, Muraoka 1985, Longacre 1989, Van der Merwe 1991. An example of the "marked" use of one the features studied in these is discussed in §3.4.3.

[15]   The thematic actor indicated by the narrator's focus is typically the character most frequently represented in a passage as subject of a clause and most commonly referred to by pronouns. Other characters in the context are typically distinguished by nominal reference. "Thematic actor" is thus a sub-class of what is called "topic" as used in Givón, 1983, so that the features noted there as indicators of topic continuity also distinguish the thematic actor (cf. Givón, 1983:8, 18). According to de Regt, 1993:151, a speaker "identifies/empathizes with" a character so distinguished, a suggestion which does not seem to fit the common meaning of those terms. For methods of distinguishing the narrator's purpose, see Longacre 1989:13-19.

1.7.4 The view that a particular feature is used to mark material as immediate can be supported, to some extent, by the demonstration that different features to which this function is ascribed are used in the same way, or in similar situations. The claim that the features in question mark the relative importance of material derives in part from the view that variation in any feature carries meaning. In precise terms, the claim made of such features is that, "If these features are not examples of free variation, their most probable function is to show that a word or a larger structure is either central or peripheral to the concerns of the speaker or narrator". Some other explanation of the features may ultimately prove more satisfactory, but, in default of evidence that they arise through error, they do require explanation. The alternative requires an assumption of free variation to an extent which study of spoken language shows to be unlikely.

1.8 The Question of Error

1.8.1 The programme just outlined must obviously deal with the possibility that a designation may result from scribal error, or may originate in a source in which usage differed from the general pattern. The question of error is intractable. Expressive usage of the kind described is virtually impossible to represent, without extensive paraphrase, in the language of a society which has no equivalent, as may be seen from an English translation of any French novel. It is probable that readers not attuned to the usage would often fail to notice the variation of form. It is doubtful whether any large proportion of a typical audience notices that the (historically) singular and plural forms of the second person pronoun are used in Shakespeare's plays in a way similar to their use in French. It is consequently unreasonable to expect (at least without the support of a study devoted to the question) that the Greek, or any other translation, should reproduce accurately any features of expressive usage which occur in the Hebrew text.[16] A knowledge of standard

---

[16]   Apart from this general consideration, it might well be argued that the language of the corpus is "early biblical Hebrew". The use of two forms of first person pronoun characteristic of this usage (see §26) was abandoned well before the time of the Greek translation. Other expressive features may also have been lost or changed. Cf. the information provided in Lindhagen, 1950:59, on the replacement

usage, such as is provided by grammars, is not adequate for the recognition of errors unless it is assumed that the writer never departs from the standard to secure an effect. It is, then, difficult to find a firm basis for the declaration that any particular form results from error. However, there seems no good reason to believe that the number of errors in the corpus is large.[17]

1.8.2 As regards sources, the general consistency of the usage in the corpus suggests that, as far as the features of interest here are concerned, if the usage of a source did originally differ from the general pattern, it was changed to fit it. There is, in fact, evidence that this was done, assuming that source material has been correctly identified. Where the narrator uses a title alone to designate a king of Judah, the form used is "the king" (המלך). For a king of the northern kingdom, the title "king of Israel" (מלך ישראל) is used, including the name of the state (as does the title used to designate a foreign king), unless the events described occur within the kingdom (see §5.2.1). The usage of speech shows that the form of the title used for the king of Judah is that used by any subject for his own king; the form which includes the name of the state is that used by a speaker for the ruler of a state of which he is not a citizen, as is the case in English and other languages. It is inconceivable that the title "king of Israel" would have been used, by a writer who was a citizen of Israel, as the regular means of reference either to the then king of that state, or to a former one. If the "political" portions of 1 Kings 20 did originate in the north, as is often suggested, the title

---

of third person deferential forms in the corpus by language more conformable to Greek usage.

[17] This is said of errors in the sense of forms unacceptable in terms of the usage of the corpus. These are not numerous, even in the notorious text of the Book of Samuel. The question of errors in relation to some earlier form of text is a quite different matter. For this study, the most important part of Barthélemy's judicious article on the masoretic text of Samuel is its closing caveat against the assuming, on the basis of the disturbed textual history of the text as seen through the witnesses to it, that anything unexpected in the masoretic form of the Hebrew text must result from error. (Barthélemy, 1980:43-4).

used to designate King Ahab must have been adapted to the Judaean
or "normative" viewpoint of the narrator.[18]

1.8.3 The accounts of the capture of Jerusalem and of King Zedekiah can be used as a practical example of the points just made. The
accounts which occur in 2K 25:1-7, Jer 39:1-7 and Jer 52:4-11 clearly
have a common basis, but the chapters in which they are set differ
each from the other. The account of these events, and much of
what follows, is closely similar in 2 Kings 25 and Jeremiah 52, but
the material which they do not share shows that the interests and
intentions of the narrator were not the same in both. If so, there is
no reason to suppose that their accounts of the events in question
should have been identical. Differences may not always have been
intentional, but it is not possible to be certain where error has occurred. It is often assumed that 2K 25:3 must originally have included "in the fourth month" (בחדש הרביעי) as do Jer 39:2, 52:6 (see
Cogan and Tadmor, 1988:315), but this view is opposed in Barthélemy, 1982:423. A verb could well be missing at the beginning of 2K
25:4, but interpretation is possible without it.[19] One could even
argue that the unusual syntax of this passage mirrors the confusion
of the participants described. The pronoun in "he went" (וילך, 2K
25:4) has no immediate antecedent, but there is no doubt as to its
referent. King Zedekiah is the thematic character in the passage, and
"the king" is mentioned shortly before the clause in question, and
shortly after.[20] The initial clause in 2K 25:7 must have been deliberately constructed in its present form, different from that of Jer
39:6, 52:10. If so, it is reasonable to argue that the use of plural

---

[18] Where the full title (as "Ahab King of Israel", 1K 20:2) was not used, usage
typical for kings of Judah would require the name (and so "Ahab") or title and
name (and so "King Ahab"), see §9.

[19] "Way" (דרך) could be understood as adverbial, head of the predicate of a
verbless clause; some verb of motion might be implied by such an adverbial, (see
GKC 119.ee, gg), allowing a translation such as "All the men of war (were on/left
on) the way of the gate..."

[20] Commentators often supply a designation of the king in this verse, and usually
some form of the verb "flee" (ברח), as occurs (in an unexpected form) in Jer 52:7
(as Cogan and Tadmor, 1988:317, who suggest both). Even if the two verses were
originally identical, however, the reconstruction of their original form is quite
uncertain, since they are unlikely to have been identical to Jer 39:4.

verbs in this and the preceding clause (where the Jeremiah passages have singular forms) was also deliberate, intended to give greater impact to the use of the singular, representing the king of Babylon, in the following clauses, which recount the blinding of Zedekiah (after his children had been slaughtered in his sight) and his exile in chains.[21] There can thus be no certainty that any one of these verses now stands in a form different from that in which the narrator used it. There is, equally, no certainty that the verses have not been changed, but this is a possibility. One of the purposes of this study is to explore the extent to which the usage of such examples, taken as intentional, can be understood as reflecting stable conventions.

1.9 The Question of Subjectivity

1.9.1 The fact that a certain proportion of the argument presented in this study is subjective is so obvious that it scarcely requires the attention given above. Some passages of this introduction may seem to indicate that any feature of the text will be made to conform to the writer's views. The justification for this attitude has been offered above: the probability that a particular form is an error can only be gauged by assessing the ways in which it could be understood as conforming to acceptable usage. The effort to see a suspect form as acceptable usage no doubt leads to the interpretation of a number of errors in that light, just as the pursuit of other views has led, in some cases, to the interpretation of acceptable usage as error. Excess on one side or the other can be avoided with certainty only by ignoring suspect use. This study relies on an objective basis as far as is possible.[22] That it must go beyond that arises from the nature of the project.

---

[21] Where a group with its leader is in question, the use of the plural does not imply that the leader is not acting, and the use of the singular does not necessarily imply that he is acting alone, but rather highlights the action. See §17.4.

[22] Undoubtedly computer assisted analysis of the text such as that being developed by Prof. Talstra will improve the objective basis of interpretation. No doubt a programme developed for the analysis of the features studied here would provide a much more reliable analysis of the context of use. A part of the purpose of this study is to show that such an initiative would be worth taking.

1.9.2 Interpretation is put forward in the study to show the basis for conclusions reached, and to show that the usage studied can be understood as self-consistent. These interpretations are not particularly clear cut. The same feature may be interpreted as having more than one value (cf. the discussion of the "introductory" or "highlighting" functions of designations in §4.13.2), and several features may be said to contribute to the same result (see §4.4.1 on 1S 30:18, §4.12.1 on Ju 4:21). The text can be read in a multiplicity of ways, depending on the assumptions and interests brought to the reading, and no interpretation can be said to be "right" or "wrong" save within the limits imposed by such assumptions or interests. It is unreasonable to say that one particular feature carries one particular meaning and no other. This study is concerned to demonstrate that designations present linguistic signals which ought to be taken into consideration in any interpretation, rather than with the interpretation of individual examples of those signals. The claims made are: that the high level of consistency typically visible in the use of designations requires that the motivation of their use be investigated; that the most probable explanation of it is to be found by assuming that designations are used in biblical Hebrew much as they are in other languages; that apparent inconsistency of usage should therefore be assumed to result from deliberate choice for expressive contrast, and be treated as error only as a last resort.[23]

---

[23] The elegant and erudite discussion of subjective interpretation in the Introduction and the Synthesis and Conclusion of the first volume of Fokkelman's masterly work on the books of Samuel (Fokkelman, 1981) goes far beyond what is said here. Much of it is nevertheless applicable to this study, despite its different purpose.

The Structure of Society and
the Designation of Its Members

2.1 Introduction

Three sets of categories appear to be used to describe the social position of characters in the narratives of the corpus. One places the character in a general way, in terms of sex and of other broad social categories. A second indicates kinship, and other forms of personal relationship, with other members of the society. A third deals with occupation and similar characteristics. More than one term from any category may be used of the same person; a character may be described both as a man (אִישׁ) and a "lad" (נַעַר). It is assumed here that terms which contrast in one situation may not do so in all, just as in English (as described in §1.5.3). The use of potentially contrasting terms depicts the individual from different viewpoints — viewpoints which should be evident from other uses of the terms.

2.2 General Categorization

2.2.1 The terms in this group represent the basic social categories: "man" (אִישׁ), "woman" (אִשָּׁה), "child" (יֶלֶד), "lad" (נַעַר), "lass" (נַעֲרה). Little personal knowledge of an individual is required for categorization on this scale, which is concerned with such features as sex, age, and dependency. The question of one's sex, and of whether or no one is dependent on employment by others for one's livelihood, can be answered by any observer. Categories based on age may be used for legal purposes, but an accurate knowledge of a person's age can not be obtained simply by observation. Consequently, apart from legal situations, age categories generally have indistinct boundaries, even in our day, when classification as child, teenager or adult often seems to depend on the context in which the person is described. It is not surprising, then, that terms often translated by English words which imply categorization by age may be used over a wide age-range in Hebrew.

2.2.2 *"Man"* (אִישׁ) *and "woman"* (אִשָּׁה) The Hebrew terms for "man" (אִישׁ) and "woman" (אִשָּׁה) basically carry the sex distinction indicated by the translation. They are generally used of persons who are adult and independent, in the sense that they are married, or of age to marry, and are not employed by others. The extent to which either of these features is relevant, however, is determined by other words used in the context. Both words are often bound to a name or a personal pronoun, in which case they function as personal relationship terms corresponding to "husband" and "wife", as described below.

2.2.3 *"Child"* (ילד) The Hebrew ילד is based on the root used to present the idea of bearing or engendering a child. It basically denotes a person seen in relation to parents. It usually corresponds to the English "child" in the sense of a person too young to marry, but, as in English, it has no specific reference to age. A person's children can be of any age. In 1K 12:8 and following, adults called on for advice are referred to as "children" (ילדים) in contrast to "old men" (זקנים). The term "old man" (זקן) is often used to designate a member of government at any level, an "elder" or "counsellor", and so carries implications of experience. The "old men" are "the counsellors who had served his (King Rehoboam's) father Solomon" (הזקנים אשר היו עמדים את פני שלמה אביו).[1] The use of the term "child" in 1K 12:8, of those whom the king preferred as advisers, can be seen as suggesting their intimacy with the king as the reason for his preference. They are "the children (his childhood playmates) who had grown up with him, who were those who stood before him" (הילדים אשר גדלו אתו אשר העמדים לפניו). Since the basic meaning of the word "child" relates the person designated to his parents, these younger advisers are also pictured as still living with their parents, and so lacking experience of the world, and of decision-making.[2]

---

[1]   The term "elder" (זקן) is used in the plural in the corpus to denote a group, as here. It is used descriptively in the singular, but not as a designation.

[2]   The antonym usually contrasted with "old man" is "lad" (נער). This term implies dependency on an employer, not on parents. Its use would have presented those designated as servants, not as companions, see §2.2.6. The term "lad" also carries implications of inexperience, but may not have suggested lack of knowledge

2.2.4 "Lad" (נער) The term "lad" (נער) basically indicates a male whose social position is subordinate, either because he is young, or because he is a servant, or is similarly dependent on an employer.[3] It is used over the same age range as "child" (ילד), but differs from that term in that it does not view the person designated in the context of his family. Thus Samson, though unborn, is called a "lad" in connection with his life's vocation as Nazirite (Ju 13:5). Ichabod is called a "lad" where named by his mother, who is dying in childbirth (1S 4:21). Hannah refers to her son Samuel as a "lad" where she speaks of his leaving the family when he is weaned (1S 1:22).[4] Samuel is referred to as a "lad" several times in the following narrative, where he serves in the temple under Eli.

2.2.5 The term "lad" is used of sons by a speaker addressing their fathers, as of Jesse's sons in 1S 16:11, or David's in 2S 13:22. Presumably this views them as subordinate to the father, but as independent of the family. Where Hannah uses the term "lad" of her own son, she can be seen as using a distanced term, deliberately avoiding the reference to relationship implicit in the terms "son" or "child", and so restraining her emotion. A similar explanation could be applied to David's use of the term "lad" for Absalom (as in 2S 14:21, 18:5) and to other uses (see §14.3.2-3). The distinction be-

---

of the world to the same extent as "child". The interpretation of "old men" and "children" in this passage which is followed here is consistent with that in Würthwein, 1977:154. Other views are discussed on pp. 154-5 there.

[3]   This definition differs from that in Stähli, 1978:275-6, chiefly in the claim that the "lad" is viewed outside the context of his natural family, which Stähli does not see as significant, and in not seeing marital status as significant (at least in the corpus), while Stähli finds it so. Probably these differences arise mainly from the fact that Stähli is interested in a context-free definition, whereas the present discussion attempts to place the word within a semantic field. Particular aspects of the meaning of "lad" are discussed in Avigad, 1987:205, MacDonald, 1976, Rainey, 1981:122-123.

[4]   Compare Gen 21:8, where Isaac is called a "child" by the narrator in connection with his weaning, where he is shown as growing up in the family. The different view taken in Barilko, 1982, of these passages (as of others discussed here), is supported by the suggestion that "the lad was a lad" (והנער נער, 1S 1:24) shows that Samuel was, for Hannah, "the lad of all lads". This seems to me inconsistent with the lack of the article on the second word. I would suggest the translation "the lad became a servant".

tween the terms used for male infants seems to be, then, that "son" (בן) indicates a specific personal relationship to either parent (see §2.3.2), "child" (ילד) views the infant as part of a family, and "lad" (נער) views him without reference to his family.

2.2.6 The term "lad" (נער) implies that the person designated, though independent of his family, is dependent in the sense that he is a servant, employed by, or otherwise under the control of, another, as is the case with "the lad" Samuel in relation to Eli in 1S 2:11. Where there is evidence of age, it can be seen that "lad" is usually used of young men, but this is not necessarily the case. Ziba, called a "lad" in 2S 9:9, 16:1, 19:18, had many children according to 2S 9:10.[5] The term sometimes appears to imply weakness or inexperience as much as youth, as with Gideon's son, who is said to have feared to act the part of a "man" (איש, Ju 8:21), because he was a "lad" (נער, Ju 8:20). A similar contrast between "man" and "lad" occurs in 1S 17:33, and Solomon requests God's support in carrying out his duties as king because he is a "young lad" (ואנכי נער קטן, 1K 3:7).[6] Where no contrast is intended, the designation of a character as both "man" and "lad" presumably shows that, like Ziba, he is adult, but dependent. Thus in 1K 11:28, Jeroboam is described as a "man",[7] but Solomon sees him as a "lad", a subordinate. He recognizes good qualities in him, and so appoints him to a position of authority. As a result, Jeroboam was a "servant" (עבד, a subordinate with a personal relationship with Solomon, see §2.3.7), when he rebelled against the king (1K 11:26).

2.2.7 Cases where the term "lad" occurs in a military context suggests to some that it denotes a member of a class of young men of

---

[5]   Avigad, 1987:205 sees the term "lad" as a title in Ziba's case, indicating an important functionary, such as the steward or agent of a landowner, although the exact function is not known. He notes the seals using this title, which is translated "intendant" in Lemaire, 1988:221, reflecting similar views. This is perfectly compatible with the view taken here, that "lad" denotes a subordinate, regardless of age.

[6]   Where "lad" is used in connection with a professional title, as with the prophet of 2K 9:4, or the priest of 1S 2:13, it may be used with the connotations of inexperience suggested above, and so have almost the meaning of "apprentice".

[7]   איש, he is also called גבור חיל, a "powerful" or perhaps "competent" man.

rank, who formed the backbone of the army.[8] The reference to "four hundred men (who were) lads" (ארבע מאות איש נער, 1S 30:17) seems to imply a class when compared with "a man (who is) a prophet" (איש נביא, Ju 6:8). Nevertheless, the suggestion seems unlikely. A "lad" may act as "squire", carrying his master's equipment (Ju 9:54, etc.), but most of the tasks "lads" are shown as performing do not suggest high status. They function as lookouts (2S 13:34), messengers (2S 1:5), or as porters, to fetch Saul's spear (1S 26:22) or carry Naaman's gift (2K 5:22). A "lad" guided the blind Samson for the amusement of the Philistines (Ju 16:26). The task of execution (2S 1:15, 4:12) or assassination (2S 13:29, 18:15) is turned over to "lads". No doubt many young men in the position of "lad" came from good families, as did Samuel, and David, but the term does not imply such origin. A "lad" may attain a relatively high position in society, as in the case of Ziba (2S 16:1-4) and Gehazi (2K 8:4), but his importance derives from his employer. The majority of the people termed "lad" belong to the lowest socio-economic class, called here the servant class, and the term "lad" is often suitably translated "servant". The phrase "man (who is a) lad" probably indicates an adult male of the servant class, just as "A woman (who is) a concubine" denotes a married woman (originally) of servant status (see אשה פילגש in §2.3.5).

2.2.8 *"Lass"* (נערה) The terms glossed "lad" and "lass" are morphologically masculine and feminine forms derived from the same base. The term "lass" is used in the corpus of a married woman (a concubine, see §2.3.5) seen in association with her father in Ju 19:3, etc., (see §14.2.3, and cf. Deut 22:15, 16, 19). It is also used of women attendant on Abigail when she goes with David's servants to be-

---

[8] The most enthusiastic presentation of this view is in J. MacDonald, 1976. However, the term "lad" does not, by itself, certainly denote a soldier or a person of rank in any passage in the corpus. The use of "lads" (הנערים) in 2S 2:14 is no doubt jocular, as is "entertain us" (וישחקו לפנינו, cf. Ju 16:25). The use of "lad" in 2K 19:6 for the king of Assyria's envoys (all officials of the highest rank, see Cogan and Tadmor, 1988:229-230, on 2K 18:17) is presumably intended to belittle them and the threat they represent. The usual term for a king's ministers is "servants" (עבדים, see §2.3.8).

come his wife.[9] A girl captured by the Aramaeans on a raid into Israel, who is presumably a slave in legal terms, is referred to as a "lass" in 2K 5:2, 4. This suggests that the term "lass" is indeed used as the feminine counterpart of "lad", denoting a woman in a subordinate position, without implications as to family associations, rank, or legal status.

2.3 Relationship

2.3.1 Terms in this group categorize one individual through relationship to another. This may be a blood relationship, natural kinship, or a relationship established through a formal agreement, through which one may join the family as kin by marriage, or join the household as a servant. Categorization in this way places the individual within a particular subdivision of the community, and so indicates his loyalties, and those from whom he may expect support. Information about the relationships of important people is likely to be important to those who have dealings with them or their dependents, and so to be public knowledge, and available for use in categorization.

2.3.2 *Natural kinship* The kinship terms used in the corpus refer to natural kin within one degree of lineal or collateral relationship: "father" (אב), "mother" (אם), "son" (בן), "daughter" (בת), "brother" (אח), "sister" (אחות), "uncle" (דוד). More distant degrees (in the few cases in which they are specifically named) are referred to by combinations of these terms. In describing lineal relationship, one degree (or more) may be ignored, so that a grandfather may be referred to as "father", a grandson as "son", and plural forms of "father" and "son" are often used with the meaning "ancestors" and "descendants". In addition to the common terms for offspring, there are specific terms for "firstborn": masculine בכור, feminine בכירה. Other children may be graded by using words for "small" (קטנה, צעיר), or the cardinal numerals, with משנה replacing the usual שני

---

9   1S 25:42. Her attendants are "lads" in 1S 25:19, where she sets out to attempt to forestall David's attack on her homestead. "Lasses" also attend Rebecca on her way to marry Isaac (Gen 24:61), and Pharaoh's daughter walking beside the Nile (Exod 2:5). The "servant" (אמה, see §2.3.9) who appears in Exod 2:5 may be one of the "lasses", but could be a servant attendant on them.

as "second". (The various terms are used in 1S 8:2, 14:49, 16:11, 17:13, 2S 3:2-5, 1K 16:34).

2.3.3 These kinship terms are used in the corpus almost exclusively to present a relationship between individuals. In this case they are bound to a noun or pronoun which designates the other member of the dyad. The terms "father", "son" and "brother" may be used where there is no kinship, particularly in address, (as their feminine counterparts no doubt could be, cf. Song 4:9 etc.). The intention seems to be to suggest that the relationship so designated approximates the ideal of the family relationship named, or ought to do so. Where "father" or "son" is used, this is, or should be, a close and benevolent relationship between a senior and a junior. Where "brother" is used, the relationship is between equals. In "sons of the prophets" (בני הנביאים), the term "son" presumably implies junior status, at least in comparison to the more important prophets designated by name. Thus one of the "sons of the prophets" mentioned in 2K 9:1 is referred to as a "lad" (נער) in 2K 9:4.[10]

2.3.4 *Kinship by marriage* A spouse is characteristically referred to with the word "man" or "woman" bound to a name or pronoun indicating the partner, as "Elkanah her husband" (אלקנה אישה, 1S 1:8) or "Uriah's wife" (אשת אוריה, 2S 11:26).[11] Special terms are available to designate lineal relationships resulting from marriage, as "husband's father" (חם, 1S 4:19, 21; the feminine equivalent occurs in the Book of Ruth), wife's father (חותן), son or daughter by marriage (חתן, כלה). These are also typically used with a name or pronoun designating the other member of the dyad so related. The terms for son or daughter by marriage are not only used as relation-

---

[10] The same usage may be found in "sons of the levites" in 1 Chron 15:15, but other uses of this phrase and "sons of the priests", appear to refer simply to descent. The more general use of "sons" to designate members of a class with no connotations of junior status, as "sons of the exile" (בני הגולה, the returned exiles, Ezra 4:1) seems to be a feature of late biblical Hebrew. In contrast, the use of "son" with the sense of "possessing a quality", as in בן בליעל "son of worthlessness, scofflaw", see §2.4.5) is early.

[11] An alternative word for the male partner, בעל, used in the Pentateuch (where "man" is also used with this value), and in some poetic and prophetic texts, occurs in the corpus only in 2S 11:26 (see §13.3.6).

ship terms in this way, but also with no following name or pronoun, in the sense of "bridegroom" and "bride".

2.3.5 *"Concubine"* (פילנש) The term "concubine" evidently denotes
a woman of "servant" status taken as a wife.[12] "Concubine" is
treated as a different category from "woman" (אשה) in the sense of
"wife" in 2S 5:13, 19:6, 1K 11:3. However, the term "her man" is
used for the husband of a "concubine" in Ju 19:3, and "woman" is
similarly used of a concubine in relation to her husband outside the
corpus.[13] The probable reason is that "concubine", like "lad" is a
designation of status.[14] Where the female partner is a "concubine",
her husband is "master" from the viewpoint of status. In this sense,
"concubine" contrasts with "woman" in the sense of "wife". However, from the point of view of personal relationship, "master" and
"concubine" are "husband" and "wife". "Concubine" also does not
contrast with "woman" in the sense of "adult female", and so may
be used in apposition to it, as in אשה פילנש, "a woman (who is) a
concubine" (Ju 19:1, also 2S 15:16, 20:3).

2.3.6 *Master-servant relationship* The term glossed "master" here is
אדון, also translated "lord" where this seems the more suitable English usage. It designates the superior in a master-servant relationship.
It is almost always used as a relationship term, bound to a name or
pronoun indicating the other member of the dyad. This subordinate
member of the dyad is termed "servant" (עבד where male, אמה or
שפחה where female. There is generally no need to specify the gender in the discussion in this study). The term "master" may be used
of the king, or of a man of a lower rank in society, as is frequently

---

[12]   Abimelek's mother is called both "concubine" (Ju 8:31) and "servant" (אמה, Ju
9:18, although the term here may be chosen mainly for its derogatory value). The
narrator refers to the levite as "master" (אדון) in reference to his "concubine" in Ju
19:26, 27, a term typically used only where the subordinate is a "servant" or "lad".
In the Pentateuch, Bilhah, called a "servant" (both אמה and שפחה are used in Gen
30:3, 4) is also called "concubine" (Gen 35:22). On these terms for "maidservant",
see §2.3.9.
[13]   As for Keturah, Gen 25:1, Bilhah, Gen 30:4. Zilpah, like Bilhah, a "servant"
(but only called שפחה, Gen 29:24, 30:9, 10, 12, 35:26), is called "woman" in relation to her husband (Gen 30:9, 37:2), but not "concubine".
[14]   Neither appears as a legal classification in the Pentateuch.

the case in deferential address, both in the corpus and in epigraphic sources.[15] The "servant" in this case may be subordinate to the master by reason of some formal relationship, or may assume that position metaphorically for purposes of ingratiating himself with the master, or persuading him to a particular course of action. The feminine counterpart, "mistress" (גבירה) which is rare in the corpus, was presumably used in the same way.[16]

2.3.7 The status of "servant" is a position of privilege, indicating a firm personal relationship with the master. This relationship involves mutual responsibilities. The "servant" provides service; the "master" gives support and protection in return. Such a relationship gives the "servant" of a person of rank a certain status in the community, derived from the power and prestige of his master, as is the case with the "lad".[17] The Hebrew words translated "servant" here do not have the pejorative connotations of "slave" in English. The terms "master-servant" and "father-son" may be used of the same relationship. Both sets of terms are used to represent the relationship between God and Israel.[18] Saul calls David "my son" in a number

---

[15] For Hebrew epigraphic sources, see Davies, 1991. For the Moabite inscription of Mesha, see Jackson and Dearman, 1989. Deferential terms are used in the Lachish letters, the Arad Inscriptions and in the Meṣad Hashavyahu plea (studied in detail in Weippert, 1990). The use of deferential address in the corpus is described in §§20-24 below.

[16] "Mistress" (גבירה) is used as the feminine counterpart of "master" (אדון) in the corpus in 2K 5:3, of a high-ranking Aramaean woman as mistress of a "lass" captured on a raid into Israel. It is similarly used in Gen 16:4, 9. It is also used in the corpus with no following name or pronoun, to designate a king's wife (1K 11:19, 2K 10:13) or mother (1K 15:13, the term "the king's mother" [אם המלך, 1K 2:19] is also used). See §5.1.2.n.

[17] This argument is presented in Lindhagen, 1950:56. These views are borne out by the usage of the corpus, see, for instance, §25.2 on the use of "my lord" (אדני) as a vocative, and cf. the promise of service to a ruler in return for various undertakings on his part in 1S 11:1, 12:10, 1K 12:4, also Gen 47:19. It is also significant that the term "servant of Yahweh" is accorded only to individuals of high status, and to few of them. See Lindhagen, 1950:277-287.

[18] "Master" and "father" are used together in Mal 1:6, but "father" is also used of God sporadically elsewhere, as in Deut 32:6. The relationship between God and King Solomon is pictured as that of father and son in 2S 7:14 (also 1 Chron 22:10, 28:6), and "son" is occasionally applied to the community Israel either in the singular, as in Exod 4:22, 23, Hos 11:1, or in the plural, as in Deut 14:1. The use of

of cases, as in 1S 24:17, and David calls him "my father" in 1S
24:12, although their relationship is usually described as that of
"master" and "servant" (as by David in 1S 24:9, 26:18). Naaman also
is "my father" to his servants in 2K 5:13.[19] The two sets of terms,
"father-son" and "master-servant", both indicate a relationship between a superior and a subordinate. They differ in that "master-
servant" terminology does not carry the implications of benevolence
and loving respect ("honour", כבוד, in Mal 1:6, reflecting the fifth
commandment) characteristic of the kinship terms. Thus David,
seeking support from Nabal (1S 25:8), and Ben-Hadad king of Aram
seeking advice from Elisha (2K 8:9), are presented as "your son", in
the hope of persuading the addressee to act benevolently. King
Ahaz, seeking protection, presents himself to the king of Assyria as
"your servant and your son", promising service, and hoping for
friendly relations (2K 16:7).[20] Ben-Hadad is presented to the king
of Israel as "your servant" (1K 20:32). He has been conquered, and
can expect no benevolence.

2.3.8 *"Manservant"* (עבד) The term for male servant (עבד) is used in
the Pentateuch to denote a slave in the legal sense (as in Exod 21:2).
It is also sometimes used with this meaning in the corpus, as in 1K
2:39-40, 9:22). The common use of "manservant" in the corpus however, is to designate a "courtier" or "minister", a man, presumably
of high rank, attendant on the king, or holding some office from
him, as with David in relation to Saul (1S 22:8, 29:3), or Achish (1S
27:12). A number of people who are not kings have "servants"
(עבדים) who may or may not be slaves in legal terms. The narrator

---

"master" (אדוני, usually translated "[my] lord") to designate God is not uncommon
(see §§15.1.2, 15.7.2).

[19]   The Hebrew is often questioned, both in 1S 24:12 and in 2K 5:13, but neither
seems in any way objectionable as far as Hebrew usage is concerned (see §25.3.2n).
The two sets of terms are similarly used in Aramaic and other cognate languages.
See the survey in Fitzmyer, 1974:213, particularly the use of both "father-son" and
"master-servant" to refer to the recipient and sender of Hermopolis West papyrus
III noted there.

[20]   The narrator has chosen this way to indicate the aspirations of Ahaz; he intended to be pro-Assyrian. The question of whether the combination of "servant" and
"son" was possible in practical diplomatic usage, or not (discussed in Cogan and
Tadmor 1988:187) is irrelevant to the understanding of the usage.

calls David's envoys "lads" (נערים) in 1S 25:9, and "servants" (עבדים) in 1S 25:10.[21] It seems likely that legal status, slave or free, had little relevance to everyday life at the lowest level of society. Typically, "servant" is used as a personal relationship term, bound to a name or pronoun designating the "master", while "lad" (נער) is used to indicate status. Thus the "Egyptian man" found by David's force (איש מצרי, 1S 30:11) describes himself in 1S 30:13 as "an Egyptian lad" (נער מצרי), thereby indicating his social status, and as "servant to an Amalekite man" (עבד לאיש עמלקי), indicating the personal relationship to his master. However, "lad" is also sometimes used as a relationship term, with a name or pronoun designating the person he serves. The two terms do not appear fully distinct in the text as it stands, but may possibly have carried different implications.

2.3.9 *"Maidservant"* (שפחה, אמה) Two terms are used to designate female "servants": אמה and שפחה. Both may be applied to the same person in deferential speech and elsewhere. It is possible that they should have carried different implications, as is expected under the assumptions governing this study, and some have argued that this is the case. It is generally agreed that (if a distinction exists) אמה indicates a form of servant superior to שפחה, and this view can be used to present an interpretation of some passages more colourful, and not less plausible, than that obtained by treating the two terms as synonyms, as in Berlin 1983, 152 n.5. However, it is not possible to demonstrate such a difference in meaning on any reasonably objective basis.[22] The biblical and extra-biblical evidence bearing on the question is carefully investigated in Cohen, 1979, with the conclusion that the two terms differ only in that the use of אמה is characteristic in legal contexts, while שפחה is more common in more col-

---

[21] Other examples are: Gideon (Ju 6:27), Mephibosheth (2S 9:12), Absalom (2S 14:30, 31), Naaman (2K 5:13). In other cases the "master" has at least quasi-royal status, as Ishbosheth in 2S 2:12, Absalom in 2S 17:20. The term "lad" (נער) is sometimes used of the servant of a king, presumably indicating a character of low rank, as David's lookout (2S 13:34), or Saul's troops (1S 21:3, 5, 6).

[22] It is argued in Sasson, 1979:53 (cf. p. 80) that the two words had a distinct meaning, but also pointed out that "in many episodes of the Bible... the two terms are freely interchanged".

loquial usage. In accordance with this view, the two words אמה and
שׁפחה are treated as free variants in this study.

2.4 Occupation

2.4.1 Terms in this group categorize the individual according to
function in society. Occupation is one of the most easily determined features by which individuals can be distinguished, and is
used for this purpose in many societies, as is evident from the study
of surnames. The corpus categorizes people at all levels of society in
this way, from those with important authority over different
aspects of the activity of their fellows, such as the king and his
officials, priests, and prophets, to those who earned their living in
more humble occupations. A few categories based on social situation or personal characteristics are also included here.

2.4.2 *King* (מלך) The king is the head of the human community,
who maintains the social system, and is the final resort of appeals
for justice by its members.[23] To this extent, he is superior to all
other citizens of the state. Master-servant terminology is typically
used in addressing the king (in the situations described in §§21-23),
even by members of his own family.[24] The members of the king's
family naturally have a share of his power and prestige, as do his
servants; the terms "son of the king", "servant of the king" and
"mother of the king" are used as titles (see §3.2.3), the mother
having a more privileged position than the dead king's other wives
(see Donner, 1959). It may be for this reason that Joab, Abishai and
Asahel are regularly called "sons of Zeruiah" (בני צרויה, as in 2S
2:18), using their mother's name in the "patronymic", instead of the
father's, as is usual. Presumably, as sister to King David, her prestige would be higher than that of her husband. Similarly, the Judaean princes, journeying to visit their counterparts in Israel, identify
themselves as "brothers of Ahaziah", no doubt expecting (wrongly,

---

[23] This is shown in 2S 15:1-6. The maintenance of justice is one of the king's
main duties. See Whitelam, 1992:44.

[24] 2S 13:24 (by a son, cf. the reference in 1K 1:19), 13:32 (nephew), 1K 1:17 (wife).
Sarah refers to Abraham as "my lord" in Gen 18:12. Otherwise a wife refers to her
husband as "my man" (אישׁי), and uses no vocative in address, as in Ju 13:6, 23, 1K
21:5, 7, and even when dictating his actions in 1K 21:15.

as it turns out) that their relationship to the king of Judah will ensure them a trouble-free passage.

2.4.3 *Priest* (כהן) The duties of the priest in regulating the observation of religious practice made him an important figure in the
daily life of the people. Eli is addressed as "my lord" by Hannah in
1S 1:15, where she rebuts his opinion of her. The priest in charge
of the Jerusalem temple no doubt had a position of similar influence
in relation to the king and his ministers, as is suggested by the actions of Jehoiada in 2K 11:4-19. Titles such as "great priest", "head
priest", and "second priest" (כהן הראש, כהן משנה, כהן גדול), suggest
a hierarchical structure for the temple attendants, but this is not
described in the corpus. Those at the lower levels of this structure,
as the "doorkeepers" were later called "levites", reserving the term
"priest" for particular families of the tribe of Levi.[25] It is clear that
lineal descent from Levi was not a requirement for undertaking
temple service, as Samuel's father was an Ephraimite (1S 1:1), although the appointing of priests from other families is mentioned
as a reprehensible act in a later context (1K 12:31). Consequently,
where the term "levite" is used in the stories in Judges 17-19, it is
taken as an epithet of occupation, indicating that the person so designated was trained to serve at a shrine, and not as referring specifically to tribal affiliation (see §14.2.1n).

2.4.4 *"Prophet"* (נביא, נביאה) *and "Man of God"* (איש האלהים) The
title "prophet" (נביא masculine, נביאה feminine) or "man of God"
(איש האלהים) denotes a person who can deliver communications
direct from God. Overall, "prophet" (נביא, נביאה) appears to designate a specific class, included within the more general category of
"man of God" (איש האלהים), but the two can be treated as free
variants for the purposes of this study (see §12.6). Such a person,
when acting as God's representative in this way, stands outside the
hierarchy of human society, and is superior to any member of it.

---

[25] The tribe of Levi was dedicated to the service of the shrine of the god of Israel
(Deut 10:8-9). "Doorkeepers" (שמרי הסף) are called "priests" in 2K 12:10, but "levites" in 1 Chron 9:18. No title is used in 2K 22:4, 23:4, 25:18. In the last two cases
they are mentioned as a category separate from the "high priest" (כהן הראש, כהן
הגדול) and "secondary priests" (כהן משנה, כהני המשנה).

This status is reflected in the deference with which a prophet is usually treated, even by kings, and is demonstrated in the stories in which a prophet rebukes a king (as in 2S 12:1-12), or frustrates the attempts of a king or his officers to control him (as in 1K 13:4-9, 2K 1:9-16). Clearly, the temporal power of a king did enable him to curb the activities of a hostile prophet, as is shown in 1K 22:26-27, Jer 26:21-23. However, the prestige of a prophet might make it very difficult to silence him, even when he had aroused considerable hostility, as was the case with Jeremiah (Jer 26:7-19, 38:1-16). The "sons of the prophets" (בני הנביאים) mentioned in the text were evidently prophets who had not achieved the pre-eminent status of the individual prophets mentioned by name, and were, in some way, junior to them, but might nevertheless be sent on important missions, as in 2K 9:1-10.[26]

2.4.5 *Other* The names of many other occupations are given in the corpus. These may be broadly divided into those designating officials of the court or of lower levels of government, and those designating workers (see §3.2.3). Titles of foreign officials (such as the emissaries of the king of Assyria mentioned in 2K 18:17), form a small separate group. A few other terms are used to categorize people by misfortune, or anti-social behaviour, as "widow" (אלמנה), "leper" (מצרע, 2K 7:8), "harlot" (זנה, 1K 3:16), and "scofflaw" (איש בליעל, also with בן or בת in place of איש).[27] Such terms help to give an idea of what was considered exceptional in the society. However they are used descriptively rather than as designations, and so are of little interest to this study.

---

[26] See §2.3.3 on "sons" in this phrase. Large numbers of people evidently used the title "prophet", see 1K 18:19, 22:6.

[27] A "harlot" was probably simply a woman who had left her husband (cf. Ju 19:2), although the social structure (combined with the general difficulty of gaining a livelihood) probably left her no recourse but prostitution or slavery if she did not return. The term translated "scofflaw" reflects "worthless" as its philological origin, and so presumably indicates someone who rejects the norms by which society in general appraises worth. The antonym of "scofflaw" (as applied to an adult male) is possibly "good man" (איש טוב, 2S 18:27) or "valiant man" (איש חיל, 1K 1:42).

2.5 Status

2.5.1 The term "status" as used here refers to the combination of factors which determines the treatment of one individual as the superior or subordinate of another, or as neither, and so as an equal. This is distinct from "rank", which refers to a position in a particular hierarchy. Power (in human terms) is, of course, an important source of status. If this were the only source, status could be measured on a simple scale, with the king at the top, followed by his family, his officials, and so on, with the servant class at the bottom. However, a prophet cannot be placed on such a scale, being in some ways more powerful than the king, in some ways less so. Kings and prophets are, therefore, considered as equals in status for purposes of this study. Samuel, a "prophet" according to 1S 3:20 (also 2 Chron 35:18), must certainly be considered the equal of King Saul in the same way. There is no evidence that priests held a similar status, but this is possible. Kinship presents another hierarchy relevant to status; respect for parents is commanded in the law. However, where the child is the king, he and his parents each have a claim to superiority, so in cases like 1K 2:1, 19, they are seen as conversing as equals.

2.5.2 The status system of the community depicted in the corpus can be described in terms of three levels. The top level is occupied by the king and by prophets (and perhaps other religious leaders), the bottom level by members of the "servant class", the middle level by others. God is above this ranking, always treated as superior. Clearly this description could be further refined. Divine messengers are subordinate to God, but are still superior to humans. A king's wife addresses him as an equal (as in 1K 21:5, 15) and Absalom, the king's son, treats Joab, the commander in chief, as a subordinate in 2S 14:29-32. It appears, then, that members of the king's family are superior in status to other subjects, although they must be considered as subordinate to the king in terms of family hierarchy. Similar gradations no doubt existed in other levels, depending on factors such as age (particularly relevant among siblings), and so on. The corpus does not provide enough information for such factors to be described in detail. Gradations within the basic status levels do not, in any case, seem to affect the features studied here. A person on one level of status is said to be "status-marked" in relation to those on lower levels, and "non-status" in relation to those above him. Where there is no formal or temporary relationship which suggests otherwise, people on the same status level are considered as equal.

2.5.3 The main effect of status on the language is seen in the convention that a speaker who is subordinate in status must use deferential language to persuade a status-marked addressee to act as he wishes, to accept criticism without taking offense, and so on (see §20.4). The value of the above outline, limited though it be, is that it presents a framework for the evaluation of the relative status of speaker and addressee in the case of any dialogue. The fact that a relatively objective evaluation of status can be reached in this way makes it possible to form some idea of the extent to which the use of deferential speech is conditioned by circumstances other than status, and the extent to which its use follows fixed patterns. This, in turn, makes it possible to relate the biblical examples to the usage of modern languages, which can shed light on the biblical usage. This is attempted in §§21-23 below.

Designations and
Related Features of Usage

3.1 Introduction

3.1.1 The designation of a character in the narrative of the corpus may be nominal, consisting of a noun or noun phrase, or it may be pronominal, consisting solely of a pronoun. In either case, the choice of designation follows conventional patterns in the majority of cases. There is, however, some scope for variation, and the choice between the possible variants is used expressively. The present chapter describes the terms which are used for designation, and describes, in a general way, the kind of information carried by the choice between them. Where a nominal designation composed of a single term is used, the choice between the available terms allows the narrator to present the character in the role best suited to his purpose. Choice between different designations composed of more than one term is also sometimes available, and has a similar function. Choice between possible pronominal designations is used to mark immediacy, to show that the designation, or the clause containing it, is important for the narrator's purpose, or is not so. Choice may also be made on what could be called a "vertical" scale. A pronoun, a single nominal term, or a combination of nominals may be used to designate a character. This choice, which governs the specificity of the designation, the amount of information it provides, and so the extent to which it unequivocally identifies a particular individual, is treated in the next chapter.

3.1.2 A single term used to designate an individual is called a "simple designation". Nominals used for this purpose can be classed as "names" and "epithets". The term "name" refers to the personal name, given, according to the narratives, at or soon after birth.[1] As a general rule, an individual in the corpus has only one personal name. The giving of a new name in response to particular circumstances is recorded in a few instances, of actual or potential rulers.[2] Epithets are titles or other terms which indicate that the individual belongs to one of the categories described in §2. The same individual is likely to be designated by different epithets in different contexts, each appropriate to the context in which it occurs. English also may use a variety of different designations for the same person, to present the particular "role" — the particular aspect of the character's identity — appropriate to the context, but this is less advanced than the biblical usage, and of course follows different patterns.[3] An example which fits the usage of both languages is the narrator's use of "his mother" in 2K 4:19 for the person he calls "the woman" in 2K 4:17. In 2K 4:19 the woman is the goal of a servant carrying her son. In either language, two or more terms may be combined to present a more complete identification of the character. Such combinations, usually the name and an epithet in biblical Hebrew, are here called "compound designations". The use of compound designations is also related to the context in which

---

[1]   The structure of the names used in biblical and extra-biblical sources, and the meaning which they convey, has been widely studied, and need not be discussed here. Noth, 1928, is the classic work. The most recent general studies are Fowler, 1988, Layton, 1990. Since the structure of names is not of interest in this study, the name of each character is given in traditional anglicized form, ignoring variant spelling. The symbol b. is used to represent בן, בת "son of, daughter of" in designations which include patronymics.

[2]   As with Gideon (Ju 6:32), Solomon (2S 12:25), Jehoiakim (2K 23:34), Zedekiah (2K 24:17). The biblical text also shows that different combinations of the same elements sometimes designate the same individual, as with Hezekiah (חזקיהו, usual in Kings, as in 2K 20:5, 20, יחזקיהו, 2K 20:10, and usual in Chronicles), Ahaziah (אחזיהו, 2K 8:25, 2 Chron 22:1) appears as Jehoahaz (יהואחז) in 2 Chron 21:17. There are also cases of the use of different names with no explanation, as with the use of Azariah (עזריהו) and Uzziah (עזיהו) for the same king.

[3]   An English speaker who uses "putting on my other hat" to mark a shift from the viewpoint of one role to that of another reflects the same sort of analytic view of his identity. The use in spoken language of epithets denoting roles, and the situations in which they are preferred to names, are discussed in de Fornel, 1987. The details of such usage are, of course, likely to be culture-specific.

they occur. They are most commonly used at the first mention of a character, where a full identification is desirable.

3.2 Categories of Epithets

3.2.1 *Patronymics* The term "patronymic" is used here of a statement of relationship which can be used in any circumstances as an epithet which identifies an individual. For men and unmarried women the epithet typically names the father, hence the name "patronymic". A married woman is usually identified by reference to her husband. A character is sometimes identified by reference to some relative other than that expected. Thus the mother's name is used for Joab b. Zeruiah (2S 2:13), presumably because her relationship to the royal family (she is David's sister) makes her his most prominent relative. Other relatives may be referred to where the relationship is relevant in the context. In 2S 13:1, David's sons are identified by the use of his name in the patronymic in the usual way. In 2S 3:3-4, the mother's name is used in the list of David's children by his various wives. In 1K 1:5 Adonijah is identified by his mother's name to draw attention to the difference in affiliation which separates him from his rival, Solomon. So also Mephibosheth is called "son of Saul" (his grandfather) where he comes to be reconciled to David in 2S 19:25 to remind the reader of his status as a potential rival to the throne.[4] Where an unexpected relationship is mentioned because it is relevant to the context in this way, the epithet is considered as a personal relationship term (see §3.2.4), not as a patronymic.

---

[4]   The names of both father (Jonathan) and grandfather (Saul) are used in the designation of Mephibosheth in 2S 9:6, 21:7 (cf. 2S 4:4). He is referred to as "a son of Jonathan's" in 2S 9:3 (no doubt in reflection of David's intention to act kindly "for the sake of Jonathan", 2S 9:1). The designation "Mephibosheth b. Jonathan" is not used in the corpus, possibly because of the overwhelming relevance of his relationship to Saul, whom David replaced as king. Jehu is named after his grandfather in 2K 9:20. Otherwise, the names of both father and grandfather are given (2K 9:2, 14). It is possible that the name of his father, Jehoshaphat, is not used alone as a patronymic from fear of confusion with Jehoshaphat King of Judah. Names other than the father's are used for a variety of reasons in Arabic speaking societies, where the use of patronymics is similar to that in biblical Hebrew. See Schimmel, 1989:8.

3.2.2 *Gentilics* A "gentilic" epithet identifies an individual as a native of some town, country, or population group. A gentilic is typically used where the family of the person named is unknown, or not well enough known (to the narrator or his intended audience) to be useful for identification. Where the family is known, the patronymic is usually used, as providing more specific identification.[5] The designation of the same character by different gentilics is unusual. "Goliath the Philistine" (1S 17:23, 21:10, 22:10) and "Goliath the Gittite" (2S 21:19) may be different individuals, as they are defeated by different people. On the other hand, the two designations may represent the same person, as Gath is given as the native city of Goliath (the Philistine) where he is introduced in 1S 17:4. If this is the case, the different gentilics can be seen as chosen to suit the contexts in which they occur. In 1 Samuel 17, Goliath is the representative of the Philistine army, so the epithet "the Philistine" is appropriate, as it is in the related passages. In 2S 21:19, Goliath is presented simply as an individual hero, so the reference to him as a native of a particular Philistine city-state is not surprising.[6]

3.2.3 *Titles* A title naming the characteristic occupation may be used as a designation for any character. The occupation named may be regular, as king, prophetess, or it may be specific to the narrative context, as "the informant" (2S 1:6, 13, 4:10 etc.). Titles of the first sort are typically used with a name in place of a patronymic as the common identifying epithet. Those used in this way in the corpus (beside "king", "prophet", "prophetess"), are "mother of the king" (אם המלך, 1K 2:19),[7] "son of the king" (בן המלך, 2S 13:4),[8] "ser-

---

[5]   A designation sometimes includes both patronymic and gentilic, as in Ju 4:17, 21, 1S 27:3, 30:5, 2S 2:2, 3:3, 11:3, 19:17, 21:8, 19, 23:11, 1K 2:8, 2K 25:23. The gentilic usually modifies the patronym, but evidently may apply to the person designated, see §13.2.4. The use of gentilics is discussed in detail in Revell, 1994.

[6]   It is, of course, possible that the two designations should reflect different sources, but the difference between them does not require this view.

[7]   The evidence collected in Donner, 1959, shows this to have been a powerful position in Israel, as in other Near Eastern states.

[8]   See Avigad, 1986:26, 27. Lemaire, 1979 shows that the contexts in which the phrase is used do not require the interpretation, suggested by some, that this title designates an official of a particular type. However, there can be no doubt that it represents a generic rather than a personal reference, like the term "prince du sang"

vant of the king" (עבד המלך, 2K 22:12), "major domo" (אשר על הבית, 1K 18:3), "Inspector of the corvée" (אשר על המס, 1K 12:18), "recorder" (מזכיר, 2K 18:18) "scribe" (סופר, 2K 18:18) "eunuch" (סריס, 2K 23:11), "city governor" (שר העיר, Ju 9:30), "commander in chief" (שר הצבא, 1S 17:55).[9] Some of these titles are also used as designations for characters who are not named, as are titles for less important occupations. Examples of these are: "nurse" (אמנת, 2S 4:4), "wet-nurse" (מינקת, 2K 11:2), "keeper of the robes" (אשר על המלתחה, 2K 10:22), "captain of a thousand" (שר אלף, 1S 17:18), "captain of fifty" (שר חמשים, 2K 1:9), "officer" (שליש, 2K 7:2),[10] "musician" (מנגן, 2K 3:15), "messenger" (מלאך, 2S 11:19), "shield-bearer" (נשא הצנה, 1S 17:7) "squire" (נשא הכלים, 1S 14:7), "lookout" (צפה, 2S 18:24), "gate-keeper" (שער, 2S 18:26), "cavalryman" (רכב, 1K 22:34), "rider" (רכב סוס, 2K 9:18), "the lad informing him" (הנער המגיד לו, 2S 1:5). Designations of the less important occupations may well have been used in place of the patronymic, as were the titles of high officials, but their greater commonness would have confined their use to a more limited circle.[11]

3.2.4 *Personal relationship terms* Any designation used with a suitable noun or pronoun indicating a second party can function as an epithet of relationship. However, the most common personal rela-

---

which he mentions (p. 65). The legend "daughter of the king", found on one seal, can be interpreted in the same way.

[9]   Many of these titles are known not only from other references in the corpus and other parts of the Bible, but also from extra-biblical sources. The corpus in Davies 1991 includes seals or bullae showing the titles "major domo", "son of the king", "servant of the king", "scribe", and "city governor", (all of which are illustrated in Avigad 1986, no. 1-10), and also "priest" (הכהן), and titles not found in the corpus, "servant of Yahweh" (עבד יהוה), "daughter of the king" (בת המלך), and "healer" (הרפא), and "doorkeeper of the harem" (שער המסנר). The biblical evidence is related to the archaeological in Avigad, 1987.

[10]   For a discussion of the more precise meaning of this title, see Schley, 1990.

[11]   No doubt some individuals were generally identified by epithets indicating lower status occupations where this was their most significant source of importance or individuality in the eyes of the community, as with master-servant relationship for Ziba (2S 9:2, 16:1, 19:18) and Gehazi (2K 5:20, 8:4). A number of seals give the title of one individual as "servant" (עבד) or "lad" (נער) of another, titles which probably reflected a relatively high status in the community. See Avigad, 1987:202-3, 205.

tionship terms, and those of greatest interest in this category, mark kinship. Such epithets, showing that two characters are related by blood or marriage, or by other association similarly close, are used by the narrator to draw attention to relationships significant in the narrative context (see §§13.3, 14.2). In quoted speech, they are common in deferential usage, and in the rhetoric of persuasion (see §§ 13.4, 25.3). That is, their use is dependent on the context in which the designation is used, rather than on any general convention governing designations. Epithets denoting relationship as master or mistress and servant are used in a similar way. "Master-servant relationship" is, like kinship, a personal relationship. In fact the relationship of master to servant was clearly seen as analogous to that of father to son. Both sets of terms may be used of the same relationship, although, of course, they carry different implications (see §2.3.7). Occupation terms bound to a noun or pronoun, as "his (or Jabin's) commander in chief" (שׂר צבא יבין, שׂר צבאו, Ju 4:2, 7), are also occasionally used as relationship terms (see §5.1.2n).

3.2.5 *Terms indicating social categories* Where the purposes of the narrator (or a speaker) do not require more precise identification (or his information is not adequate for it), an individual may be designated by a term representing a broad social category, as "man" (אישׁ), "woman" (אשׁה), "child" (ילד), "lad" (נער), "lass" (נערה). Some similar categories, as "concubine" (פילגשׁ), "widow" (אלמנה) are used in the same way. The way in which these categories were defined is not always certain, but the terms are typically used distinctly, as is demonstrated in §2.2. An adjective or other epithet is often added to a term of this sort to provide a more precise identification, as "old man" (אישׁ זקן, Ju 19:16), "wise woman" (אשׁה חכמה, 2S 20:16), "young lad/girl" (נער קטן, נערה קטנה, 1S 20:35, 2K 5:2). These terms are most widely used for unnamed characters.

3.2.6 *Nonce epithets* A word or phrase describing a character in relation to a particular situation is sometimes used as a designation in quoted speech, as "My remaining ember" (גחלתי אשׁר נשׁארה, 2S 14:7, the Tekoite referring to her son), or "This son of a murderer" (בן המרצח הזה, 2K 6:32, Elisha referring to the king). In cases like "this dead dog" (הכלב המת הזה, 2S 16:9, Abishai referring to Shimei), one of several similar expressions, the designation itself may be conventional.[12] However, the use of these expressions, too, results from a particular situation, not a settled convention, so that they can reasonably be called "nonce designations" in contrast to those regularly used in a variety of situations. Similar usage occurs in narration in the form of the use of a noun carrying affective meaning in place of a standard form of designation, as "their hero" (גבורם, 1S 17:51, designating Goliath from the point of view of the Philistines). Nonce designations reflect the opinions or emotions of the speaker, but their expressive value is evident in their lexical content, so their use is only noted in particular circumstances (as when used as vocatives, see §25.5.2).

3.2.7 *Unnamed characters* Many characters who are mentioned in the narrative are not identified by name; some other designation, usually indicating occupation or general social category, is used. Personal names may sometimes have been lost, either before or after the time of the narrator. Generally, however, an individual who was not named was not sufficiently prominent in the narrative, or in the history of the community, to warrant specific identification. Thus the claim made by the king of the b. Ammon in Ju 11:13 provides the motivation for Jephthah's important speech, and his refusal to listen the motivation for Jephthah's subsequent action, but he never appears in person. He merely represents a hostile power. His name is irrelevant unless it is noteworthy in some other context. Such contexts of course include the Bible outside the corpus, as with Moses (Ju 1:20). They are presumably not confined to the Bible, as the information provided there would scarcely justify the naming of Tibni b. Ginath (1K 16:21, 22), or of So King of Egypt (2K 17:4). It is, of course, possible that these names were used simply because they were available to the narrator, but this study assumes that the use of such designations in the corpus reflects the narrator's assumption of general historical knowledge in the reader.

---

[12] The term "dog" (כלב) is used as a derogatory epithet in 1S 24:15, 2S 9:8, 16:9 in combination with "dead" (מת), and in 1S 17:43, 2S 3:8, 2K 8:13, and also in a conventional formula in Lachish 2:4, 5:4, 6:3, without it. Cf. also Exod 11:7, Deut 23:19. The Amarna letters show that this sort of use of the term had a long history in the area.

3.3 Pronouns and Variation in Concord

3.3.1 A pronoun identifies the individual it is used to designate only through concord. Concord is here understood as the indication that one word has the same referent as another word by giving it the same classification (insofar as the language allows) in terms of number, gender, and person. Hebrew nouns have morphological features which are commonly said to represent one of four classes: masculine or feminine gender, each of which may be singular or plural in number. This morphological classification usually corresponds with the facts of sex and number in the natural world, but this is not always the case. Thus the words "fathers" (אבות) and "women" (נשׁים) have "feminine plural" and "masculine plural" endings respectively. "God" (אלהים), commonly used to refer to the unique God of Israel, is "plural" in form. The form of a noun is thus arbitrary, and does not necessarily reflect the facts as perceived by the speakers of the language, as stressed in Waltke and O'Connor (1990) §6.3.1.

3.3.2 It is consequently true that the classification of a noun in terms of number and gender is revealed only by coreferents which show concord with the noun: nouns (adjectives or participles) used attributively or predicatively, or, more commonly, pronouns. Such coreferents show that "fathers" (אבות) is masculine in gender, "women" (נשׁים) is feminine, and "God" (אלהים) is singular.[13] As these examples suggest, where a noun denotes a human or divine being, (the area to which this study is limited), concord is consistent with reality as perceived by the speakers of the language.[14] The language treats common nouns as it does proper names, which are often not marked for gender. Similar direct relation to physical reality also occurs in pronouns or adjectives which refer to speaker or addressee; there is no grammatical basis for the choice of number and gender. In general, then, coreferents mark the number and gender of nouns denoting humans according to the perceived nature of the referent.

---

[13] "God" (אלהים) with a singular referent occasionally has plural coreferents, see §15.1.1.n.

[14] See Albrecht, 1896:66, who considers this relationship "self-evident". Details of the morphology of nouns in relation to referent and gender are given there.

3.3.3 The classification of a noun in terms of number and gender may vary. With nouns representing humans, such variation is limited to number.[15] Coreferents of "collective" nouns, which represent groupings of humans, such as a tribe, may be of either number. Such nouns are typically "singular in form"; descriptions usually regard the use of singular coreferents as determined by grammatical convention, the use of plural coreferents as determined by the physical facts. (A tribe is made up of a number of individuals; plural coreferents show "notional" concord, "constructio ad sensum"). The above argument shows, however, that the form of a noun has no relevance for its number or gender. As with other nouns, the grammatical classification of a collective can be determined only through its coreferents. It must be regarded as indeterminate as to number, with the choice of the number of its coreferents reflecting the ideas or perceptions of the speaker or narrator.

3.3.4 This conclusion is supported by the fact that a coreferent of a collective is regularly singular only where the coreferent is an attributive which applies to the group, but not to its individual members, such as "large". This fact obviously arises from the speaker's intention, not from the influence of grammar in the abstract. Moreover, the dichotomy "grammatical" x "other" is not easily applied to the similar variation in the grammatical number of coreferents of compound nominals, nor in the less common cases where an individual is addressed in the plural (as in 1K 3:26) or where a group represented by a plural nominal is addressed, or refers to itself, in the singular (1S 5:10-11). The variation in person found in direct speech where the speaker (1st person) or addressee (2nd person) is represented by a nominal (3rd person) is also difficult to see in such terms.

3.3.5 Variation in number or person of the sorts referred to is not to be seen as "correct" versus "incorrect", or as "standard" versus "substandard" but as "marked" versus "unmarked". Where a choice of person or number is possible, the choice made reflects the ideas or perceptions of the speaker or narrator. More precisely, the

---

[15] A few nouns representing animals may be used with coreferents of either gender, see Albrecht, 1896:68.

choice of person or number in such cases is designed to enhance the impression or information which the speaker or narrator desires (consciously or unconsciously) to convey; it is expressive.[16] The basis of this design, the "meaning" of the choice, is, however, neither clear-cut nor obvious. An English speaker may refer to a baby a few days old as "it", or to a pet as "he" or "she", but this can hardly be taken as showing that the baby is considered as non-human, or the pet as human. Similarly, reference to an addressee in the third person in Hebrew does not show that the speaker is ignoring his presence. The use of the singular for the verbs in "David and his men went... and attacked... (...וילחם...ואנשיו דוד וילך, 1S 23:5) does not show that only David was active. Similarly, the use of a singular or plural coreferent for a collective does not show that the speaker had in mind a single group or a number of individuals respectively. The factors determining such choice are more complex than is suggested by the conventional labels of the grammatical classifications in question.

3.4 Immediacy and Its Opposite

3.4.1 An understanding of the basis of the choice among possible coreferents in such cases is clearly important not only for the understanding of the way the language is used, but also for an understanding of the way the users of the language thought about the people to whom the words refer. This understanding can only be obtained from a study of the choices made in relation to the contexts in which they are made. One study (Wales, 1983:116) shows that, in one society, the singular x plural contrast may reflect relative social status (singular is used to inferiors, plural to superiors); absolute status (s is used within the lower class, p within the upper); physical context (s is used in private, p in public); social context (s is used in informal or intimate situations, p in formal or neutral ones). Finally, the use of one where the other is expected reflects the speaker's attitude (s expresses contempt or scorn, p respect

---

[16] Variation in person and number for rhetorical purposes (which some Arabic grammarians have called "departure from what is expected") is also found in the Qur'ān. According to Zamakhsharī, such variation is used as "This is more likely to raise the interest of the listener than it would if it were all in a uniform style" (see Abdel Haleem, 1992:431).

or admiration). More than one of these categories may be relevant in any given speech. Where such complexity occurs, the choice can not be a matter of convention. It necessarily carries information about the speaker's attitudes and intentions. A speaker addressing, in private, a close relative who is also his employer, may use the singular, reflecting friendly intimacy, or may use the plural, out of respect, or fear that the choice of singular would seem presumptuous, and cause offence. The complexity of the motivation of usage of this sort is important, since it means that, even though the general pattern is well known, the usage required in a given situation may not be clear even in spoken language (for examples, see Mühlhäusler and Harré, 1990:145).

3.4.2 In biblical Hebrew, the possible variations in number and person typically involve pairs of contrasting forms, as with the use of singular and plural noted in §3.4.1.[17] It is thus reasonable to present the meaning of the usage in terms of binary contrast, although the information conveyed by the usage may reasonably be categorized differently in different situations (as with the binary contrast discussed in §3.4.1). Binary contrasts of this sort in the corpus are said to indicate "immediacy" or "non-immediacy" (see §1.7.2-4). The term "immediate" is used here to designate material which is presented as the significant core of a communication, the essence of what a speaker or writer wishes to convey. In narrative, this covers not only the main sequence of events, but also other details which, while not presented as part of that sequence, are nevertheless important to the narrator's purpose. Such details are marked as "immediate" and so drawn to the reader's attention.

3.4.3 An example of a detail which is not presented as part of the main line of events, but which is nevertheless marked as immediate, is provided by "His concubine was with him" (ופילגשו עמו) in Ju 19:10. This is a verbless clause, a structure which typically presents "background" (Longacre, 1989:81). The presence of the concubine

---

[17]   Variation in concord in gender does not seem relevant to this study. Where the use of masculine pronouns in place of feminine was seen as intentional in Slonim, 1939, 1942, 1944, the referent is typically non-human or plural. For further discussion of variation in gender see Levi, 1987, and the work referred to there.

could have been indicated in the preceding clause "With him was a pair of donkeys". The fact that she is presented in a separate clause, terminal to the grammatical unit of which her husband, referent of "his" and "him", is subject, draws the reader's attention to the information, and so highlights it. This clause foreshadows the part played by the concubine in the climax of the story. It is rendered prominent by its subject-predicate order and by its terminal position.[18] "Narrative prominence" or "immediacy" of this sort, then, differs from the (grammatical) "foreground" of those who define grounding in terms of clause structure. Discourse analysis may well find it desirable to use terms which distinguish the marking of material belonging to the main story line, from the marking of incidental details as of particular significance (cf. the term "local grounding" used in Thompson, 1983). The necessary analysis is not attempted here. The marking of prominence of any sort is regarded as the marking of "immediacy". Material not so marked is termed "non-immediate".

3.4.4 In speech, what is "immediate" is material which is central to the concerns of the speaker, and so requires the attention of the addressee. Such material can sometimes be identified on the basis of clause structure, but the use of other features, particularly variation in person or number, is more common in speech. Speech which is marked as non-immediate (or is not marked as immediate), avoids the common forms of direct address, as with the use of forms such as "your servant" and "my lord" to represent speaker and addressee, and the accompanying use of third person pronouns in place of first or second. The effect of such usage is to "distance" speaker from addressee by not treating the two as forming a dyad. Such distancing is used to show deference; it suggests that the speaker is too humble to be treated as a person on the same social level as the addressee.

---

[18]   Verbless clauses in which the predicate is composed of a preposition and a pronoun referring to the thematic actor in a verse, as is the case here, typically have the order P – S (see §28.6.4). Circumstantial clauses of this sort most commonly occur within a section of narrative. Placing them at the end of a section gives them a prominence in the same way as does the use of "end-focus" in a clause, as suggested in Revell, 1993:80 n17. Other examples occur in 1S 30:18 (see §4.4.1), 1S 25:19 (see §13.3.7).

Where such distancing is expected, but the direct forms are used, the speaker expresses urgency, or other forms of emotion. That is, the speech is marked as particularly important to the speaker. It is presented to the addressee as "immediate", despite the difference in their relative status, which normally requires the expression of deference. That is, the expression of emotion or urgency, or of politeness, deference, or distance, can be achieved by the marking of speech as immediate or non-immediate.

3.5 Conclusion

The division of the text into "narration" and "speech" obscures the fact that many features characteristic of narration also occur in speech. That is, a speaker is not restricted to the use of the first or second person, but may also use the third, as does the narrator. If this were not so, it would not be reasonable to use the terminology of immediacy and distance in both categories. Since the narrator is restricted to the third person, however, a more restricted range of expressive variation is available to him than is available to a speaker. Narration also provides the context within which speech must be interpreted. For these reasons, this study will concentrate on the usage characteristic of narration before moving on to consider usage unique to speech.

The Use of Nominal
and Pronominal Designations

4.1 Introduction

4.1.1 Both nominals and personal pronouns are used to designate individuals, as described in §3. On the level of structure, a personal pronoun is simply a substitute for a nominal. In terms of usage, a personal pronoun is one of the group of words and phrases which are commonly used to designate any individual. The words which make up such a group are partial synonyms, since they have the same referent. However, they are not free variants; it is not possible to choose any one of them for use in any position in which a designation of that individual occurs. Obviously, a pronoun cannot be used unless it can easily be related to a nominal in the preceding context which designates the same individual. However, the same is true, to some extent, of those nominal designations which have anaphoric value. Designations like "the man" or "the king" can only be usefully used in a context in which the referent has been more specifically designated, and the anaphoric reference is clear.

4.1.2 Personal pronouns and the various nominals used to designate an individual thus differ in the extent to which the designation is specific. A personal pronoun used in narration indicates only the gender and number of the individual, and so has very wide potential application. Terms denoting social categories are also very widely applicable, although even in the case of "man" and "woman", some features of status are indicated, as well as number and sex (see §2.2.2). Other nominal designations, such as occupation terms, have a more limited potential application, much more so in the case of "the king", and some other titles. The personal name is the most specific simple designation available for most individuals, but it, too, may be applicable to more than one individual, even in a small community. Compound designations are the most specific; they have the highest degree of referentiality and individuation.[1] It is unlikely that a designation like "Ehud b. Gera" or "Zebul the city governor" could be applied to more than one individual within a community. The way in which the narrator uses the different levels of specificity provided by pronouns, simple nominals, and compound nominals is described in this chapter. The basis for the choice of the terms used as simple and compound designations is discussed in succeeding chapters.

4.1.3 The use of different forms of designation in the Joseph story has been discussed in Longacre, 1989:141-157, in his chapter on participant reference. His interest is to relate these to the "ranking" of participants and the operations of participant reference, a subject pursued further in de Regt, 1993, which deals with particular topics over a much wider range of text, and so in less detail. The intent here is to gain a general view of the values of the different forms of designation, and of the extent to which such values can be considered as used consistently in the corpus. The designations are initially categorized on a purely formal basis as compound, simple, or pronominal. The purpose of this chapter is to evaluate, in general terms, the function of each category. It is evident that Longacre's views are generally valid. For instance, simple designations can usually be classed as names, titles, relationship terms, or social category terms. The first two correspond to category 2 in the list of participant reference resources in Longacre, 1989:141-2, the second two to category 3. However, the Joseph story and the corpus reflect different forms of society. The compound designations characteristic of the corpus are not used in the Joseph story. They would fit Longacre's category 1, defined as including designations which present more than one item of information about the character designated,

---

[1]   "Referentiality" is the property of having a specific referent (Hopper and Thompson, 1980:288); "individuation" is the marking of an item as having a specific referent (see Khan, 1991:235). These features determine the extent to which a designation is useful as a "recognitional" (as defined in Sacks and Schlegoff, 1979: 17). The term traditionally employed in this area was "definiteness". Here "specificity" is used to describe the degree to which a designation can be recognized as referring to a particular individual, ranging from "unspecified" (the designation is a third person pronoun with no nominal antecedent) to "highly specified" (it includes a name and one or more epithets).

but further division might be justified (see §12.3.1n). Longacre's analysis of pronominal designations also goes beyond the purpose of this work. Different types of pronominal designation are considered here only in the discussion of the use of demonstrative rather than personal pronouns in §13.5.3.

4.2 The Use of Nominals to Introduce Units of Content

4.2.1 In general, it can be said that, once a character has been designated by a nominal, a pronoun is used for further references as long as it would not be ambiguous. This can be considered as describing the unmarked use of the choice between nominal and pronominal designations. In fact, however, the use of pronouns is typically more limited than this implies. There is a tendency (in much of the corpus) to avoid long strings of pronominal reference. A nominal designation is often used to remind the reader who is acting, even where the use of a pronoun would not be ambiguous. Such usage often coincides with a new aspect of the character's activity. In Ju 8:24 Gideon asks for gold rings; the repetition of his name in Ju 8:27 introduces the description of his making an ephod with them. Abimelech's name is used in Ju 9:48 first with the verb describing his ascent of Mount Salmon, then with that describing what he did there. Jephthah is mentioned by name in Ju 11:29, 30, 32, and 34, introducing successively the description of his march against the b. Ammon, his oath, his victorious battle with the b. Ammon, and his return home. The repetition of a verb of speaking within a speech by one character is sometimes similarly used to draw attention to the introduction of a new topic, a recapitulation of the character's speech, etc. In Ju 8:23-24, Gideon's speech (introduced by "Gideon said to them") first refuses an invitation to rule, and then (after the same introduction is repeated) asks for gold rings.[2] A designation

---

[2] The repeated verb is usually accompanied by a repeated nominal designation of the speaker, and (less commonly) by a repeated designation of the addressee. Other examples with repeated nominal subject occur in 1S 16:11, 17:10, 37, 26:10, 2S 15:4, 27, 16:11, 17:8, 24:23, 1K 2:44, 3:24, 22:5, 2K 6:28. The source of the communication is often similarly restated in speeches by God through his representatives, as in 1S 2:30, 2S 12:11, 2K 3:17, 19:32 (see §15.5.3), and also with repeated verb of speaking in the Hebrew text, but not in the Greek, in the instructions given by God to Elijah in 1K 21:19.

repeated in this way, where a pronoun could have been used, can be seen as marking the introduction of a new topic, a different phase of the action.[3]

4.2.2 A nominal designation presents a character to the reader more precisely than does a pronoun. The use of a nominal where a pronoun is adequate thus draws attention to the character designated. It "higlights" the character designated. This highlighting of the character can be seen as the basic meaning of the marked usage, the choice of a nominal where a pronoun would not be ambiguous. As Siewierska (1988:11) says of the usage of languages generally: "It has been observed that, once a referent is established as given, it will tend to be pronominalized or elided unless its identification is impeded by the presence of competing discourse participants, or the nature of the reference warrants highlighting for reasons of contrast, emphasis, or the like." The introduction of a new phase in the action of the narrative is only one of the purposes for which the narrator highlights the designation of a character by using a nominal where a pronoun would not be ambiguous. He may repeat the nominal designation of a character within a clause where that explanation would not apply, as in the repetition of the name of God in 2S 17:14. The following paragraphs survey such unexpected uses of nominal designations.

4.3 The Choice of Nominals to Introduce Speech

4.3.1 Dialogue provides an easily recognized situation in which the choice of noun or pronoun for designation can be further explored. The use of one or the other to designate speaker and addressee in the first speech of a dialogue is affected by the way they are referred to in the preceding context, but nominal designations are quite often used for both. Either or both may also be designated by

---

[3]   Phenomena of this sort have been widely noted elsewhere, e.g. in Clancy, 1980:160, for English and Japanese usage, in Givón, 1983:7, with a more general description under the name "thematic paragraph". Longacre, whose work is referred to there, surveys "paragraph types" in Longacre 1989:60-62, and illustrates them in the following chapters; the phenomenon described here corresponds to Longacre's process R (1989:143). Similar views, also using the term "paragraph", are presented in de Regt, 1993:156.

a nominal in the introduction to succeeding speeches, although, as in other languages, pronouns may be used without ambiguity. Nominals used in this way draw attention to speaker and addressee, and so mark the speech so introduced as important. A striking example occurs in 1S 17:32-37, where David and Saul are both designated by name in the introduction to four successive speeches. These speeches present David's offer to fight Goliath (17:32), Saul's rejection of him as unequal to the task (17:33), David's assertion that, with God's support, he will win (17:34-36, recapitulated in 17:37), and Saul's acceptance of his offer (17:37).[4] This dialogue is clearly crucial to David's career as presented by the narrator. It opens the way to his defeat of Goliath, which demonstrates to the reader that his anointing has indeed ensured that God's spirit is with him.[5] This victory also brings David fully into court circles, and so opens the way for his rise towards the throne. The reason of the highlighting of the speeches is thus easily appreciated.

4.3.2 The significance of the form of introduction used within a dialogue is discussed at length in Longacre, 1989:158-184, where it is seen as determined by the internal dynamics of the dialogue. Thus Saul's first speech in 1S 17:32-37, and David's second, can be called confrontational, and Saul's second speech can be said to re-direct the dialogue. In Longacre's view, these terms represent the reason why an introduction naming both speaker and addressee is used in each case. Clearly, however, introduction in that form can, in itself, only be said to have a general meaning, such as "important interview between two important people" (as suggested above, and presented as default in Longacre, 1989:184 D.1). The specific reason why the speech and the participants are important must be deter-mined from the context. Similarly, "He said to his master's wife" (Gen 39:8), and "She said to her father" (Ju 11:37) are both said to mark the speech as "addressee dominant" (D.5). This is true in so-cial terms in both cases, but hardly otherwise. moreover, speech to

---

[4]   The recapitulation of David's speech in 1S 17:37 is introduced by "David said" (ויאמר דוד) repeating the verb used in v. 34 (cf. note 2).

[5]   See 1S 16:13. Such demonstration is also provided, soon after their being anoin-ted, for Saul (his defeat of Nahash, 1 Samuel 11) and Solomon (his famous judg-ment, 1K 3:16-28).

a dominant addressee is not always introduced in this way, as with David's speech to Saul in 1S 17:37, and use of this form of introduction does not always show that the addressee is dominant, as with "he said to his lad" in Ju 9:13. Joseph's speech in Gen 39:8 is, in fact confrontational ("He refused" וימאן), and that in Ju 11:37 redirects the dialogue from consideration of Jephthah's situation to that of the speaker, his daughter, so that one might expect the use of nominal designations for both participants in both cases. In fact, the form of introduction used in these two cases, and in Ju 19:13, is consistent with the typical use of relationship terms, which is conditioned by the thematic status of the characters involved, as described in §13.3.2. That is, factors other than the internal dynamics of the dialogue also condition the use of the different forms of introduction. It is reasonable to argue that the choice of a nominal or pronominal designation in an introduction to speech has the same basic function as elsewhere (as suggested in de Regt, 1993:158). Where a pronoun could have been used, the use of a nominal draws attention to the name in connection with the action, here the speech, marking it as deserving attention, as important in its context. The internal dynamics of the dialogue form one of the reasons why such highlighting may be desirable.

4.4 The Marked Use of Nominals Elsewhere

4.4.1 A nominal designation may also be repeated (where a pronoun could have been used) to impress on the reader's mind the connection of the person designated with events other than speech. In Ju 4:23-24, the designation "Jabin King of Canaan" is used in three successive clauses, so that the reader has no chance of overlooking his complete downfall. In 1S 19:7, the use of the name "Jonathan" in three successive clauses impresses on the reader the fact that it was Jonathan who effected David's reconciliation with Saul. The involvement of Abner with Asahel is similarly highlighted in 2S 2:18-19. In the clauses "David saved all that Amalek had taken, and his two wives David saved" (ויצל דוד את כל אשר לקחו עמלק ואת שתי נשיו הציל דוד, 1S 30:18), the repetition of "David" as subject combines with several other features to draw attention to the event described

in the second clause.[6] The name "Absalom" is used six times in 2S
13:23-27 (compared to four pronouns representing him), showing
the reader that it is important to bear in mind that Absalom engin-
eered Amnon's presence at his feast. The reiteration of the title "the
king" for David in 1K 1:1-40 constantly impresses on the reader
that Solomon was anointed as David's successor through the exer-
cise of the proper authority.[7] Similar examples of the reiteration of
designations to connect characters with important events can be
found in 2K 16:10-18, 22:8-12 and elsewhere (see §§4.11.1-2).

4.4.2 Such repetition of nominal designation is used throughout the
corpus, both in narration and in speech, and may occur in any
situation. The designation "Ahab b. Omri" is used three times in
the introduction to Ahab's reign in 1K 16:29-30. The wording used
to introduce the descriptions of reigns is often spoken of as "formulaic", but the use of designations in this way is without parallel,
and is no doubt evoked by the unique significance of this reign in
the history of the kingdom. The name of God is frequently repeated where a pronoun could have been used, as in the speech of Jephthah's daughter: "Father, you have opened your mouth to Yahweh,
do with me what your mouth expressed, since Yahweh has done for
you vengeance on your enemies, the b. Ammon" (אבי פציתה את פיך
אל יהוה עשה לי כאשר יצא מפיך אחרי אשר עשה לך יהוה נקמות מאיביך
מבני עמון, Ju 11:36). Here the repetition of "Yahweh" draws attention to the fact that God has provided victory for Jephthah, who is

---

[6]   Not only is the same nominal subject used in both clauses, but their verbs
derive from the same root. The chiastic patterning draws attention to the phrase
"his two wives" in the second clause (and marks it as "focus"), a feature which is
doubly striking, since "all that Amalek had taken" in the first clause would include
them. The structure and position of the clause draw attention to the contents in
much the same way as in the circumstantial clause in Ju 19:10 discussed in §3.4.3.
[7]   The use of the title in five successive clauses in 1K 1:15-16, and four in 1K
1:28-29, are merely the most concentrated examples of this reiteration. See §5.3.1.
The idea that the repetition of nominal designations is used to call attention to
important events is suggested in Longacre, 1989:30, 145, and carried further in de
Regt, 1993:168-70.

consequently obliged to fulfil his promise.[8] The idea of his corresponding obligation is also stressed by the repetition of "your mouth", and of forms of the verb "do". Such careful formulation is no doubt designed to endow the apparently simple words with the maximum impact. Similar care in the formulation of English wording typically avoids repetition, so it is scarcely possible for an English speaker to evaluate the impact of the Hebrew usage, or to gauge its effect. Nevertheless, the choice of the words for repetition, and the pattern they create, can still be appreciated.

4.5 Styles of the Use of Nominals

4.5.1 The forms of repetition described above are typical of the most common style of composition in the corpus, in which long strings of clauses in which a character is designated only by pronouns are avoided. In Ju 11:1-12:7, an example of this style, Jephthah is designated in narration in 30 verses, but is represented by a pronoun and not by a nominal only in 11:15, 33, 35, 36, 38. A different style, in which pronominal designation is the rule, is less common.[9] An example occurs in the first part of Judges 8. Gideon is designated in 18 of the first 20 verses, but a nominal is used only in 8:4, 7, 11, 13.[10] In the common style of composition, where nominal designations occur frequently, they must be used at almost every opportunity if their use is to attract particular attention. Where nominal designations are used sparingly, as in the second style, a moderately frequent use will attract attention. In Ju 16:25-30, the narrator designates Samson by name once in each verse. This contrasts with the use of only six nominal designations in the 21 verses in which he is designated in Ju 16:1-24. The use of nominal designations in Ju 16:25-30 is not dense in comparison to many

---

[8]   The name of God is similarly repeated, for example, in Ju 2:15, 18, 3:7, 9, 12, 15, 4:14, 1S 1:28, 2:20, 3:7, 7:9, 10:22, 1K 11:6, 9, 12:15, 24, 13:21, 26, 2K 10:10, 18:6, 25. The name "Allāh" is similarly often used in the Qur'ān where a pronoun would suffice. See Abdel Haleem, 1992:428.

[9]   This second style dominates where the narrator concentrates on a single character, as in the stories of Samson, Elijah, and Elisha. Strings of pronominal designations are also sometimes used in the presentation of dialogue (as for Gideon in Ju 6:13-18) and other forms of reciprocal action.

[10] Contrast the remaining 15 verses of Judges 8. Gideon is designated in 13, but by a pronoun alone only in 8:26, 31.

passages, but it is dense in contrast to usage in the earlier parts of the Samson story, and so draws the reader's attention to Samson's heroic death, the crowning event of his career.[11]

4.5.2 Where the narrator's use of nominal designations is relatively sparing, as in the stories of Samson, Elijah, and Elisha, the correspondingly greater use of pronouns provides greater potential for confusion.[12] Loose use of pronouns is most common in such passages, but there are cases throughout the corpus in which the referent of a pronoun can only be determined through interpretation of the context.[13] One similarly finds pronouns with no antecedent used in speech.[14] In most cases the referent of the pronoun is clear from the situational context of the speech, so no nominal antecedent is needed, as is often the case in spoken language. In some cases, it is reasonable to suggest that the narrator is indifferent to the realism of his presentation, and uses a noun in the narration as antecedent for a pronoun in quoted speech. The reverse, a pronoun used in narration with its apparent antecedent in quoted speech, can also be

---

[11] Since the use of nominal designations is not homogeneous throughout the corpus, any attempt to identify the specific reason for individual examples of the marked use of nominals must be limited to homogeneous units of narrative. For this reason, terms as "highlighting" which are valid generally, are used in this study (as in §4.2.2). The ranking of participants, together with the operations of participant reference established as in Longacre, 1989:142-3, would clearly provide much of the motivation for the highlighting, but it seems probable that factors external to the narrative would also be involved (see §4.11.1).

[12] For instance, a pronoun is not coreferent with the nearest possible antecedent in "and he drank" (וישת, Ju 15:19), "to him" (אליו, 2K 1:5), "he (sent) again" (וישב, 2K 1:11, 13), "to meet him" (לקראתו, 2K 4:31), "he called" (ויקרא, 2K 4:36).

[13] As in "he fell" (ויפל, 1S 4:18), "he sent" (שלח, 1S 13:2), "he said" (ויאמר, 1K 22:19). This is particularly common where the pronoun is plural, as in "they got up" (וישכימו, 1S 1:19), "they sacrificed" (וישחטו, 1S 1:25), "all of them" (כלם, 1S 26:12), "between them" (ביניהם, 1S 26:13), and elsewhere where the reference is more general, as with the plural verbs in 1S 10:21-23.

[14] As "he has told" (הגיד, Ju 16:18), "they" (הם), and the objective pronoun in "we will draw him out" (נתקנהו, Ju 20:32), "let him go aside" (יסב, 2S 14:24), "he" (הוא, 2K 4:9), "let him come" (יבא, 2K 5:8), "he will come out" (יצא, 2K 5:11).

found.[15] Such imprecise use of pronouns is not to be considered marked and meaningful. The usage, though technically ambiguous, is not so in practical terms. The narrator relies on the reader's comprehension, a phenomenon which could easily be paralleled in the literature of other cultures.[16] It is probable that a detailed description of the use of pronouns in the corpus (following and expanding the initiative in Longacre, 1989) would provide much information on the narrator's methods of composition and presentation of his narrative, but this would go far beyond the limited scope of the present study. Some particular features of the use of pronouns are treated in later parts of the study. The present survey of their use is only intended to show that the use of a nominal or pronominal designation often represents a significant choice. Where a pronoun would suffice, the choice of a nominal highlights that designation.

4.6 Compound Designations

4.6.1 Where a nominal is used to refer to any character, a single term — a "simple designation" — is most commonly chosen, typically the one which carries the most precise information, and so the personal name for a named character.[17] In most cases, however, a personal name can identify a particular individual only within a limited circle of family and friends. In a wider circle, more information is needed to avoid the possibility of confusion between two characters with the same name. In the narratives of the corpus, such

---

[15]   As in "he took her" (ויקחה, 2S 3:15). The pronoun refers to Michal. David's speech about her in the preceding verse provides the motivation for the action described by this verb. Other examples are "him" (אתו, Ju 16:24), "to him" (אליו, 2K 1:9), "he said" (ויאמר, 2K 4:41), "to meet him" (לקראתו, 2K 8:9).

[16]   Cf. the comment "Inexplicit forms of reference are used for the current hero, at times despite ambiguity..." in Clancy, 1980:195, describing the usage of English and Japanese material studied there. The ignoring of potential ambiguity in the use of pronouns referring to an established topic is likewise noted in Givón, 1983:14. Some examples in the corpus, where the antecedent of a pronoun is genuinely uncertain, as in "they took" (ויקחו, Ju 7:8), may result from disruption of the text.

[17]   This is the consistent with the preference for "minimization" and "recipient design" noted as characteristic of spoken language in Sacks and Schlegoff, 1979. Reference is typically made with a single term chosen to enable the addressee easily to identify the person referred to, avoiding the use of unnecessary words.

information is typically provided by the use of two or more terms
— a "compound designation" — where a character is first mentioned.[18] A simple designation is usually used after a character has
been securely identified in this way, but further compound designations may be used. The use of compound as opposed to simple
nominal designations thus parallels the use of nominal as opposed
to pronominal designations. The use of compounds may reflect the
need to provide precise or detailed information, but they may also
be used where the provision of such information is not necessary.
In the latter case, the use of a compound rather than a simple nominal draws attention to the designation, and highlights it in relation
to its context, in the same way as does the use of a simple (or other) nominal rather than a pronoun.

4.6.2 A compound designation is most commonly composed of the
name with a patronymic, a gentilic, or a title. Designations of this
sort probably provided the standard form of identification within
the community.[19] Further epithets, or different epithets, may be
used as is appropriate to the context. For instance, a relationship
term may be combined with the personal name (with or without
other epithets) to indicate a relationship significant for the narrative
at that point. The following description of the use of compound
designations is based on the use of the standard or general purpose
forms: the name with patronymic, gentilic, or title, ignoring the use

---

[18] Cf. the introductory designations "Mesha b. Kemosh[ ] King of Moab, the
Dibonite" (משע בן כמש[ ] מלך מאב הדיבני), "Omri King of Israel" (עמרי מלך ישראל)
in the Mesha inscription (lines 1 and 4). Hopper, 1990, briefly describes the use, in
a traditional Malay folk-tale, of a number of forms of reference for the leading
character. These correspond to the compound, simple, and pronominal designations used in the corpus. There appear to be general similarities, but culture-specific differences between the usage discussed there and that discussed here.

[19] The designations on all the bullae described in Avigad, 1986, are composed of
name and patronym, as are the majority of compound designations on the other
Hebrew seals represented in Davies, 1991. The numbers which do and do not have
"son of" (בן) between the two names are roughly equal. Patronyms with "daughter" (בת, 11 cases) and "wife" (אשת, 4 cases) also occur. A small number include
both patronym and title, or a second patronym, or simply a title, beside the name.
A substantial number (but less than one fifth of the total) show only one name.
Gentilic epithets do not occur in compounds, but are used occasionally as simple
designations, as בעלמעני.

of additional epithets or of other forms. It is also based on use in narration, although use in the speech of other characters is also noted. The view of the use presented is substantially the same as that of D. Clines' study of the use of designations composed of a name and a patronymic (Clines, 1972), though less minutely classified.

4.7 The First Mention of a Character

4.7.1 In most cases, the first mention of a named character is made in the form of a compound designation including the name and a patronymic, gentilic, or title, as Barak b. Abinoam (Ju 4:6), Heber the Kenite (Ju 4:11), Jabin King of Canaan (Ju 4:2).[20] Further information may be added, either through the use of additional epithets, or in other ways, as is described below. A few characters are first designated by name with a relationship term. A king who succeeded his father is regularly introduced with a statement of that relationship (see §§9.2.2, 10.3.4n, and cases with foreign kings in 2S 10:1, 2K 19:37, and the Mesha inscription l. 6). Presumably this reflects the importance of the relationship in political or cultural terms. A woman is sometimes introduced in relation to her husband, even where the woman has the more important role in the narrative, as with Hannah (1S 1:2) and Abigail (1S 25:3. Cf. Naomi in Ruth 1:1-2).

4.7.2 A few major male figures other than kings are similarly introduced in relation to a father of lesser importance, as Gideon (Ju 6:11), Saul (1S 9:2). The same effect is achieved by the narrative of the anointing of David (1S 16:1-13), and (with relationship to both parents) in the narratives of the birth of Samson (Judges 13) and Samuel (1 Samuel 1). Some officials are introduced in relation to the ruler who appointed them, as are named servants in relation to

---

[20]   This applies to the mention of a character as a participant in the narrative, not necessarily elsewhere. Thus a full designation is used for "Eli the priest" where he is first mentioned as a participant in 1S 1:9, but "the two sons of Eli" are mentioned in 1S 1:3.

their masters.[21] A number of other characters of minor importance
in the narrative are also introduced through relationship to their
fathers, as Eleazar (son of the Abinadab who first housed the ark on
its return from the Philistines, 1S 7:1), Genubath (son of Solomon's
enemy Hadad, 1K 11:20), and Abiram and Segub, whose father Hiel
defied Joshua's curse, and rebuilt the walls of Jericho (1K 16:34).[22]
The relationship marked by an introductory designation of this sort
is sometimes significant for the status or actions of the character in
the narrative (as with kings), but introduction in this way is not
directly related to the part the character will play in the narrative.

4.8 Characters First Mentioned By Name Alone

4.8.1 In a small proportion of the cases, a character is designated,
where first mentioned, by name alone. This is easily understood in
the case of the great figures of the past: Abraham, Isaac, Jacob/
Israel, Aaron, Moses.[23] Their names were so well known in the
community that further identification was superfluous. Joshua is
mentioned by name alone in Ju 1:1, 2:6, 7, 7, before the compound
designation "Joshua b. Nun" is used in Ju 2:8, but this simply reflects fact the Book of Judges is the continuation of the Book of
Joshua in the text as it stands. In a few cases, some information in
addition to the name is given, but in an unusual way. In the case of
Amasa (2S 17:25) and Hiram (1K 7:13) the initial use of the name
alone is followed by some details of parentage. Ishbi (2S 21:16) and
Saph (2S 21:18) are identified by relative clauses as belonging to "the
offspring of the Raphah". In a few cases a prepositional phrase is
possibly used in place of a gentilic, as where they brought the ark
"to the house of Abinadab in Gibeah" (אל בית אבינדב בגבעה, 1S
7:1). A phrase introduced by "in" (-ב) carrying the information

---

[21] Officials: Sisera (Ju 4:2), Zebul (Ju 9:28, in speech), Shobak (2S 10:16), Naaman
(2K 5:1), Bidkar (2K 9:25), Nebuzaraddan (2K 25:8). Servants: Purah (Ju 7:10, in
speech), Zibah (2S 9:2), Gehazi (2K 4:12).

[22] This would include names which appear in lists of Saul's children (1S 14:49),
David's wives and children (2S 3:2-5), and similar lists.

[23] Ju 1:16, 2K 13:23, and in speech in 1S 12:6, 8, 1K 18:36.

"who lived in", may possibly modify the introductory designation in the case of Delilah (Ju 16:4) and Ishbi (2S 21:16) as well.[24]

4.8.2 The name alone is used for the first mention of a character in a few other cases. Jonathan is associated with Saul by the context in 1S 13:2, 3, but their relationship is not stated until 1S 13:16. The narrator probably assumed that Jonathan was so well known that a compound designation was unnecessary in 1S 13:2-3, where he is only mentioned incidentally.[25] The designation "Abishai b. Zeruiah, brother of Joab" makes clear that the patronym "b. Zeruiah" would identify Joab as well, but the form of designation certainly suggests that Joab is well known in his own right. One would otherwise expect "Abishai brother of Joab b. Zeruiah". The compound designation "Hazael King of Aram" is first used in 2K 8:28. He is designated as "Hazael" in several previous cases, including the first mention of him (1K 19:15, 17, in speech, also 2K 8:8, 9, 13, 15). These uses of the name as a simple designation occur in stories of Elijah or Elisha, and so might reflect characteristics of a source from which those stories were taken. It is equally likely, however, that the narrator knew nothing of the background of the usurper Hazael, and so had no way of providing a compound designation before he became king.[26] The name Rei, listed among those who did not support Adonijah in 1K 1:8, is not mentioned elsewhere, and there is no indication which of the men named Shimei that name in that

---

[24]   If the phrase denoted the location of Abinadab's house, one might expect the repetition of the preposition "to" (אל), or the use of the directional suffix (ה‬ָ) See §5.4.2. In 2S 6:3, a relative clause "the house of Abinadab which is in Gibeah" (בית אבינדב אשר בגבעה) is used, but the context is different, so this cannot settle the question. The preposition "from" (מן) is often easily taken as modifying the verb, as with Barak in Ju 4:6, Hiram in 1K 7:13, but it, too, can introduce a phrase which replaces a gentilic, as with Elisha in 1K 19:16. This may be its function in 1S 25:43, where Ahinoam is introduced.

[25]   A standard compound designation is first used for Jonathan in 1S 14:1, at the beginning of a chapter in which he first plays a central role independent of his father. A prepositional phrase "in Gibeah of Benjamin" (בגבעת בנימין) is used in 1S 13:2, but it is unlikely that it was intended to replace a gentilic in the case of a character so well known. The context, too, is different from that of the similar phrases in Ju 16:4, 1S 7:1, 2S 21:16.

[26]   Compound designations are used for Jehu and Elisha, mentioned for the first time in 1K 19:16, in the same speech in which Hazael first appears.

verse refers to. It is reasonable to assume that nothing further was known to the narrator. The narrator's standard practice is, then, to use a compound designation, or provide equivalent information, at the first mention of a character. He sometimes fails to do this when introducing a character who is well known but is not an important participant in the narrative, and sometimes where his information was inadequate.[27]

4.9 Delayed Use of the Name

4.9.1 In quite a number of cases a named character is first designated by a general term (usually denoting a social category), and the name is supplied in a following clause, as in "There was a man/woman, and his/her name was PN". Other information about the character is usually supplied. The first clause is often used to present information significant for the narrative context, such as home community as with Delilah (Ju 16:4, presumably marking her as a Philistine), Kish (1S 9:1, a Benjaminite), personal relationship, as with Doeg (1S 21:8, one of Saul's servants), Tamar (2S 13:1, Absalom's sister), Hadad and Rezon "opponents" to Solomon (שָׂטָן, 1K 11:14, 23), or even character, as with Sheba, a "scofflaw" (אִישׁ בְּלִיַּעַל, 2S 20:1). The second clause may give the name alone (as with Delilah), but typical forms of compound designation are often used (as with Sheba).

4.9.2 The characters introduced in this way are mostly, in their different ways, of considerable importance. Many are enemies, hos-

---

[27] No patronymic is used for the usurpers Zimri and Omri, in striking contrast to the usual usage for kings of Israel, see §10.3.4. Hephzibah is the only one of the mothers of the kings of Judah named for whom no information on family or local origin is given; possibly information was lacking here also. The failure to use a compound designation at the first mention of Jehoiada (2K 11:4) may possibly result from disruption of the text. A compound designation is used for the first mention of him in the parallel in Chronicles (2 Chron 22:11 = 2K 11:2), where Jehosheba is said to be "wife of Jehoiada the priest". Compound designations are often not used in lists, but the context in which a list was made provides some background information about the individuals named in it.

tile to the community in general, or to one of its leaders.[28] Their
part in the narrative is not necessarily large, but it is evident, in
most cases, that they had a significant impact on events. Some others are fathers of important characters.[29] The remainder are characters of different sorts who play a notable part in the events nar-
rated.[30] An introduction of this sort delays the identification of a
character; the expectation thus induced draws attention to the
name, as noted in de Regt, 1993:166. The distance between the initial designation and the use of the name may be widened, develop-
ing the form to build up expectation, as in the case of Abishag (1K
1:2-3) and Bathsheba (2S 11:2-3), and particularly of David (1S 16:11-
13). The use of a name is sometimes delayed in the typical way
where a leading protagonist is introduced at the beginning of a section of narrative.[31] Such delay is more often used to introduce a
new character within a section. Attention may be drawn to the
name in a similar way where the birth of an important character is
recorded.[32] It seems reasonable to suggest, then that the use of an
introduction of this sort to draw attention to the name is a way of
alerting the reader to the importance of the character so introduced
for the events related.

---

[28]   Delilah (Ju 16:4), Goliath (1S 17:4, also 17:23), Doeg (1S 21:8), Nabal (1S 25:3),
Baanah and Rechab (2S 4:2), Shimei (2S 16:5), Sheba (2S 20:1, also in the speech of
Joab, 2S 20:21), Hadad (1K 11:14), Rezon (1K 11:23), Jezebel (1K 16:31).

[29]   Manoah (Ju 13:2), Elkanah (1S 1:1), Kish (1S 9:1), also Jesse, where he is reintroduced into the narrative in 1S 17:12. Cf. the introduction of Elimelek, a father-
in-law, in Ruth 1:1. Ithra (2S 17:25) could possibly be added to this group.

[30]   Abimelek (Ju 8:31), Micah (Ju 17:1), Saul (1S 9:2), David (1S 16:11, 12, in
speech, then in narration), Abiathar (1S 22:20), Asahel (2S 2:18), Rizpah (2S 3:7),
Mephibosheth (2S 4:4), Ziba (2S 9:2), Bathsheba (2S 11:2), Solomon (2S 12:24),
Tamar (2S 13:1), Abishag (1K 1:3), Josiah (in speech, 1K 13:2), Micaiah the prophet
(1K 22:8, in speech).

[31]   Elkanah (and Hannah), Kish (and Saul), Manoah (and his wife), Nabal (and
Abigail). Cf. Elimelek (and Naomi) in Ruth 1:1. Job is also introduced in this way
(Job 1:1).

[32]   "She bore a son and she called his name PN", as with Samson (Ju 13:24), Samuel (1S 1:20) Solomon (2S 12:24). Compare the use of the name as direct object of
the verb "bore" in the case of the less important character Genubath (1K 11:20).
Possibly Ichabod should be included here, but the announcement of his birth is
made by characters, that of the name by the narrator (1S 4:20-21).

4.10 First Mention in a New Context

A compound designation is often used where a character is reintroduced into the narrative after a period of absence (operation T in
Longacre 1989:143), as with Achish (1S 27:2), Mephibosheth (2S
19:25), Elijah (1K 21:17, 2K 1:3). The space between these examples
and the last appearance of the character in question as a participant
(1S 21:15, 2S 9:13 [cf. 2S 16:4], 1K 19:21, 21:28, respectively) leaves
no doubt that the character is being reintroduced in a new narrative
context, but the context can often be considered as changed where
there is no such hiatus. In 2S 7:17-18 we read "...thus spoke Nathan
to David. And King David came and sat before the Lord" (כן דבר...
נתן אל דוד: ויבא המלך דוד וישב לפני יהוה). The first clause ends the
description of the presentation of God's message to David, the
second begins the narration of David's response to it in prayer. It is
reasonable to see these as two different topics, and so to classify the
compound designation in the second clause as used to introduce
David in the new context. Other examples of the use of compound
designations at shifts in context of this sort occurs in 2S 16:5 (beginning a scene with David and Shimei after one with David and
Ziba), 1K 9:26 (beginning the notice about Solomon's fleet), 1K
22:10, 29 (beginning the scene of Micaiah's prophecy, and that of
the battle with Aram). A compound designation is regularly used
for a king where events are dated by his regnal years (see §§9.2.1,
10.3.1). This can be considered as a special case of introduction in
a new context.[33]

---

[33] Examples of compound designations used to draw attention to the participation
of a previously named character in a new context occur in Ju 3:17, 4:17, 23, 5:1,
8:13, 29, 9:1, 35, 57, 1S 17:55, 18:20, 22:9, 11, 18, 23:6, 16, 25:14, 26:14, 27:2, 3,
30:5, 7, 2S 2:2, 8, 10, 12, 3:3, 14, 4:4, 8:12, 12:25, 13:1, 37, 14:1, 16:9, 16, 17:15,
18:2, 19, 19:12, 17, 22, 25, 20:23, 21:17, 21, 23:24, 24:11, 1K 1:5, 7, 8, 15, 22, 36,
2:13, 23, 25, 26, 29, 35, 39, 46, 4:4, 19, 7:13, 9:11, 15, 26, 10:13, 16, 21, 23, 11:1, 15,
23, 12:2, 18, 14:18, 25, 27, 31, 15:22, 27, 29, 16:12, 34, 20:1, 2, 13, 21:1, 17, 28, 22:2,
10, 24, 29, 2K 1:3, 3:7, 5:8, 6:24, 8:7, 28, 29, 9:1, 14, 16, 21, 27, 10:13, 23, 11:2, 9,
15, 12:3, 18, 19, 13:3, 22, 24, 25, 14:8, 15, 17, 16:5, 6, 7, 10, 15, 18:9, 14, 17, 26, 37,
19:5, 20, 36, 20:1, 11, 14, 22:8, 12, 23:29, 24:12, 25:1, 8. Statements introducing the
reign of a king could be added.

4.11 Repeated Use of Compound Designations

4.11.1 It can, in fact, be argued that the shift in context which induces another use of a compound designation may occur only a few clauses after the last. In 2K 22:3 The king sends "Shaphan b. Azaliah b. Meshullam the scribe", to instruct the High Priest to have repairs carried out in the Temple. In 22:8 the priest tells "Shaphan the scribe" that he has found a scroll of the Torah. He gives it to "Shaphan" and "he" reads it. In 22:9, "Shaphan the scribe" goes to the king, "he" reports and "he" says that the king's instructions have been carried out. In 22:10, "Shaphan the scribe" informs the king of the discovery of the scroll, and "Shaphan" reads it to the king. In 22:12, the king instructs "Shaphan the scribe" (along with other dignitaries) to enquire of God about the significance of the find. In 22:14, where they go to carry out the king's instructions, the members of the group are designated by name only (except for their leader "Hilkiah the priest"), and the group is represented by a pronoun thereafter. A compound designation is thus used for Shaphan at the beginning of each stage of the narrative: the initial mission, the revelation of the discovery, the report to the king, and the mission to enquire of God. References within these stages are by name or pronoun. The narrative occupies only a short section of text, and could be seen as dealing with a single topic. The topic, however, is one of extreme importance: the discovery of information which led to a necessary reform of the state religion. The repeated use of the compound designation "Shaphan the Scribe" impresses on the reader the identity and high office — the unimpeachable authority — of the person so closely involved in the events.[34]

4.11.2 The designation of Hilkiah the High Priest, the other person crucially involved in this discovery, is similarly treated in this passage. The same sort of repetition occurs with the designation of Gaal b. Ebed, the potential nemesis of Abimelek, in Ju 9:26-35; of Michal b. Saul where she reacts with scorn to David's dancing before the ark in 2S 6:16-23; of Zadok the priest and the other officials involved in the anointing of Solomon in 1K 1:32-39; of

---

[34]   That is, the motivation for the type of reference used derives primarily from the value of the narrative to the community, not from the value of the characters in the narrative.

Benaiah b. Jehoiada where he disposes of the enemies inherited by
Solomon from his father in 1K 2:25-46; of King Amaziah, and of
King Jehoash whom he rashly challenges, in 2K 14:8-13; of King
Ahaz and Uriah the Priest where they make changes at the temple
in Jerusalem under foreign influence in 2K 16:10-18. Simple designations could be used for the second and succeeding mention of these
characters. Repetition of a compound designation in these situations
is clearly a choice, and potentially carries meaning. Each of these
events is of considerable importance either to the history of the
community, or, as in the case of Gaal, to the narrative. Repetition
of the compound designation impresses the name on the reader's
mind in connection with the event. It seems reasonable to suggest
that the highlighting of name and event is the purpose or "meaning" of this use of compound designations.

4.12 Use to Highlight One Act in a Series

4.12.1 A compound designation may be used in this way to draw
the reader's attention to a particular act in a series performed by the
same character. In Ju 4:18, "Jael" comes out to meet Sisera, and
"she" performs other acts in that verse and the following, but it is
"Jael the wife of Heber" who takes up the tent peg in Ju 4:21. The
use of a compound here draws the reader's attention to her action,
as does the "slow-motion" quality of the description of her movements.[35] Both features impress the importance of the action on the
reader. "The king" questions Ziba in 2S 9:2-4, but "King David"
sends to fetch Mephibosheth in 2S 9:5. The importance of the event
is also indicated by the compound designation of Mephibosheth
marking his arrival. Elijah is usually designated simply by name, but
"Elijah the Prophet" approaches God to offer his crucial prayer in
1K 18:36. The significance of the prayer is also marked by the unusual designation of God which he uses (see §15.6.4). Ben-Hadad is
usually designated by name in 1 Kings 20, but the designation "Ben-
Hadad King of Aram" in 1K 20:20 is used to draw attention to his

---

[35] The actions are described in detail, with a low proportion of verbs in comparison to other words. The same occurs at a similar juncture in Ju 3:21. Contrast the
use of many verbs and few other words in Ju 9:27, to inform the reader of acts unimportant in themselves, which are presented to provide a context for the following action.

escape amid the destruction of his army, the significance of which
is stressed by the prophet's warning in 1K 20:22. "Naboth" refuses
Ahab's request in 1K 21:3, but, where Ahab's reaction is shown in
1K 21:4, the significance of the refusal for the narrative is marked
by the use of the designation "Naboth the Jezreelite", and by the repetition of Naboth's words.

4.12.2 A compound designation may be used in this way after introductory material, to draw attention to the more important action
which that material introduces, as in "All the elders of Israel came
to the king, to Hebron, and King David made a covenant with
them in Hebron before the Lord" (ויבאו כל זקני ישראל אל המלך
חברונה ויכרת להם המלך דוד ברית בחברון לפני יהוה, 2S 5:3).[36] The
narrator refers to Solomon by name from his anointing in 1K 1:39
until 1K 1:53, where a compound designation is used with his decis-
ive action in sending to arrest Adonijah. Jehu is similarly designated
by name alone in 2K 9:5-13, but by a compound designation where
he rebels against his master, the act which marks the beginning of
his career as king (2K 9:14). Such usage can be related to the practice of introducing a king with "PN his son ruled after him" in the
description of his father's reign, immediately followed by a standard
compound designation beginning the description of his own, as in
1K 15:8-9, etc. It is also analogous to the "delayed use of the name"
described in §4.9, but the usage described here does not always entail the use of a more specific designation after a more general one.
In 2K 24:10, "At that time the servants of Nebuchadnezzar King of
Babylon came up to Jerusalem", the compound designation is the
first mention of the king in the new context of the reign of Jehoiachin. In the next verse, the compound designation in "Nebuchadnezzar King of Babylon came up against the city" marks the decis-
ive action following this introduction.

4.12.3 A compound designation is also sometimes used to draw
attention to the name where action results from previous action, or
from speech, another form of marking a more significant action

---

[36] The use of an unmarked form in introductory material of this sort, and a
marked form in the more significant material it introduces, is found with a variety
of features, see §28.5.1.

after an introduction. In Ju 8:12 "Zebah and Zalmunna" flee, but Gideon captures "the two kings of Midian, Zebah and Zalmunna". God orders the anointing of "Elisha b. Shaphat from Abel Meholah" in 1K 19:16, and, in 1K 19:19, Elijah encounters "Elisha b. Shaphat" as a result. In 2K 9:21, "Jehoram King of Israel" drives out in the chariot that "Jehoram" ordered to be prepared. In 2K 12:18, "Hazael" determines to attack Jerusalem, but in 2K 12:19, a bribe is sent to "Hazael King of Aram" by Jehoash King of Judah. In 2K 18:37, officials come to "Hezekiah" with a message. When "King Hezekiah" hears it in 2K 19:1, he tears his clothes in despair. In 2K 21:23, his servants kill "the king", but in 2K 21:24, the people strike down all who conspired against King Amon". These are all cases in which the narrator draws attention to a name in connection with a significant event by the unexpected use of a compound designation soon after another designation of the same character.[37]

4.13 The Function of Compound Designations

4.13.1 The significance of the use of a compound designation compared to that of a simple one cannot be evaluated in absolute terms. It must be related to the frequency with which compound rather than simple designations are used for the character in question, as is the case with nominal designations and pronouns. Where a character is well-known, and his participation in the events of a continuing narrative is not in doubt, a compound designation is not needed to draw the attention of the reader to his mention in a new context, just as a pronoun may be adequate to identify a character on whom the narrator is concentrating, even though the nearest possible antecedent does not represent that character. For this reason compound designations are relatively rarely used for well-known characters, like David, Joab, Samuel, or Solomon, in comparison to

---

[37] Other examples of this kind of usage occur in Ju 3:12, 14 (Eglon); 1S 11:1, 2 (Nahash); 1S 21:11, 13 (Achish); 2S 8:9, 10; 2S 19:16, 17 (David); 2S 21:8, 10 (Rizpah); 1K 2:20, 22; 1K 2:23, 25; 1K 5:26, 27; 1K 6:1, 2; 1K 9:26, 28; 1K 10:10 (Solomon, also 1K 8:1-2 where the repetition of "King Solomon" doubly emphasizes the importance of the assembly with the King); 1K 12:18; 1K 12:21 (Rehoboam); 1K 15:16, 17 (both Asa and Baasha); 1K 15:18, 20; 1K 15:22 (Asa); 1K 21:16 (Naboth); 2K 8:29 (Jehoram); 2K 12:7, 8 (Jehoash); 2K 11:4, 9 (Jehoiada); 2K 25:21, 22 (Nebuchadnezzar); 2K 25:23, 25 (Ishmael); 2K 25:27 (Jehoiachin).

others. The same can be said of designations of God, see §15.8.1. For the same reason, a relatively high proportion of those compound designations is used within a series of designations of the same character, and not where the character is reintroduced in a new context. The fact that the appearance of such characters in the narrative is expected does not affect the narrator's need to mark some events in which they are involved as particularly significant, as "immediate" for his purposes (see §1.7.3), and this can be achieved by the use of compound designations in this way.

4.13.2 A compound designation (rather than a simple one) is conventionally used where a character is first mentioned, or is mentioned for the first time in the context of a particular topic. Such "introductory" uses (about 80% of the examples of compound designations) can be seen as necessary to the clear presentation of the narrative; the more specific designation provides the information which enables the reader to identify the characters correctly. This use can be seen as a parallel to the use of a simple (or other nominal) designation rather than a pronoun where the latter would be ambiguous. Where a compound designations is used within a series of designations of the same character the main motivation cannot be precise identification; the higher specificity is unnecessary. Such usage is marked in comparison to "introductory" uses, and so carries additional meaning, as does the use of a simple designation where a pronoun would not be ambiguous. Such use highlights the designation and its relation to the events in the context. This use for highlighting is not wholly different from the introductory usage; in both situations, the participation in the narrative of the character in question is drawn to the reader's attention, marked as immediate. Moreover the distinction between "introductory" and other use of compound designations must depend on an arbitrary definition of the size or nature of the thematic paragraphs which are said to be introduced. Nevertheless, it is evident that the need for precise identification is dominant in determining the choice of a compound designation in some situations, the need for highlighting in others. Between the two is a "grey area" (as is not unusual in cases of binary choice) in which both motivations no doubt play a part in determining the usage.

4.13.3 Compound designations are used in speech in the same way as in narration. Most examples can be attributed to the need for precise identification. The common use of compound designations in isolated reference in speech (as for Michal in 2S 3:13, Abner in 2S 3:23, Hanun in 2S 10:2, Abimelek in 2S 11:21) is typical of this. Compound designations are also used where precise identification seems unnecessary, or of no particular value, as in 1S 15:32, 22:22, 2S 3:28, 12:9, 1K 1:11, 26, 51, 2:22, 2K 19:10, etc. Such examples are reasonably explained as intended to highlight the use of the name in the context for the benefit either of the addressee in the narrative, or of the reader, or both. Compound designations may also be repeated in speech in the same way, and for the same purpose, as they are in the narrative, as in 2S 3:25, 15:35, 1K 1:45, 12:27.

4.13.4 The use of a compound designation rather than a simple one thus parallels the use of a simple (or other nominal) designation rather than a pronoun. A compound designation is most commonly used where the narrator needs to present more precise or complete identification of a character than is provided by a simple designation, just as a simple designation is most commonly used where a pronoun will not identify the character clearly. Either simple or compound designations may be used within a series of nominals designating the same character, to draw attention to the name in connection with a particular event. The choice of a simple or compound nominal for this purpose depends, to a large extent, on the general use of nominal designation for the character. If compound nominals are not often used, the repetition of simple ones, with or without a compound among them, is enough for such highlighting. Where compound designations are used, the clauses in the passage can be marked in descending order of importance to the narrator's purpose by the use of a compound nominal, a simple nominal, or a pronoun, to designate the character in question, as can be seen in the analysis of 2K 22:3-14 in §4.11.1 (cf. the schema in Longacre, 1989:141-2). The use of a compound designation is thus marked in contrast with the use of a simple one in much the same way as is the use of a simple (or other nominal) designation in contrast with the use of a pronoun. In both cases, the more specific form of designation, providing greater individuation, is used where the narrator's purpose requires that the involvement of the character in the narrative must be marked as immediate, and so more forcefully impressed on the reader.

II NAME AND NATURE: RULERS

The Designation of Rulers: Introduction

5.1 Introduction

5.1.1 The previous chapter shows that a compound designation can be used for almost every named character. The name, or any epithet used to form such a compound may be used as a simple designation for the same character. Titles — epithets of occupation — are more commonly used in this way than are other epithets, and the titles of rulers provide the bulk of the evidence on the use of titles in the corpus. The designation of rulers is, therefore, the best area in which to begin the investigation of the basis of the choice between the different terms available for the designation of an individual. Only rulers for whom the title "king" (מלך) is used by the narrator are considered in the following discussion. Those of whom the root מלך is used in other ways, like Ishbosheth (2S 2:10), Absalom (2S 15:11), Adonijah (1K 1:11), are not included. The rulers surveyed here are generally designated by title or by personal name, and these two possibilities form the basis of the discussion in this and the following chapters. However the use of other terms as simple designations, and the form and use of compound designations is also surveyed.

5.1.2 The basic title of a ruler is "the king" (המלך).[1] This form is used where the context of its use is limited to the ruler and his subjects, or to others who identify with the community he rules. Where non-subjects are, or are expected to be, involved, the name

---

[1]   The term "king" is used in this chapter with specific reference to the Hebrew word מלך. The title of the queen was evidently גבירה (1K 15:13, 2K 10:13, Jer 13:18, 29:2), but the term was not restricted to royalty (see §2.3.6n). The only example of its use as an epithet is with Tahpenes, the Egyptian queen, 1K 11:19. Others for whom the title might have been expected have their status shown through relationship to the king (as "mother of the king" in 1K 2:19, or the "wife of Jeroboam" in 1K 14:1-17), or not at all. The term מלכה (a feminine form noun with the same base as מלך "king") is used only of the Queen of Sheba (1K 10:1-13), and, apart from the parallels in Chronicles, in the Book of Esther.

of the state or people ruled is added, as "the king of Aram" (מלך
ארם), "the king of the b. Ammon" (מלך בני עמון).[2] The title is used
with the personal name to make up the usual compound designation for a ruler. Where the title includes the name of the state, the
order is name – title + state. Where it is not, the order is typically
title – name, occasionally name – title. The latter order, which is
more common in the Book of Chronicles than in the corpus, and
became standard in later times, has been seen as usage of a later
period, intrusive in the corpus. With titles other than "king", however, the order name – title is standard. It is quite possible that the
placing of the title "king" before the name was originally marked,
but came to be the unmarked order through excessive use, with
position after the name becoming the marked order (see §28.3.5).
Because of this possibility, the combination of title and name in
either order is treated as a standard compound designation.

5.2 The Designation of Rulers: a Synopsis

5.2.1 The narrator's viewpoint has a considerable effect on the designations of rulers, as can be seen from the table below. This shows
the use of title and name, alone or in combination, in the designation of various individuals or groups of rulers. The table includes
uses in narrative only, not uses in speech.[3] PN represents the name,

---

[2]   The title "commander in chief" (שר הצבא) is used in much the same way.
Where used alone, it designates an officer of the state of which the speaker, or the
subject of the clause, is a member (as in 1S 17:55, the case in 2K 4:13 possibly
represents the addressee's viewpoint), or with which the narrator identifies (and so
an officer of the United Monarchy or of the Kingdom of Judah). A noun or pronoun bound to it typically shows that the officer commands the army of the northern kingdom, or of some foreign state (and so marks the attitude of the narrator,
or of David, to Saul's rule in 1S 14:50, 26:5, see §§7.2.4, 7.3). In 1K 2:32, both
Israel and Judah are mentioned, to mark the contrast, as is common with kings
(e.g. 2K 14:8-11).
[3]   Figures for the title do not include cases in which the use of the name is not
an option, as in "the royal residence/palace" (בית המלך). Figures for Saul and David are limited to their actual reigns: 1S 11:15-31:8, 2S 3:12-1K 1:48. Epithets other
than title and name are ignored; a designation composed of a name with a patronymic or relationship epithet is simply listed as the use of a name. The figures for
foreign kings do not include designations which include the word "Pharaoh"
(פרעה, discussed in §11.4).

T the use of "king" (המלך) alone, and TS the use of "king" with the name of the state or people ruled.

	PNTS	TPN	TS	T	PN
Saul	–	1	–	14	235
David	–	21	–	159	206
Solomon	–	32	–	46	97
Kings of Judah	53	30	1	41	150
Kings of Israel	30	4	43	36	227
Foreign kings	70	–	59	2	68

5.2.2 The fact, shown in the first column, that Saul, David, and Solomon, are not designated by PNTS, the form of compound designation most often used for other rulers, might possibly reflect a difference between the sources describing the reigns of those three rulers and those of the bulk of the Book of Kings. More probably, it is due firstly to the tendency (noted in §4.13.1) to use few compound designations for well-known figures, and secondly to the fact that the three rulers named are rarely mentioned in dates, or shown in association with foreign kings.[4] These factors also account for the rarity of the use of designations of the form TPN for these characters, in comparison to the proportion of compound designations used for other kings.

5.2.3 The third and fourth columns show the use of the title, in its two different forms, as a simple designation. They confirm the fact that the kings of the United Monarchy are treated differently from others, and show that the kings of Judah receive similar treatment in the use of the title. The form of title typically used for rulers of Judah, like that of the three rulers of the United Monarchy, does not include the name of the state. This is the form of title used by subjects; these are rulers of the community with which the narrator

---

[4]   See §§9.2, 10.3. Philistine speakers refer to "Saul King of Israel" (שאול מלך ישראל) in 1S 29:3. The designation "David King of the Land" (דוד מלך הארץ, 1S 21:12, also in speech by Philistines) uses a form of title for which there is no parallel, so its significance cannot be assessed.

identifies.[5] The form of title used for rulers of the northern kingdom, Israel, most commonly includes the name of the state, as is
the case with the titles of foreign rulers. This feature clearly reflects
the narrator's Judaean (or "normative") viewpoint.[6] A ruler of the
northern kingdom is referred to as "the king" (המלך), without the
addition of the name of the state, where the narrative concerns matters within his kingdom (see §10.1.1). The same is true of (other)
foreign rulers, although they are rarely shown in situations of this
sort, and so rarely designated simply as "the king" (see §11.1.1).

5.2.4 The final point of interest shown by this table is the fact that
the narrator uses the title "king" for Saul very much less frequently
than for other rulers. This is not likely to reflect a source which
avoids the title, since in quoted speech it is used for Saul much as
for other rulers (see §7.3). The narrator's general avoidance of the
title for Saul is no doubt another reflection of his own viewpoint.
It is likely that, for him, David was the first fully legitimate ruler of
the community.

5.3 The Significant Choice of Title or Name

5.3.1 The narrator's viewpoint is clearly evident in the broad patterns illustrated above. It is also revealed in the way he uses name
or title to designate a particular ruler. The table above shows that
the narrator uses these two possibilities for King David in roughly
equal proportions. This general equality is not, however, characteristic of all sections of the narrative. In 1 Kings 1, the narrator designates David by his title alone in 19 cases, by his name alone in one.
Name and title are combined in four cases. The relationship term
"his father", used once, is the only other nominal designation. In 2
Samuel 11, the narrator does not use the title "king" among his 25

---

[5]　The one case anomalous use of the title "king of Judah" occurs in 2K 3:9, (cf.
2K 3:12).
[6]　This viewpoint is also reflected in the use of the title "commander in chief"
(see note 2), and in the use of gentilics (see Revell, 1994, para. 11-14). The form of
title including the name of the state is also used in the inscription of Mesha King
of Moab (l. 10) to designate "the king of Israel".

nominal designations of David.[7] The personal name is used in 23 cases, the relationship term "his master" in two.

5.3.2 This sharp difference in usage correlates, in a general way, with the content of the chapters. 1 Kings 1 is mainly concerned with political matters, the transfer of power from King David to his successor, Solomon. 2 Samuel 11 deals mainly with David's affair with Bathsheba, and so with matters personal to the ruler. This can provide only a partial explanation, however. 1 Kings 1 opens with the story of the provision of a personal "care-giver" to keep the failing David warm. 2 Samuel 11 deals not only with David's affair, but also with its consequences in the political sphere. The choice of designation does not reflect a conventional suiting of the designation to the content of the immediate context. It represents a deliberate attempt to keep King David in the reader's mind in a particular role.

5.3.3 In 1 Kings 1, the narrator is anxious to show that, although David was failing, the transfer of power to Solomon was made through the deliberate act of the proper authority.[8] The narrator rarely misses a chance to remind the reader that David is "the king". In the key verses, from 1:15, where Bathsheba begins the process of persuading David to act, to 1:33, where he finally orders the anointing of Solomon, the narrator uses 17 nominal designations for King David, all containing the title, two combining it with the name. A pronoun alone is used to represent David in "The king said 'What's the matter?' and she said to *him*..." (ויאמר המלך מה לך ותאמר לו, 1K 1:16-17) and in "King David responded and *he* said...", and "the king promised and *he* said..." (ויען... ויאמר... וישבע... ויאמר, 1K 1:28, 29). Thus the title is used five times in successive clauses in

---

[7]   It is assumed that "the king's house" (בית המלך, 2S 11:2, 8, 9) and "the king's portion" (משאת המלך, 2S 11:8) are fixed phrases. The personal name is not a possible choice (see §6.6.1).

[8]   It is reasonable to assume that many of the facts recorded in these narratives were common knowledge, as suggested in McCarter, 1984:15. If so, the narrator could not avoid acknowledging David's physical debility, and so giving additional interest to the question of authority. The same highlighting of authority can be seen in the use of the designations "Zadok the priest" and "Nathan the Prophet" in this chapter (see §12.8.1).

1K 1:15-16, four in 1K 1:22-23. Such frequent repetition is not common even in biblical Hebrew (where repetition of the sort was clearly not felt to be distasteful, as it is in English). Opinions on the narrator's intention in using the title "king" may vary, but there can be no doubt that his concentration on it is deliberate.[9]

5.3.4 In 2 Samuel 11, the narrator exerts himself to keep the reader's mind fixed on David's personal responsibility for the actions described. This can be seen in his reference to King David's servants as "the servants of his (Uriah's) master" (עבדי אדניו) in 2S 11:9, 13. This phrase represents Uriah's viewpoint, suggesting his loyalty to David, and so, by the contrast, drawing attention to David's callous selfishness in bringing about Uriah's death.[10] The use of the term "servants of David" (עבדי דוד, 2S 11:17) to describe those killed along with Uriah as a result of David's orders, is unmarked (see §6.6.2). The same is true of "servants of the king" (עבדי המלך, 2S 11:24), used in the speech of Joab's messenger to describe the same group. The language of the messenger is deferential, and subjects typically do not refer to their ruler by name (as with Joab in 2S 11:19, 20). Nevertheless, the narrator, too, could have used the term "Servants of the king" in 2S 11:17, as he does in 1K 1:9, and in 2S 15:15, etc. The fact that he does not do so would, in itself, have a certain significance (see §1.5.1). The significance of his choice is enhanced by the fact that the phrase "the servants of David" עבדי (דוד) is used to provide a closer definition of "the people" (העם) who died along with Uriah. The redundancy of the expression

---

[9] The narrator's use of other designations is also of interest. In "his father never restrained him" (ולא עצבו אביו מימיו, 1K 1:6) the use of the relationship term reminds the reader that it is a father's duty to discipline his son. In "David's heroic warriors" (הגבורים אשר לדוד, 1K 1:8) the choice of the personal name shows these men as bound to David by personal loyalty. The term "servants of the king" (עבדי המלך, 1K 1:9) is rare in comparison to "servants of David" (see §6.6.2), and so stands out in expressive contrast. It can be seen as referring to mere government employees, who supported the office, not the individual.

[10] The use of "his master" to designate the king in this phrase (rather than the name or a title) occurs elsewhere only in 2K 9:11, where it designates the fellow officers to whom Jehu returns after being privately charged by a prophet to annihilate the descendants of Ahab, including "his master". On the use of "my master's servants" by Uriah in 2S 11:11, see §6.8.3.

draws attention to it, again highlighting David's callous indifference to loyal subordinates.

5.4 The Conventional Basis for the Use of the Title

5.4.1 The usage in 2 Samuel 11 and 1 Kings 1 demonstrates the use of title and name for expressive purposes, but such usage is not the norm. In other passages, the narrator's use of name and title to designate rulers of the community with which he identifies typically reflects a common convention, which is quite closely related to the presentation of the ruler in the clause as "agent" or "patient". The term "agent" as used here must include not only the subject of a clause, but also position as actor where the action is represented by some structure other than a finite verb, as in "the king's command". The term "patient" must include not only the object of a verb, but also any situation in which the ruler is shown as recipient or goal of action by another. In general, a ruler represented as agent is designated by his personal name; a ruler represented as patient is designated by title. Exceptions are not uncommon. A ruler presented as agent may be designated as "king" where the narrator has reason to stress his status; a ruler presented as patient may be designated by name where his status is irrelevant. The general pattern is, however, clear: an agent is designated by name, a patient by title.

5.4.2 This convention reflects an important principle of biblical Hebrew usage. A clause typically reflects the viewpoint of the subject. The verbs בוא and יצא are not used according to the speaker's viewpoint, as are "go" and "come" in English, but according to the viewpoint of the agent, the person going or coming.[11] Where both a general and a specific goal for movement is given, Hebrew typically views both from the viewpoint of the subject, and indicates movement "towards" both, as in "She went... to her father's house, to Bethlehem" (ותלך... אל בית אביה אל בית לחם, Ju 19:2).[12] English

---

[11] Thus the closest English equivalents for בוא and יצא are "arrive at/enter" and "leave/go out of", as the dictionaries show.

[12] Thus the preposition אל is used before the nouns representing both goals in Ju 19:2, 21:8, 2S 17:23, 23:13; "directional" ה_ is suffixed to the first, and אל used before the second in 1S 2:11, 22:9, 1K 2:40, and the reverse order is used in 2S 5:3, 17:20, and (where the preposition is -ל) 2S 13:10.

typically sees the one in relation to the other, as "She went to her father's house in Bethlehem". The use of relationship terms also typically reflects the viewpoint of the subject of the clause, see §13.3.2. The concord of pronouns with a nominal representing speaker or addressee is somewhat similarly conditioned, see §20.2. In the same way, a ruler approached or addressed by a subject is typically designated as "king" because it is in this capacity that the subject approaches him. The title represents the role relevant to the agent. If the ruler is approached or addressed by a rebel, or by a prophet acting as God's servant rather than as his, or by God himself, the title is not used; the status, or role, which it represents is irrelevant. The title is equally not used in most cases where the ruler is subject of a clause. It can be assumed that, for the Hebrew speaker, the person acts, not his office. The title is, however, used where the office is particularly relevant to the action, as where the ruler is acting as judge, deciding the fate of a subject.

5.4.3 The existence of seals inscribed both "servant of the king" and "servant of PN", where the name evidently designates a king, might seem to conflict with the conclusion that name and title are used with distinct values. That conclusion, of course, relates to the corpus as a literary work. Information from the world it describes is not necessarily relevant. The evidence listed in Lemaire, 1978:13-14 shows that the question is not confined to the areas using the Hebrew language. We lack the information needed to evaluate the significance of the existence of the two legends even for the world that produced them, let alone for the usage of the corpus. The assumption that the legends "servant of the king" and "servant of PN" would not be used as free variants on seals, even where title and name represent the same individual, is not, of course, self-evident, but neither is the assumption that they were so used.[13]

5.5 Conclusion

This description shows that these designations act in the same way as lexical items covering the same semantic field. Their use is, in

---

[13] The designation "servant of PN" might, of course, relate to the time before the person named became king.

general, governed by convention. However, the user may choose not to comply with the convention in any particular instance. The use of a non-conventional term, marked usage, then carries expressive meaning related to the value of the term and the reason for the choice. The following sections illustrate the conventional usage in the corpus, and discuss exceptions to it. Uses in narration are treated first, then uses in speech. The discussion also offers interpretation of the meaning presented by the choice (as was done above). Such interpretation is offered here with the intention of showing that the usage described can be understood as self-consistent, not with the intention of promoting a particular understanding of the text (see §1.9.2). The necessary basis for any understanding of these designations is detailed knowledge of the way they are used. The primary purpose of the following chapters is to provide this.

The Designation of King David

6.1 Introduction

This chapter describes the designations used for King David in detail. They are more numerous than those used for any other ruler, and so provide the best illustration of the use of designations for an individual, while also illustrating the patterns characteristic of the designation of rulers generally. The narrator occasionally designates King David by a relationship term, or by a compound designation.[1] For the most part, however, he uses a simple designation: either the name "David" (דוד), or the title "the king" (המלך), so the use of these two terms is described first, starting with the cases in which King David is "patient".

6.2 Obeisance, Approach, or Speech to King David

6.2.1 A character bows to (השתחוה ל־) "the king", not to "David".[2] Clearly the verb implies recognition of his status, which is represented by the title. The same would apply to the act of "falling before" (נפל לפני Shimei, 2S 19:19). In fact, where a subject does something "before" (לפני) King David, the title is generally used, as with the verbs "pass on" (עבר, 2S 15:18), "cross (?)" (צלח, 2S 19:18) "go out" (יצא, 2S 24:4), and "stand" (עמד, 1K 1:28); come before (בוא לפני, 1K 1:28 and elsewhere) is treated in §6.2.2. The subject of the verb in these cases designates a person or group (troops, subjects, Joab, and Bathsheba respectively) interacting with King David as director of the affairs of court, or as commander of the army, not as a private person. Such people naturally view their actions as concerned with "the king"; the use of the title reflects their viewpoint.

---

[1] A relationship term is used (usually in speech) in a dozen cases alone, in combination with the title in 48, in combination with the name in four, and in combination with both name and title in four. A compound designation composed of name and title is used in 24 other cases.

[2] Absalom, 2S 14:33, Ahimaaz, 2S 18:28, Araunah, 2S 24:20, Bathsheba, 1K 1:16, 31, Nathan, 1K 1:23.

6.2.2 Those who "approach" King David (בא ל-/לפני, any verb with לקראת) are typically said to approach "the king" for the same reason. They wish to make arrangements which require the king's permission (Absalom, 2S 13:24, Joab, 2S 14:33). They have a problem that he must decide as judge, or a plea to present ("any man" 2S 15:2, "all Israel", 2S 15:6, Bathsheba, 1K 1:15, Nathan, 1K 1:23). They have been summoned (Absalom, 2S 14:33, Bathsheba, 1K 1:28, Zadok and others, 1K 1:32). They wish to recognize him as king, or be reconciled to him (2S 5:3, 19:9, 16, 25, 26). Complaint or reproach is brought to "the king" by Joab (2S 3:24, 19:6), or "all the men of Israel" (2S 19:42), over problems which, as king, he could remedy, or could have remedied. King David's son, Absalom, in disgrace, is not allowed into the presence of "the king" (2S 14:24, 28), and attempts to send Joab to "the king" as a result (2S 14:29). Presumably King David is seen as judge, or this is a court, not a family matter. The fact that Abishag is brought to "the king" in 1K 1:3, despite the personal nature of her intended duties, may represent her viewpoint, or may be expressive, representing the narrator's insistence on David's royal status in this chapter (see §5.3.3).

6.2.3 Where a character is said to approach "David" the royal status is sometimes clearly irrelevant. Abner is not a subject in 2S 3:20. The same is true of "all the tribes of Israel" in 2S 5:1.[3] Nathan is sent to "David" as God's representative, not as a subject (2S 12:1), and Gad approaches "David" (2S 24:13, 18) in the same capacity. Michal also approaches "David (2S 6:20); she regards his actions as unworthy of a king, and is thus presented as one for whom he is not king (see §6.8.6). Messages are brought, to "David" in several cases. In 2S 11:22 this reflects the narrator's desire to concentrate on David as person in this chapter (see §5.3.4). The fact that the informant comes to "David" in 2S 15:13 suggests that, in his view, David has lost his throne. The speech of Mephibosheth reported in 2S 16:3, and that of Shimei (2S 16:8), clearly present this view. This effective deposition explains David's abandonment of Jerusalem; without it, his precipitate flight is insufficiently motivated. David's situation at this juncture is presented as equivocal. He is treated as

---

[3] In 2S 5:3, where the elders approach "the king", they are going to arrange formal recognition of a fact already accepted.

king by his own supporters (2S 15:15), and even by some of those of Absalom (2S 17:2), but he is portrayed as desponding even to the extent of using the title "king" for Absalom in 2S 15:19 (cf. 2S 15:35).[4] The narrator always treats David as king. His indication of the contrasting view of his characters adds a realistic tension to the narrative. In 2S 9:6, Mephiboshet is said to come to "David", probably in recognition of the personal reasons behind the summons.[5] In 2S 23:13, the fact that the three heroes come to "David" may indicate the personal nature of their loyalty (see §5.3.3n on 1K 1:8).

6.2.4 Speech addressed to King David is treated in much the same way as is approach. Subjects — those who regard David as their king — are said to address "the king" (32 cases in all).[6] Those who are not subjects are said to address "David", as does Abner in 2S 3:12, 21, Jebusites in 2S 5:6. Such characters would use the name, not the title, in their speech (see §6.9.1). God is said to address "David" in 2S 5:19, as are the prophets Gad (2S 7:17, the verb is דבר) and Nathan (2S 12:7, 13) representing God. The prophet Nathan addresses "the king" in 2S 7:3. This may well be an indication that, despite his speech, he is not, in fact, speaking as God's representative (see 2S 7:5). In 2S 24:22, Araunah addresses "David" where

---

[4]   Absalom is, after all, supported by "all the men of Israel" 2S 16:15, 17:14, etc., who had anointed him (משׁח, 2S 19:11). Fokkelman (1981:181-2) argues that David's use of the title in 2S 15:19 represents the viewpoint of the addressee, but failure to refer to "the king of Gath" (or to "your master", as in the similar situation in 1S 29:10, cf. 29:3) would be highly unusual, even if Ittai were regarded as that king's subject. It is much more likely that the use of the title does reveal David's state of mind. David's despondency is also reflected in his speech by his view of his future as unpredictable (2S 15:20, 26), his reaction to Shimei's curse (2S 16:10-12), and in his actions in 2S 15:30.

[5]   "David" also speaks to him, see §6.4.5, though he was sent for by "King David", 2S 9:5.

[6]   Speech is introduced by a form of אמר, either alone or in combination with some other verb: 2S 4:8, 7:3, 9:3, 4, 11, 13:6, 35, 14:4, 9, 22, 15:7, 15, 21, 16:3, 9, 18:28, 19:20, 31, 35, 42, 21:5, 24:3, 23, 1K 1:23, 36. (Cases in 2S 3:24, 13:24, 19:6, 1K 1:31 where a verb describing obeisance or approach to "the king" is one of a series introducing speech have been treated in §§6.2.1-2.) The case in 2S 19:15, where וישׁלחו "they sent" with no following form of אמר introduces speech, and where ויגד "he informed" (2S 18:25), or מדברת עם "was speaking with" (1K 1:22), with no following quoted speech, can be included.

he opposes the offer to buy his property (and is thus not acting as a subject).[7] In 2S 17:21, messengers inform "King David", but speak to "David", probably reflecting the equivocal nature of his situation at that point (see §6.2.3 on 2S 15:13). In 2S 11:5, 10, 11, 23, subjects are said to address "David" in conformity with the narrator's concentration on David as person in that chapter.[8]

6.3 King David as Patient in Other Situations

6.3.1 Elsewhere where King David is "patient", usage is the same. A person acting in the capacity of "subject" interacts with "the king".[9] Those who have never been subjects interact with "David".[10] The same is true of those who reject his authority, as Shimei in 2S 16:6, "all the men of Israel" in 2S 20:2. Similarly Joab leaves "David" in 2S 3:26, determined to contravene his wishes, although in 3:24, as a subject with a complaint, he approached "the king". Rechab and Baanah, who bring the head of a murdered rival to "David" (2S 4:8) are similarly contravening his wishes. In a few other cases, the use of the name "David" probably represents a fixed usage. Thus "David" is anointed as king (2S 5:3), and children are borne to "David" (2S 5:13, 12:15). The statement that the crown of the king of Rabbah "was on the head of David" (ותהי על ראש דוד, 2S 12:30) may also represent conventional language, but the use of "the king" would, in any case, be ambiguous. In 2S 16:23, "the advice of Ahitophel to David and to Absalom" treats the two contestants for the crown impartially; neither gets the title. Where an impersonal subject is used, there is no actor to whom King David's status could be relevant. Consequently "rumour" comes to "David"

---

[7]   But in 2S 24:23, he addresses "the king" in performing the act of a true subject in blessing him.

[8]   Cases in 2S 5:1, 6:20, 13:30, 15:13, 24:13, 18 where a verb describing obeisance or approach to "David" is one of a series introducing speech have been treated in §6.2.3.

[9]   Barzillai (2S 19:32, 33), other supporters (2S 19:16, 41, 20:2), Joab (2S 20:22, 24:9), Abishag (1K 1:4, 15). The title is also used where King David or his actions are presented through the perception of a subject in 2S 3:36, 37, 14:1, 19:2, 3, 24:20.

[10]   Abner, 2S 3:22, various foreign groups or rulers, 2S 5:11, 11, 17, 10:17, 21:16, (also cases in which the action is perceived by such people in 2S 5:17, 8:9, 10:6), God, 2S 8:6, 14, 24:1, or his representatives, 2S 7:17, 12:1.

(השמועה באה אל דוד, 2S 13:30), and unknown actors inform "David" (as with וַיַּגִּדוּ 2S 10:5, וַיֻּגַּד 2S 10:17, 21:11).

6.3.2 A few of the other cases of the use of the name do not fit clearly into the pattern described. The fact that they summoned Ziba to "David" (2S 9:2) probably reflects the fact that his interest in Ziba is of a personal nature. The use of the title is expected, so the use of the name is marked, carrying expressive meaning, as with its use in the cases described in §§6.4.2-3. The same would be true of Joab's sending to "David" about Uriah in 2S 11:6, 18, but the use of the name is characteristic of this chapter, so that individual examples cannot be considered significant. Barzillai and his colleagues bring supplies to "David" in 2S 17:29, reflecting the equivocal nature his position at this point (see §6.2.3). Foreign groups who submit to King David become servants to "David", not to "the king" (2S 8:2, 6, 14, cf. 1K 5:1). Their relationship is seen as personal, not as institutional, just as is that of an individual servant. It may be that the feeding of "David" (2S 3:35), and the bringing of water from Bethlehem to "David" (2S 23:16) were seen as acts of a personal nature. The fact that Joab sends messengers to "David" about the progress of the war (2S 12:27) seems certainly anomalous.

6.4 King David as Agent: Speech

6.4.1 Where King David addresses others, the choice of designation is determined by the relevance of his royal status to the speech. God is addressed only by "David". Where humans are addressed, the choice of designation correlates generally with the status of the person addressed, and the nature of the speech. The "nature" of the speech can, to a considerable extent, be determined objectively, on the basis of clause types classified as modal, interrogative, or declarative (see §1.7.1). The description is based on this classification, although it is clear that it is the content and intention of the speech which determines the choice of designation, not the form. Speeches using modal verbs, and speeches which convey instructions in other ways, are both treated in the same way.[11]

---

[11] The same feature appears in deferential speech, where deferential forms are used in requests presented with indicative verbs as they are in requests presented with modal verbs. See §23.4.

6.4.2 Where the first clause of a speech has a modal verb, marking
it as a request (on the term, see §1.7.1n), the speaker is generally
designated as "the king", as in "The king said 'Let him return to his
house'" (ויאמר המלך יסב אל ביתו, 2S 14:24), and "The king said to
Zadok 'Take the ark of God back to the city'." (ויאמר המלך לצדוק
השב את ארון האלהים העיר, 2S 15:25).[12] The designation "king" is
similarly used where an exclusive first person plural modal is used
to refuse a request in 2S 13:25, and where the modal request is
introduced by a question in 2S 15:19, 27, or a statement in 2S 14:21.
"David" is said to address a modal clause to Ishbosheth, who is not
a subordinate, in 2S 3:14. The speaker is also designated as "David"
where the request indicates benevolent intentions to the addressee:
to Mephibosheth (here a subordinate) "Do not fear" (2S 9:7); to
Tamar, granting her brother's request that she be sent to him (2S
13:7); to Ittai, rescinding a previous command at his request (2S
15:22); and similarly where the speaker uses an inclusive first person
plural modal to subordinates (2S 15:14).[13] The command to Joab
and others to mourn for Abner (2S 3:31) can be included here.
These requests are perhaps not "kinglike" because the speaker is
making concessions which are not required of him by his position
or by the circumstances. The cases in 2S 11:8, 12, where "David"
speaks using modal forms, are no doubt examples of the narrator's
concentration on David as person, not as king, in that chapter.

6.4.3 Where a speech by King David begins with a question, he is
designated as "the king" where the question introduces a request
(see §6.4.2). The same is usually true elsewhere where the addressee
is one of his subjects. In most examples the addressee is presenting
a plea, or is otherwise in the position of a supplicant under judg-
ment, as in "The king said to him 'Why did you not come with
me, Mephibosheth?'" (ויאמר לו המלך למה לא הלכת עמי מפיבשת, 2S

---

[12]   Other examples occur in 2S 10:5, 14:8, 18, 15:9, 18:30, 19:34, 20:4, 24:2, 1K
1:33; also in 2S 7:2, where the initial verb is indeed modal, but simply presents a
request for attention.
[13]   Thus voluntarily abandoning the marks of status, condescending, see §18.2.9.
The choice between the two forms of first person singular pronoun may also reflect condescension, see §26.2.1.

19:26).[14] The speaker is designated as "David" in other situations. The speech expresses benevolent intentions in 2S 9:1 (David wishes to help Jonathan's descendants), and in 2S 21:3, where the question "What shall I do for you" expresses willingness to accede to a plea. In 2S 19:23 the question "What have I to do with you" rebuking the b. Zeruiah, introduces another rejecting the idea of executing any of the rebels now in his power. Here also speech by "David" expresses clemency atypical in a king. In 2S 16:10, the same question was put by "the king". The circumstances which give rise to it are similar in the two passages, but King David, returning in victory in 2S 19:23, is fleeing in despair in 2S 16:10. It is possible that, in the latter case, where David's status is equivocal (see §6.2.3), the narrator takes this opportunity to remind the reader that David is the king, at least as far as the b. Zeruiah, his supporters, are concerned. A question is put by "David" in 2S 12:19 in asking for information on a personal matter. In 2S 11:10, the use of the name is consistent with the narrator's intention in the chapter.

6.4.4 Where the speech does not begin with a question or a modal verb, the designation "king" is used where the speech conveys instructions, or decides the fate of a subject, usually a supplicant. Examples are: "The king summoned Ziba servant of Saul, and said to him 'All that belonged to Saul and his whole family I give to the son of your master. You will work the land for him...'" (ויקרא המלך אל ציבא נער שאול ויאמר אליו כל אשר היה לשאול ולכל ביתו נתתי לבן אדניך ועבדת לו את האדמה..., 2S 9:9-10); "The king said to Araunah 'No. I will indeed buy from you at a fair price...'" (ויאמר המלך אל ארונה לא כי קנו אקנה מאותך במחיר, 2S 24:24).[15] Other uses are possibly to be seen as deliberate choice of marked usage for ex-

---

[14]   Other cases occur with "his servants" in 2S 3:38, with Ziba, 2S 9:2, 3, 4, 16:2, 3; Absalom, 2S 13:26; the Tekoite, 2S 14:5, 19; Ahimaaz, 2S 18:29; the Kushite, 2S 18:32; Mephibosheth, 2S 19:30; and Bathsheba, 1K 1:16. The question to the b. Zeruiah in 2S 16:10, is treated below.

[15]   Other examples occur in 2S 14:10, 21 (noted in §6.4.2), 16:4, 19:24, 39, 21:6. The title is also used where the giving of instruction is indicated by the use of the root צוה (2S 18:5, 21:14), or by the phrase "the word of the king" in 2S 24:4. "David" issues instructions using an indicative verb in 2S 11:25, showing the use of the name characteristic in the chapter (cf. §6.4.2 on its use with modal forms in 2S 11:8, 12).

pressive purposes. The fact that "the king" laments over Abner (2S 3:33) may be intended to stress the public nature of the event (as indicating the extent to which Abner was honoured), or possibly to draw attention to its political implications.[16] King David's responses to the news provided by the lookout in 2S 18:25, 26, 27, are spoken by "the king", presumably showing him as a commander, awaiting the outcome of a crucial battle.[17] The speech by "the king" in 2S 18:2 expresses his own intentions to his subjects, so the use of the title is not surprising. The fact that "the king" abandons these intentions on the advice of others in his speech in 2S 18:4 is surprising; it appears to conflict with the usage in 2S 15:22 (see §6.4.2). There, however, the intention which King David abandoned affected a subject; here it affects only himself.[18] The use of "the king" in 1K 1:29 reflects the narrator's preoccupation with David's status in that chapter.

6.4.5 In other cases, King David as speaker is designated as "David", as in "David said 'To buy the threshing floor from you'" (ויאמר דוד לקנות מעמך את הגרן, 2S 24:21). Here the speech is intended to persuade, not, as that in 2S 24:24, to command (note the absence of modal forms). The same is true of the speech in 2S 15:33-36, persuading Hushai not to accompany him in his flight. It is true the speech includes instructions which are eventually carried out, but the use of conditional clauses presents compliance as an option. The fact that speech intended to confirm identity is addressed by "the king" to Ziba in 2S 9:2, but by "David" to Mephibosheth in 2S 9:6 represents a conflict if the address to Mephibosheth is understood as a question. The conflict could be resolved by the argument that

---

[16] Cf. the use of a compound designation, highlighting the king's participation in the funeral, in 2S 3:31 (see §6.7).

[17] In 2S 18:19-32, the narration of how the news of the death of Absalom and the defeat of his army was brought to King David is drawn out, creating suspense in anticipation of his reaction (cf, the bringing of news of a disaster to Eli in 1S 4:12-18). The narrator uses the designation "king" throughout this passage to heighten the irony of the fact that the king's optimism is justified in political, but not in personal terms. (On the continued use of the title in the following chapter, see §6.5.2.)

[18] It is also possible that the use of "the king" may be a reminder of David's status in his equivocal situation, as suggested for 2S 16:10 in §6.4.3.

the use of the name in 2S 9:6 reflects David's benevolent intentions. The failure to use the title with the root צוה "command" in "David commanded the lads" (ויצו דוד את הנערים, 2S 4:12) does seem anomalous. Even if other dubious examples are added to this, however, they form a negligible proportion of the total. The argument that the use of name or title to designate King David as speaker is generally determined by the status of the addressee and the nature of the speech is clearly justified.

6.5 King David as Agent: Other Actions

6.5.1 Where the action is other than that of speaking, King David as agent is typically designated as "David" (95 cases). The narrator uses the title "king" in 1K 1:4, 15, as is typical in that chapter, to draw attention to King David's status. Elsewhere, the title can be seen as used to highlight action incumbent on, or characteristic of a ruler. "The king" continues the conquest of the land by attacking Jerusalem (2S 5:6); resolves to act as king and so sets out to "sit in the gate" (2S 19:9); proceeds on his return to his capital (2S 19:16, 40, 41); deals with concubines as the situation requires (2S 20:3); or acts to relieve the country of famine (2S 21:2, 7, 8). "The king" makes a promise in 2S 19:24, suggesting that his royal status is a guarantee of performance. The same is possibly intended where "the king" kisses Absalom in reconciliation (2S 14:33), or Barzillai in farewell (2S 19:40, signalling confirmation of his undertaking in 2S 19:39).

6.5.2 The title is also used where the action is not characteristic of a ruler, to draw attention to the contrast between the acts of the person and those expected of a ruler. This is most poignantly shown in the description of King David's reaction to the news of Absalom's death (2S 19:1-5). Other examples of emotional reaction by "the king" occur in 2S 13:31, 36. The fact that "the king" publicly displays emotion which would normally be limited to the private individual, "David", increases the impact of the event on the reader. In 2S 19:1-5, the use of the title can additionally be seen as heightening the irony of the fact that, though a credit to his feelings as father, King David's emotional reaction to Absalom's death threatens to cost him his position as king.[19] In the same way, "the king" abandons Jerusalem and flees (2S 15:16, 16, 17, 23), or is in distress (2S 16:14). The use of the title draws attention to King David's critical situation. The fact that "the king" goes to visit Amnon (2S 13:6) may be an ironic reflection of the fact that King David showed more concern in family matters than is expected of a king, but the usage may be anomalous. The title is also used to show acts not characteristic of a king in a more positive light. The mourning for Abner is discussed above (§6.4.4). In 2S 7:1 "When the king sat in his house" highlights the fact that, though an active ruler, he can stay at home, because God's support has rendered his country secure, as the verse goes on to say.[20] The statement that "The king stood by the gate" as his troops went out to battle (2S 18:4) may be similarly intended to highlight the concern of his troops for him (2S 18:3), but is one of several oddities in the passage (cf. §6.4.4 on the speech in 2S 18:2, 4).

6.5.3 The discussion of the mourning for Abner exemplifies the feature which conceals the expressive meaning from readers not accustomed to usage of this sort. The meaning is not conveyed, like lexical meaning, by the form of the word, but by contrast, by its use where another word is to be expected. Thus where the use of the title is normal, as for a speaker giving instructions, the unexpected use of the name draws the reader's attention to the unkinglike command to mourn for a leader of hostile forces (2S 3:31). Where the use of the name is normal, as for a speaker who is neither instructing nor questioning, the title is used to draw attention to the unkinglike display of emotion (2S 19:1-5). The ideas that the narrator intended to arouse by drawing attention to these actions could be fully determined only by a member of his intended audi-

---

[19] In 2S 12:16-20, where "David" displays grief at the death of his son, the scene is private; the events have no political implications. The narrator thus shows the grief as personal, just as he concentrated on the personal responsibility for the acts in the preceding chapter, of which the death of the child is the result. The view in Fokkelman 1981:262 that "David the father" acts in 2S 19:1, in contrast to "David the King" acting in 2S 15:30 conflicts (at least in terms of the surface) with the designations actually used in the passages.

[20] Contrast 2S 11:1, where "David stayed in Jerusalem", at ease, while Joab was campaigning.

ence, familiar with the culture. The value of the suggestions on his intentions made here is uncertain, but there is no reason to doubt that the contrasting usage has the same purpose in both cases: to draw attention to the unusual nature of the action in the circumstances. (See §1.5.2).

6.6 Simple Designations in Nominal Phrases

6.6.1 The choice of name or title to designate King David in a nominal phrase is determined in much the same way as in a clause. In some uses, the choice is fixed by convention. In narration, the phrase "the house of PN", using the king's name, typically denotes people: the king's family, household, or descendants, as "the house of Saul (בית שאול) in 2S 9:1-3. The phrase בית המלך "house of the king" denotes a building, as in 2S 11:2. The phrase may also be used to refer to the king's family, as in 2S 19:19, where it reflects the viewpoint of the agents, those transporting the family. Subjects typically use the title to refer to the king (see §6.9.1). The use of "the house of the king" (בית המלך) to denote a source or recipient of information (as in 2S 15:35, cf. 2K 7:11) no doubt has a similar origin. The phrases שלחן המלך "the king's table" (2S 9:13, cf. 2K 25:30) and משאת המלך "the king's provision" (2S 11:8) are probably also conventional names for ways in which a ruler could provide food to a subject as a mark of favour. If the use of the ruler's name in these phrases was a possibility, the use of the title in the examples listed is easily understood as expressive. The phrase "David's provision" would give little idea of the nature of the supplies provided. "The king's provision" suggests a rich temptation to Uriah to indulge himself, as the luxury enjoyed by kings is proverbial (see 1S 25:36).

6.6.2 The personal name is typically used in phrases expressing kinship, or other personal relationship. Thus King David's servants are normally referred to as עבדי דוד "David's servants".[21] The phrase עבדי המלך "the king's servants", using the title, occurs in 2S 15:15, where the narrator uses it (and uses the speech by the serv-

---

[21] The phrase "David's servants" is used (after David has become king) in 2S 3:22, 10:2, 4, 11:17, 12:18, 18:7, 9. The name is also used where similar relationship is shown with different syntax in 2S 20:26, 23:8, 1K 1:8.

ants) to assure the reader that David really is king, despite his flight before Absalom, and in 1K 1:9, where it is also expressive (see §5.3.3n; on עבדי המלך דוד, 2S 16:6, see §6.7). The name is typically used in expressions of kinship, including patronymics, and in בני דוד "David's sons" (2S 8:18, cf. 2S 3:2). The phrase בן המלך "son of the king", which contrasts with the typical use of the name to express kinship, is a title (see §3.2.3). Where the narrator uses the phrase to designate David's children, the use of the title can be seen as expressive. In 2S 13:36, for instance, the use of the title can be seen as drawing attention to the fact that events which should not occur in any family are occurring within the royal family.[22]

6.7 Other Forms of Designation

The only other simple designations used by the narrator for King David are the relationship terms אדניו "his lord" (2S 11:9, 13) and אביו "his father" (1K 1:6), the expressive function of which is noted in §§5.3.3n, 5.3.4. The narrator uses a compound designation in 21 cases: דוד המלך in 2S 13:39 (see below), המלך דוד elsewhere. Examples which can reasonably be classed as "introductory" uses (see §4.13.2) introduce noteworthy incidents: David's reaction to God's promise of a successful life and a flourishing dynasty (2S 7:18), his stoning by Shimei (2S 16:5), the events leading up to Solomon's succession (1K 1:1), the promise to Bathsheba that Solomon will succeed (1K 1:28), the command for his anointing (1K 1:32). Most other examples also highlight notable incidents: the mourning for Abner (2S 3:31, see §6.4.4), the covenant making David king of the northern tribes (2S 5:3), the motivation to resume bringing the ark to Jerusalem (2S 6:12), the incident which blocks the transmission of Saul's blood through David's progeny (2S 6:16). Similarly, "King David" summons Mephibosheth (2S 9:5), hears of the rape of Tamar (2S 13:21), attempts reconciliation with Judah, and the replacement of Joab (2S 19:12). Shimei acts to reconcile himself with "King David" (2S 19:17), and Solomon is conveyed to the anointing ceremony on the mule of "King David" (1K 1:38). In 2S 13:39, the text is obscure, but presumably indicates that David came to desire re-

---

[22] Cf. §6.5.2. Other relationships expressed by the use of the name include "sons" (2S 8:18), "brother" (2S 13:3, 32, 21:21), "counsellor" (יועץ 2S 15:12), "companion" (רעה 2S 15:37, 16:16), "seer" (חזה 2S 24:11).

conciliation with Absalom.[23] The final example occurs in 2S 16:6, where Shimei stones "David and all the servants of King David" (ויסקל באבנים את דוד ואת כל עבדי המלך דוד). It could be argued that the narrator is highlighting the actual stoning, and contrasting Shimei's perception (David is not his king) with reality (David's entourage is that of a ruler), but the example is better regarded as anomalous. Other examples of the compound designation occur where two kings interact, in 2S 8:8, 10, 11, as with other kings (see §§9.2.2-3, 10.3.2-3). In 2S 17:17, where Jonathan and Ahimaaz approach "King David", the title is used because they approach as subjects, but the name David is added, as "the king" might refer to Absalom. In these four examples, then, the main motivation for the use of the compound designation is the need for precise identification.

6.8 Designations in Speech: Address

6.8.1 The most common designation of King David used in address to him is the compound אדני המלך, "my lord the king", which is used nine times as a vocative (on which see §25), and 34 times in deferential third person address (on which see §§20-23). The two components of the compound are each used as a simple designation. אדני "my lord" occurs once as vocative, four times in third person address. המלך "the king" occurs in address twenty-two times.[24] The only other designation of King David used in address to him are "the king of Israel" (מלך ישראל, 2S 6:20), which is used ironically (see §§1.4.2-3), and "the anointed of Yahweh" (משיח יהוה, 2S 19:22), which presents the king in terms of his relationship to God rather than to humans.

6.8.2 Typically, the compound designation "my lord the king" (אדני המלך) is used as the first designation of the king in a speech, in-

---

[23] The designation is here "David the King" (דוד המלך). The fact that this is subject of a feminine verb no doubt reflects some error, but this does not necessarily involve the form of the designation. The unusual word order, placing the name before the title, can be read as reflecting the fact that David's desire for reconciliation with Absalom was atypical for a king. See §28.3.6.

[24] This does not include the first case of המלך in 2S 24:23, which appears to be an error, see §§25.7.3, 27.2.1. Two of the 22 cases are vocatives.

cluding a unit of speech within a dialogue.[25] The same designation
may be repeated within such units (as in 2S 14:17, 19, 15:21, 19:28,
28, 29, 24:3, 1K 1:25). The first designation in the speech is "my
lord" (אדני) where "my lord the king" is used in 2S 13:33, 19:20, 1K
1:18, 20, 20, 21); "the king" (המלך) where it is used in 2S 18:36, 38).
The contexts in which the reiteration of "my lord the king" occurs
suggest that it indicates a particular effort by the speaker to influence the king. The use of the title indicates proper recognition of
the king's status. The use of "my lord" expresses fealty, and also
claims the addressee as protector (see §2.3.7). Where a speech includes two or more designations, the last is also sometimes compound, apparently with the same purpose, as in 2S 19:21, 28, 1K
1:2, 27.[26] The initial position of "my lord" in "my lord the king",
preceding the title, is typical for deferential relationship terms (see
§13.4.6). The same components are used in the reverse order in 2S
14:15. Here, the speaker is explaining her action in coming to the
king. The initial position of the title highlights the role relevant as
the goal of her action, the king who is to judge the case, just as the
compound designation is highlighted by its position before the
direct object: "I came to make to the king (who is my lord) this
speech..." (באתי לדבר אל המלך אדני את הדבר הזה....).

---

[25] 2S 3:21, 9:11, 14:9, 12, 17, 18, 19, 15:15, 21, 16:9, 18:31, 32, 19:27, 31, 38, 24:3,
21, 22, 1K 1:2, 13, 24, also the case in 2S 14:15. In 2S 14:22, 16:4 and 18:28, it
follows the communication, giving it prominence (the first two cases are vocatives,
the significance of their position is treated in §§25.8.4-5). A final case occurs in the
speech of Rechab and Baanah in 2S 4:8. Here "my lord the king" is neither initial,
showing that a display of deference is important, nor does it clearly highlight a
particular clause. Its position may be intended to suggest that the speech is presumptuous.

[26] This usage recalls speeches in which the words used at the beginning are repeated at the end (often with some variation) to make a point forcefully ("inclusio",
or "envelope structure") as in "Uriah the Hittite you struck down with the
sword... and him you killed with the sword of the b. Ammon" (את אוריה החתי
הכית בחרב... ואתו הרגת בחרב בני עמון, 2S 12:9, other examples occur in 1S 19:4-5,
28:19, 2S 13:32-3, 19:35-6, 2K 5:18, etc.). A compound designation is occasionally
used in a terminal position in narration as in Ju 4:24, 9:57, 2S 3:37, 21:11, etc. Such
usage is noted as a mark of closure in Mirsky, 1977, and also in Khan, 1988:88,
where the fact that it is a form of inclusio is noted.

6.8.3 "My lord" (אדני) is used at the beginning of a speech or a division of a speech, as is the compound designation. The following designation, where one occurs, is compound. It is used by Shimei (2S 19:20) pleading for his life, and by Bathsheba (1K 1:17) pleading for the recognition of her son as king. Jonadab, the king's nephew, uses it in his attempt to quiet the king's fears that all the princes have been murdered (2S 13:32). The Tekoite uses it to introduce the flattering description of the king's wisdom with which she follows her admission that she has been tricking him (2S 14:20). Use in these contexts suggests that the omission of the title makes the designation more personal, and is intended to make the speech more persuasive (see §25.2.5). The final example of its use is Uriah's reference to "my lord's servants" (עבדי אדני) in 2S 11:11. Since he might have used "the king" or a pronoun instead of "my lord" (see 2S 18:29, 19:8), it seems probable that this expression is intended to enhance the contrast between Uriah's personal loyalty to David and David's callous treatment of Uriah in the same way as is the narrator's reference to "his master's servants" (עבדי אדניו) in 2S 11:9, 13 (see §5.3.4).

6.8.4 "The king" (המלך) typically occurs within a speech, following the use of "my lord the king" (אדני המלך), or "my lord" (אדני). Cases where "the king" occurs in a new speech, but the speaker has used "my lord the king" earlier in the dialogue (as in 2S 14:11, 18:29, 19:29, 24:23) can be included here. "The king" (המלך) is thus the form regularly used for address by subordinates after the tone of the speech has been set by the use of "my lord" or "my lord the king".[27] It is occasionally used where one of these more deferential terms does not precede it. In 2S 16:2, the designation "the king's house" (בית המלך), denoting his family, is already deferential (see §6.6.1); a more personal reference might well be out of place (see §13.4.2). In 2S 19:35, the speech refuses an invitation; the initial "the king" (המלך) is followed by the use of "my lord the king",

---

[27] Such default usage carries no particular implications. However, in a situation like "What other right do I have for further appeal to the king" (ומה יש לי עוד צדקה ולזעק עוד אל המלך, 2S 19:29), where it is used in a despairing statement and contrasts with repeated earlier use of "my lord the king", it may be felt to express distancing and humility.

indicating a desire to remain on good terms. In 2S 19:42, the speech criticizes the king's actions. The omission of "my lord" reflects the fact that the speaker is opposing the king, and so not acting in accordance with the relationship which the use of "my lord" would imply (see §§22.1, 28.2). It also provides a term which is less specific than "my lord the king", and so distances the speaker. Distancing can be used to show deference (see §3.4.4) or rejection (see §23.8.2); the speaker's intention can only be determined from other features of the context. In the request "Help, oh king" (הושעה המלך, 2S 14:4), the usage reflects the highly deferential tone general in the Tekoite's speech, contrasting with the use of "my lord the king" in the same request in 2K 6:26 (see §25.2.3). In Absalom's invitation to the king his father "May the king come..." (ילך נא המלך, 2S 13:24) the omission of "my lord" may be intended to express deference of this sort, or may reflect indifference to the king's reaction.

6.8.5 The pattern typically followed in the use of the common designations is exemplified in: "Let not my lord impute to me guilt, and do not remember that your servant erred on the day when my lord the king left Jerusalem, by the King's keeping it in mind" (אל יחשב לי אדני עון ואל תזכר את אשר העוה עבדך ביום אשר יצא אדני המלך מירושלם לשום המלך אל לבו, 2S 19:20); "Let them search for an unmarried girl for my lord the king, and she will stand before the king and be a care-giver for him and she will lie in your bosom and my lord the king will be warm" (יבקשו לאדני המלך נערה בתולה ועמדה לפני המלך ותהי לו סכנת ושכבה בחיקך וחם לאדני המלך, 1K 1:2). The difference in value between "my lord the king", "my lord" and "the king" is perhaps not great, but it is reasonable to suggest that the different forms of designation do carry different implications, and that these are used consistently.

6.8.6 In 2S 6:20, Michal addresses her husband, King David, scornfully with "How noble today is the king of Israel" (מה נכבד היום מלך ישראל). The usage here is clearly ironic. A subject typically does not include the name of the state ruled in the title of her king (see §5.1.2). The noble conduct implied by the title "king of Israel" is here contrasted with David's conduct in dancing before the ark, which is, in Michal's view, unworthy of a king. The fact that she is said to approach "David" and not "the king" with this speech reflects this view (see §6.2.3, and cf. §7.2.1). In 2S 19:22, Abishai says to King David "Will Shimei not be put to death in account of this: that he has cursed the anointed of Yahweh?" (התחת זאת לא יומת שמעי כי קלל את משיח יהוה). This allusion to David as God's appointee presents Shimei's action in the worst possible light. Abishai thus makes a stronger case for punishment than where he used the designation "my lord the king" in his similar question in 2S 16:9.

6.9 Designations in Speech: Reference

6.9.1 The title המלך "the king" is the usual designation used where King David is referred to in speech between subjects (34 cases). The name דוד "David" is used mainly by those who are not subjects (12 cases).[28] A subject occasionally refers to King David by name. In 2S 17:16, this avoids ambiguity (the title "king" is used for Absalom in 2S 15:19, 16:16, see §6.2.3); King David is referred to by title once the referent has been made clear. The title "king" is not applied to Sheba by the narrator. However, he led "all the men of Israel" (2S 20:2); it is likely that his followers regarded him as king. It is thus reasonable to assume that in 2S 20:11, where people are asked to choose between him and King David, the designation of the latter by name is also intended to avoid ambiguity. The compound designation "King David" is used by Joab in addressing the wise woman from the city in which Sheba has taken refuge (2S 20:21), and by Nathan addressing Bathsheba in 1K 1:13, where confusion with Adonijah is possible (cf. 1K 1:5, 11). The main motivation for the use is probably to avoid ambiguity in both cases. In 2S 19:44, the clause containing the name "David" is parallel to the preceding, in which the designation "the king" is used. The two clauses thus form a unit containing the composite designation המלך דוד "King David", used here probably simply to highlight the designation of King David in the context of the claim of his close association with the speakers. The designation "David b. Jesse" is pres-

---

[28]   Those who have rejected David as king (2S 17:1, 20:1), foreigners (2S 3:17, 5:6, 10:3, 3), God (2S 16:10, 24:12, and, with the epithet עבדי "my servant" 2S 3:18, 7:5, and elsewhere after his reign). David addressing God, refers to himself by name in 2S 7:20, and as עבדך דוד "your servant David" in 2S 7:26 (see §27.2.1).

ented (by a speaker who rejects David as king) in parallelism of this sort in 2S 20:1.[29]

6.9.2 King David is referred to as "our lord David" (אדנינו דוד) by Nathan in 1K 1:11, and, with the addition of the title, by Jonathan (1K 1:43, 47), as is "my lord King David" (אדני המלך דוד) by Bath-sheba (1K 1:31), and Benaiah (1K 1:37). The name is no doubt used in each case to distinguish the referent, as the term "king" in those contexts might also be used to designate Adonijah or Solomon. Jonathan's use of the first person plural pronoun is inclusive, reflecting the fact that he and his addressees hold that David still has the power to make Adonijah his successor. Nathan is speaking to Bathsheba as a courtier, and so as a subordinate (see §2.5.2), not as God's representative. In his speech, the pronoun is exclusive, the plural pronoun representing a deeper form of humility than would the singular (see §18.2.2). In the cases of Bathsheba and Benaiah, the designation is used in a wish spoken in the king's presence. There is no example of a subject addressing a king by name, and the personal name is rarely used as a term of address in other circumstances (see §25.4; even reference to a superior by name is unusual, see §13.4.3). For this reason such wishes are not treated as examples of address, but as examples of reference, as would clearly be the case if they were not spoken before the king (see also §8.3n on 1K 1:51, and §10.4.3 on 2K 9:13).

6.9.3 King David is designated as אב "father" (with an appropriate pronoun suffixed) in 2S 13:5, by Jonadab advising Amnon how to use King David to make Tamar visit him, and in 2S 16:21, 21, where Ahitophel advises Absalom to show his break with the king as definitive by publicly visiting his concubines. The title "the king" is used by Tamar speaking to Amnon (2S 13:13), and by Absalom speaking to Joab (2S 14:32, 32), where it can be seen as representing their father as the authority who can decide their fate. Ahitophel,

---

[29]   This is one of a variety of forms of poetic parallelism in which the components of fixed phrases are divided between parallel stichs (see Watson, 1985:133, 328-332). Various features characteristic of poetry occur sporadically in prose, most commonly in speech. Other examples of names treated in this way in speech occur in 1S 10:11, 1K 12:16, and cf. Ju 9:28, 1S 25:10.

speaking to Absalom in 2S 17:2 predicts striking down "the king" alone, suggesting the removal of the authority against which Absalom is rebelling. In the preceding verse he referred to him as "David" presenting him as a private person, devoid of royal power.[30] The two examples of the designation "father" can reasonably be seen as contrasting with these cases in which it might have been used but is not. It can be seen as presenting the suggested action as a family matter, and so as easy.

[30] This is consistent with the usual treatment by the narrator of rulers whose position was, in his opinion, illegitimate. He never uses the title for Athaliah (2K 11:1-16), who ruled independently for six years, nor for Sheba (who was probably considered as king by his followers, see §6.9.1), and only sparingly for Saul and the kings of the northern kingdom generally, see §§7.1.1-2, 10.1-2. See also §9.3.2 on the Rab Shakeh's failure to use the title for King Hezekiah in 2 Kings 18.

The Designation of King Saul

7.1 Designation in Narration

7.1.1 During his description of the reign of Saul (1S 11:15-31:8), the narrator designates him by name in 206 cases, by title in 14 (6%). He combines the two only in 1S 18:6. King Saul is thus clearly treated differently from King David in general, and this can be confirmed in detail. The name is used where subjects approach or speak to King Saul (as in 1S 16:20, 21, 17:15, 32), and where King Saul gives instructions to subjects (as in 1S 14:17, 34, 38, 42, 43). In both situations, the title is typically used to designate King David (see §§6.2, 6.4.2). Where King Saul is designated by title, the situation is generally one in which its use would also have been expected for King David, but use is made of it only in particular instances of such situations.

7.1.2 The narrator uses the title in the greatest concentration where King Saul summons Ahimelek, (a priest who had helped David under the impression he was on a mission from the king), and then has him and his family slaughtered (1S 22:11, 11, 14, 16, 17, 17, 18). He also uses the title where "the king" instructs Abner to find out who David is (1S 17:56); where David decides to become son-in-law to "the king", and acts accordingly (1S 18:26, 27, 27); where "the king" sits to eat at the time of the new moon (1S 20:24, 25); and where "the king" tells the witch of Endor not to worry after she has discovered his identity (1S 28:13). This last passage shows Saul in a bad light. Even though the witch now knows that he is the king who banned her activities, he confirms his promise that she will not be penalized, becoming accessory to the breaking of his own laws.[1] Saul is also shown as unworthy to be king in his deal-

---

[1] The promise in 1S 28:10, that she will not suffer as a result of carrying out his wishes, is made by "Saul". The title (clearly a marked usage where designating Saul) is used for the more reprehensible confirmation of this promise in 1S 28:13, when the woman has realized who he is, in much the same way as a compound

ing with Ahimelek (1S 22:11-18). The maintenance of justice is one of the king's main duties (see §2.4.2). Saul not only condemns an innocent man, he slaughters a whole family of "priests of Yahweh".[2] The other examples of the use of the title occur at important points in the career of David. In 1S 17:56 "the king" takes notice of him, leading to a permanent position at court.[3] In 1S 18:26-27, David becomes a member of the royal family. In 1S 20:24-25, David is shown as expected to participate in a ceremonial meal along with Abner and Jonathan, who are both military commanders, and close relatives of the king. The narrator uses the marked designation "king", and the implications it carries, to draw attention to Saul's unworthiness for the kingship on the one hand, and to David's rise through society towards the throne on the other.

7.1.3 The narrator' single use of a compound designation combining name and title is consistent with this suggestion. The women come out to greet "Saul the King" (שאול המלך, 1S 18:6) with song on his return from battle. The order name – title is unusual, suggesting that the title is of secondary importance, not central to the women's perception of Saul.[4] The fact that they do not refer to Saul as "the king" may reflect the conventions of this sort of song (see §7.2.2n), but the fact that they treat David as his equal or superior

---

designation is used after introductory material to highlight a significant act, see §4.12.2, cf. §28.5.1.

[2]   Note the use of "the servants of the king" (עבדי המלך) in 1S 22:17. The use of the title in this phrase is marked (cf. §§6.6.2, 8.1.1). "The king" has decided on this atrocity, but even "the servants of the king" (government employees, who serve the institution but have no loyalty to an individual cf. §5.3.3n) have principles superior to his, and refuse to carry out his orders. The unusual term "priests of Yahweh" (only used in 1S 22:17, 21) is no doubt also intended to draw attention to the sacrilegious aspect of Saul's act. Cf. the term "prophets of Yahweh" used to highlight the relationship to God for similar negative reasons in 1K 18:4, for positive ones in 1K 18:13.

[3]   Note that, as in 1S 28:13 (see note 1) the title is not used at the beginning of the incident, where Saul's interest is first displayed, in 1S 17:55, but in 1S 17:56, where he takes effective action as a result.

[4]   See §28.3.6. The verse is usually emended, and the title ignored (as in McCarter, 1980:310-311). Fokkelman (1986:216, and note 18) argues that the order of the words gives extra emphasis to Saul's capacity as king, but does not support this from consideration of other uses.

shows their lack of respect for Saul.[5] The use of the compound designation here, then, draws attention to this expression of the feelings of Saul's subjects towards him, and, by the unusual order of its components, helps to illustrate it.

7.1.4 The only other designations used by the narrator are relationship terms. King Saul is designated as "Saul his father" (שָׁאוּל אָבִיו) where his son Jonathan's address to him is introduced in 1S 19:4, 20:32, but not in 1S 14:43, 20:28. In 1S 19:4, Jonathan speaks in favour of David to Saul, and persuades him to allow David back to court. In 1S 20:32, Jonathan makes a similar attempt which is a striking failure. The term "father" draws attention to the relationship which should have precluded disagreement between Saul and Jonathan, and so reminds the reader of the problems of the triangular relationship between Jonathan, Saul, and David. In 1S 14:43, 20:28, Jonathan is replying to Saul's questions, acting in the position of the accused or his advocate addressing a judge. Saul is referred to as "his father" (אָבִיו) in 1S 14:27, 20:33, where he has acted against Jonathan's interests. In 1S 14:27 he did not ensure that Jonathan had important information.[6] In 1S 20:33 he determined to kill David, Jonathan's protégé.[7] Here, also, the use of the relationship term highlights the fact that Saul's relationship with his son is far from ideal. The case in 1S 20:33 can be seen as a deliberate contrast to that in 1S 19:4, drawing attention to the hardening of Saul's atti-

---

[5]   He is certainly treated as an equal, as is noted in McCarter, 1980:312, quoting D.N. Freedman. Fokkelman, 1986:214-217, takes a similar view, quoting the extensive discussion in Harran, 1970.

[6]   Jonathan should get the information as a leading figure in Saul's army (1S 13:2, 22), not only as his son, but note the repeated reference to the relationship in 1S 14:39, 40, 42, where Saul seeks to conceal his fault behind a display of impartiality and unnecessary rigour.

[7]   David is clearly Jonathan's subordinate. Jonathan is the king's son. Moreover, he equips David (1S 18:4), and is in a position to give him leave of absence (1S 20:5) and to be held responsible for that absence (1S 20:27). David's subordinate position is also shown by the fact that he uses deferential language to Jonathan (1S 20:7-8, see §20.3). The fact that David's name follows Jonathan's when the two form a compound also suggests his subordinate status (see Revell, 1993:72-3), but this could simply be due to Jonathan's relationship to the king (see §2.5.2).

tude towards David. The general use of relationship terms is discussed in §13.3-4.

7.2 Designation in Speech

7.2.1 Address The terms "our lord, my lord" and "my lord the king" are used in second or third person address to King Saul in much the same way as to King David.[8] The same is true of the use of the title "king". The title is relatively more common in requests to Saul than in those to David, but this can be attributed to the fact that the requests are not personal to the speaker.[9] David twice uses the title "king of Israel" in addressing Saul (מלך ישראל, 1S 24:15, 26:20). As where David is addressed in this way (see §6.8.6), the usage is ironic, contrasting Saul's ignoble actions with the conduct expected of an ideal king of Israel. The conventions followed in address to Saul appear, then, to be the same as those followed in address to David.

7.2.2 Reference In speech among subjects, King Saul is usually referred to as "the king" (המלך, eleven cases).[10] Philistine speakers refer to him as "Saul King of Israel (שאול מלך ישראל), the standard form of compound designation used by foreigners, in 1S 29:3. Otherwise, the name alone is used by those who do not recognize him as their king: by Goliath (1S 17:8), by God (1S 15:11, 16:1), by Samuel (presumably as subject to God rather than to Saul, 1S 16:2), by the witch of Endor (who has rejected his decree, and so does not act as a subject (1S 28:9, 12). Jonathan never refers to King Saul as "the king". He refers to him simply as "my father" in 1S 19:3, 3, 20:2, 2, 9, 12, 13, 13, where he promises David to speak to King Saul on his behalf, or to bring him information from the king. The

---

[8]　"My lord the king" (אדני המלך, 1S 24:9, 26:17, 19) "my lord" (אדני, 1S 26:18), and "our lord" (אדנינו, 1S 16:16). The use of the plural pronoun in the latter is unusual, even where there is more than one speaker, and probably reflects fear that the speech may annoy the addressee, King Saul (see §18.3.1).

[9]　The title "king" (המלך) is used in requests in 1S 19:4, 22:15, 23:20, 20, and in other address, in 1S 17:55, 18:18, 22:14, 26:22, and also in "the king's table" (שלחן המלך, 1S 20:29), which is probably a fixed phrase.

[10]　1S 12:2, 13, 17:25, 18:22, 22, 23, 25, 25, 20:5, 21:3, 9, 26:14, 16. Samuel's use of "the king" in 1S 12:14, and of "their king" in 1S 12:25, presumably refers to any king.

use of the term may hint that Jonathan's relationship as son of King Saul will ensure his success, or may possibly be intended to reflect Jonathan's acceptance of David as the true king. Jonathan uses "Saul my father" (שאול אבי) to begin his attempt to reconcile David to King Saul in 1S 19:2, and in 23:17, 17, where he definitely declares his loyalty to David, in opposition to Saul's wishes. Here, too, the reference to family relationship instead of to royal status can be variously interpreted, but it seems likely that, in 1S 23:17, it can be taken as reflecting the fact that Jonathan is not treating Saul as his king. Where David refers to Saul by name (see §7.2.3), he, too, has rejected him as king. Saul's name is also used in 1S 13:4, 15:12, 19:24, where the speaker is not indicated (see §6.3.1), and in the women's song in 1S 18:7, repeated by Philistine speakers in 1S 21:12, 29:5.[11] Again, the conventions followed in the designation of King Saul and King David in speech do not seem to differ significantly.

7.2.3 David refers to Saul by name when speaking to God (1S 23:10, 11, 12), to his own followers (1S 22:22, 26:6), and to himself (1S 27:1,1). He refers to Saul as "the king" in speaking to Saul's servants (1S 18:23), and to Ahimelek the priest (speaking as one sent on a mission by the king, 1S 21:3, 9). In speaking to Saul's commander-in-chief Abner he refers to Saul as "your lord the king" (1S 26:15, 15), and as "the king" (1S 26:16).[12] David thus refers to King Saul by title when he himself is still acting as a subject, or when he is speaking to someone who regards Saul as king. He refers to Saul by name when he has left the court, rejecting him as king, and is speaking to someone who does not regard Saul as his king. Accordingly, David refers to King Saul as "the king" when speaking to Jonathan of his duty to sit with "the king" in 1S 20:5. "The king" is

---

[11]   In 1S 19:24, "Is Saul also among the prophets?" is the second of the two parallel questions given in 1S 10:11. The first of those questions contains a patronymic, so the parallelistic structure presents a compound designation appropriate in the situation (see §6.9.1n), as Saul is not yet king. Saul does not take umbrage at the use of his name with no title by the women in 1S 18:7, suggesting that the usage was characteristic of such songs.

[12]   "Your lord" (אדניך) precedes the title in the first case in 1S 26:15, and follows it in the second. On the significance of their relative positions, see §13.4.5.

here the relevant role. However, he refers to Saul as "your father" in speaking to Jonathan elsewhere (אביך, 1S 20:1, 3, 6, 8, 10).

7.2.4 David refers to Saul as "the anointed of Yahweh" (משיח יהוה) in speaking to his own followers, 1S 24:7, 26:9, 11, 2S 1:14, 16, to Abner, 1S 26:16, and to Saul, quoting his own thoughts, in 1S 24:11, and, in third person address, 1S 26:23. He thus recognizes Saul as appointed by God (cf. Samuel's usage in 1S 12:3, 5), but avoids recognizing Saul as his king. David combines "my lord" (אדני) with "the anointed of Yahweh" in 1S 24:7, 11, but not in 1S 26:9, 11, 23. Thus he still recognizes the mutual obligations of master and servant (the public perception of his relationship with Saul, see 1S 29:4) in 1 Samuel 24, where he is led to effect some form of reconciliation (1S 24:23). In chapter 26, his attitude has changed. He addresses Saul with the conventional master-servant terminology in 1S 26:17-19, but his strong language in 26:19-20 shows his real feelings. In 1S 26:21, Saul confesses his error, and appeals for David's return, addressing him as "my son" to suggest the benevolence of his feelings (see §25.3.3). David confirms his alienation by ignoring this appeal, using distancing third person address to "the king" (see §23.8.2). The terms used for reference or address to King Saul by David are thus carefully chosen to show his feelings and attitude towards the king.[13]

7.3 Conclusion

The designation of King Saul can thus be seen as based mainly on the same conventions as govern the designation of David. In narration, an additional factor, irrelevant to the designation of David, dominates the designation of Saul. The use of the title is avoided (in general) in narration, as in other cases in which the narrator does not regard the character in question as a legitimate king (see § 6.9.3n). The narrator does use the title for King Saul in some situations consistent with the common conventions, but the choice of these situations is not conventional. It promotes the view of the

---

[13]   The difference in David's attitude to Saul in 1 Samuel 24 and 1 Samuel 26 has been noted, as in Garsiel, 1985:125-6, Fokkelman, 1986:461-6, 544-51. The latter gives some attention to the way in which the designations are chosen to illustrate this.

narrator that Saul was unworthy to reign, and draws attention to the rise of David, who has been anointed to replace him. Apart from the use of "the Lord's anointed", the conventions followed in the use of designations for King Saul in quoted speech do not differ significantly from those reflected in the designation of King David. This shows that the narrator intended to present the speech of his characters as "natural", as usage typical of the situation. It also confirms the conclusion that the designations used in the narrative sections do not follow different conventions from those used for David. The different pattern which they show arises from the manipulation of the standard conventions to promote the narrator's views.

The Designation of King Solomon

8.1 Simple Designations

8.1.1 The narrator uses the title "king" (המלך) for King Solomon proportionately less commonly than for King David (see §5.2.1), reflecting the fact that Solomon is less often shown interacting with his subjects than is David. The basis of the use of the title is the same for both rulers. Where King Solomon is patient, and the agent is one of his subjects, he is designated by the title. Where the agent is not his subject, he is designated by name. The use of the name is noteworthy in a few cases. In 1K 2:1, David addresses his son, and so "Solomon", not "the king". The whole country approaches "Solomon" to hear his wisdom (1K 5:14), presumably because wisdom is characteristic of the individual, not of the office.[1] Jeroboam is "servant to Solomon" (עבד לשלמה, 1K 11:26), because the master-servant relationship is seen as personal.[2] The statement that "Adonijah feared Solomon" (ואדניהו ירא מפני שלמה, 1K 1:50) reflects the ambiguity of the situation. Adonijah's attempt to become king is not settled until King Solomon sends for him, and he bows to King Solomon in 1K 1:53, and the narrator does not use the title for Solomon until this point. The name is also used where King Solomon receives information from an unnamed agent.[3]

8.1.2 The use of the title also requires comment in a few cases. Jeroboam is said to attack "the king" (1K 11:26, 27), representing the general perception of the action. The use of the title here draws attention to the gravity of the action, (as does the use of the name of God in 1S 22:17, 21, see §7.1.2n). The use of the name, while indi-

---

[1]   Thus the phrase "wisdom of Solomon" (חכמת שלמה) occurs in 1K 5:10, 14, 10:4; "wisdom of the king" does not occur.
[2]   As with David, see §6.6.2. Population groups are treated in the same way in 1K 5:1, cf. §6.3.2.
[3]   1K 1:51, 2:41, cf. §6.3.1. A compound designation is used in 1K 2:29, introducing the narration of the end of Joab's career, see §8.2.

cating rejection of Solomon as king (see §6.2.3), would suggest only a quarrel between two private individuals.[4] The Queen of Sheba comes to "Solomon" (1K 10:2), but speaks to "the king" in praise (1K 10:6), and gives "the king" valuable gifts (1K 10:10). Possibly the intention is to show that she began to appreciate his kingly qualities after meeting him. Hiram King of Tyre also presents gold to "the king" (1K 9:14), and "the king" has "ships of Tarshish" at sea with the ships of Hiram (1K 10:22), although Hiram's other dealings are with "Solomon" (1K 5:15, 22, 24, 9:11). Possibly the intention is to show that in 1K 9:14, 10:22, the two are acting together as kings, while elsewhere they are acting as friends, or as merchants. "Solomon" as agent directs action towards "the king" as patient in "Solomon collected chariotry... and stationed them... with the king in Jerusalem" (ויאסף שלמה רכב ופרשים... וינחם... ועם המלך בירושלם, 1K 10:26) "The king" here represents the purpose of the arrangement, or the viewpoint of those being stationed: they were to be with "the king". Similar usage occurs in "Solomon had twelve prefects... and they maintained the king and his household" (ולשלמה שנים עשר נצבים... וכלכלו את המלך ואת ביתו, 1K 4:7), and "Solomon convoked the elders... to King Solomon in Jerusalem" (אז יקהל שלמה את זקני ישראל... אל המלך שלמה ירושלם, 1K 8:1). Cf. also 1K 12:21 (see §9.2.5).

8.1.3 Where King Solomon speaks, he is designated by title, as "the king", when issuing instructions to, or giving judgment on, a subject, and also where the verb "command" (צוה) is used in 1K 2:46, 5:31 (see §6.4.4n). The name "Solomon" is used where the speech does not instruct or judge, or the addressee is not a subject.[5] Exceptions occur in 1K 1:53, 2:29, where instructions, using modal verbs, are said to be given by "Solomon". In 1K 1:53, the use of the name reflects the "unkinglike" benevolence Solomon displays in sparing Adonijah's life (see §6.4.2). In 1K 2:29, the use of the name possibly indicates that the action is unkinglike because ineffective (see §

---

[4] Subordinates are also said to attack "the king" in 2K 14:5, 21:23-24. The use of the name in 2K 12:21 seems anomalous (see §9.1.1).

[5] The title is used in 1K 2:20, 26, 31, 36, 42, 44, 3:23, 24, 25, 27, and also as subject of the verb "command (צוה) in 1K 2:46, 5:31. The name is used in 1K 1:52, 3:6, 5:16, 8:12.

28.2.1). "The king" speaks in 1K 2:31, where the renewed command is effective. The choice of name or title to represent King Solomon as speaker thus follows (with one possible exception) the same pattern of usage as does the choice for King David.

8.1.4 Apart from speaking, King Solomon as agent is designated as "the king" where he appoints officials (1K 2:35, 35), travels to Gibeon to sacrifice (1K 3:4), provides materials or technology for his building (1K 7:46, 10:12, 27), or objects for the royal ceremonial (1K 10:17, 18), has ships for international trade (1K 10:22). He is also designated by title as agent where "all Israel" is either joint agent, or is patient, in the ceremony described in 1 Kings 8. The examples are: "The king turned and blessed the whole congregation of Israel" (ויסב המלך את פניו ויברך את כל קהל ישראל, 1K 8:14); "The king and all Israel with him were sacrificing before Yahweh" (והמלך וכל ישראל עמו זבחים זבח לפני יהוה, 1K 8:62); and "The king and all the b. Israel inaugurated the temple of Yahweh" (ויחנכו את בית יהוה המלך וכל בני ישראל, 1K 8:63). The title is also used in "On that day the king sanctified the interior of the court..." (ביום ההוא קדש המלך את תוך החצר, 1K 8:64). King Solomon is also designated by title where the action is presented through the perception of a subject in 1K 3:28. The name "Solomon" is used to represent him as agent elsewhere.[6]

8.1.5 It is reasonable to argue that these examples show that the title is used to designate King Solomon as agent where the royal status is involved, the name where it is not. This argument would assume that the journey to Gibeon was made so that King Solomon could perform a ceremonial act, not offer a personal sacrifice, and that the examples in 1K 8:14, 62, 64, also depict ceremonial acts, not personal worship. The designation "Solomon" is used in two contexts similar to these. "Solomon slaughtered (as) the peace offerings which he offered to Yahweh 22,000 oxen and 120,000 sheep" ויזבח שלמה את זבח השלמים אשר זבח ליהוה בקר עשרים ושנים אלף)

---

[6] The agent is designated as "Solomon" in 1K 2:12, 27, 3:1, 3, 4, 10, 15, 4:7, 5:25, 25, 6:14, 21, 7:1, 8, 47, 48, 51, 8:22, 54, 63, 65, 9:1, 10, 17, 21, 22, 9:25, 10:3, 26, 11:2, 5, 6, 7, 28, 40, 42, 43, also in 1K 11:27, where the action is building, but the statement is retrospective, providing background to the rise of Jeroboam.

וצאן מאה ועשרים אלף, 1K 8:63), describes the munificence of Solomon's provision for sacrifice, seeing it as a personal act, and so performed by "Solomon", as are other actions directed towards God in
1K 8:12, 22, 54. In "Solomon kept the festival at that time, and all
Israel with him... before Yahweh our God..." (ויעש שלמה בעת ההיא
...את החג וכל ישראל עמו... לפני יהוה אלהינו, 1K 8:65) the use of the
name contrasts directly with the use of the title in 1K 8:62, but
there the performance of the action is described. In 1K 8:65, the
narrator looks back on the sacrifice, using the designation "Yahweh
our God", unique in the corpus, to present himself and his readers
as part of the community keeping the festival on that inaugural occasion.[7] Solomon is presented as a worshipper among worshippers;
his royal status is irrelevant in the context.[8]

8.1.6 In nominal phrases, King Solomon is typically designated by
name (28 cases). The title is used in "the royal merchants" (סחרי
המלך, 1K 10:28), mentioned in the context of the acquisition of
horses, and so of public rather than private activity. The title is also
used in "companion of the king" (רעה המלך, 1K 4:5). This contrasts
with the use of the name in "companion of David" (רעה דוד, 2S
15:37, 16:16, see §6.6.2n). "Companion of the king", using the title,
is perhaps itself to be considered a title rather then a descriptive designation.[9] A compound designation, including title and name, appears to be used in nominal phrases to draw attention to King Solo-

---

[7]   Cf. the remark in Long, 1984:107, "The author-editor asserts common heritage
with events and his audience".
[8]   It is also possible that the unexpected designations for King Solomon and for
God in this verse reflect the fact that it is a late addition, as is often suggested. The
question cannot be decided objectively. The meticulous analysis in Talstra, 1993,
does not provide a basis for relating the use of designations to the stages through
which the material in this chapter developed, but that could scarcely be expected,
since only three designations (representing two different stages) are covered. The
situation for the remainder of the chapter is summed up by the comment in Long
1984:94, "The evidence for a complicated history of redaction is clear, but a consensus on the lines of that history eludes us".
[9]   That is, the reference may be generic rather than personal. "Companion of the
king" and "companion of PN" might have been used to designate the same person,
but, if so, would presumably have been used in different contexts.

mon's reputation for the luxury of his table (1K 5:7, 10:21), and his generosity (1K 10:13).

8.2 Compound Designations

The narrator uses compound designations more frequently for King Solomon than for King David, but uses them in the same way: to draw attention to significant events. They are used freely in connection with the fate of Adonijah (1K 1:53, 53, 2:19, 22, 23, 25), the building and inauguration of the temple (1K 5:27, 6:2, 7:13, 14, 40, 45, 51, 8:1, 2, 5), other glories of Solomon's kingdom (1K 9:26, 28, 10:10, 13, 13, 16, 21, 23). The rest are used at the beginning and end of the description of King Solomon's administration (1K 4:1, 5:7, 7); where his concessions to Tyre are mentioned (1K 9:11); where his building programme is summarized (1K 9:15); at the beginning of the narration of the end of Joab's career (1K 2:29); of Solomon's misdeeds and their consequence (1K 11:1). A compound designation is also used in 1K 12:2, where King Solomon must be distinguished from the new king, Rehoboam.

8.3 Designation in Speech

Most of the few designations used by speakers addressing or referring to King Solomon require comment. The woman pleading for her son's life uses a particle before the term "my lord" at the beginning of her speech (בי אדני, 1K 3:17, 26). The particular humility which this particle indicates is suitable to her desperate need to persuade the king (see §15.7.3). King Hiram addresses King Solomon as "my brother" (אחי, 1K 9:13). This treats him as an equal, but is also a typical example of the use of kinship terms in language intended to persuade (see §25.3). A composite designation "King Solomon" (המלך שלמה) is used for reference by speakers in 1K 1:34, 39, 51, 51, where Solomon is king, but David is still alive, so "the king" might be ambiguous.[10] In 1K 2:45, it is used to ensure that

---

[10] Adonijah's use of the designation "King Solomon" in 1K 1:51 shows that his speech is directed to the messengers, not to Solomon (see §6.9.2). The speech is presented in "semi-indirect" form (see Goldenberg, 1991:81-3). Adonijah's name is used to avoid ambiguity (as is Solomon's in 1K 1:34, 39) in the wish "Long live King Adonijah" (יחי המלך אדניהו, 1K 1:25), contrasting with the usual form "Long live the king" (יחי המלך, 1S 10:24, 2S 16:16, 2K 11:12).

the person to be blessed is correctly identified. The unusual order "Solomon the King" (שלמה המלך) is used by Adonijah in 1K 2:17. This form recognizes Solomon as king, but gives precedence to the name (see §28.3.6), and so evokes the family situation within which his request is made, in the hope of making his speech more persuasive. In her reply, Bathsheba refers to "the king" (1K 2:18), not to "my son", showing that she does not regard this as a family matter. She chooses the term typically used in speech between subjects, but, in the context, it can be regarded as showing at least lack of enthusiasm, if not hostility. A prophet, quoting God, refers to Solomon by name in 1K 11:31. A subject uses "my lord the king" (אדני המלך) in third person address to King Solomon in 1K 2:38, and refers to him as "the king" (המלך) in 1K 2:30, in accordance with the usage described for King David.

8.4 Conclusion

The designation of King Solomon appears to follow the same patterns of usage as does the designation of King David. The few features in which it differs can be seen as reflecting the difference in the contexts in which the two kings are shown as acting. King David is more frequently shown in personal relationship to others. The material on King Solomon is more concerned with his building programme, and with ceremonial actions. Where the contexts in which the designations of the two kings are used can be directly compared, the common basis of the usage is evident. It is consequently reasonable to suggest that the designations of King Solomon described in §8.1.4-5 also reflect this basis, even though the corresponding interpretation of their use can sometimes only be offered hesitantly. The alternative suggestion, that 1 Kings chapter eight was not originally part of the corpus, would not be less speculative.

The Designation of Kings of Judah

9.1 Narration: Simple Designations

9.1.1 A king of Judah as patient is designated by title (המלך) where the agent is one of his subjects (1K 12:16, 2K 11:11, 17, 17, 19, 21:23, 22:9, 9, 10, 10, 20). The same designation may be used where the agent is not his subject if the royal status is of particular significance. In 2K 15:5, God strikes "the king" with leprosy. The title reminds the reader that this renders King Azariah unfit to act as king. In 2K 18:18, the envoys of the king of Assyria "call to the king" (ויקראו אל המלך); they are on a mission to "King Hezekiah" (2K 18:17), so "the king" is the role relevant to them. In 2K 25:5, 6, Chaldaean troops pursue and capture "the king"; the significance of the event lies in the capture of the head of state. Elsewhere where the agent is not a subject, the king is designated by name (20 cases).[1] The name may also be used for expressive purposes where the agent is a subject. In 2K 18:37, the officials who received the king of Assyria's domineering message come to "Hezekiah" to report. The use of the name suggests that they regard him as if already dethroned by the Assyrians; their tearing of their clothes reflects similar despair.[2] The use of the name in 2K 12:21, where his servants conspire and kill "Jehoash", seems anomalous. A king attacked by servants is usually designated by title.[3]

---

[1] The agent is a rebel, 1K 12:3, 12; a foreign ruler, 1K 15:6, 7, 16, 32, 22:4, 8, 18, 30, 50, 2K 9:23, 16:5, 20:12, 23:34, 34, 24:15, 17; a prophet (representing God), 2K 19:20, 20:16.

[2] This usage heightens the contrast provided by the use of a compound designation in 2K 19:1, where "King Hezekiah" takes effective action.

[3] See §8.1.2. There is possibly some significance in the fact that the description of the death of Joash is placed after the standard formula ending the description of the reign.

9.1.2 A king of Judah as agent is designated as "the king" where he issues instructions to a subject (6 cases);[4] where he is answering a plea (i.e. acting as judge, 1K 12:13, 15); and where his action is presented through the perception of subjects (1K 12:16, 2K 11:14, 14). The title is also used where the king effects changes in the Jerusalem temple (2K 16:12, 12, 12), or in other places of worship set up by former kings (2K 23:12, 13), or convenes the elders and conducts an important ceremonial in the temple (2K 23:1, 2, 3). The repeated use of the title in these passages ensures that the reader will take note of the royal status, reflecting the importance of the king's part in the national religion, whether he was doing right (as in 2 Kings 23) or wrong (as presumably in 2 Kings 16).[5] The king's reaction to the content of the scroll found in the temple (tearing his clothes, foreshadowing his determination to conform to its rules, 2K 22:11) can be included here. The use of the title in "after the king lay with his fathers (אחרי שכב המלך עם אבתיו, 2K 14:22), seems anomalous. The use of the title in 2K 3:9 is also anomalous, and its form, "the king of Judah" (מלך יהודה) is not used elsewhere by the narrator as a simple designation. The name is expected, as in 2K 3:12.[6]

9.1.3 A king of Judah as agent is elsewhere designated by name (79 cases). The following cases might be considered to conflict with the above description, but should probably be seen as consistent with the general pattern of usage. "Amaziah" (2K 14:8) and "Ahaz" (2K 16:7) speak using a modal verb, but the addressee is not a subject. In 2K 12:5, "Jehoash" gives instructions to priests. Possibly they were not considered as subjects; possibly the instructions were seen as "benevolent" (see §6.4.2). In 2K 20:12 the "king of Babylon" sends an embassy to "Hezekiah". The use of Hezekiah's name here pos-

---

[4]   He speaks using modal verbs in 1K 12:12, 2K 22:3. The designation is subject of the verb "command" (צוה) in 2K 22:12, 23:4, 21, and represents the agent in the phrase "the king's command" (מצות המלך, 2K 18:36).
[5]   "Solomon" convenes the elders in 1K 8:1, "the king" in 2K 23:1. However, in 1K 8:1, Solomon's royal status is stressed in what follows. The employment of expressive usage is obviously not a matter of convention, but of option.
[6]   The use of "the king of Judah" in 2K 3:9 is possibly due to the influence of "the king of Israel" and "the king of Edom", which precede and follow it. In a further usage in 1K 14:28, the title presumably indicates any king of Judah, not an individual.

sibly reflects the nature of the mission. It is not a matter of state policy, but exploratory, and had no practical results. In 1K 15:13, "Asa" deals with the objects used in his mother's heterodox worship. In 2K 23:16, 19, "Josiah" deals with an altar at Bethel and shrines elsewhere in the northern kingdom. The name is also used in 2K 23:24, where he roots out various aberrant practices which had appeared in the land of Judah and in Jerusalem. It appears that the name was used to designate a ruler reforming the religious practice of the land, unless he was dealing with shrines patronized by former kings of Judah.

9.1.4 A king of Judah is usually designated by name where the designation follows a construct noun, as in "the servants of Amon" (עבדי אמון, 2K 21:23), and the common reference to the "rest of the acts of PN" at the end of the description of a reign, (e.g. "the rest of the acts of Rehoboam, יתר דברי רחבעם, 1K 14:29). The title is used where "the king" represents the relevant role, in "the king's command" (מצות המלך, 2K 18:36). "The mother of the king and the wives of the king" (ואת אם המלך ואת נשי המלך) are said to be exiled along with "Jehoiachin" in 2K 24:15. King Jehoiachin is designated by name because (from the narrator's point of view) the royal status is not involved. Where his mother and wives are mentioned, he is designated by title (or one could say that his mother's title is used, see §3.2.3). Their status is no doubt indicated in this way to draw attention to the completeness with which the kingdom was despoiled. Cf. the similar usage in the statement in 2S 17:6 that Shimei stoned "David and all the servants of King David" (see §6.7).

9.2 Narration: Compound Designations

9.2.1 The common form of compound designation used for a king of Judah is composed of name and title. A compound of this sort is regularly used in dating by regnal year. The title includes the name of the state where the event dated occurred outside Judah, as "in the second year of Asa King of Judah" (בשנת שתים לאסא מלך יהודה, 1K 15:25, and 21 cases in all).[7] This format is also used in 2K 8:16,

---

[7]   1K 15:25, 28, 33, 16:8, 10, 15, 23, 29, 22:52, 2K 3:1, 13:10, 15:8, 13, 17, 23, 27, 17:1, 25:27. A patronymic is included in 2K 1:17, 13:1, 14:23, see §9.2.5.

where the regnal year of a king of Judah is added to that of a king
of Israel in dating the accession of a king of Judah.[8] Where the
event dated occurred within Judah, the title does not include the
name of the state, as "in the fifth year of King Rehoboam" (בשנה
החמישית למלך רחבעם, 1K 14:25, also 2K 12:7, 18:13, 22:3, 23:23,
25:2). This format is also used for dating the final Assyrian attack
on Samaria in the description of the reign of Hezekiah King of
Judah (2K 18:9). The personal name alone is used in dating the fall
of Samaria in the following verse. More surprisingly, the personal
name and patronymic "Jotham b. Uzziah" is used in the description
of the reign of a king of Israel to date his murder (2K 15:30). Possibly the title has fallen out. A patronymic is sometimes used in other forms of compound designation used in dating, see §9.2.5.

9.2.2 A new king of Judah is regularly introduced at the end of the
description of his father's reign with the statement "And PN his
son became king in his place", as for Rehoboam, וימלך רחבעם בנו
תחתיו (1K 11:43).[9] The synchronistic date statement is thus not the
first mention of a king; it introduces his name in a new context: the
description of his reign. Compound designations composed of name
and title are used in other situations where the name is introduced
in a new context in some 26 cases.[10] The name of the state is included in the title where the king of Judah is involved with the
king of Israel or another foreign king, but not where he is involved
with his own subjects, or the concerns of his kingdom. The name
of the state is not used in 2K 16:10, where the king of Judah goes
to see the king of Assyria in Damascus (the passage concerns inno-
vations in the Jerusalem temple), in 2K 18:17, where the king of

---

[8]   This unexpected usage occurs where the kings named are Jehoram b. Ahab
King of Israel, Jehoshaphat King of Judah, and Jehoram b. Jehoshaphat King of
Judah. The usage no doubt reflects a desire to prevent confusion between kings of
the same name in the two kingdoms, see §9.2.5.
[9]   Also 1K 14:31, 15:8, 24, 22:51, 2K 8:24, 12:22, 15:7, 38, 16:20, 20:21, 21:18, 26,
24:6. Where the succession was arranged through some unusual agency (the people,
2K 14:21, 23:30; a foreign king, 2K 23:34, 24:17) the relevant information is given
in a different form.
[10]   1K 12:6, 18, 15:22, 22:2, 10, 29, 2K 3:7, 9:16, 21, 27, 10:13, 11:2, 12:8, 19, 13:12,
14:15, 16:10, 15, 18:14, 17, 20:14, 23:29, 24:12, 25:27. A patronymic is included in
2K 8:29, 14:17, see §9.2.5.

Assyria sends envoys to him in Jerusalem, or in 2K 23:29 where he goes to attack Pharaoh Necho at Megiddo (presumably within his own territory). These three cases occur in the description of the reign of the king of Judah concerned, and were possibly viewed as domestic matters.[11]

9.2.3 A compound designation composed of name and title may be used to draw the reader's attention to some item of significance in a passage in which the king has already been mentioned. The name of the state is included where foreigners or external events are involved (five cases).[12] A sixth case occurs in "Hezekiah cut away the doors of the temple of the Lord... which Hezekiah King of Judah had overlaid, and gave them to the king of Assyria" (את חזקיה קצץ 2K 18:16), דלתות היכל יהוה... אשר צפה חזקיה מלך יהודה ויתנם למלך אשור. Here the title is used to contrast the reprehensible despoiling of the temple by "Hezekiah" with its ornamentation, an act worthy of a king of Judah. The name of the state is not included in the title where the context is limited to the kingdom of Judah (14 cases in all, including 1K 15:20, where a foreign king responds positively to a request by the king of Judah). A compound designation composed of name and title is most commonly used to draw attention to an event with political implications. In "Jehosheba daughter of King Jehoram sister of Ahaziah" (יהושבע בת המלך יורם אחות אחזיהו, 2K 11:2) the feature highlighted by the compound designation of Jehoram is obviously the relationship. This shows that Jehosheba, as a senior resident of the palace, would be in a position to hide Joash, and (along with the term "sister") indicates her motivation: the preservation of the Davidic line to which she belonged.

9.2.4 A compound designation made up of name, patronymic and title is typically used in the statement of synchronistic date which

---

[11] The inclusion of the name of the state in the title in 2K 14:17, where, in the description of his own reign, the life-span of a king of Judah is given with reference to the reign of a king of Israel, suggests that there was a grey area in which either form of title might be used. Such minor irregularities might, of course, have arisen through change occurring after the narrator's time.

[12] The name of the state is used in the title in 1K 15:17, 2K 14:9, 11, 13, 18:14, (also 2K 18:16, see below). It is not used in 1K 12:18, 14:27, 15:18, 20, 22, 2K 11:2, 16:10, 11, 11, 16, 17, 19:1, 5, 21:24.

begins the description of the reign of a king who succeeded while
the northern kingdom was in existence, as with "Jehoram b. Jehoshaphat King of Judah" (יהורם בן יהושפט מלך יהודה, 2K 8:16). In the
statement for Rehoboam (for whom no date is given, 1K 14:21) and
for Jehoshaphat (1K 22:41), the designation does not include the
title.[13] This has been supplied in composite designations used earlier (1K 12:23, 27, in speech; 22:10). No patronymic is used in the
synchronistic date beginning the description of the reigns of Abijam
and Asa (1K 15:1, 9). This is possibly because their reigns are described immediately after that of Rehoboam, the first king of Judah,
their father and grandfather respectively. The designation of Abijam
also omits the title, stating that "Abijam became king over Judah"
(מלך אבים על יהודה). The second synchronistic date given for Ahaziah (2K 9:29) is also given in this form.[14]

9.2.5 The patronymic used in the synchronistic date statement
draws attention to the regular succession of descendants of David
on the throne of Judah. A compound designation composed of
name and patronymic is used in 2K 11:2, 23:30, 34, in other situations in which it is important to show that a person who came to
the throne in an unusual way also had ancestry suitable for a king
of Judah. In 1K 12:21, where "Rehoboam" sets out to "return the
land to Rehoboam b. Solomon" the use of the patronymic reminds
the reader that such a return would maintain the former rights of
the Davidic line.[15] The use of the patronymic in "Ahaziah b. Jehoram King of Judah" (2K 8:29) in describing Ahaziah's visit to Jeho-

---

[13]   In these two cases, the position of the date and the name of the king of Judah
relative to the verb is reversed. The name precedes the verb in these cases, follows
it in the standard statement.

[14]   The first synchronistic date for Ahaziah (2K 8:25) is given in the standard form
"In year n of PN b. PN King of Israel, PN b. PN King of Judah became king",
and serves the standard function of opening the description of his reign. The second date (2K 9:29) follows the description of his death at the hands of Jehu. A date
for the beginning of Jehu's reign in Israel, which might have been expected at this
point, is nowhere given. This can be calculated from the second date given for
Ahaziah, but there seems no reason why the date should not have been provided
in the usual way.

[15]   Cf. the similar usage where King Solomon performs acts of which he is the
ultimate goal, described in §8.1.2.

ram King of Israel is no doubt intended to avoid confusion between kings of the same name in the two kingdoms.[16] The unexpected use of patronymics in the designation, in dates, of Jehoram (2K 1:17), Jehoash (2K 13:1), and Amaziah (2K 14:23, also, not in a date, in 2K 14:17) is probably similarly intended to impress the identity of the king in question on the reader's mind, because either he or his father has the same name as a king of Israel (cf. §§9.2.1n, 10.3.1-2). The use of a second patronymic as well as the title in the designation of Amaziah in 2K 14:13, naming both father and grandfather, is probably intended to relate the incident recorded there to the struggle of Jehu with the descendants of Ahab, which resulted in the death of Ahaziah, Amaziah's grandfather (see §10.3.2). On the placing of the title in this designation between name and patronymic, see §28.3.4.

9.3 Designations in Speech

9.3.1 *Address* The only example of address to a king of Judah is the use of his personal name as a vocative by the king of Israel in warning him of danger (2K 9:23). The use of the personal name probably reflects the danger of the situation, possibly also the intimate relationship of the two kings, who are cousins (see §25.4.2).

9.3.2 *Reference* The personal name of a king is used by God, speaking to Isaiah in 2K 20:5, where neither speaker nor addressee is one of the king's subjects. The king of Judah is referred to as "the king" in 2K 11:7, 8, 8, 12, as is usual where speaker or addressee is his subject. To omit the title in this situation is to disregard the the king's status (cf. such omission by the narrator or by a speaker noted in §§6.9.3, 11.3.2, 11.5.2, 13.4.3). Such disregard can represent

---

[16]   The patronymic is omitted where Ahaziah's visit is mentioned in the context of the activities of Jehu in 2K 9:16. The repetition of the content of 2K 8:29 in 2K 9:15-16 is a typical example of resumptive repetition used to bring together characters who must initially be treated separately. (Another case, in Ju 17:5, 11, is described in §14.3.1n.) Thus the story of the kings of Judah and Israel is suspended while Jehu is introduced, just as the story of the Midianites is suspended while Gideon is introduced (cf. Ju 6:33, with 7:1, 8, 12), and that of Goliath is suspended (cf. 1S 17:4 with 17:23) while David is introduced. On resumptive repetition in general, see Talmon, 1978.

deference to an addressee who is not a subject, as where his brothers refer to Ahaziah King of Judah by name only in speech to Jehu,
the hostile king of Israel by whom he was killed (2K 10:13), or
where King Hezekiah's envoys address a plea to Isaiah, representing
God (2K 19:3). Disregard of a king's status can also signal disre-
spect, as where the Rab-shakeh, the king of Assyria's envoy, refers
only to "Hezekiah" in speaking to his subjects (2K 18:19, 22, 29, 30,
31, 32). His disregard of Hezekiah's status as king adds a significant
psychological element to his argument on the weakness of Hezekiah, and the futility of opposing the king of Assyria. Where speaker or addressee is a foreign king, the formal designation "PN King
of Judah" is used in 2K 3:14, 19:10, possibly reflecting the language
of international diplomacy. The same form of title is used by Jeroboam King of Israel in internal speech in 1K 12:27. His use of the
designation "Rehoboam King of Judah" is probably intended to suggest that he respects or fears that king. The title alone is more usually used among friends to refer to a rival king, as in "the king of
Aram" in 1K 20:22.[17]

9.3.3 In 1K 12:23, God directs a message to "Rehoboam b. Solomon
King of Judah". The use of the patronymic stresses the continuity
of the Davidic line of kings; the use of the name of the state in the
title restricts their rule to the southern kingdom, a limit made clear
in the message. A designation composed of name and title is used
where God speaks through prophets in 2K 21:11, referring to "Manasseh King of Judah". The title alone is used in 2K 22:16, 18, referring to Josiah as "the king of Judah". This usage probably represents deliberate distancing, speaking as of a foreign king, in order to
enhance the impact of the threat of punishment to the realm. Such
distancing is also evident in the fact that King Josiah is first referred
to as "the man (אִישׁ) who sent you" (2K 22:15). Cf. the designations
God is represented as using where the message to be sent is intend-

---

[17]   Other examples occur in 1K 22:3, 31, 2K 3:7, 5:5, 6:11, 12, 7:6, 16:7, 25:24; also
in the Rab Shakeh's representation of such speech in 2K 18:30, and in the speech
of God to a king in 2K 19:6, 20:6, 18. Cf. also "the king of Israel" in the inscription of Mesha King of Moab, l. 10. It is also true, however, that a compound designation is often used in speech for an isolated reference to an individual (see §
4.13.3), and this could account for the first compound designation in 1K 12:27.

ed to encourage: "your lord" (אדניכם, 2K 19:6) and "Hezekiah, leader of my people" (חזקיהו נגיד עמי, 2K 20:5).

9.4 Designations in the Book of Jeremiah

9.4.1 The events described in the book of Jeremiah mostly occurred during the reigns of the last kings of Judah, and the king is designated in over 100 cases. The book presents the orations ascribed to the prophet, and first person descriptions of experiences related to them; it also includes a good deal of third person narration similar to that of the corpus. The common simple designation used in the narration is "the king" (המלך). In chapters 36, 37, and 38, this is used (17 cases) to represent the king both as agent and as patient. The name "Zedekiah" is used to designate the goal of Jeremiah's response to a request made to him by "the king" in Jer 38:15, and to a promise made to him by "King Zedekiah" in Jer 38:17. The name "Zedekiah" is also used in Jer 38:24 to represent the king as speaker. The initial clause of his speech has a modal verb, but the king is asking a favour of Jeremiah, not giving a command as a superior. In speech, the King is addressed as "my lord the king" (אדני המלך) in a plea in Jer 37:20 (by Jeremiah), and in Jer 38:9 (by an official). He is referred to as "the king" by officials (Jer 26:21, 36:16, 38:25, 25, and by Jeremiah replying to them in Jer 38:26; the last three examples are presented in speech by the king). King Hezekiah is referred to as "the king of Judah who sent you" (מלך יהודה השלח אתכם) by God directing his reply to the king's enquiry through his messengers in Jer 37:7. The same phrase designates King Josiah in 2K 22:18, and the explanation offered in §9.3.3 could apply to both cases. Hezekiah refers to himself as "the king" in Jer 38:5, representing his addressee's viewpoint (as does King David in 2S 19:12-13, see §27.2.3). He is referred to by name by Jeremiah, instructing officials to reply to the king's enquiry of God (Jer 21:3), by God in speech to Jeremiah (Jer 36:2), and in a prophecy quoted by the king (Jer 32:5). A king's name is also used in a prophetic comment in Jer 22:28.[18]

---

[18] Name and title both occur as simple designations in Jer 39:2, 5, 6, 7, 52:1, 2, 3, 8, 9, 10, 11, in verses with parallels in 2K 24:18-25:7. The only significant difference in usage occurs where 2K 25:2, Jer 52:5 have "King Zedekiah" in a date by regnal year, but Jer 39:2 uses only the name (much as in 2K 18:10).

9.4.2 A compound designation in the form "the king PN" (as המלך
צדקיהו, Jer 21:1) is used in twelve cases in narrative (referring to
events occurring within the kingdom, see §9.2.2), and three times in
speech by subjects referring to the current king.[19] The reverse
order, "PN the king" is used in Jer 29:2, in third person narrative
introducing Jeremiah's letter to the exiles (a form of prophecy), and
in Jer 3:6, in an introduction (presented as a first person statement
by Jeremiah) to a speech by God. This form of designation is
known in the corpus, but is rare (see §§6.7, 7.1.3, 8.3, 10.3.3). The
title can be seen as used to provide a fuller designation, but its position shows that it is the individual, not his status as king, which is
the focus of it, see §28.3.6. A designation in the form "PN King of
Judah" is used in nine cases in narrative (typically where foreigners
are referred to in the context, see §9.2.3), and twice in speech, by
subjects referring to a past king. It is used once in narrative presented as spoken by Jeremiah, and twelve times in speech ascribed to
God.[20] A patronymic is added to a designation of this sort in Jer
36:9 in giving a date by regnal year at the beginning of a section of
narrative, and in ten further cases in third person narrative introducing prophecy. It is used in eight cases for various forms of reference in prophetic speech, including designation of the intended addressee (Jer 22:11, 18, cf. §9.3.3 on 1K 12:23), and a date (Jer
25:3).[21] A designation composed of name and patronymic is used
twice in Jer 37:1 in a succession statement. The word "king" which
precedes the first example is not part of the designation, but is used
to delay the use of the name (see §4.9).

9.4.3 It is clear that the different forms of designation used in Jeremiah for kings of Judah are, in general, used in different contexts.
Their use in third person narrative, and in the speech quoted in it,

---

[19] In narrative in Jer 21:1, 34:8, 37:3, 17, 18, 21, 38:5, 14, 16, 19, 41:9, and 52:5
(=2K 25:2); in speech in Jer 26:21, 22, 23.
[20] In third person narrative in Jer 29:3, 32:1, 3, 34:6, 36:32, 39:1 (cf. 2K 25:1),
39:4, 49:34, and 52:31, 31 (=2K 25:27); speech by subjects Jer 26:18, 19; narrative
by Jeremiah, Jer 28:1; speech by God, Jer 21:7, 24:8, 27:3, 12, 32:4, 34:2, 21, 36:28,
29, 30, 44:30 (reference), and 34:4 (address).
[21] In narrative in Jer 36:9; introducing prophecy in Jer 1:2, 3, 3, 25:1, 26:1, 27:1,
35:1, 36:1, 45:1, 46:2; in prophetic speech in Jer 15:4, 22:11, 18, 24, 24:1, 25:3,
27:20, and 28:4.

is much the same as in the corpus. The simple designations used in address are typical for subjects when pleading before the king, see §25.2.2. This is Jeremiah's role in Jer 37:20. In spoken reference, God, and Jeremiah speaking as his representative in Jer 21:3, use the name, the simple designation typical for non-subjects, while officials use the title, as is typical for subjects, as described in §9.3.2. The general use of the title as a simple designation in the narration of chapters 36-38 can be seen as representing the viewpoint of a subject (rather than that of an omniscient narrator), consistent with the view that the material in these chapters originated with Baruch the scribe. The three uses of the name in narration treat Jeremiah as God's representative, and so as a non-subject. Compound designations used in narrative, and in the speech quoted in it, are used in generally the same way as are those described in §9.2. Thus the uses of name and patronymic in Jer 37:1 are comparable to those in 2K 23:30, 34 (and cf. 24:17), see §9.2.5. Points of contact between the usage of the corpus and the prophetic speech in Jeremiah, or the narrative introductions to it, are too few to justify a definite statement about the relationship of the conventions of usage reflected. The use of designations in the narrative material in Jeremiah appears, in general, to reflect the conventions characteristic of the corpus, with the difference that the narrator's viewpoint is that of a subject. However, some usage is unexpected, and, taken with features of the designation of foreign kings, suggests that additions reflecting a different convention have been made (see §11.6).

9.5 Conclusion

The evidence available on the designation of kings of Judah is scarcely adequate to support some of the suggestions made above on the expressive value of their use, but further support can be obtained from the use of designations for David and Solomon. The designations of these two kings show the same patterns of usage as do the designations of the kings of Judah, both in speech and in the usage of the narrator. The use of both patronymic and title to designate some kings of Judah has no parallel in the usage for David and Solomon, but there is no reason to think it inconsistent with the general basis of the usage. The standard compound designation is made up of name and title. The patronymic is added in contexts in which the information it provides can be seen as particularly significant.

The Designation of Kings
of the Northern Kingdom, Israel

10.1 Simple Designations in Narration: the Title

10.1.1 The title of the king Israel is "the king" (הַמֶּלֶךְ) where the narrative concerns events within his kingdom, or where the king is involved only with a prophet or a subject (34 cases).[1] The form "king of Israel" מֶלֶךְ יִשְׂרָאֵל, is used where he is involved with the king of Judah, or other foreign kings, in 43 cases, including 2K 13:16, 18, where the involvement with the king of Aram is only implied.[2] In some cases the use of the title "king of Israel" is due only to the involvement of a foreign king in the narrative.[3] The narrator naturally draws attention to the royal status of both kings. In most other cases the title (in either form) is used to draw attention to the power and prestige of a prophet (see §10.1.2). The use of the title in 1K 12:28 is a striking exception. Here "the king" determines to subvert what is, for the narrator, the true religion. The use of the title thus draws attention to the wickedness of Jeroboam by showing "the king" committing an act which it was, in fact, his duty to prevent, as in some cases of the use of the title for Saul (see §7.1.2).

10.1.2 A King of Israel is almost always designated by title where he is involved with a prophet. In the narratives where the title is used, the prophet dominates the king. He passes judgment on the king (1K 13:11, 20:38-43, 2K 1:15-16), afflicts and restores his hand (1K 13:4-6). He is offered hospitality, which he roundly refuses (1K 13:7-9). He makes predictions which are fulfilled (1K 13:3-5, 20:28, 22:28, 2K 6:28-7:18), gives the king divine advice, or other miraculous help against his enemies (1K 20:14, 2K 3:13, 6:21, 13:16-18). In 2K 8:3-6,

---

[1]   1K 12:28, 13:4, 6, 6, 7, 8, 11, 20:38, 39, 39, 22:15, 15, 22:16, 35, 37, 37, 2K 1:15, 5:8, 6:28, 30, 7:2, 12, 14, 15, 17, 17, 18, 8:3, 4, 5, 5, 6, 6, 13:16.
[2]   1K 20:4, 7, 11, 21, 22, 28, 32, 40, 41, 43, 22:2, 3, 4, 5, 6, 8, 9, 10, 18, 26, 29, 30, 30, 33, 34, 45, 2K 3:4, 5, 9, 10, 11, 12, 13, 13, 5:6, 7, 8, 6:9, 10, 21, 26, 13:16, 18.
[3]   Examples occur in 1K 20:4, 7, 11, 22:3-10, 45, 2K 3:4-12, 6:9, 26.

the king asks that the prophet's marvellous acts be recounted to him, and, having interviewed a woman who was a favoured beneficiary of the prophet, grants her request with remarkable generosity. The power of the prophet to benefit his supporters is here shown in a less direct way.

10.2 Simple Designations in Narration: the Name

10.2.1 A king of Israel is designated by name in situations in which the narrator's purpose does not call for the use of the title. This includes all situations in which foreign kings or prophets are not involved (except 1K 12:28). The name is used both where the king is approached by a subject and by a non-subject, both where he issues commands to a subject, or makes a statement to a non-subject. The name is also used in a few cases in narratives in which a foreign king is involved. It is stated that "there was war between Rehoboam (or Abijam) and Jeroboam (מלחמה היתה בין רחבעם ובין ירבעם), in 1K 14:30 15:6, 7. In 2K 8:28 "Jehoram" is defeated by the Aramaeans, in a verse in which the king of Aram is mentioned. The king of Israel is introduced in the verse as Jehoram b. Ahab", an ally with whom the king of Judah went on campaign, continuing the narrator's concentration on that king's relationship with the royal family of Israel (see §10.3.5). In 2K 13:25, "Jehoash" is said to have defeated Ben-hadad b. Hazael three times, but neither here nor elsewhere is this Ben-hadad given the title "king of Aram". In 2K 15:19, "Menahem" bribes Pul King of Assyria to be his ally. In 2K 17:3-4 Hoshea submits to Shalmaneser King of Assyria, and the king of Assyria finds him untrustworthy. In most of these cases there would be little point in using the title if its use were intended to enhance the prestige either of one king or of the other.

10.2.2 The narrator always designates the king of Israel by name in 1 Kings 18. In 1K 18:3, 5, 6, 16, 45, King Ahab is acting within his own realm, and no prophet is involved. In 1K 18:2, 16, 17, 17, 20, 41, 42, 46, Ahab is directly involved with the prophet Elijah. His involvement is, however, marginal to the narrative, and he is submissive to the prophet. The hostility with which Obadiah credits him (1K 18:9-14) is expressed in an insult (1K 18:17), but after that, he obeys Elijah's orders without question (1K 18:19-20, 41-42) and goes home with Elijah running before him (1K 18:46). Ahab is thus shown to be dominated by Elijah, but this is only a background to the central drama of the chapter: Elijah's demonstration of the power of the God of Israel and the impotence of Baal, and the consequent slaughter of the priests of Baal (1K 18:21-40). The benefit which Ahab gains, rain for his parched land, results from a prior decision by God (1K 18:1). It can be argued here that Ahab is acting like a true worshipper of God, not as is typical of a "king of Israel", hostile to the true religion, and to God's chosen rulers, the kings of the Davidic line. There is, then, some basis for the suggestion that the designation of King Ahab in this chapter does not conflict with the pattern established elsewhere.

10.2.3 The king is designated by name in 1K 20:14, where "Ahab" asks for further information after "Ahab King of Israel" is informed by a prophet that God will give him victory where defeat seemed certain (1K 20:13). This, again, correlates with a submissive and helpful attitude, not a hostile one. As in 1 Kings 18, this may be the reason for the use of the name rather than the title. King Ahab is again not acting like a king of Israel, but like a worshipper of God. The use of the title where a similar announcement is made in 1K 20:28 may be intended to presage Ahab's failure to follow God's instructions in prosperity as he did in adversity.[4]

10.3 Compound Designations in Narration

10.3.1 A compound designation is typically used for the king of the northern kingdom where a date is given in terms of his regnal years. The designation takes the form name - title + state, as "Jeroboam King of Israel" (ירבעם מלך ישראל) in 1K 15:9, 22:41, 2K 15:1, 29, 18:10. A patronymic is added to this in "Jehoram b. Ahab" (2K 8:16, 25), "Jehoash b. Jehoahaz" (2K 14:1, 17), Pekah b. Remaliah (2K 15:32), and Hoshea b. Elah (2K 18:1, 9). In the case of Jehoram, the patronymic seems to be used simply to draw attention to his relationship to the wicked King Ahab, which caused his downfall (see §9.2.5). In other cases, the patronymic is probably used to guard against the possibility of confusing people with the same or

---

[4]   It is unlikely that the fact that the speaker in this case is designated "man of God" (איש האלהים) rather than "prophet" (נביא) is relevant to the question. See §12.6.

similar names. Jehoash was a younger contemporary of Jehoash b. Ahaziah, King of Judah (see §9.2.5). Pekah is similarly likely to be confused with the preceding king of Israel, Pekahiah; despite the English spelling, they probably use different forms of the same basic name.[5] The patronymic is possibly used for Hoshea to differentiate him from the prophet Hosea, whose name has the same spelling in Hebrew.[6] The title is not used in dates by the regnal years of Jehoram (2K 9:29), Pekah (2K 16:1), and Hoshea (2K 17:6). I can see no reason for its omission, save possibly in the case of Hoshea, who was no longer acting as king, having been imprisoned by the king of Assyria. The designation used for the first king of the northern kingdom in the date in 1K 15:1 "King Jeroboam b. Nebat" (המלך ירבעם בן נבט), is also anomalous, see §10.3.3.

10.3.2 Other compound designations including name and title are used to provide clear identification of the king in question in the description of the reign of a king of Judah, or in other passages in which foreign kings are involved. The examples in 1K 15:16, 20:2, 13, 2K 8:26, 13:14, 21:3, draw attention to the first mention of the king in a new context. The designation of Ahab in 1K 21:1 is similarly introductory, but the title "King of Samaria" (מלך שמרון) used here is unusual.[7] The use of a title other than "the king" where no foreign king is involved is also unusual. The designation "Baasha King of Israel" (1K 15:32) is presumably used because Baasha's reign has not been described.[8] In 2K 14:8, it is stated that Amaziah (the king of Judah) challenged "Jehoash b. Jehoahaz b. Jehu King of Israel". The two patronymics not only avoid confusion between this king of Israel and Jehoash father of Amaziah (see §10.3.1); they also

---

[5]   Designations of Pekah include the patronymic in 2K 15:25, 27, 32, 37, 16:1, 5. His name is used without patronymic only in 2K 15:29, 31, where his identity is made clear by the preceding patronymics.

[6]   A patronymic is used in the designation of Hoshea in 2K 15:30, 17:1, 18:1, 9. His name is used without patronymic in 2K 17:3, 4, 6, 18:10, again where his identity is made clear by preceding patronymics.

[7]   It is also used in speech in 2K 1:3, see §10.4.4. The Assyrians used the title "King of Samaria" for kings of the northern kingdom, see Cogan and Tadmor 1988:25-26.

[8]   Jeroboam's name alone is used in similar statements in 1K 14:30, 15:6, 7, after his reign has been described.

portray the encounter as a further stage in the conflict between Jehu and the descendants of Ahab.[9] The other designations which include the name and the title "king of Israel" are used in the usual way to highlight particular events: Baasha's advance on Judah (1K 15:17), Jehoram's going out to meet Jehu (2K 9:21; Jehu killed him), and the events in the fight between Jehoash and Amaziah (2K 14:9, 11, 13, see §4.11).

10.3.3 The designation "King Jehoram" (המלך יהורם, 2K 3:6), unique for a king of Israel, is used by the narrator to shift his focus from the king of Moab (whose dealings with the king of Israel are described in 2K 3:4-5) to the King of Israel and the campaign he undertakes with other kings, eventually with the aid of the prophet Elisha. The designation "Jehoram the King" is used in describing that king's return to Jezreel to recuperate (יורם המלך, 2K 8:29, also 9:15, where the statement is recapitulated in shortened form, see §9.2.4n). The unusual position of the title (see §28.3.6) might reflect the fact that the action was considered personal,[10] but the wider context deals with political matters. The designation "King Jeroboam b. Nebat" (המלך ירבעם בן נבט, 1K 15:1) also occurs in a situation in which a title including the name of the state is expected (see §10.3.1). I can suggest no reason for the failure to use a title in the expected form.

10.3.4 A compound designation composed of name and patronymic is typically used in the statement of synchronistic date which begins the description of each reign, as "Nadab b. Jeroboam" (נדב בן ירבעם, 1K 15:25).[11] The title is added in the designation of Jeroboam II (2K 14:23), undoubtedly to distinguish his father from Jehoash, father of his contemporary, Amaziah King of Judah (see

---

[9] Ahab was Amaziah's great great grandfather. The narrator does not use more than one patronymic in a designation of Jehoash elsewhere (2K 13:10, 25, 14:1, 17).

[10] The title is not used for Jehoram in connection with the visit of Ahaziah King of Judah (2K 8:29, 9:16) possibly indicating that the visit is social (the kings are cousins), not political.

[11] As with kings of Judah (see §9.2.2), this statement is not the first mention of the king, but the first mention in the new context of the description of his reign. It is regularly preceded by a statement that he succeeded his father, or that he gained the throne by violence.

§9.2.5). No patronymic is used for Zimri or Omri, either in this statement, or elsewhere in the corpus.[12] The synchronistic date is typically accompanied by a statement of length of reign.[13] The king is usually designated only by a pronoun in this statement, but King Ahab is designated by name and patronymic (1K 16:29), undoubtedly to draw the reader's attention to his name (see §10.3.5). No statement of synchronistic date is provided for Jeroboam, the first king of the northern kingdom, or for Jehu (cf. §9.2.4n).

10.3.5 The designation "Ahab b. Omri" is used not only in the statement of synchronistic date in 1K 16:29, but also in the following statements of the length of his reign, and the assessment of his reign as evil (1K 16:29, 30). Clearly the narrator is highlighting the name of this despicable king at the beginning of his description of his reign.[14] Most other examples of designation by name and patronymic can also be classed as "introductory".[15] In 2K 9:14 "Jehu b. Jehoshaphat b. Nimshi" is said to have conspired against the king. The additional patronym used here (the only compound designation used by the narrator for Jehu) correlates with the fact that, where Jehu is designated with one patronym, the name of his grandfather is used. The narrator is presenting complete information

---

[12]   Probably the information was not available to the narrator. The failure to use a patronymic for Omri contrasts sharply with the use of one for Tibni b. Ginath, the rival he defeated (1K 16:21, 22), who is never given the title "king".

[13]   Where the name precedes the verb in the date statement (1K 15:25, 16:29, 22:52, 2K 3:1, 15:13) the length of reign is given in a clause, otherwise (1K 15:33, 16:8, 15, 23, 2K 13:1, 10, 14:23, 15:8, 17, 23, 27, 17:1) in a phrase. I can suggest no motivation for the variation.

[14]   The tendency to draw attention to the acts of villains (as well as of heroes) can be noted elsewhere, e.g. in the references to Jabin King of Canaan (Ju 4:23-24). The Midrash characteristically emphasizes the wickedness of the villains of history, consistent with the view (expressed in *Bereshith Rabba* 49:1) that they should be cursed when mentioned. The king is typically designated by a pronoun in the statement of the length of his reign and in the assessment of it as evil. The use of the name for Jeroboam, 1K 14:20, and Jehu, 2K 10:36, correlates with the unusual placing of the length of reign statement. The use of Omri's name in 1K 16:25 is the only other case where a pronoun is not used in the assessment of the reign.

[15]   1K 12:2, 15, 15:27, 22:50, 2K 8:28, 13:25, 14:27, 15:10, 14, 25, 30, 37, 17:21.

at the beginning of Jehu's career.[16] In 2K 8:29 "Jehoram the King" goes to recuperate in Jezreel, but the king of Judah goes to visit "Jehoram b. Ahab" there. The use of the patronymic in the second case draws attention to the relationship to Ahab (and so to Jezebel), and so foreshadows the events of the following chapter. (On the failure to use the title for Jehoram here, see §10.3.3n.) The compound designation "Shallum b. Jabesh" occurs three times, highlighting the main events of his career (2K 15:10, 13, 14). The only other nominal designation is the use of his name in the closing formula (2K 15:15). The similarly frequent use of the designation "Pekah b. Remaliah" is probably intended to avoid confusion between him and Pekah (see §10.3.1).

10.4 Designations Used in Speech

10.4.1 *Address* A king of Israel is addressed by subjects as "my lord the king" (אדני המלך) in 2K 6:26, 8:5. Prophets (false ones) giving advice at his request, use "the king" (המלך) in third person address in 1K 22:6, 12, as does Micaiah, a prophet of the true God when imitating them in 1K 22:15. A king of Judah uses "the king" in third person address to his ally, a king of Israel in 1K 22:8. This may reflect the fact that the king of Israel is leading the expedition, but lack of parallels makes evaluation impossible. On the forms of address used to Jehu in 2K 9:22, 31, see §§25.4.4, 25.5.2.

10.4.2 *Reference* A king of Israel is referred to as המלך "the king" by subjects speaking among themselves (1K 16:16), or to those they believe should regard him as king (1K 22:13, 2K 10:13). The usage is the same in messages from the king to such people (1K 22:27, 2K 1:9, 11, 9:18, 19). The prophet Elisha similarly refers to "the king" in address to a subject with the implication that the king might do something for her (2K 4:13). Elijah's reference to "the king who

---

[16] The grandfather's name may be used to avoid confusion between the father's name and that of the Jehoshaphat who had lately been king of Judah, but the usage possibly reflects factors known to the intended audience, but not to us. Jehu is also designated with two patronyms in speech, where Elisha orders that he be anointed (2K 9:2). The designation "Jehu b. Nimshi" is used (also in speech) in 1K 19:16, 2K 9:20. A compound designation is usual where a future king is presented as a conspirator against his predecessor (1K 15:27, 2K 15:10, 25, 30).

sent you" in addressing envoys (2K 1:6) is perhaps similarly polite, perhaps ironic. The term "King of Israel" (מלך ישראל) is used for reference by foreigners speaking among themselves, and in speech by or address to foreign kings.[17] The personal name is used for reference by God, or by prophets representing God, or by other non-subjects.[18] King Jeroboam refers to his wife as "the wife of Jeroboam" (אשת ירבעם, 1K 14:2) in speaking to her, but representing the viewpoint of other people. Presumably he has in mind those who, like the prophet Ahijah whom he wants her to visit, do not regard him as king.

10.4.3 Obadiah, one of King Ahab's officials, refers to "Ahab", showing the viewpoint of a non-subject, in claiming that the king will kill him (1K 18:9, 12). He uses "my lord" (אדני) in referring to the king's international search for the prophet Elijah, to whom both speeches are addressed (1K 18:10). In reply, Elijah uses the non-committal "your lord" (אדניך, 1K 18:8, 11, 14), as does Jehu (2K 10:2, 3, 6) in speaking to officials whose allegiance to the king he hopes to subvert. The prophet Elisha uses "his lord" in reference to the king (whom he also designates by a derogatory epithet) when speaking of one of his servants (2K 6:32). On Jehu's use of his own name where describing his intended action (2K 10:18), see §27.2.2. The acclamation "Jehu reigns" (מלך יהוא, 2K 9:13), spoken by prospective subjects, uses the name to identify the ruler they now support in place of Jehoram, whose throne Jehu intends to usurp. Solomon's name is used similarly in 1K 1:34, 39, as is Adonijah's in 1K 1:25 (see §8.3n).

10.4.4 Compound designations used in speech generally follow the principles outlined above. The name, with a patronymic or relationship term, is used by non-subjects. The king of Judah uses name and title in asking the king of Aram to break his treaty with "Baa-

---

[17] 1K 22:31, 32, 2K 5:5, 6:11, 12, 7:6, 16:7, and, in the plural with general reference "Kings of the house of Israel" in 1K 20:31.
[18] 1K 14:7, 10, 10, 10, 11, 13, 13, 14, 16, 16:3, 4, 18:1, 44, 21:21, 24, 29, 22:20, 2K 9:8, 8, 9, 25, 10:18, 30.

sha King of Israel" and help him against him (1K 15:19).[19] The use
of a compound designation for clear identification in such isolated
references is common in speech as in narration. Compound designations are often used in spoken reference to past kings (as in 1K
21:22, 22, etc.), but not always (e.g. 2K 21:13). In 2K 1:3, an angel,
speaking to the prophet Elijah, refers to "the messengers of the king
of Samaria".[20] God refers to "Ahab King of Israel" in speaking to
the prophet Elijah in 1K 21:18. In both these cases the prophet is to
denounce the king, but this is not so where God refers to "Ahab"
in 1K 18:1. However, the name is used in the body of a message,
whether hostility or benevolence is expressed (1K 21:21, 24, 29), so
the use of the title in these two cases is possibly to be regarded as
ironic.

10.5 Conclusion

10.5.1 The designations of kings of Israel show the same dichotomy
as those of Saul. Designations used in speech follow the common
pattern, exemplified by the designations of David; designations used
by the narrator do not. The narrator's use of the title, including the
name of the state, where the "king of Israel" is involved with foreign kings, reflects his Judaean (or normative) viewpoint. A king of
Judah is often designated by name in such situations. This shows
that the narrator does not identify with the northern community
which the king of Israel rules. The use of the title where a king of
Israel is involved with a prophet enhances the prestige of the prophet, and the form of religion he supports, since the prophet is shown
to dominate the king in such cases. This recalls the narrator's use of
the title for Saul in order to draw attention to David's rise through

---

[19] This may represent the standard language of international diplomacy (see
§9.3.2). A later king of Judah is less specific, using the title alone, in a request for
similar help where no treaty is involved in 2K 16:7.
[20] The use of "Samaria" (consistent with Assyrian usage) rather than "Israel" to
designate his realm may possibly be intended to belittle him by depicting him as
the ruler of a city state, rather than of a part of God's chosen community. This explanation could be applied to the other use of this form of title in 1K 21:1 (a surprising use in narration, see §10.3.2). However, the name of the capital city seems
to be used as a free variant of a wider designation in the title of some other kings,
see the examples in §11.5.3n. The use of one rather than the other may, of course,
originate in particular sources.

society. The use of the title in 1K 12:28 draws attention to a particularly heinous act by King Jeroboam. The title is used for Saul in just the same way (see §7.1.2).

10.5.2 The contrast between the general similarity of the use of spoken designations for all the kings described, and the differences in the usage of the narrator, emphasizes the significance of that usage. The treatment of the same material in different ways reflects (in general) the narrator's viewpoint, not that of his sources. Some other differences in the treatment of kings of Israel and Judah may well be source-related. In the regnal resumé which provides the framework the descriptions of the reign of the kings of both kingdoms, the narrator provides more information on kings of Judah.[21] That he can give details of their burials where they died by violence probably reflects the more stable political situation in the south. The giving of age on accession, and the name of the mother, shows that he was more interested in the southern kingdom than in the northern, and probably also that he had better information about the affairs of the former.[22] The inclusion of these two items creates the main difference in the basic structures of the resumés. It seems possible that Jehu's struggle for the throne, and the six-year interregnum to which it gave rise in Judah, disrupted the keeping of

---

[21] "Regnal resumé" is the term used in Long, 1984, where these are summarized on p. 160-161. Bibliography on studies of these resumés is provided by Long, also in Nelson, 1981 and Provan, 1988. The few statements characteristic of these resumés found in the material on Saul, David, and Solomon (1S 13:1, 2S 5:4-5, 1K 2:10-12, 11:41-43) are usually ignored in such studies. However, the only information regularly provided in the regnal resumé for a king of Judah which could be provided for these kings, but is not, is the age of accession for Solomon, and the mother's name and "rest of the acts" statement for Saul and David. Some of this information is given in the narrative, not in the formulaic statements of the resumé, but information on the reigns of kings of Israel and Judah is sometimes treated in this way as well (see §9.2.4, and the discussion in Nelson, 1981:32-36).

[22] His information on the king's mother is limited to her name alone only in the case of Hephzibah, mother of Manasseh (2K 21:1). The Mother of Jehoram is the only one whose name is not given (2K 8:17).

records or caused their loss in both kingdoms. Similar factors may have caused the loss of the patronymics of Zimri and Omri.[23]

---

[23] Nelson, 1981:35 suggests that the "texture of the history" rendered an introduction or conclusion to the description of the reign of Jehu unnecessary, but there is a remarkable concatenation of unusual features in the treatment of both kingdoms at this time. This could, of course, be due to later disturbance of the narrator's work, but the uniformity of other features suggests that this was not a major factor.

The Designation of Foreign Kings

11.1 Simple Designations: the Title

11.1.1 The form of title used for the ruler of a state other than Israel or Judah typically includes the name of the state or people ruled, as "the king of Moab" (מלך מואב, 1S 22:3), "the queen of Sheba" (מלכת שבא, 1K 10:1). The title "the king" (המלך), without the name of the state, is used for a foreign king by the narrator only in 2K 8:8, 25:30.[1] In both cases the context deals with events occurring within the king's realm. Both references are unambiguous. No other king is mentioned in the context in 2K 8:8. In 2K 25:30, although the title has been used for other captive or subordinate kings, there is no doubt that "the king" designates the king of Baylonia as the source of Jehoiachin's provisions.[2] The word "Pharaoh" (פרעה), usually used in designations of a king of Egypt is discussed in §11.4. The few designations of kings of Egypt in which this word is not used are included in the general description.

11.1.2 The title is sometimes the only designation used for a ruler, as with the "king of the b. Ammon" with whom Jephtha negotiates (Ju 11:12, 13, 14, 28), or the "queen of Sheba" (1K 10:1, 4, 10, 13). In some cases, no doubt, the name of the ruler was unknown. In some cases, as with the "king of Aram" in 1K 22:31, or "the king of Assyria" in 2K 18:7, the ruler in question can be identified with some probability, and it seems most likely that the name was omitted as unimportant. In such cases, the title simply represents a threatening foreign power. The name of the ruler who directs it is not relevant to the narrator's purpose. In passages in which a for-

---

[1]   In "their king" (מלכם, 2S 12:30), the pronoun represents (the people of) Rabbah, the capital, used to designate the state ruled (as with Ahab, see 1K 21:1, and with others, see §11.5.3n).

[2]   The king of Babylon is the thematic actor in Jer 25:27-30. The narrator relies on the reader's comprehension, as he sometimes does with pronominal anaphora (see §4.5.2).

eign king is named, the simple designation used for kings of Assyria, Babylonia, or Egypt, is regularly the title. The use of the name "Pul" for a king of Assyria (2K 15:19) is the only exception in the usage of the narrator. The title is only used as a simple designation for a named king of a foreign country other than these in 2K 3:5, where "the king of Moab" is presumably Mesha, named in 2K 3:4, and in 2K 13:4, 7, where "the king of Aram" is presumably Hazael, who is mentioned in 2K 13:3. All three examples show the foreign king as agent, acting successfully against the king of Israel.

11.2 Simple Designations: the Name

11.2.1 The name is used as a simple designation for named kings of Aram, Aram-naharaim, Gath, Hamath, Midian, Moab, and Tyre, states on the borders of Israel, or not distant from them. The case of "Pul" in 2K 15:19, is the only exception. The states listed presumably used forms of north-west Semitic language related to Hebrew. If this was not the case in Gath, the names of its kings would at least have been familiar to many Hebrew speakers. The conventional structure of Mesopotamian names would have been unfamiliar, as would the language.[3] The same is true of Egyptian names. It may have been this cultural difference which determined that the personal name was not used as simple designations for Mesopotamian and Egyptian rulers.[4]

11.2.2 It is a striking fact that, after 2K 12:18, the name is not used by the narrator as a simple designation for a foreign king with the exception of Pul in 2K 15:19, but this is largely because the foreign powers with which Israel and Judah were involved in the periods represented were Mesopotamian or Egyptian states. The title is used

---

[3]   In general, the masoretic form of Mesopotamian and Egyptian names differs much more from the (supposed) original than does that of north-west semitic names, as a result of this unfamiliarity. The name "Pul", exceptionally used to designate a king of Assyria in 2K 15:19, is of Mesopotamian origin (see Millard, 1976), but the form, though unusual for a name, is not strikingly foreign to North-west Semitic. Cf. "Noah" (נוח), "Og" (עוג) and "Shua" (שׁוע).

[4]   The same is true for "Nebuzaraddan the 'chief cook'" (נבוזראדן רב טבחים), designated by this compound in 2K 25:8, 11, 20, by title in 2K 25:10, 12, 15, 18. Other Assyrian officials are designated only by title.

as a simple designation for the king of some other state (for whom the name is expected) in only three cases. The designation of Mesha as "King of Moab" in 2K 3:5 may have been intended to draw attention to the fact that he rebels successfully, becoming an independent ruler. However, it seems less likely that the reference to Hazael as the "King of Aram" in 2K 13:4, 7, had expressive intentions of this sort. Possibly the use of the title in all three cases is not intended to do anything more than distance the king, to show that it was not important to connect the event with the name.

11.3 Compound Designations

11.3.1 Foreign kings are often designated by name and title, as Toi King of Hamath in 2S 8:9 (59 cases in all). A compound designation including name and title is characteristically used where a king is first mentioned, as with Hiram King of Tyre in 2S 5:11, and where he is re-introduced in a new narrative context, as with Hiram in 1K 5:15, 9:11. Such "introductory" uses would include isolated references, as that to Hadadezer King of Zobah in 1K 11:23, or the reference to Nebuchadnezzar King of Babylon in the date in 2K 25:8. The bulk of compound designations of this sort have this introductory function. The main purpose of such usage is no doubt to provide clear identification. Where the name of the king is familiar in the context, a compound designation of this sort may be used to draw attention to a significant event, as the defeat of "Jabin King of Canaan" in Ju 4:24, the escape of "Ben-hadad King of Aram" in 1K 20:20, or the arrival of "Nebuchadnezzar King of Babylon" at Jerusalem in 2K 24:11.

11.3.2 A compound composed of name and gentilic is used for "Nahash the Ammonite" in 1S 11:1, 2. The narrator omits the title, as would a speaker who does not recognize the person referred to as king (see §§6.9.3, 11.5.2). Samuel speaks of a "Nahash, King of the b. Ammon" in 1S 12:12, in describing the people's reaction to an invasion. The designation represents their perception of Nahash as leader of that invasion. A compound composed of name and patronymic is used of Ben-hadad b. Hazael in 2K 13:3, 25. The context shows that he was king of Aram, but the narrator never gives him the title. A patronymic is included with the name and title in the designation of Achish in 1S 27:2, 1K 2:39, Hadadezer in 2S 8:3, 12,

Talmai in 2S 13:37, and Berodach-baladan in 2K 20:12.[5] Two patronymics are used with name and title for Ben-Hadad in 1K 15:18. If these examples reflect the importance of the patronymic in the context, the reason is not apparent from the corpus. These designations are all used in connection with events that can be considered particularly noteworthy. The "weightier" form of designation is probably intended to draw attention to the name in connection with the event described. The unusual repetition of the title in the designation "King Nebuchadnezzar, King of Babylon" (used in 2K 25:8 to introduce the description of the destruction of the temple, houses, and walls of Jerusalem) no doubt had the same purpose.

11.4 The Designation "Pharaoh" (פרעה)

Designations of kings of Egypt usually include the word "Pharaoh".[6] The word (פרעה) alone is used as a designation in 14 cases.[7] It is also used with a title, as "Pharaoh King of Egypt" (פרעה מלך מצרים, 1K 3:1, 9:16, 11:18, 2K 17:7, 18:21), with a name, as in "Pharaoh Necho" (פרעה נכה, 2K 23:33, 34, 35), and with both name and title, as "Pharaoh Necho King of Egypt (פרעה נכה מלך מצרים, 2K 23:29). The use in combination with a name makes it highly unlikely that "Pharaoh" itself was regarded as a name. This view is supported, outside the corpus, by the use of the term in third person address (Gen 41:10, etc.), and in reference by subordinates (Gen 40:11, etc.). The word "Pharaoh" appears to have been understood by the narrator as specifically denoting a ruler of Egypt, just as "Tsar" denotes a ruler of Russia. The use of "Pharaoh" alone thus represents the use of the title as a simple designation standard for kings of Egypt and Mesopotamia. "Pharaoh King of Egypt", effectively using two titles, is used as a compound designation would

---

5   The name "Berodach-baladan" reflects the Babylonian original "Marduk-apla-iddina" (apart from the initial letter, an error internal to the Hebrew, cf. Isa 39:1). Patronymics were not normally used in Babylonian names, so the epithet "b. Baladan" may also have arisen through error. The name of Merodach-baladan's father is not known from cuneiform sources, unless it was one Erba-Marduk, more probably his grandfather. See Brinkman, 1964, Millard, 1971.

6   "King of Egypt" (מלך מצרים) is used as a simple designation in 2K 24:7, 7, and is combined with the name Shishak in 1K 11:40, 14:25, the name So in 2K 17:4.

7   1S 2:27, 6:6, 1K 3:1, 7:8, 9:24, 11:1, 19, 20, 20, 20, 21, 22, 2K 23:35, 35.

be, where the ruler of Egypt is first mentioned in a new context. "Pharaoh Necho King of Egypt" is used where Necho is first mentioned in 2K 23:29, and so draws attention to his killing of Josiah King of Judah.[8] "Pharaoh Necho", corresponding to "Necho King of Egypt", the typical form of compound designation, is used, as might be expected, to draw attention to his further interference in the domestic affairs of Judah in 2K 23:33, 34, 35. The use of designations including the word "Pharaoh", then, appear to follow much the same patterns as the designations of other foreign kings.

11.5 Designations in Speech

11.5.1 *Address* A foreign king is addressed as "My lord the king" (אדני המלך) by a subject, or by a foreigner who treats him as overlord (1S 29:8, 1K 20:4, 2K 6:12, also in 1K 20:9, where the address is through messengers). Ehud, whose position is less dependent, addresses Eglon as "king" (המלך) in Ju 3:19.

11.5.2 *Reference* A foreign king is referred to by title (including the name of the state he rules) where speaker or addressee is an independent king (18 cases).[9] The Rab-shakeh, an official of the king of Assyria, uses the same form to refer to his king in speaking to the people of Judah (2K 18:31, 33, and, with "my lord" in apposition, in 2K 18:23). He uses "the king", without the name of the state, in the same context (2K 18:29), after he has used a compound designation. A foreign king is referred to by name in the speech of non-subjects in Ju 4:7, 8:6, 7, 15, 15, as is typical of spoken reference to any king (see §§6.9.1, 7.2.2, 9.3.2, 10.4.2). A king uses his name himself where he uses the conventional introduction to a message "Thus says Ben-hadad" (1K 20:3, 5). Ben-hadad's messengers refer to him by name when presenting his plea for his life to Ahab King of Israel (1K 20:32, adding "your servant" to indicate his submission), and where they accept Ahab's offer to treat Ben-Hadad as a "brother", a friendly equal (1K 20:33). The use of the title, presenting him

---

[8]   Cf. the use of two titles for the king of Babylonia in 2K 25:8, noted in §11.3.2, to draw attention to an even more horrifying event.

[9]   Ju 11:17, 17, 17, 1K 20:22, 22:3, 2K 3:7, 16:7, 18:30, 19:6, 10, 13, 13, 13, 20:6, 18, 25:24, and, with "his lord" added, 2K 19:4. The reference to "Pharaoh" in 1S 2:27 can be included.

as an independent monarch, would be out of place in the context of these personal relationship terms. Hezekiah King of Judah refers to "Sennacherib" in prayer to God (2K 19:16), whereas he would normally use the title to humans, as in 2K 19:4. This startling contrast with the narrator's practice (see §11.1.2) presumably represents "Sennacherib" as a person under the control of God. The designation "the king of Assyria" is used to represent a threat (as in 2K 19:4). It distances the individual. A foreign ruler is referred to as "my lord" by a subject in 2K 5:18, 18:24, 27, and as "their lord" by a non-subject speaking to or of that ruler's subjects in 2K 6:22.

11.5.3 Where a speaker uses a compound designation for a foreign king, the intention may be merely to provide clear identification, as Jephtha's reference to "Sihon King of the Amorites, King of Heshbon" in Ju 11:19.[10] However, it is usually also easy to understand the intention as also including the highlighting of the name of the king. Thus in Ju 8:5, Gideon's reference to "Zeba and Zalmunna, Kings of Midian" not only identifies his quarry, but indicates the importance of his expedition to the men of Sukkoth. In 1S 15:20 Saul is presenting his capture of "Agag King of Amalek" as evidence that he has carried out his orders. Other examples occur in 1S 15:32, 2K 19:20; the reference to "Pharaoh King of Egypt" in 2K 18:21 can be added. In 2K 8:9, Hazael's reference to "Your son Ben-Hadad King of Aram" presents his master to the prophet Elisha first as "your son", a dutiful subordinate approaching a benevolent adviser (see §13.4.4), and then uses his name and title, the usual way of making first reference to a foreign king. The Rab-shakeh uses "the great king, king of Assyria", a common Assyrian form of designation in such introductory situations (המלך הגדול מלך אשור, 2K 18:19, 28). In 2S 10:2, David refers to "Hanun b. Nahash" in speaking to himself or his followers. The failure to use a title probably indicates that he is treating this as a personal, not a political matter,

---

[10] The need for clear identification is probably mainly the narrator's. The use of the two titles identifies him as the same Sihon for whom either may be used, as Num 21:21, Deut 2:26. The two designations for his state are often related to Sihon in other ways, as in Num 21:34, Deut 2:24. Cf. the use of either "Hazor" the capital, or "Canaan", the state, in the designation of Jabin in Ju 4:17, 23, combined in Ju 4:2, where he is first mentioned.

but may be connected with the fact that the narrator never uses the title for Hanun.

11.6 Foreign Kings in the Book of Jeremiah

Foreign kings are regularly designated in Jeremiah by title, as "the king of Babylon" (מלך בבל, Jer 20:4), or by name and title, as "Nebuchadnezzar king of Babylon" (נבוכדראצר מלך בבל, Jer 21:2). The use of the term "Pharaoh" is likewise consistent with the standard usage of the corpus described above. Nebuchadnezzar is designated by name alone in Jer 29:1, in the introduction to Jeremiah's letter (a form of prophecy), in Jer 32:1 (introducing a more typical form of prophecy), and in the narrative of Jer 52:28, 29, 30, recounting the numbers exiled on different occasions. Jer 52:1-27 corresponds to 2K 24:18-25:21, but the Kings account continues with a consideration of the situation in Judah. The replacement of this by the statements on the numbers exiled reflects the different interests of the narrator in Jeremiah. The designation of a mesopotamian king by name, virtually unknown in the corpus (but common in the book of Chronicles), suggests that Jer 52:28-30 had an origin different from that of the preceding narrative material.[11] The designations of Nebuchadnezzar by name in prophetic materials probably have similar implications. The use of the name alone in Jer 39:2 does not seem remarkable. However, the use of the name alone in giving a date by regnal year in Jer 32:1 is certainly surprising (cf. Jer 25:1), as is the fact that the name is used there for a character who has not been mentioned for some time, and is designated by title in what follows (Jer 32:3, 4). It seems probable, then, that, although the designation both of kings of Judah and of foreign rulers in the narrative materials in Jeremiah generally reflect the conventions characteristic of the corpus, a few examples reflect different conventions, and so presumably occur in additions to the basic material. The situation is probably much the same in the prophetic passages and the introductions to them.

---

[11] The designation of King Zedekiah by his personal name in Jer 39:2 may also reflect conventions different from those of the corpus. The wording of the context differs from that in 2K 25:2 and Jer 52:5. 2K 18:10 might be adduced as a comparable example of the use of the name alone in a date, but the date in Jer 39:2 seems more prominent.

11.7 The Designation of Rulers, Conclusion

The material surveyed in §§5-11 shows that rulers are treated in the corpus in three groups. Where a simple designation is used for David, Solomon, and the Kings of Judah, the legitimate rulers of the community with which the narrator identifies, name or title is chosen to nuance the description of their conduct, or to suggest the narrator's attitude to it. Saul and the kings of the northern kingdom ruled the same people, or a division of it, but rejected God's commands, and so could not be considered legitimate rulers of the community. The choice between name and title for their designation is rarely used to illuminate their own conduct. For the most part the title is used to draw attention to unkinglike actions by these rulers, or to enhance the presentation of characters encountered by them who stand in a good relationship to God. The designation by name or by title of the third group, rulers of foreign states, is typically predictable on the basis of the state ruled. The conduct of such rulers is quite beyond the interests of the narrator, and it is doubtful whether the choice of simple designation for them is ever used expressively. Compound designations are also used differently for the three groups, although less clearly so. The main difference is the restriction (almost complete) of designations in the form "the king PN" to members of the first group. The designation of rulers in the Book of Jeremiah appears to be based on the same conventions, as might be expected in material covering part of the same period, and largely presented as the work of participants in the events described. It is significant that the work of the Chronicler does not reflect the same convention, one of the factors which suggests that the features of usage described here were, to a large extent, characteristic of early biblical Hebrew, and were absent from, or used differently in the later forms of the language. Some of the exceptional uses of designations in the Book of Jeremiah may represent such later forms of usage. The same could be true of some uses in the corpus, but most examples of unexpected usage there are plausibly explained as "marked". The contrast with the standard pattern of usage is deliberate, and is intended to convey some expressive meaning. Thus the designation of rulers in the corpus can reasonably be seen (barring some few anomalies) as reflecting a single self-consistent system of usage.

III NAME AND NATURE: OTHERS

The Designation of Priests and Prophets

12.1 Introduction

The only other groups of named characters for whom both title and name are commonly used as a simple designations are priests and prophets. The use of titles for these groups differs somewhat from their use for kings, no doubt in part because their situation in society was different. The title "king" is unique, in the sense that it is typically applicable only to one person in any state. The title "the king" denotes the same individual for all citizens of that state, and all would speak about him in much the same way. As a result, where the language concerns a king of a state of which the speaker is a member, or with which the narrator identifies, the use of the title can be linked quite closely to grammatical features. The narrative shows that the number of priests and prophets was not similarly restricted. The title alone can thus only denote a particular individual within a limited context. For this reason, the name is the common simple designation for members of these groups. The use of the title is relatively rare, and can not be linked to grammatical features in the same way as it can for David, Solomon, and the kings of Judah. Usage is less consistent, more a matter of the use of marked forms for expressive purposes. Similar differences are not evident in the use of compound designations.

12.2 Priests: Simple Designations

12.2.1 Where the title is used as a simple designation, the term "priest" (כהן) is usually adequate to indicate the position of the holder without addition. It is occasionally qualified to indicate rank in the Jerusalem temple, as "high priest, second priest" (כהן הגדול, 2K 22:4; כהן משנה, כהן הראש, 2K 25:18). The deity served may be indicated, as in "priests of the Lord" (כהני יהוה, 1S 22:17, where it is used to emphasize the vicious nature of Saul's crime in slaughtering them, see §7.1.2n), or in "Mattan, priest of Baal" (מתן כהן הבעל, 2K 11:18, where it is used to make a necessary distinction). The title "the priest" may be used to designate an unnamed character, as in the narrative in Judges 18, described in §14.3.1. As a general rule, however, an individual priest who participates in a narrative is named, and, where names are not given, the title is used in the plural, as in 1K 8:3, 2K 12:5, 17:27, 23:2.

12.2.2 The title is used as a simple designation for a named priest in 9 cases, as opposed to over 50 uses of the name; it is clear that its use is marked. As with "the king", the use of the title "priest" draws the status of the character in question to the reader's attention. This is usually done where the clause shows the character acting in a priestly function, but the title may also be used to contrast the event described against the ideal represented by the title "priest". Both uses are shown in "Saul said to Ahijah 'Bring up the Ark of God'... but while Saul was speaking to the priest, the tumult in the camp of the Philistines kept on increasing, and Saul said to the priest, 'Hold your hand!'" (ויאמר שאול לאחיה הגישה ארון האלהים... ויהי עד דבר שאול אל הכהן וההמון אשר במחנה פלשתים וילך הלוך ורב ויאמר שאול אל הכהן אסף ידך, 1S 14:18-19). Saul is said to speak to "the priest" in the temporal clause in 1S 14:19, suggesting the usual respect for the office. This exemplifies the expected usage, but in an introductory or background situation. A worthy ruler would obtain God's advice in this way, but Saul prevents "the priest" from providing it, addressing Ahijah not as a priest, but as a subordinate. This second use of the title "priest" is thus unexpected, and the use of a nominal designation for the addressee is unnecessary. This marked usage in the main clause highlights Saul's improper action, to presage the fact that his subsequent decision, taken without God's advice, leads to failure. The passage exemplifies the narrator's use of expressive features to present Saul in a bad light.[1]

12.2.3 Another example of the expressive use of the title occurs in the story of David and the priest Ahimelek in 1S 21:2-10. "Ahimelek" comes to meet David (1S 21:2), but "the priest" speaks of "sanc-

---

[1] A title is used (in a compound designation) where a priest is asked to obtain advice from God in 1S 23:9, 30:7. The unworthiness of Saul is also highlighted by the use of the title "king" (see §7.1.2) and possibly by the designation of God in relation to Saul (see §15.4.3).

tified bread" (לחם קדש), and gives it to David when told that he can properly receive it (1S 21:5, 7). David reassures "the priest" in the matter of the bread (1S 21:6), but he asks "Ahimelek" for weapons (1S 21:9). In these cases, the title is used where the context deals with a priestly function, not where it does not. Where the title "the priest" is used in 1S 21:10, however, Ahimelek does not perform a priestly function; he gives the sword of Goliath to David. This last example, then, contrasts with the expected usage and so draws attention to the event, suggesting its importance. The narrator has already hinted that Saul will learn of this action (1S 21:8). No doubt the wording in 1S 21:10 is intended to stimulate expectation of his reaction (and speculation on it).[2] Elsewhere, the title is used as expected. "The priest" suggests seeking advice from God in 1S 14:36. "Jehoiada" sends for soldiers in 2K 11:4, but "the priest" is concerned with ceremonial, and the purity and security of the temple, in 2K 11:10, 15, 18.[3]

12.3 Priests: Compound Designations

12.3.1 The narrator refers to a priest with a compound designation, composed of the name and title, in some 35 cases. Most of these occur where an individual is first mentioned, or in other cases classed as "introductory".[4] Uses which are not reasonably classified as introductory can readily be seen as drawing attention to the name in the context of a particular event. A compound designation is used in this way for "Zadok the priest" (צדוק הכהן) where King David gives him the significant order to take the ark back to Jerusalem (2S 15:27), and where he sets out ceremonially and anoints Solomon as king (1K 1:38, 39). A compound designation is always used for "Uriah the priest" to draw attention to his part in the changes made in the Jerusalem temple (2K 16:10, 11, 11, 15, 16, see §4.11.2). Hilkiah, who played an important part in the discovery of the scroll in the temple, is similarly treated (see §4.11.2). A simple designation,

---

[2]   Fokkelman 1986:391, argues that the gift of the sword to David had a "sacral" character.

[3]   In 1S 2:13, 14, 15, and 2K 12:11, it is assumed that the title does not represent a particular individual, but "any" priest or high priest.

[4]   With the priest Eli, the title occurs in the second mention (1S 1:9), not in 1S 1:3 (see §4.7.1n). On the first mention of Jehoiada (2K 11:4), see §4.8.2n.

his name, is used only in 2K 22:8, following the use of the compound "Hilkiah the high priest" (חלקיהו הכהן הגדול) in the same verse.[5]

12.3.2 The compound designation of a priest almost always includes the title, as in the examples above. The only acting priest designated by name and patronymic by the narrator is Abiathar. Where Abiathar is first mentioned, he is introduced as "a son of Ahimelek b. Ahitub" (1S 22:20). There is no particular reason to use the title here; the use of the patronymic asserts the identity of this Ahimelek with the priest slaughtered by Saul, which is significant for the fact that Abiathar joins David, as is described in that passage. Abiathar is designated by name and patronymic (1S 23:6) or by name alone (1S 22:21, 22) until 1S 23:9, where the compound designation "Abiathar the priest", using the title, draws attention to the first time he is asked to act as a priest. Name, patronymic and title are used to introduce Abiathar in a new context in 1S 30:7, confirming that both forms of designation represent the same individual (as in other cases where an individual is designated in different ways, see § 11.5.3n). After this, the common form of compound designation for priests, composed of name and title, is used for him. A designation composed of name, patronymic and title is also used for Ahimelek, Abiathar's father, in 1S 22:11, where it draws attention to Saul's summons which results in the slaughter of Ahimelek and his family. Patronymics are not used in the designation of other priests, presumably because their genealogy was well known.

12.3.3 In 1S 30:7, the components of the designation of Abiathar are given in the order name – title – patronym. Here he is asked to obtain advice from God as to whether David should pursue the raiders who had carried off the women from Ziklag. That is, he is asked to

---

[5]   The full title "Hilkiah the high priest" is used where he is first mentioned (2K 22:4, in speech), where he first appears in connection with the discovery of the scroll (2K 22:8), and where he is ordered to remove improper objects from the temple (2K 23:4). Elsewhere the compound is "Hilkiah the priest", using name and title, as for other priests (2K 22:10, 12, 14, 23:24). The fuller form is thus used in relation to the ordinary form much as is a compound designation in relation to a simple one (cf. §4.13.4).

act in his priestly capacity. The same three components are used to designate Ahimelek in 1S 22:11, but there the order is name – patronym – title. In 1S 22:9, Doeg tells Saul of David's visit to "Ahimelek b. Ahitub" ignoring his priestly status (see §12.4). As a result, Saul summons "Ahimelek b. Ahitub the priest" (1S 22:11). The addition of the title, acknowledging the priestly status which Doeg ignored, is probably intended to remind the reader that Saul ought to treat Ahimelek with respect. It thus heightens the impact of the injustice which Saul actually shows. However that may be, it is clear that Ahimelek's priestly role is irrelevant here; he is summoned to answer a charge of treason. The position of the title relative to the patronym in a combination of this sort thus correlates with its relative significance in the context (cf. §28.3.4). The same could be said of "Jonathan b. Abiathar the priest" (1K 1:42), but here the title "priest" probably relates to Abiathar, not to Jonathan, who is not elsewhere given this title.

12.4 Priests: Designation in Speech

The priest Eli is addressed deferentially as "my lord" by Hannah, rebutting his suggestion that she is drunk (1S 1:15, see §25.2.6). The only other examples of a designation of a priest used in address occur in speech by Saul to Ahimelek. Saul uses the patronym "ben Ahitub" when he first speaks to him (1S 22:12), and his name when he sentences him (1S 22:16). The significance of the use of these forms is discussed in §§25.4.2, 25.5.1). Spoken reference to priests is typically made with the standard compound designation, made up of name and title (12 cases).[6] The personal name is used (in speech by King David) in 2S 15:36, following the compound designations in the preceding verse, just as it would be in narration. In 1S 22:9, Doeg refers to "Ahimelek b. Ahitub". His use of a compound designation is typical of such situations, where precise identification is needed. His failure to use the title is striking. It is possibly intended to show that, as an Edomite, he is a pagan, more probably to show him as a true "servant of Saul", irreverent like his master.

---

[6] 2S 15:35, 35, 1K 1:19, 25, 26, 32, 34, 44, 45, 2K 22:10, and 2K 22:4, where the title is "high priest" (הכהן הגדול).

12.5 The Designation of Priests: Conclusion

The designation of priests, then, shows clear patterns. The title is typically used in spoken reference; failure to use it suggests lack of the respect due to the holder of the office. The office is typically indicated where a priest is first mentioned in narration. The usual simple designation is the name. The title is used to draw attention to the priestly status, either to highlight the performance of some priestly function, or to highlight events unexpected in the context of the activity of priests. The narrator resorts to these exceptional uses to reinforce the impression that he wishes to present of the qualities of the characters in his narrative. The few cases of the use of patronymics can also be seen as the result of careful choice, intended to carry particular implications.

12.6 Prophets: the Form of the Title

12.6.1 The title used in the corpus for the people included in this section on the designation of prophets is either "man of God" (איש האלהים), or "prophet" (masculine נביא, feminine נביאה). These titles are not mutually exclusive. Both are applied to Elijah by himself (1K 18:22, 2K 1:10), to Elisha (2K 5:8, 14), and to "the man of God who came from Judah" by the "old prophet" (1K 13:18, 26).[7] However, the use of the title "prophet" (נביא/נביאה) is often associated with the delivery of a message from God, or with successful prayer.[8] The major exception (where an alternative designation is available) is the repeated reference to "Nathan the prophet" (נתן הנביא) in 1 Kings 1 (9 cases, against two of the name alone). This can be seen as reflecting the narrator's desire to emphasize the involvement of the highest authorities in the transfer of power from David to Solomon (see §12.8.1). The title "man of God" can be used for a character who delivers a message of the same sort as does a

---

[7]   The otherwise consistent use, in this chapter, of the term "man of God" for the visitor from Judah, and "prophet" for the resident of Bethel, is probably intended to distinguish the two characters, not to show that they followed different branches of the profession. It is noteworthy that in 1K 13:20, 21, 23, 25, 26, where confusion between the two would be easy, the narrator does not rely on these terms alone to distinguish them, but adds some further description.

[8]   2S 24:11, 1K 11:29, 14:2, 18, 16:7, 18:36, 2K 14:25, 19:2, 20:1, 11, 14, 22:14.

"prophet".[9] However, the title "man of God" is not closely associated with any particular activity. The use of the term by Samson's parents for a stranger who made a prediction without naming God as his authority (Ju 13:6, 8) suggests that it had a general application, and did not refer to a specific occupation.

12.6.2 The term "prophet" (נביא/נביאה) can be used of adherents of a particular deity, as the "prophets of Baal" (נביאי הבעל, 1K 18:22). Where an individual is designated, the phrase "prophet for Yahweh" is used (נביא ליהוה, 1S 3:20, 1K 18:22, 22:7, 2K 3:11). In the contexts in which this phrase is used, "prophet" could well be translated "spokesman", a value of the term perfectly exemplified by its use of Aaron in relation to Moses in Exod 7:1. The term "prophet" is also used to represent a person who is enabled, as a result of close association with God, to direct the use of superhuman power on behalf of humans. Thus Elisha indicates that the king's despair over the demand that he cure leprosy is unwarranted, saying "Let him come to me and learn that there is a prophet (נביא) in Israel" (2K 5:8). That is, Elisha can, as a result of his association with God, produce effective advice. This is the factor which makes the designation of Elijah as "prophet" significant where he approaches God with his crucial prayer in 1K 18:36. His association with God will ensure that his prayer is effective. Such varied examples suggest that the term "prophet", while generally use in association with the presentation of a message from God, was not restricted to a particular kind of message, or a particular context of presentation.

12.6.3 Both terms, then, denote an agent or representative of God. The term "prophet" implies that the holder represents God through the spoken word, but this is not excluded in the case of a "man of God". It seems quite likely that the use of the terms in the text as we have it reflects some change in the categorization of such representatives over the period between the occurrence of the events described, and the final formulation of the description of them in the corpus. The statement in 1S 9:9 that the term "prophet" (נביא) was the equivalent, in the writer's day, of the older "seer" (ראה) shows

---

9   Compare 1S 2:27 with Ju 6:8, 2K 6:9 with 1S 22:5, 1K 20:28 with 1K 20:13.

that such change did occur. The evidence of Chronicles suggests that the use of "man of God" there is not due to the Chronicler, but reflects his sources.[10] A title is more freely used for some prophets than for others, and it seems possible that some cases of its use, at least, represent updating of earlier usage. However, the evidence is not adequate to show clear historical patterning. As far as the usage of the Bible generally is concerned, "man of God" (איש האלהים) appears to be a general term, which would include the more specific "prophet" (נביא) as a hyponym. For purposes of the present study, the two titles are considered as free variants.

12.7 Prophets: Simple Designations

12.7.1 Where the narrator uses a simple designation for a prophet, he typically uses the name (as is also the practice in the books of the "writing" prophets). The title is used only for Elisha, who is called "man of God" (איש האלהים) in 20 cases, "Elisha" in 46. Clearly, the use of the title is marked. It seems to be intended to draw attention to Elisha's special relationship with God, and to the powers he can wield as a result. The use of the title as a simple designation sometimes represents the viewpoint of some other character who is agent of the clause, as where a woman informs "the man of God" of what has occurred (ותבא ותגד לאיש האלהים, 2K 4:7). Other examples occur in 2K 4:21, 25, 27, 42, 5:15. The fact that Naaman washes "according to the word of the man of God" (...וירד ויטבל כדבר איש האלהים, 2K 5:14) probably represents Naaman's viewpoint as agent of the main clause. He is now viewing Elisha as able to speak for God.[11]

---

[10] "Man of God" is used 56 times in the corpus. Of the 16 other uses in the Bible, six refer to Moses (Deut 33:1, Jos 14:6, Ps 90:1, Ezra 3:2, 1 Chron 23:14, 2 Chron 30:16), three to David (Neh 12:24, 36, 2 Chron 8:14). The title "man of God" is also used for a man whose sons or descendants had a chamber (לשכה) used by Jeremiah (Jer 35:4), for Shemaiah (2 Chron 11:2 = 1K 12:22), who is called "prophet" (נביא) in 2 Chron 12:5, 15, in material not found in Kings, and for an unnamed character who advised King Amaziah in 2 Chron 25:7, 9, 9, also in material not found in Kings. The term נביא occurs in the Lachish letters (3:20, 16:5).

[11] The same is possibly true where the woman of Shunem acts "according to the word of the man of God" (2K 8:2, see §12.7.4), and where the king sends to "the place which the man of God mentioned" (2K 6:10). In the only example in which the name Elisha is used in a situation of this sort, the verb is passive (2K 2:22), or the agent is God (2K 6:18).

12.7.2 In these two chapters of 2 Kings (four and five), the prophet as patient is designated as "Elisha" where he is first approached: by the woman in 2K 4:1, by Naaman in 2K 5:9. This is easily understood as expressive usage. Initially they think of him only as "Elisha"; after he has helped them, they realize that he is indeed a "man of God" (2K 4:7, 5:14, 15). The title is also used to designate the prophet as agent in 2K 4:25, 27. Here, too, the usage can be seen as expressive. "The man of God" is shown as not knowing why the Shunammite is coming to see him, a phenomenon which surprises him, as his speech in 2K 4:27 shows. The designation "man of God", used in 2K 4:25, 27, draws attention to the prophet's special relationship with God, which should have prevented this ignorance, and so suggests that the relationship may no longer be in effect. The suspense raised over the question of whether Elisha still has the power to help the woman adds to the impact of the story. Elsewhere in these chapters, the name is used as a simple designation for the prophet as agent (2K 4:2, 8, 17, 32, 38, 5:9, 25).

12.7.3 In 2K 7:2, an officer answers "the man of God", but his answer shows disbelief in Elisha's prediction, so that the title cannot be said to reflect his viewpoint. Its use can be seen as intended to raise expectations for the following narrative, and so to add to its impact. The circumstances under which the prediction is made (detailed in 2K 6:24-30), suggests that the fulfilment of Elisha's prediction is impossible. This conflicts with the expectations raised by use of the designation "man of God", which reminds the reader of Elisha's powers, an example of which has just been given (in 2K 6:32-33). The uncertainty induced by the conflict, and the consequent suspense, is not allayed until 2K 7:16. The title "man of God" is also used at the end 2 Kings 7, where the essential events of the story are recapitulated. It represents the agent in 2K 7:18, the patient in 2K 7:19, where 2K 7:2 is repeated. The intention is, no doubt, to drive home the lesson presented in the story. The repetition of the title highlights the fact that Elisha is shown acting as a "man of God", as God's representative. In 2K 6:24-7:20, the name is used as a simple designation only in 6:32, 7:1, where the prophet is agent.

12.7.4 The title is used in 2K 8:2, where the woman of Shunem acts "according to the word of the man of God" (כדבר איש האלהים). In

2K 8:3, the narrator introduces the possibility that her following the instructions of the man of God may lead to her losing her property. In 2K 8:4, the king asks "Gehazi, servant of the man of God" (נחזי נער איש האלהים) to tell him about the marvellous acts of Elisha. This suggests to the reader that Elisha's special relationship with God will enable him to surmount this problem too, and so any uncertainty and suspense raised by the possibility of the woman's loss is quickly allayed. The use of the title is probably mainly intended to impress on the reader the fact that a "man of God" can help those in his favour in any sort of problem. In this story (2K 8:1-6), the narrator only designates the prophet as "Elisha" in 2K 8:1, where he is agent.

12.7.5 The title is also used to designate Elisha as agent in 2K 6:6, and in 6:9, 10, and in the designation of his servant in 2K 6:15, where it may be used to stimulate the reader's interest in the possibility of the solution thus presaged, and the manner of it, as in 2K 7:2. Elsewhere in 2K 6:1-23, the name is used as a simple designation, whether the prophet is agent (2K 6:17, 18, 18, 19, 20) or patient (2K 6:1, 17, 21). Elisha as agent is also designated as "man of God" in 2K 8:11 and 13:19. The use of the title here appears simply intended to point out that "the man of God" is making the prediction described. This fosters the belief that what he foresees will happen, and thus induces the reader to participate in Elisha's emotions. Elsewhere in 2K 8:7-15, 13:14-21, the narrator designates the prophet as "Elisha".[12]

12.7.6 There is little in the way of objective evidence to support the argument that the narrator deliberately uses the title "man of God" as suggested, to add to the interest and impact of the stories about Elisha. The usage is not strikingly consistent; it seems to have been applied in different ways in different stories. It is possible, then, that the use of the title derives from a stage in the development of the individual stories prior to the work of the narrator. The Elisha stories would then have to be viewed as deriving from a context in

---

[12] As agent in 2K 8:7, 10, 13, 14, 13:14, 15, 16, 17, 20, as patient in 2K 8:14, and in the two nominal phrases in 2K 13:21, where the identification provided by the name is required.

which the title was used as a simple designation for a prophet, unlike the contexts in which the stories of the other prophets were produced. This seems rather unlikely, especially as the term "man of God" is used in spoken reference for Elijah as well as Elisha. The assumption made here is that the narrator used the title to enliven some of the stories of Elisha, particularly in relation to striking or miraculous acts and predictions. There was little need for this in stories of other prophets.[13]

12.8 Prophets: Compound Designations

12.8.1 The majority of compound designations used for prophets by the narrator occur in situations classed as "introductory".[14] Where this classification does not seem reasonable, the compound designation can be seen as used to draw attention to the use of the name in connection with a significant event. "Nathan the prophet" was not invited to Adonijah's feast (1K 1:10), showing that his allegiance to David was not questioned. "Nathan the prophet" is also mentioned in 1K 1:38 (with "Zadok the Priest", see §12.3.1) as a significant figure among those representing the divine authority behind the anointing of Solomon (see §5.3.3). "Elijah the prophet" approaches God with a crucial prayer (1K 18:36, the only place where this designation is used). The designation "Jehu b. Hanani the prophet" draws attention to the denunciation of Baasha recapitulated in 1K 16:7 after it was presented as "the word of God to Jehu b. Hanani about Baasha" (1K 16:1).

12.8.2 The form of compound designation most widely used by the narrator is made up of name and title. The title is usually "prophet"

---

[13]   The narratives of the activities of other prophets contain few examples of situations similar to those in which the title is used for Elisha. The clearest example occurs where a character is said to act on the word of "Gad" (2S 24:19) or of "Elijah" (1K 17:15). The title is use for Elisha in similar situations, see §12.7.1n.

[14]   1S 22:5, 2S 7:2, 12:25, 24:11, 1K 1:8, 22, 11:29, 12:15, 22, 14:18, 15:29, 16:1, 17:1, 19:19, 21:17, 28, 22:11, 24, 2K 1:3, 5:8, 9:1, 14:25, 19:2, 20, 20:1, 11, 14, 22:14, see also Ju 4:4. A compound designation for Elisha is strikingly absent in 2K 13:14.

(נביא), less commonly "man of God" (איש האלהים).[15] A patronymic is added to the name and title in the case of Jehu b. Hanani (1K
16:7), Jonah b. Amittai (2K 14:25), Isaiah b. Amos (2K 19:2, 20:1)
and Huldah wife of Shallum (2K 22:14), as is a gentilic in the case
of Ahijah the Shilonite (1K 11:29). In all these cases, the title is
"prophet" (נביא). The extra identification is usually added where the
prophet is first mentioned, to provide a more complete identification. In the case of Huldah, her husband is identified by two patronymics and his own title, presumably to indicate as precisely as possible the social context of the woman who made the important prediction in 2K 22:15-20. In the case of Jehu, the patronymic is not
used where he is first mentioned, but is added where his prophecy
is recapitulated, presumably indicating its importance for the coming narrative. For Isaiah, the patronymic is used both where he is
first mentioned, and (in 2K 20:1) to introduce him in a scene in
which his initial prediction is dramatically reversed.

12.8.3 As in the designation of priests (§12.3.3), the title may precede or follow the patronymic or gentilic where both are used in
the same designation. Where the title precedes the patronymic, the
prophet is approached by envoys from the king to ask for help or
advice from God (2K 19:2, 22:14). No such approach is made where
the title follows (1K 16:7, 2K 20:1); the prophet is, in fact, agent.
Thus the placing of the title before the patronymic reflects its importance, in that it represents the role significant for an agent who
comes to consult the prophet (see §28.3.4). The case of "Deborah,
a woman (who was) a prophetess, wife of Lapidoth" (דבורה אשה
נביאה אשת לפידות, Ju 4:4) does not agree with this suggestion. It can
be argued that אשה נביאה "a woman (who was) a prophetess" is a
descriptive phrase; the epithet takes the form הנביאה "the prophetess" for women (2K 22:14), as הנביא "the prophet" for men.[16] This

---

[15] "Prophet" is used for Gad (1S 22:5, also, with a relationship term, 2S 24:11),
Nathan (2S 7:2, 12:25, 1K 1:8, 10, 22, 38), Ahijah (with a relationship term, 1K
14:18), Jehu (1K 16:12), Elijah (1K 18:36), Elisha (2K 9:1), and Isaiah (2K 20:11, 14).
"Man of God" is used for Shemaiah in 1K 12:22, and for Elisha in 2K 5:8, 20.
[16] The term "woman prophetess" (אשה נביאה) occurs only in Ju 4:4. The masculine equivalent (איש נביא) also occurs only once (Ju 6:8), where it designates an unnamed character.

descriptive phrase is, no doubt, placed immediately after the name to indicate the significance of her prophetic function for the following story. However, the context is not that of the use of epithets in a designation, so that this example should not be seen as conflicting with the suggestion made above.

12.8.4 Compound designations which do not include a title are also used for prophets. Ahijah is designated by name and gentilic where his speaking the word of God is recalled in 1K 12:15, and (with a relationship term) in 1K 15:29. The prophet Jehu is designated by name and patronymic where the word of God comes to him in 1K 16:1 (the first mention of him). The narrator uses the name and gentilic "Elijah the Tishbite" where Elijah speaks God's word in 1K 17:1 (where he is first introduced), and where the word of God comes to Elijah in 1K 21:17, 28, 2K 1:3.[17] Elisha is designated as "Elisha b. Shaphat" where Elijah is about to call him as a prophet (1K 19:19) After that, the compound designations used by the narrator include the title (2K 5:8, 20, 9:1). Isaiah is designated as "Isaiah b. Amoz where he speaks the word of God in 2K 19:20. It is reasonable to suggest, then, that a compound designation composed of name and patronymic is used where the character has not achieved the status of prophet (as Elisha in 1K 19:19), or where it is unnecessary, as the context shows him receiving or speaking the word of God. A designation composed of name and title is typically used where the prophet is involved with humans otherwise than specifically as speaking God's word, or where he prays to God (1K 18:36, 2K 20:11).

12.8.5 The designation "Zedekiah b. Chenaanah" (1K 22:11, 24) does not fit this view, but he is clearly not a "prophet of the Lord" (1K 22:7-8). It is probable that he is not given the title "prophet" for this reason. A compound designation composed of name and title is used for a prophet who receives or speaks the word of God in the case of Gad (2S 24:11), Shemaiah (1K 12:22), Ahijah (1K 14:18),

---

[17] No addressee is indicated for Elijah's speech in 1K 17:1. The sentence is presumably introductory to the following narrative. The same designation is used in speech in 2K 9:36, where Jehu recalls the word of God spoken through "his servant Elijah the Tishbite".

and Jehu (1K 16:12). Among these, a patronymic or gentilic is used in the corpus only for Jehu, suggesting that the narrator lacked the necessary information for the other three. It is possible, then, that the narrator used designations composed of patronymic and gentilic, and those composed of name and title, in different contexts where his information made this possible, so that (within these limits) he used the title where he wished to remind the reader of the character's status. In this case, the designation of Jehu in 1K 16:12 is an anomaly.[18]

12.9 The Designation of Prophets in Speech

12.9.1 *Address* The forms of spoken designation used for prophets are conditioned by the attitude of the speaker to the addressee, as in the case of kings. Those who accept a prophet as God's representative address him as "man of God" (איש האלהים), or as "my lord" (אדני), or use the two combined.[19] "My lord" is also used by Obadiah, a senior official of the king of Israel, addressing Elijah in 1K 18:13, after he has addressed him as "My lord Elijah" in 1K 18:7. His use of the name rather than a title in 1K 18:7 is surprising (see §§25.2.4, 25.4.1), but, since he shows himself to have been a devoted supporter of Elijah's colleagues (1K 18:13), it may reflect intimate friendship. The name alone is used as a vocative by God addressing Elijah in 1K 19:9, 13, by the king of Israel addressing Micaiah in 1K 22:15, and by Elijah addressing Elisha in 2K 2:4. Elijah's use of the name is probably to be taken as the use of an intimate form to add to the persuasive force of a request. This is possible in the speech of the king, but, since he is hostile, his use of the name more probably belittles the prophet. The use of the name by God may similarly reflect the usage of parents admonishing their children (see §§25.4.2-3, 25.8.2). A king addresses Elisha as "my father"

---

[18] See §12.8.1 on 1K 16:1. A designation including both title and patronymic is used in connection with the speaking of the word of God for Jehu (1K 16:7) and Isaiah (2K 20:1).

[19] "Man of God" is used for Elijah in 1K 17:18, and, for Elisha, "man of God" in 2K 1:9, 11, 13, 4:40, "my lord" in 2K 2:19, 4:28, 6:5, 15, and also in deferential use by Hazael, consulting Elisha on behalf of his master, in 2K 8:12. Elisha is addressed as "My lord the man of God" by the Shunammite woman in 2K 4:16.

(אבי), treating him as a benevolent superior, in 2K 6:21, 13:14, and Elisha uses the same term to Elijah in 2K 2:12.

12.9.2 *Reference* A title is used as a simple designation in spoken reference to a prophet by those who accept him as God's representative, including the prophet himself, and foreigners, but not including a king of Israel (10 cases).[20] A composite designation which includes the title is used by various speakers in the court of Judah to refer to Nathan (1K 1:23, 32, 34, 44, 45), by Jeroboam King of Israel speaking of his wish to consult Ahijah, the prophet who predicted his rise to the throne (1K 14:2), and by a servant telling the king of Aram of the powers of Elisha (2K 6:12). These, too, accept the person named as God's representative. The name is used by a speaker who can be considered benevolent or intimate, or by others, including a king of Israel (13 cases in all).[21] A composite designation which does not include the title is used by a king of Israel, or by subordinates speaking to him, in 1K 22:8, 9, 2K 1:8, 3:11, 6:31, and, with "his (God's) servant" added, 2K 9:36.

12.9.3 It can be concluded that the use of a title in spoken reference marks the respect due to a "prophet" or a "man of God". Such formal demonstration of respect is not to be expected from their servants or other close associates. Since those who do use the title include foreigners (2K 5:13, 6:12, 8:7, 8), the fact that the title is typically not used in speech by or to a king of Israel stands out. The kings of Israel who do use the title, or otherwise recognize the prophet's mission, are those appointed as king of Israel by God through a prophet (Jeroboam, 1K 14:2, Jehu, 2K 9:36, 10:10, using "his [God's] servant" to show the prophet's calling, as does a title). Failure to use a designation which includes a title is thus probably

---

[20] Elijah and Elisha are referred to as "Man of God" in 1K 17:24, 2K 1:10, 12, 4:9, 22, 8:7, 8; "prophet" in 1K 18:22, 2K 5:3, 8, 13, and also, in speech to or by subordinates, as "lord" (אדון, 2K 2:3, 5, 16, 5:20, 22).

[21] Obadiah uses Elijah's name in foreseeing his speech to King Ahab (1K 18:8, 11, 14). God uses the name in 1K 19:17, as does Elisha when calling on God in 2K 2:14. Lesser prophets use the name in 2K 2:15, 15, as does Gehazi in 2K 8:5. The king of Aram uses it in 2K 8:14. A servant of a king of Israel uses the name in speaking to his master (2K 3:11), as does a king of Israel himself in 1K 22:26, 2K 8:4, and, referring to him as "his (God's) servant Elijah", in 2K 10:10.

intended to reinforce the presentation of the kings of Israel as refusing to follow the true religion, unlike the kings of Judah, who do use titles recognizing the status of prophets in their speech.

12.10 Conclusion

The use of the different possible designations for prophets, then, seems less consistent than the use of those for priests and kings. This lack of consistency appears mainly in the fact that the narrator uses the title as a simple designation only for Elisha, and in the use of two titles: "prophet" (נביא) and "man of God" (איש האלהים), as (apparently) free variants. The use of these two titles may reflect the historical development of the terminology, although this is not clear. The failure to use a title as a simple designation for prophets other than Elisha might suggest that the prophets, like Moses and the patriarchs, were generally so well known in the community as to be commonly referred to by name alone (see §4.13.1). However, the use of composite designations does not bear this out; they are not notably sparse. Moreover, the use of designations in speech appears to be uniform, and generally consistent with expectations derived from the designations of kings. It appears, then, that the inconsistency in the use of simple designations is limited to the designation of Elisha in narration. It seems most probable that this represents the work of the narrator.

Other Forms of Designation
of Named Individuals

13.1 Introduction

A few titles other than "king", "priest", "man of God", or "prophet" are used with a name to form compound designations, but the narrator rarely uses them as simple designations for named characters. A named character who does not have one of these titles is typically referred to by name if a simple designation is used, whether in narration or in speech. Some other form of designation, a patronymic, gentilic, relationship term, or general social categorization, is occasionally used. Their use is surveyed here, as is the use of relationship terms in combination with other forms of designation.

13.2 Patronymics and Gentilics

13.2.1 As the text stands, "b. Saul" (בן שאול) in 2S 4:1, 2, is an example of a patronymic used by the narrator as a simple designation for a character whom he also designates by name. It could be understood as used to present a distanced and impersonal picture of the diminished state of the House of Saul even before the further blow inflicted by Rechab and Baanah. However, such usage is unexpected (cf. the use of "House of Saul" [בית שאול] in the similar picture in 2S 3:1), and most argue that a personal name originally preceded the patronymic.[1] "Uriah's wife" (אשת אוריה, 2S 11:26, 12:15) is the only other example which could be listed here. Its classification as a patronymic is debatable, but it would be equally unusual as a relationship term. It is clearly intended to keep Bath-sheba's relationship to Uriah in the reader's mind. Nathan, representing God, speaks to David of "the wife of Uriah the Hittite" (אשת אוריה החתי, i.e. Bathsheba, 2S 12:10) for the same reason. The expected designation in

---

[1]   The absence of the preposition expected as a prefix to the designation in 2S 4:2 supports this view. Hebrew texts from Qumran, and Greek texts, show a name, but not that expected. The evidence is presented in Ulrich, 1978:42-45.

this case is certainly "your wife" (אשתך, see §13.4.2). The designation "wife of Uriah the Hittite" is chosen not to refer to the woman alone, but also to the fact that David caused the death of Uriah
to secure her.

13.2.2 Designation by patronym is more common in speech. A patronymic is occasionally used in address, apparently to show scorn,
as where Saul addresses the priest Ahimelek as "b. Ahitub" (1S
22:12, see §25.5.1).[2] Saul, in speaking to his followers refers to David as "b. Jesse" (1S 20:27, 30, 31, 22:8, 9, 13). Designation by patronymic alone treats the person designated as a member of a group,
not as an individual. This use thus distances the speaker from the
addressee; it shows "non-intimacy", as would the use of a title. Since
it is clear that David usually was referred to by name (as in 1S
18:25, 19:4-5, 22, 20:28, 22:14), there can be little doubt that the use
of the patronym reflects Saul's attitude to David, and that disparage-
ment is intended, as is usually suggested.[3] The wife of Jeroboam
has no role as a personality in the narrative in 1 Kings 14. She is
merely a vehicle for Jeroboam's enquiry and the prophet's reply,
"agent" in the terms of Berlin, 1989:32. She is consequently not
named, so the narrator's use of the designation "the wife of Jeroboam" (אשת ירבעם, 1K 14:4, 17), functionally a patronymic, is not
surprising. The use of the same phrase in address to her (1K 14:6),
and in spoken reference (1K 14:2, 5) is more surprising, but probably reflects her lack of importance in the context. The designation
"wife of Jeroboam", ignoring her status as queen, is expected for

---

[2]   There is no example of the title "priest" used as a term of address, so it is not,
in fact, certain that the use of this title is possible here. Other possible terms
would each carry some message as to the king's relationship or attitude to the
priest. Most address does not use a vocative (see §25).
[3]   E.g. Fokkelman, 1986:330, 334, 381, 388, 393. As Clines points out, all cases of
designation by patronym are not to be read as disparaging (Clines, 1972:282-287).
A request for identification asks for the father's name where the name of the addressee is unlikely to carry any useful information, as in 1S 17:55; also Gen 24:23,
and cf. the reply giving relationship, not names, in 2K 10:13. It is concluded in
Naveh, 1990:123, that there is no evidence that the failure to use a personal name
is significant in particular contexts. However, as is indicated there (p. 116) particular usage is characteristic of particular situations. Change in the usage characteristic
for a situation is significant.

non-subjects (God and his spokesman the prophet, 1K 14:5, 6). Where her husband uses it in 1K 14:2, it can be understood as representing the view of the agents of the clause "So they don't know that you are the wife of Jeroboam". These are the people from whom she is to disguise herself, presumably the prophet and his associates, whose indifference to her rank is probably to be seen as disrespectful.[4]

13.2.3 A gentilic is used as a simple designation for a named character in the case of Goliath (in narration in 1S 17:10 etc., in speech in 1S 17:26, etc.), of Ishbi, who is also called "the Philistine" by the narrator (2S 21:17), and of Shimei, who is referred to as "the Benjaminite" by David (2S 16:11). Again the effect is one of distancing, since the personal identity of the individual is not recognized. David's intention is no doubt to refer to Shimei's relationship to Saul, thereby portraying him as a natural enemy. The individual is represented as a member of a hostile group in the other two cases also, where this represents their most significant role in the narrative.[5] The gentilic "the Kushite" (הכושי) is used to designate a character, otherwise unnamed, used by Joab as a messenger in 2S 18:21-32. Presumably his social status was too low for his name to be of general interest, while his foreign origin provided a convenient means of specific identification.[6] A few seals show a gentilic as the only designation (see §4.6.2n).

---

[4]   It is unlikely that the speech is intended to represent Jeroboam's view of her status, and consequently of his own, but the narrator is possibly presenting his own view here, rather than the language Jeroboam is likely to have used (see § 1.6.2).

[5]   This is also true for Shimei, but one might also draw conclusions from the fact that David does not use some more emotive designation, such as "warrior" (cf. איש מלחמה, 1S 17:33), or "champion" (cf. גבורם, 1S 17:51).

[6]   The designation "the Kushite" (הכושי) occurs seven times with the article (marked once by a vowel, otherwise by a consonant as well) and once without it (2S 18:21). It is sometimes called a "personal name" (though possibly not defined as in §3.1.2), as in Layton, 1990:119. It is unlikely to be a "name" (as defined there) since no form of compound designation or equivalent information is given for this character. See §4.7-8.

13.2.4 A designation sometimes includes both a patronymic and a gentilic. The gentilic always follows the patronymic in this situation. It may certainly apply to the person named in the patronymic, as is shown in "Abigail wife of Nabal the Carmelite" (אביגיל אשת נבל הכרמלי, 1S 30:5), where the gentilic is masculine. It evidently can also apply to the person designated by the name. "Adriel b. Barzillai the Meholathite" (2S 21:8) corresponds to "Adriel the Meholathite" (1S 18:19). Consequently the use of a feminine gentilic in "Abigail the wife of Nabal the Carmelite" (אביגיל אשת נבל הכרמלית, 1S 27:3) represents acceptable usage, even though it contrasts with three examples where the adjective is masculine.[7]

13.3 Relationship Terms: Narration

13.3.1 A relationship term is a term indicating kinship, master-servant relationship, or occupation, which designates one member of a dyad, and to which is bound a pronoun (or occasionally a noun) referring to the other member. The character represented by the relationship term is thus viewed in relation to the other member of the dyad, not independently, and can be called the "adjunct". The other member of the dyad, who is represented by a nominal designation or a pronoun, is called the "principal".[8] The terms "principal" and "adjunct" have been used in relation to compound nominals (see §17.2.1). Where these terms refer to the components of a compound nominal, the principal in terms of relationship structure is also the principal of the compound, as in "Saul and Jonathan his son" (1S 13:16, 22). The character termed "principal" is the more important. This may be true in terms either of the narrative, or of the culture it reflects, or of both, as in "Saul said to Jonathan his son". Saul is more important in terms of the culture as he is the father, and of the narrative as he is the agent.

---

[7]   Designations including both patronymic and gentilic occur in Ju 4:17, 1S 27:3, 30:5, 2S 2:2, 3:3, 19:17, 21:8, 19, 23:11, 1K 2:8, 2K 25:23, also, with two patronymics, 2S 11:3.

[8]   Compare the presentation of two brothers separately, as "Absalom b. David" and "Amnon b. David" in 2S 13:1, where each acts independently of the other in the following narrative, with the usual treatment of such pairs as principal and adjunct.

13.3.2 Where both principal and adjunct are designated in a clause, the principal is typically agent. Thus the relationship is usually presented from the viewpoint of the agent, as in "Tamar went to the house of Amnon her brother" (ותלך תמר בית אמנון אחיה, 2S 13:8). The adjunct may have any function in the clause other than agent, including subject of a subordinate clause, as in "He removed the stele of Baal which his father had made" (ויסר את מצבת הבעל אשר עשה אביו, 2K 3:2, other examples occur in 2S 11:26, 2K 21:21). Where neither principal nor adjunct acts as agent, the principal, but not the adjunct, is mentioned in the preceding context, as in 1K 11:20, 15:3, 2K 23:30. Where the adjunct is subject of the clause, the focus of the narrator's interest is naturally shifted to the adjunct from the principal. The principal is typically thematic character in the preceding context, as in "The king of the b. Ammon died, and Hanun his son reigned in his place" (וימת מלך בני עמון וימלך חנון בנו תחתיו, 2S 10:1), or "Eliab his elder brother heard" וישמע אליאב אחיו הגדול..., 1S 17:28), where David, the principal, is thematic character in the preceding verses.[9] A clause with the adjunct as subject is often used to introduce speech by the adjunct, responding to speech or other action by the principal, as "Elkanah her husband said to her" (ויאמר לה אלקנה אישה, 1S 1:8, 23, other examples occur in Ju 14:3, 2S 13:20, 1K 21:5, 7). An original adjunct who becomes agent in a further clause typically also becomes principal, represented by the pronoun, while the original principal becomes the adjunct, and is represented by the relationship term, as in "The lad said to his master... His master said to him... He said to his lad..." (ויאמר הנער אל אדניו... ויאמר אליו אדניו... ויאמר לנערו..., Ju 19:11-13.[10] Where the adjunct is subject, the principal is typically represented in the same clause by a pronoun, as in the above examples. The name "David" is used in 1S 19:11, mainly, no doubt, to avoid ambiguity (a pro-

---

[9] Other examples occur in Ju 3:25, 6:11, 14:4, 10, 1S 7:1, 17:28, 19:11, 25:37, 2S 3:16, 1K 1:6, 21:25, 2K 23:30, in clauses of various types. The fact that the relationship term is used to shift topic in this way presumably accounts for the high proportion of clauses in which it forms the first constituent, including the examples in Ju 13:9 and 19:10 in which it precedes a prepositional predicate (see §28.6.5).

[10] An example with named characters occurs in Ruth 2:18-20. In the dialogue quoted by Judah in Gen 44:20-23, where the participants are equal in thematic status, the relationship term always designates the addressee from the viewpoint of the speaker, who is represented by a pronoun.

noun could refer to Saul). However, there need be no reference to the principal in the clause, other than in the designation of the adjunct, as in Ju 3:25, 6:11, 1S 7:1.

13.3.3 The use of a relationship term as a simple designation presents one character merely as the adjunct of another, not as an independent individual, and so, in some way, as of secondary interest in the context. A character treated in this way is usually not an important participant in the context in which the term is used, or the participation in that context is of little importance for the narrative. Thus in Ju 11:37, which opens "she said to her father", Jephthah's daughter has become the thematic character. Jephthah holds this position in Ju 11:35 and before, and in Ju 12:1 and following, but in Ju 11:36-40 his part is clearly secondary to that of his daughter, and the use of the relationship term reflects this. In "His mother used to make a small cloak for him, and bring it up to him... when she came with her husband..." (...ומעיל קטן תעשה לו אמו והעלתה לו בעלותה את אישה..., 1S 2:19) "his mother" and "her husband" are Hannah and Elkanah. Both were important participants in chapter 1, but that is no longer the case. Apart from the mention of Elkanah as recipient of Eli's blessing in 1S 2:20, neither appears again. A relationship term may also be used to designate an important participant where the narrator wishes to draw the relationship to the reader's attention, as where "his father" is used to designate Saul (1S 14:27, 20:33, see §7.1.4) or David (1K 1:6, see §5.3.3n), or where Bathsheba is called "the wife of Uriah" in 2S 11:26, 12:15 (if this is not considered a patronymic, see §13.2.1).[11]

13.3.4 A compound designation formed of a name and relationship term is, like others, usually used in situations of the sort called "introductory", as in "Tamar went to the house of Amnon her brother" (ותלך תמר בית אמנון אחיה, 2S 13:8), which opens the story

---

[11] A kinship term is used as a simple designation for a named character in Ju 11:37, 39, 13:6, 10, 14:3, 10, 19, 1S 1:23, 2:19, 19, 20, 17:15, 18:2, 20:33, 25:37, 2S 3:16, 11:26, 26, 12:15, 1K 1:6, 22:53, 53, 2K 3:2, 2, 2, 21:21, 23:20. A term indicating master-servant relationship is used in this way in Ju 3:25, 2S 11:9, 13, 2K 9:11. The examples in 2K 4:38, 43, 6:15 should perhaps be added, but it is not clear that they designate a named character (Gehazi).

of her effort to help him, with its tragic result. A compound of this sort is sometimes used for the first mention of a character, as with Gideon (Ju 6:11), Eleazar (1S 7:1), and, regularly, a king who succeeds his father (see §§9.2.2, 10.3.4n, and cases with foreign kings in 2S 10:1, 2K 19:37). As these examples show, an introduction of this sort provides background information about the character (as does a patronymic). Where the designation is not introductory, but serves to draw attention to the name, the relationship indicated is generally of greater significance for the events in which the character participates, as in "She (Tamar) brought (the food) to Amnon her brother in the chamber" (ותבא לאמנון אחיה החדרה, 2S 13:10). The use of the relationship term here, rather than at the beginning of the verse, brings the relationship, with the questions it raises, into the reader's mind at the point when Amnon's plan to seduce his sister appears to be working. Similarly, in 2S 13:20, Tamar stays "in the house of Absalom her brother" (בית אבשלום אחיה), repeating the relationship term with which Absalom was introduced at the beginning of the verse. This repetition here, and the several other allusions to this relationship made in this chapter, leave the reader no chance of overlooking it. It is, of course, of central importance. It motivates Absalom's murder of Amnon, and so sets him off on his career of opposition to his father, King David.[12]

13.3.5 Where a relationship term is added to a compound designation it is reasonable to assume that the relationship is of considerable significance. Thus in 1S 26:5, the information that Abner b. Ner, Saul's commander in chief (אבנר בן נר שר צבאו) is lying beside Saul in the camp enhances the picture of the security of Saul's camp which the narrator builds up, and so suggests to the reader (as does another feature, see §16.3.5) that no ordinary person could expect

---

[12]   The relationship is pointed out in 2S 13:1, where the unusual use of predicate-subject order in the verbless clause draws attention to it. It is again highlighted by unusual wording in 2S 13:4, where Amnon describes his problem in the words "I love Tamar, sister of my brother Absalom", where he could have said "my sister". It is probably alluded to again in the reference to "Tamar his sister" (2S 13:22), where the pronoun is likely to refer to Absalom, who is agent in the main clause. The narrator does not mention the relationship where Amnon is designated by name as agent in 2S 13:10, 15, 15, nor where Absalom is in 2S 13:22, possibly because they are not acting as brothers should (see §§28.2.1).

to breach that security as David is to set out to do. Similarly in "Jo-
zabad b. Shimeath and Jehozabad b. Shomer, his servants, murdered
him" (יוזבד בן שמעת ויהוזבד בן שמר עבדיו הכהו, 2K 12:22 in the Le-
ningrad Codex), the relationship term, repeating, and so stressing,
information already given, makes it clear, with minimal wording,
that King Joash died in a palace revolt. However, relationship to
King David, or to Joab, his commander in chief, which is indicated
by relationship terms attached to compound designations in 1S 26:6,
2S 13:3, 32, 17:25, 18:2, 21:21, seems to have little relevance to the
narrative context. It seems likely that the narrator intended the
reader to connect it with background knowledge not presented in
the immediate context, and quite possibly not in the corpus, as is
also the case with the designation of Joshua b. Nun as "servant of
the Lord" in Ju 2:8.[13]

13.3.6 In most cases the relationship term used is conventional, but
there is some scope for expressive choice. In 2S 11:26, "the wife of
Uriah" is said to "mourn for her lord" (ותספד על בעלה) because she
had heard of the death of "her husband" (אישה). Everywhere else in
the corpus, the word corresponding to "husband" is "man" (איש),
including the example in this verse. The term "lord" (בעל) corresponds to "husband" in Deut 24:4, which deals with the relations of
a woman with her first husband after having married a second, in
Gen 20:3 and Deut 22:22, which deal with actual or potential adul-
tery, and in some proverbs, where a good wife is said to be the
"crown" of her husband (Prov 12:4) who relies on her, is renowned
on her account, and praises her (Prov 31:11, 23, 28). Later readers
will have seen the term against both sets of examples. The evocation of at least the pentateuchal set (in some form), was presumably
intended by the narrator. In 2K 4:43, the word "servitor" (משרת)
used to designate Elisha's servant in place of the usual "lad" (נער)
implies considerable intimacy. The narrator thus suggests that even

---

[13] A relationship term is used with a compound designation in Ju 2:8, 1S 21:8,
26:5, 6, 29:3, 2S 2:8, 11:21, 24, 13:3, 32, 15:12, 16:16, 17:25, 18:2, 21:11, 21, 23:18,
24:11, 1K 11:23, 14:18, 15:29, 2K 5:20, 9:36, 11:2, 12:19, 22, 14:25, 22:14, 25:8.

Elisha's most intimate associate doubted his powers. The impact of the miraculous distribution of food is thus enhanced.[14]

13.3.7 Where a relationship term is combined with a simple or compound designation, the relationship term usually follows the other item. In narrative, the only exception involving a kinship term is "Her husband Nabal she did not inform" (ולאישה נבל לא הגידה, 1S 25:19). The unusual order, which draws attention to the kinship term, suggests that the narrator intended to indicate that Abigail did not tell "even her husband", so there is no chance of help for her if her mission is unsuccessful.[15] A term indicating master-servant relationship is placed before other items in the designation in "According to the word of Yahweh which he spoke through his servant Ahijah the prophet" (כדבר יהוה אשר דבר ביד עבדו אחיהו הנביא, 1K 14:18), and in similar examples in 1K 15:29, 2K 14:25. It seems most likely that this positioning reflects that usual in the spoken use of these terms by a subordinate in address or reference to a superior (see §§13.4.1, 13.4.5).

13.4 Relationship Terms: Speech

13.4.1 *Address* A kinship term is quite often used as a vocative, mostly, it appears, in the hope that recollection of the relationship will stimulate the addressee to do what the speaker wants. The more direct appeal to the persuasive force of relationship made with

---

[14]   The effect is similar in 2K 6:15, where "the servitor of the man of God" (משרת איש האלהים), afterwards merely "his lad" (נערו), is alarmed by the sight of foreign troops until Elisha persuades God to allow him to see the true state of affairs. In 2S 13:17, Amnon orders "his lad, his servitor" (נערו משרתו), later "his servitor" (משרתו, 2S 13:18), to put Tamar out. Otherwise the term is used in the corpus of Samuel serving God (1S 2:11). Outside the corpus it is used of Joshua as servitor of Moses (as Num 11:28), or of the service of the Temple or of God.

[15]   Note that phrase is highlighted by its initial position in the clause, and the clause is highlighted by its terminal position in the unit describing Abigail's preparations, preceding that describing her encounter with David and his men (see §3.4.3). The narrator is at pains to point out Abigail's danger, and to suggest that her mission will fail, by describing the arming of David and his force, and its numbers in detail (1S 25:13), and by placing the verses describing David's motivation and bloodthirsty intent (1S 25:21-22) after she encounters him, but before the result of the encounter is described, thus raising suspense.

the phrase "my bone and my flesh" (עצמי ובשׂרי) is combined with a kinship term used in this way in 2S 19:13 (cf. 2S 19:14, Ju 9:2). The kinship term used in this way may refer to real or metaphoric relationship. There are more examples of the latter than the former in the corpus. The use of a kinship term implies that the relationship between speaker and addressee is an ideal example of the relationship named, so either a superior ("my father, my mother"), a subordinate ("my son, my daughter"), or an equal ("my brother, my sister"), may be addressed in this way. The terminology of master-servant relationship, which is used in address in both second and third persons, is described in detail in §§20-23. Only the superior ("my lord" אדני) is addressed by a vocative. The corresponding terms for subordinates are not used for address. It is noteworthy that where a relationship term is used in a compound designation functioning as a vocative, it is nearly always the first component (19 cases). The only exception is "Samuel my son" (שׁמואל בני), used by Eli in calling Samuel in 1S 3:16. In this situation, the name, giving the identity, is clearly more important than the relationship. Where the relationship term precedes the name, the term is "my lord" (אדני) in 15 cases (cf. the predicative "my lord Elijah" in 1K 18:7). Clearly the initial position of the term reflects its importance in marking the speech as deferential. The same need to impress the implications of the term on the addressee is evident in the other four cases, where it is "my son" (בני) used in an attempt to persuade (1S 24:17, 26:17, 21, 25). The relationship term similarly always precedes the title in "my lord the king" (אדני המלך) used in deferential third person address (41 cases).

13.4.2 *Reference* Spoken reference to another character is usually by name unless there is a personal relationship between speaker or addressee and the person referred to. Where the character referred to belongs to the same family as the speaker or the addressee, a kinship term is commonly used for reference.[16] Thus Elisha, rejecting a request by the king of Israel, tells him "Go to the prophets of your father and the prophets of your mother" (2K 3:13), rather

---

[16] It seems probable that the personal name was usually used for reference to coevals or juniors within a family, as is illustrated by Saul's words "Jonathan should not know this" (as depicted by David, 1S 20:3).

than naming the couple as Ahab and Jezebel. However, the recognition of relationship is optional for a speaker (as for the narrator), and is abandoned where inappropriate. Thus it is not used in references to Absalom or Adonijah to or by their father, King David, when they are rebelling against him (as in 2S 15:13, 14, 1K 1:13, 24). Conversely, the use of a relationship term typically indicates that the members of the dyad share a relationship consistent with the ideal represented by the term, so the designation "Absalom her brother" (אבשלום אחיה) points out that Absalom is acting towards Tamar as a brother should in 2S 13:20, 20. The two possibilities, name and kinship term, are contrasted expressively in Jotham's exhortation to the men of Shechem. In his first reference to his father, Jotham presents himself as a disinterested observer, speaking of "Jerubbaal and his house" (Ju 9:16). However the thought of the murder of his brothers arouses his emotions, and he digresses to recount the benefits conferred on his audience by his father, which should have held them back from murder (Ju 9:17-18). In accordance with this display of emotion, he refers to "my father" in these verses. Eventually he masters himself, and regains his line of argument by quoting the statement that preceded the digression, including the reference to "Jerubbaal".[17]

13.4.3 Where the character referred to is the superior in a master-servant relationship with speaker or addressee, the name is typically not used, unless it is needed to distinguish him from others (see §§ 6.9.1-2, 8.3, 10.4.3).[18] The Rab Shakeh's reference to King Hezekiah by name in his speeches to his envoys and his people is clearly intended to belittle him so as to suggest that his position is unten-

---

[17] Note also the reference to "Jonathan" not "your son" by the people objecting to Saul's decision to kill him (1S 14:45). They treat him as independent where Saul has been treating him as an adjunct (1S 14:39-42). Saul's reference to "David" (1S 16:22) rather than to "your son" (cf. 1S 16:19) similarly treats David as independent, and so as able to leave his father's family. See also §14.3.3 on David's use of "lad" in 2S 12:16.

[18] Reference to a superior by name is regarded as a serious offence in Talmud Sanhedrin 100a, which may well reflect an attitude long prevalent in the area.

able.[19] A superior may be referred to as "your lord" or "my lord" in speech to or by a subordinate, as by the Rab Shakeh speaking of Hezekiah, and of the king of Assyria, to the envoys of Hezekiah in 2K 18:27. A subordinate may refer to "our lord" (אדנינו), as does a servant of Nabal speaking of him to Abigail, his wife, in 1S 25:14, 17, Nathan speaking to Bathsheba of King David in 1K 1:11, and Jonathan speaking to his associates in 1K 1:43, 47.[20] The term "your servant" may similarly be used by one subordinate speaking of another to their common superior. Such usage is a mark of deference, usually supported by other deferential features in the speech (see §20.1), as in David's reference to his father in speaking to King Saul in 1S 17:58.[21] A superior, speaking of one subordinate to another, typically avoids the use of terms which the subordinate would not use. Thus David speaks to Abishai of "your master's servants" (2S 20:6, other examples occur in 1S 29:10, 1K 1:33. In contrast, one superior speaking of his subordinate(s) to another uses "my servant(s)".[22]

13.4.4 A combination of name and relationship term is quite often used for spoken reference, exemplifying the tendency to use precise identifications in speech (see §4.13.3). A kinship term usually follows the name (some 35 cases), consistent with the fact that the

---

[19] 2K 18:19, 22, 29, 30, 31, 32. Cf. the reference to "your lord", the standard usage, in 2K 18:27, in a speech which is impromptu, not designed as propaganda, and the designation "Hezekiah King of Judah" used in a normal diplomatic exchange (albeit threatening) in 2K 19:10.

[20] In 1K 1:43, 47, the pronoun is inclusive; the speaker is showing solidarity with those he is addressing. In the other cases it is exclusive, expressing a deeper level of humility than that implied by the use of the singular (see §18.2.2).

[21] "My/your lord" is used in reference to a third person in 1S 26:15; 2S 9:9, 10; 1K 18:8, 10, 11, 14, 20:9, 2K 5:22, 10:2, 6, 18:27, "your servant" is used by one subordinate of another in 1S 17:58, 22:14; 2S 11:21, 24, 14:19, 20, 19:38; 1K 1:19, 26, 3:6, 8:24, 25, 26 20:32; 2K 4:1, cf. "servant of the king" (עבד המלך) in third person address in 2S 18:29. "His lord" or "his servant" is similarly used in reference to third parties, as in 1S 19:4, 2K 9:36, 19:4.

[22] In 2S 19:27, 1K 5:20, 23, 20:6, 22:50, 2K 5:6. God is portrayed as referring to his human servants in the same way in speech to a prophet or to a king in 2S 7:5, 8, 1K 11:13, 32, 34, 2K 21:8. In 1S 22:8, Saul uses "my servant" of David, in complaining to his subordinates that Jonathan has treasonably conspired with David. The intention is clearly derogatory.

identity of the individual is the prime interest, the relationship secondary.[23] Where the kinship term is placed first, it is reasonable to
argue that the relationship is deliberately highlighted. Thus David,
identifying the individual who is to succeed him, speaks to Bathsheba of "Solomon your son" (שלמה בנך, 1K 1:13 etc.). His use of the
standard order reflects the fact that he is primarily interested in a
particular individual; the relationship to Bathsheba simply provides
supplementary identification. The prophet Nathan advises Bathsheba to save "the life of your son Solomon" (נפש בנך שלמה, 1K 1:12),
giving initial position to the relationship as the more persuasive
factor. Bathsheba does the same in "my son Solomon (בני שלמה, 1K
1:21); for the mother, the relationship is of primary importance, the
specific identification secondary.[24] Other examples of the marked
order, with the kinship term preceding the name, occur in "my eld-
est daughter Merab" (1S 18:17, Saul's concern is that David should
marry into his family, rather than whom he should marry); "your
son, David" (1S 25:8, David wishes to present himself as a suitable
candidate for Nabal's benevolence, not to identify himself); "my
wife Michal" (2S 3:14, the relationship justifies David's request that
she be returned to him);[25] "my father David" (1K 2:32, Solomon's
concern is to show that no guilt for the murders of Abner and
Amasa should attach to David's descendants). A kinship term is
placed first in a longer designation for the same reason in "your son
ben Hadad King of Aram" (2K 8:9), where Hazael presents the king

---

[23]   Where two relationship terms are used, and neither is deferential, both follow
the name, as in "Michal his daughter, wife of David" (מיכל בתו אשת דוד, 1S 25:44),
and in other cases where the first functions as a patronymic, as "Jehosheba, daughter of King Jehoram, sister of Ahaziah" (יהושבע בת המלך יורם אחות אחזיהו, 2K
11:2).

[24]   The significance of word order in such situations was pointed out in Peretz,
1968:131. Bathsheba's maternal feelings may, of course, be strengthened by the fact
that, if her son becomes king, she will be "mother of the king", a powerful position according to Donner, 1959.

[25]   "Give up (object) my wife, (object) Michal" (תנה את אשתי את מיכל), with a preposition before each component of the designation. The same usage is found in 1S
25:8, and (where master-servant terminology is used) in 1S 19:4, 2S 7:5, 8. It does
not occur where the relationship term follows the name, that is, it does not occur
in what is, overall, the unmarked order. It is, therefore, reasonable to assume that
it gives additional prominence to the relationship term. A similar observation is
made in Peretz, 1968:133.

as a friendly subordinate to persuade Elisha to provide the information he wants.

13.4.5 Where master-servant terminology is used, the relationship term is similarly placed before the name in speech by a subordinate to or about a superior, as in "your servant David" (עבדך דוד, 2S 7:26), "my master Joab" (אדני יואב, 2S 11:11).[26] This order (marked overall, though unmarked where a subordinate uses a deferential relationship term) draws attention to the deference implied in the use of the term. A deferential relationship term follows the name in "Solomon your servant", where the speaker's purpose is to point out that this particular individual has been ignored (1K 1:19, 26). The deferential term also follows the name in "Moses your servant" (1K 8:53) used in reference to past history, where the speaker has no personal involvement (contrast 1K 8:24, 25, 26). It follows the title in "the king my lord" (2S 14:15), where there is similarly no need to draw attention to the relationship term (see §6.8.2).

13.4.6 Where the speaker is not subordinate, the relationship term typically follows the name, as in "Naaman my servant" (נעמן עבדי, 2K 5:6) and in eleven other cases, mostly in speech ascribed to God.[27] The relationship term is placed first in speech ascribed to God in 2S 7:5, 8, 1K 11:32, 2K 21:8. In 2S 7:5, 8, God possibly highlights David's status as "my servant" as this service motivates the promise that follows. There seems no plausible reason for the use of the marked order in the other two cases. Compare "for the sake of my servant David" (למען עבדי דוד, 1K 11:32) with "for the sake of David my servant" (למען דוד עבדי) used in the same context in 1K 11:34, and also in 1K 11:13, 2K 19:34. In 1S 26:15, where David taunts Joab, he uses both orders in a neat turn of phrase "Why did you not guard your master the king, for one of the people came to destroy the king your master" (ולמה לא שמרת אל אדניך המלך כי בא אחד העם להשחית את המלך אדניך). The first designation, in the order standard for speech by a subordinate, draws

---

[26] Other examples occur in 1S 19:4, 2S 11:24, 14:19, 20, 18:29, 1K 1:11, 43, 47, 20:32, 2K 9:36, 10:10, and in speech to God in 1K 3:6, 8:24, 25, 26.

[27] 2S 3:18, 9:10, 1K 11:13, 34, 36, 38, 2K 19:34, 20:5. Also in speech between equals in Ju 9:18, 1S 26:15, 2K 19:4.

attention to the relationship which motivates Joab's duty to guard Saul, his master. The second highlights the title, drawing attention to the fact that Joab's failure might have resulted in the death of the king (cf. §6.8.2 on 2S 14:15).

13.5 Non-Specific Designations

13.5.1 A term denoting a social category is occasionally used to designate a named character. Those used in this way are "man, woman, lad, girl," (איש, אשה, נער, נערה). Most commonly, one of these terms — the least specific nominal designation possible — is used where a pronoun is not adequate, but the position of the character in the narrative does not justify the attention which the use of a more specific designation would attract. Thus in 1S 1:18, "the woman went..." (ותלך האשה...) the use of a nominal subject marks a new topic; the scene in the temple is over. Hannah is still agent, however, and what is presented is not some significant new action, but a comment on the difference in her condition from what was related earlier. In 1S 1:23 "the woman stayed..." (ותשב האשה...), the narrator uses a nominal subject to turn his focus back to Hannah from her husband, but the content of the clause, that she did what she had suggested and he had accepted, requires no prominence.[28]

13.5.2 A term of this sort may be used to represent the viewpoint of a character who does not know the name of the person designated. Thus in 2S 11:2 David sees "a woman" as he looks down from his roof, not "Bathsheba".[29] Another special use of social category terms, to draw attention to the introduction of a new character, has been mentioned above (§4.9.1). Jael uses a similar technique when she says to Barak "Come and I'll show you the man you are

---

[28]   In a few cases a social category term may be used to avoid some ambiguity that the use of a pronoun would entail, as in 1S 3:8, where "Eli understood that Yahweh was calling to the lad" is not ambiguous, whereas "was calling to him" would be. A social category term is used in place of a name to mark the clause as non-prominent in the way described in Ju 17:11, 1S 1:18, 23, 24, 25, 2:11, 3:8, 16:11, 25:3, 2S 3:8 (in speech), 11:5, 18:32, 1K 1:4, 14:3, 12, 17, 2K 5:7, 6:17.

[29]   Other examples occur in 1S 17:24, 2S 11:2, 3, 1K 1:3. Such terms are also naturally used by a speaker who does not know the name of a person to whom he refers in 1S 17:25, 33, 55, 56, 58, 28:14, 1K 1:2.

seeking" (Ju 4:22). The use of the periphrastic description demands more attention for the speaker than might be forthcoming if she used the shorter name "Sisera". A similar periphrastic designation is used to impute guilt without naming names where David speaks of "evil men who slaughtered a righteous man" (2S 4:11), and where Elisha speaks to Gehazi of "a man" who turned from his chariot (2K 5:26). Where a demonstrative is added, a social category term of course becomes specific. Where Eli addresses Elkanah, he cannot use the expected term "your wife" to refer to Hannah, as this could refer to Elkanah's other wife, Peninah. Eli's choice of "this woman" (האשה הזאת, 1S 2:20) enables him to use a specific designation without breaching the convention (see §13.4.2) by using Hannah's name in speech to her husband.

13.5.3 The demonstratives זה and זאת (translated "this") are occasionally used in speech to designate a named individual. These demonstratives are not used precisely as is English "this" (see Waltke and O'Connor 1990 §17.3); they present the person designated as "the one before us" or "the one under discussion". Where reference would typically be made with some other form, the use of a demonstrative is marked, as in "Am I a god... that this (person) is sending to me to remove a man's leprosy?" האלהים אני... כי זה שלח אלי לאסף איש מצרעתו , 2K 5:7, "the king of Aram" is expected, as also in 1K 20:7); "Please get this (person) away from me into the street" (שלחו נא את זאת מעלי החוצה, 2S 13:17, "my sister" or "this woman" is expected). Such usage is often seen as pejorative (cf. Joüon, 1991, §143d). However, where the speech requests hostile action, or asks a critical question, as in these cases, even the standard form of reference is likely to be perceived as ironic or otherwise impolite. In "Surely for nothing have I guarded all that belongs to this (person)..." (אך לשקר שמרתי את כל אשר לזה, 1S 25:21), the use of "Nabal" or "this man" in place of "this (person)" would not change the obvious fact that the speaker is expressing dislike or contempt. Other cases occur in 1S 10:27, 21:16, 16, 29:4, 1K 22:27. Where the context does not express disapproval or hostility, the demonstrative is not seen as pejorative, as "This (person) shall reign over my people" (זה יעצר בעמי, 1S 9:17), even though a name, or at least "this man"

or "this woman" might have been used.[30] The use of the demonstratives זה and זאת in place of the expected reference form adds to
the impact of any aversion expressed in the clause in which the use
occurs. In the same way, in "Did they not chant of this (person) in
the dances 'Saul has killed his thousands, and David his Myriads'"
(1S 21:12, הלוא לזה יענו במחלות לאמר הכה שאול באלפיו ודוד ברבבתיו),
the use of the demonstrative in place of the name adds to the impact of the admiration and fear expressed by the speech. The demonstrative itself, however, is neutral in emotional content.

---

[30]   Similar examples occur in 1K 3:23, 14:13. The lack of pejorative value is obvious where the demonstrative is used as subject with a predicate which identifies an
individual, as "this (person) is he" (1S 16:12; other examples 1S 21:12, 29:3, 5, 2S
18:26) or states something good of him, as "This (person) is a good man" (איש טוב
זה, 2S 18:27).

The Designation of Unnamed Characters

14.1 Introduction

14.1.1 An unnamed character may be designated by any type of term used for named characters except a personal name. It has already been noted that "the Kushite" (הכושי, 2S 18:21-32) is the only example of a gentilic used to designate an unnamed character (see §13.2.3). The use of a patronymic is also rare (see §13.2.1). An example is provided by "the wife of Jeroboam" (1K 14:2-17). A married woman is typically identified by an epithet of this sort in place of a patronymic, for which reason such epithets were classed with patronymics in §3.2.1. The distinction from what is here called a "relationship epithet" lies in the fact that the latter is used to mark relationship significant for a particular context, and is not used for general identification. If this is the criterion, other statements of relationship which are used for general identification, rather than to highlight a specific relationship, can also be classed with patronymics. Examples used to designate unnamed characters are "daughter of Pharaoh" (בת פרעה, 1K 3:1, 7:8, 9:24), "sister of Tahpenes" (אחות תחפניס, 1K 11:20).

14.1.2 An unnamed character is often designated by an occupation term or title. This may designate a regular occupation, as "captain of fifty" (שר חמשים, 2K 1:9), or one arising from the circumstances of the narrative, as "the lad informing him" (הנער המגיד לו, 2S 1:5, 6, see §3.2.3). Relationship terms, and terms denoting general social categories are also commonly used to designate unnamed characters. The use of such designations does not differ significantly whether the character is named or unnamed. Identity is viewed analytically, even where a character is unnamed. As a result, the designation of an unnamed character may change in accordance with the circumstances of the narrative. Unnamed characters usually play only limited parts in any narrative, so the variation is rarely remarkable. Where their participation is more extensive, the variations consequent on the choice of relationship or social category terms to reflect their different roles can be surprising. The outstanding examples are discussed below.

14.2 The Characters in Judges Chapter 19

14.2.1 *The levite* The narrative in Judges chapter nineteen involves a number of different characters, mostly related to each other, none of whom is named. The central character in the chapter is a levite, whose actions form the chain of events around which the description of the actions of the other characters is organized. He is introduced as "A man (who was) a levite" (איש לוי, Ju 19:1), naming his occupation, the most specific identification of him available.[1] This term is also used where he is reintroduced in Ju 20:4 as appearing before the assembly as a result of the events of chapter 19. He is there further described as "the husband of the murdered woman" (איש האשה הנרצחה) in allusion to those events. This represents his role as far as the assembly is concerned. Between the two ends of his story, the man is never shown acting as a levite, so the term is not used, but is replaced by other designations.

14.2.2 The narrator moves from the introduction of the levite to the statement that his concubine had left him and had gone to her father's house, and that the levite went after her to bring her back. In this context he is referred to as "her husband" (אישה, Ju 19:3). This designation, which is not used for him elsewhere, presumably is intended to point out to the reader that he is acting as a husband should. The couple is received hospitably and remains a few days with the girl's father. After this the levite wants to go home, but the girl's father persuades him to delay. In this context, the father-in-law speaks to "his son-in-law" (חתנו, Ju 19:5). This designation, not used for the levite elsewhere, is similarly presumably intended to point out that he is acting as a son-in-law should, in complying with his father-in-law's wishes. After this episode, the father asks "the man" (האיש) to stay longer. This is the most common designa-

---

[1]   In origin, "levite" denotes a member of the tribe of Levi, but it appears to be used in the corpus primarily as a designation of occupation: a person qualified to attend a shrine (see §2.4.3). The indications that the levite who figures in Judges 17-18 was associated with Judah (Ju 17:7) and Manasseh (Ju 18:30) must reflect such a view, whether they are original, or (as is often suggested) not.

tion for the levite, the "default", but it is not neutral. The limits imposed by the use of other designations give the use of "the man" (האיש) a meaning of its own. It represents the levite where he either has no relationship to any other character mentioned in the clause (Ju 19:17, 28), or is not acting according to the ideal of that relationship, and so not doing what his father-in-law wants (Ju 19:7, 9, 10, or not disposed to do it, 19:6), or acting brutally to his concubine (Ju 19:25). Other designations present the levite as "his master" (אדניו, Ju 19:11, 12) in relation to his servant, or as "her master" (אדניה), representing the point of view of his concubine when she is trying to get to him (Ju 19:26), and where the focus subsequently shifts from her actions to his (Ju 19:27).

14.2.3 *The concubine* The girl, whose murder forms the significant event of the chapter, is introduced as "a woman (who was) a concubine" (אשה פילגש, Ju 19:1). The term designates her social position as wife of the levite, but of servant status (see §2.3.5). The next designation of her, "his concubine" (פילגשו, Ju 19:2) is that used whenever she is shown in association with the levite. In grammatical terms, it is used wherever one is agent and the other patient, including subordinate clauses where that situation obtains in the main clause (Ju 19:2, 9, 10, 24, 25, 29). In relation to her father, she is referred to as "the lass" (הנערה, Ju 19:3, 5, 6, 8). This probably recognizes the fact that she has left home (in contradistinction to "daughter", בת, see §2.2.8). Elsewhere, she is designated "woman" (אשה). This term is used in Ju 19:26, as subject of a clause which includes no reference to any person to whom she is related. It is used again in Ju 19:27, where her husband sees her dead; "his concubine" is used in apposition, to include the role related to him. Finally, she is referred to as "the murdered woman" (האשה הנרצחה), the role relevant for the assembly, in Ju 20:4. In short, the term "woman" represents her as an independent individual, as does "man" for the levite.

14.2.4 *The concubine's father* The concubine's father is designated only by relationship terms, indicating his relative lack of importance in the chapter (see §13.3.1). In Ju 19:2, he is presented as "her father" (אביה), where the concubine is agent and he is patient in Ju 19:2, 3. Where he is agent, he is referred to as "the girl's father"

(אבי הנערה) where he first sees the levite (Ju 19:3), and where he makes hospitable suggestions to him as "his son-in-law" (Ju 19:5), or as "the man" (Ju 19:6, 8). He is designated "his father-in-law" (חתנו, Ju 19:7) where he successfully urges him to accept one of these suggestions, which he initially rejected. The two designations are combined as "his father-in-law, father of the girl" where he first encounters the levite in Ju 19:4, and at his last appearance (Ju 19:9) where he makes a last, unsuccessful, attempt to delay the levite's departure.[2] It appears, then, that his "default" identity is as father of the girl. His resultant relationship to the levite is mentioned along with this at the beginning and end of the period in which the levite joins his daughter as his guest. Where, by a special effort, he persuades the levite not to leave (Ju 19:7), he is designated only by his relationship to the levite.

14.2.5 *The old man* After leaving the girl's father, the levite and his party reach a town where they get lodging for the night. Their host is introduced as "an old man" (איש זקן, Ju 19:16). This phrase is used where the man questions the levite, and offers him lodging (Ju 19:17, 20), but the adjective is omitted where there is no danger of confusing the two (Ju 19:16, 26). Where the men of the town surround the house, he is designated as "the householder", representing their point of view, although "the old man" is added to it, to confirm that the two roles pertain to the same individual (האיש בעל הבית הזקן, Ju 19:22). He is also called "The householder" (האיש בעל הבית) where he comes out to speak to the men of the town in Ju 19:23. In Ju 19:26, where the concubine is agent, the old man's house is called "the house of the man where her lord was" (בית האיש אשר אדניה שם), so that he is obliquely designated from her viewpoint.

14.2.6 *Conclusion* The only other actor in this chapter is the levite's servant. He is designated as "his lad" (נערו) in clauses in which the levite is agent, or is principal in a compound which represents the agent (Ju 19:3, 9). He is called "the lad" (הנער) where he addresses an independent suggestion to the levite in Ju 19:11. This is only a

---

[2]   Using the two designations in combination here (as for the concubine in Ju 19:27) shows that the two role are combined in the same individual, see §11.5.3n.

pale reflection of the variation found in the designation of the more prominent characters, but it is of a piece with it. The designation of each character is related to the context in which it occurs in a way which is quite complex, but remarkably clear. The choice of designation is mainly controlled by the tendency to suit the designation to the role of the character in the context, and to do this according to the point of view of the agent in the clause, factors show to be equally important in the choice of designations of named characters.

14.3 Analytic Designation of Unnamed Characters Elsewhere

14.3.1 There is no other passage which shows the range of variation found in Judges 19, but similar usage can be seen, on a reduced scale, elsewhere. The principal character in Judges 17-18 is introduced as "a lad from Bethlehem in Judah... who was a levite" (נער מבית לחם יהודה... והוא לוי, Ju 17:7). He is generally referred to as "the levite" during the first section of the story, where he goes with Micah, who has offered to employ him as "father and priest", and where he accepts the offer (Ju 17:10, 11), and also where Micah installs him (Ju 17:12), and where he refers to him in speech (Ju 17:13). He is called "the man" (האיש) when he sets out from home to seek his fortune, and so is independent, and is not viewed in connection with a shrine (Ju 17:8). He is referred to as "the lad" (הנער) where his relationship to Micah, his employer, is described (Ju 17:11, 12).[3] He is referred to as "the levite lad" (הנער הלוי), reflecting the introductory description, at the beginning of each of the remaining two sections in which he participates in the narrative (Ju 18:3, 15), typical "introductory" use of a compound designation.

---

[3] It seems to me probable that the statement that he became "as one of his (Micah's) sons" (ויהי הנער לו כאחד מבניו, Ju 17:11) resumes the statement that Micah consecrated "one of his sons" as a priest (וימלא את יד אחד מבניו ויהי לו לכהן, Ju 17:5), showing that both designations refer to the levite. The narrative follows the characteristic practice of treating sets of contemporaneous events separately until the point at which they converge (for other examples, see §9.2.5n). The establishment of the shrine is treated from Micah's point of view in Ju 17:1-6, from the levite's in Ju 17:7-11. The two treatments are brought together in Ju 17:11, which repeats Ju 17:5 with suitable variation. Boling, 1975:256 is the only scholar I have noted who argues that "one of his sons" refers to the same person in the two verses. The ambiguity is in part due to the fact that the narrator has to refer in Ju 17:5 to a character he has not yet introduced.

Within these sections, he is referred to as "the priest" (הכהן) by the narrator, where he acts as a priest in delivering advice from God (Ju 18:6), and also where he does not act as priest in Ju 18:17, 18, 20, 27, since this is the role in which he is of interest to the other participants, Micah and the b. Dan. He refers to himself as "priest to Micah" in speech to representatives of the b. Dan in Ju 18:4, and Micah refers to him as "the priest" in Ju 18:24.

14.3.2 The narrative surveyed is of particular interest as it gives a clear idea of the relative values of "man" (איש) and "lad" (נער) as terms for social categories. A view of the distinction between "lad" (נער) and "child" (ילד) can be obtained from a survey of 2K 4:17-37. As a result of Elisha's promise, the Shunammite woman bears a son (בן, 2K 4:17). The next verse states that "the child grew up" (הילד, 2K 4:18). The term "child" here probably represents him as living as a member of the family (see §2.2.3). The story goes on to relate that the boy falls ill, and dies (2K 4:20), but the mother appeals to Elisha, who eventually revives him. The term "lad" (נער) is used where Gehazi lays Elijah's staff on the boy's face, and when Elijah finds him dead (2K 4:31, 32), where the child acts without reference to other characters (sneezes and opens his eyes, 2K 4:35), and where Gehazi and Elisha discuss him between themselves (2K 4:29). The term "child" (ילד) is used where he grows up (2K 4:18), and where Elisha stretches out over him, and, as a result, his flesh becomes warm (2K 4:34, 34). It is thus arguable that the term "child" depicts him as a member of a family, or (as where Elijah stretches out over him) as recipient of parent-like care. The term "lad", which depicts him free of family associations, is more distanced and impersonal. The mother naturally speaks of the boy as a "son" (בן, 2K 4:28), and this term is also used, with an appropriate suffix, where Elisha speaks to her of the boy (see §13.4.2), and where she is agent and the boy patient (2K 4:36, 37).

14.3.3 There is a little support for this view of the relation of "lad" and "child" in the story of the boy revived by Elijah under somewhat similar circumstances (1K 17:17-23). This boy is referred to as "son" (בן) when associated with his mother, otherwise as "child" (ילד). He is never shown in the sort of circumstances which give rise to the use of "lad" (נער) in 2K 4:17-37. The first child borne to

David by Bathsheba is referred to as "son" where his mother is agent and he patient (2S 11:27), and in speech directed to his father (2S 12:14). Elsewhere, he is referred to as "child", depicting him as a member of David's family, save in 2S 12:16, where David is said to "beseech God on behalf of the lad" (ויבקש דוד את האלהים בעד הנער). The choice of the more distanced term "lad" presumably reflects David's speech, suggesting that he is taking the stance of a disinterested third party for the purpose of his plea (see §13.4.2 on Ju 9:16), or possibly to conceal his grief (see §2.2.5).[4] The use of "child" for the contemporaries of Rehoboam, to whom he turned for advice when dissatisfied with that of the elders, is discussed in §2.2.3. The discussion above provides a fuller basis for the conclusion reached in §2.2.5: the term "son" (בן) presents a child in association with his mother or father. The term "child" (ילד) shows him as a family member. The term "lad" (נער) shows him free of family associations; if he is associated with anyone, it is as a servant.

---

[4] The named character, Abijah, is similarly referred to as "lad" by his father when asking his mother to find out from a prophet how his illness will turn out (1K 14:3, also by the narrator recording his death, 1K 14:17). The prophet, foretelling the boy's death to his mother, refers to him as "the child" (1K 14:12), a somewhat less emotive term than "your son" which might have been expected.

The Designation of God

15.1. Introduction

15.1.1 The designation of deities is much like that of humans. A name or epithet may be used alone as a simple designation, or the name may be combined with one or more epithets in a compound designation. The most common epithet is the word "god" (אלהים), which can be treated as a title. It is plural in form, but coreferents are typically singular where it refers to an individual deity.[1] "God" as a title may be used alone, or the name of the state or people by whom the god is worshipped may be added to it, much as with the title "king". The corpus mentions a number of deities worshipped in territories surrounding Israel, as "Ashtoreth god of the Sidonians, Chemosh god of Moab, and Milcom god of the b. Ammon" (1K 11:33). There is not enough information to make it worth treating these foreign deities as a separate group, so they are ignored. The discussion below deals only with the designation of the God of Israel, to whom the word "God" in this section refers.

15.1.2 The name of the God of Israel, spelled YHWH (יהוה), is vocalized "Yahweh" by a long-standing consensus of academics. The vowelling of the masoretic text reflects the use of the word "(my) lord" (*'ădonāy*) as a surrogate, an ancient custom, probably reflected in the use of "lord" (κυριος) in the Greek translation.[2] The written

---

[1] A plural coreferent is used in the corpus where the referent appears to be singular in 2S 7:23, possibly also 1S 4:8, see §15.1.3.

[2] The word "lord" (אדון) derives from the terminology commonly used of the relationship between human masters and servants in the Bible and in epigraphic sources. The word אדני presumably originated as the plural of the word "lord" with a first person pronominal suffix, as argued in Brettler, 1989:41-42. (The use of *qameṣ* as the vowel of the final syllable, rather than the *pataḥ* expected in this form, most probably represents the use of the "pausal" form in all situations, as יהונתן from נתן; the change is rare in less common names ending in *yod* other than in full pausal situations, but cf. שׂרי, Gen 11:29. This final vowel, marking the word as plural, shows that the word designates God, as opposed to "my lord" ad-

form of (*ădonāy*) "(my) lord" (אֲדֹנָי) is used in address, where it has
a value distinct from the name "Yahweh". It is also occasionally
used in spoken reference, where its value is uncertain, and in narration. The latter use shows no particular pattern, and so is treated
here as a free variant of the name "Yahweh".[3] The standard compound designation, presenting a precise identification of God, is
"Yahweh God of Israel" (יהוה אלהי ישראל). Where the use of the
name of the people "Israel" is not required, the word "God" is
sometimes used alone, as in "Yahweh (the) God" (יהוה אלהים, 2S
7:25). More often, a pronominal suffix, or some nominal other than
"Israel" is used to mark the relationship between God and the
speaker, addressee, or some third party. The word צבאות, translated
"hosts", is sometimes used in the designation of God, most commonly in the form "Yahweh of hosts" (יהוה צבאות, as in 1S 1:3). Its
actual reference is obscure.

15.1.3 Where a simple designation for God is used by the narrator,
or by a speaker who is a member of Israel, the name is nearly always chosen. Where the title is used as a simple designation, the
word "God" (אלהים[ה]) is usually used alone.[4] The fuller form
"God of Israel" (אלהי ישראל) is rarely used unless it is necessary to
make clear that some other deity is not intended, as in the speech
of the Philistines in 1S 6:5. However, it is used as a simple designation by the priest Eli in 1S 1:17 (in reference), and by Solomon in
1K 8:26 (as a vocative). It is used by the narrator only in the phrase

---

dressed to a human, which has the same spelling אדני, but represents (*ădoni*), with
ḥireq in the final syllable.) Other surrogates, similarly designed to recognize and
protect the uniqueness of the name, came into use later.
[3]   "(My) lord" (אֲדֹנָי) is used in narration in 1K 3:10, 15, 2K 7:6, in spoken reference in 2K 19:23, and as a vocative in Ju 6:15, 13:8. The compound "(my) lord
Yahweh" (אֲדֹנָי יהוה, where "God", אלהים, is traditionally used as a surrogate for
the name) is used in spoken reference in 1K 2:26, as a vocative in eight cases (see
§15.7.2). The compound "(my) lord God" (written as such, אֲדֹנָי אלהים) is used as
a vocative in 2S 7:25. (In the spoken reference in 1S 6:20, "God" heads a descriptive phrase.) On the value of the first person pronoun in "(my) lord", see §15.8.2.
[4]   Forms with and without the article appear to be used in free variation in the
text, so the difference is ignored in this study.

"the ark of the God of Israel" in 1S 5:8.[5] The Philistines speak of "the ark of the God of Israel" (ארון אלהי ישראל, 1S 5:7, 8, 8, 10, 11, 6:3, 5), and the Assyrians speak of "the God of the land" (אלהי הארץ, 2K 17:26, 26, 27). Foreign speakers also use the title in the form "God" (אלהים) alone (as Ju 1:7, 7:14, 1S 30:15). The referent is not clear except where a plural coreferent, showing that the title does not designate the God of Israel, is used in an oath by Jezebel (1K 19:2), and by the king of Aram (1K 20:10). The use of "God" with plural coreferents in the speech of the Philistines in 1S 4:8, where the word does refer to the God of Israel, is perhaps intended to reflect foreign patterns of thought. Foreign speakers occasionally refer to God by the name Yahweh, just as the narrator may use the name of a foreign deity, as "Dagon" in 1S 5:2.[6]

15.2 Simple Designations: Nominal Structures

15.2.1 The possibility that the use of the title as a simple designation has a value distinct from the use of the name (as in the case of kings), is most clearly evident in nominal structures. An "angel of Yahweh" (מלאך יהוה) is typically an envoy with a mission, as in the first example in the corpus: "An angel of Yahweh came up from Gilgal to Bochim and said..." (ויעל מלאך יהוה מן הגלגל אל הבכים ויאמר..., Ju 2:1).[7] An "angel of God" (מלאך ה[א]להים) is most commonly mentioned as a standard of comparison, as in "his appearance was like that of an angel of God" (ומראהו כמראה מלאך האלהים, Ju 13:6, other examples occur in 1S 29:9, 2S 14:17, 20, 19:28). Where the phrase "angel of God" denotes an envoy, he appears to be act-

---

[5]   This usage can be understood as representing the Philistine viewpoint, but may well have arisen through the influence of the previous two uses of the phrase (in speech by Philistines) in the same verse. "God of Israel" is also used in 2S 23:3, in a poetic passage.

[6]   Achish King of Gath swears by "Yahweh" in 1S 29:6; Hiram King of Tyre gives thanks to him in 1K 5:21, as does the queen of Sheba in 1K 10:9. The use of the name in these situations possibly reflects the extent to which these foreigners were considered well-disposed to leaders of Israel, and so as having a high regard for the state religion. Araunah's statement to David that "Yahweh your God will bless you" (יהוה אלהיך ירצך, 2S 24:23, a wish using the indicative for distancing to show deference, see §23.4.1) does not necessarily reflect Araunah's attitude to God.

[7]   "Angel of Yahweh" occurs in Ju 2:1, 4, 5:23, 6:11, 12, 21, 21, 22, 22, 13:3, 13, 15, 16, 16, 17, 18, 20, 21, 21, 2S 24:16, 1K 19:7, 2K 1:3, 15, 19:35.

ing beyond the requirements of his mission. In Ju 6:20, he instructs Gideon (whom he has come to inspire as a "judge") what to do with an offering. In Ju 13:9, he reappears to repeat the message he has already delivered.

15.2.2 A "spirit of Yahweh" (רוח יהוה) is typically a positive force, promoting heroic acts, as in "The spirit of Yahweh was upon him, and he judged Israel, and went to war..." (ותהי עליו רוח יהוה וישפט את ישראל ויצא למלחמה, Ju 3:10).[8] The phrase is also used to represent the power of God to remove his human agents from the scene of their former activities (to "spirit them away") in 1K 18:12, 2K 2:16. The phrase "spirit of God" (רוח אלהים) is used almost exclusively in connection with Saul. While it may inspire positive action (as in 1S 11:6), it more usually induces the state called "acting like a prophet" (התנבא) in which he was led to attack David.[9] Other uses refer to the need for soothing music to banish this state. In Ju 9:23, "God sent an evil spirit" (וישלח אלהים רוח רעה) similarly refers to a force which produced irrational dissension between a superior and his subordinates. The term "spirit of Yahweh" is used of Saul in 1S 10:6, where Samuel, after anointing him, predicts the coming of the spirit to him, in 1S 16:14, where the "spirit of Yahweh" is said to leave Saul, to be replaced by "an evil spirit from Yahweh", and in 1S 19:9, where it is qualified as "evil" (רעה).

15.2.3 The ark, the wooden box in which the tablets of the law had been placed, which symbolized the presence of God, is designated as "the ark of God" (ארון ה[א]להים) where it is described as being captured by the Philistines, or as being in a location, or being moved to one with no particular ceremony.[10] This term also desig-

---

[8]   Other examples occur in Ju 6:34, 11:29, 14:6, 19, 15:14, and in Ju 13:25, 1S 16:13, where the heroic result is potential. In 1K 22:24 it refers to the spirit which produces prophecy.

[9]   1S 10:10, 18:10, 19:23, also inspired in Saul's messengers, 1S 19:20. The Hebrew term is generally regarded as indicating a visibly abnormal state, like the trance or frenzy in which some prophets delivered their messages. In the case of Saul, however, no divine communication is implied. The other examples of the phrase "the spirit of God" (1S 16:15, 16, 23) also refer to this force which disturbs Saul.

[10]   Captured, 1S 4:11, 17, 18, 19, 21, 22, 5:1, other uses 1S 3:3, 4:13, 5:2, 10, 10, 14:18, 2S 6:2, 3, 4, 6, 7, 12, 12, 7:2, 15:24, 25, 29.

nates the ark as a subject of concern to Eli (1S 4:13), as called for by
Saul (1S 14:18), and as the cause of Yahweh's blessing on the house
of Obed Edom (2S 6:12). The designation "ark of the covenant of
God" (ארון ברית האלהים) is used where the ark is mentioned in
such contexts in connection with priestly attendants.[11] The term
"ark of Yahweh" (ארון יהוה) is used where the ark is viewed, either
by Israel or by the Philistines, as a source of power, usually dangerous power.[12] The term "ark of Yahweh" is also used where the ark
is described as being transported with fitting ceremony (2S 6:13, 15,
16, 17, 1K 8:4). The designation "ark of the covenant of Yahweh"
is used where the ark is brought to the camp of Israel as a means of
ensuring God's support and so Israel's victory.[13] The designation
"ark of the covenant of Yahweh" is also used of the final placement
of the ark in the temple (1K 6:19, 8:6), and introduces the description of Solomon's ceremonial moving of it (1K 8:1). The related
term "the ark of the covenant of (my) Lord" (ארון ברית אדני) is
used by the narrator in connection with Solomon's sacrificing in Jerusalem before the building of the temple (1K 3:15). The sacrifice is
presumably an expression of thanks to God for his promise of support for Solomon personally, given in 1K 3:12-14. Finally, Solomon
speaks of "the ark of (my) lord Yahweh" in referring to Abiathar's
services (ארון אדני יהוה, 1K 2:26). This designation, referring to
Solomon's personal relationship to God, presents Abiathar's service

---

[11] Ju 20:27, 1S 4:4, 2S 15:24. The ark was used by priests in obtaining counsel
from God. Such counsel is requested in the context in Ju 20:27, and the need for
it is implicit in the other two cases.

[12] By Israel, 1S 6:15, 18, 19, 21, 7:1, 1, 2S 6:9, 10, also 2S 6:11, where it is a source
of blessing; by the Philistines, 1S 4:6, 5:3, 4, 6:1, 11. Philistine speakers even use
the term "ark of Yahweh" in 1S 6:2, 8, although they more usually use "ark of the
God of Israel" (1S 5:7, 8, 8, 10, 11, 6:3).

[13] 1S 4:3, 4, 5. The designation presumably alludes to the specific relationship of
God with Israel which will ensure the provision not just of counsel, but of active
support. The expanded designation "The lord of hosts who sits (between) the cherubim" (יהוה צבאות ישב הכרובים), a reference to the position of the ark (conceived
of as used as a throne) in the temple, is used in designating the ark in 1S 4:4
(where the ark is taken from Shiloh), and 2S 6:2 (where David sets out to bring it
up to Jerusalem). Both appear to be typical uses of a more weighty designation to
draw attention to an event of particular significance. The cherubim are also referred to in a designation of God used as a vocative in 2K 19:15, where the ark is
not mentioned.

to "(my) lord Yahweh", as to "my father David", as the motivation
for his decision to spare Abiathar's life.

15.2.4 It is reasonable to interpret the designation of the ark as "the
ark of God" as showing that it is viewed simply as a physical object, as in "The Philistines took the ark of God, and brought it to
the temple of Dagon" (ויקחו פלשתים את ארון האלהים ויביאו אתו בית
דגון, 1S 5:2). Viewed as representing God's power, or as a medium
for transmitting it, the ark is called "the ark of Yahweh", as in
"There was Dagon fallen forward on the ground before the ark of
Yahweh" (והנה דגון נפל לפניו ארצה לפני ארון יהוה, 1S 5:3).[14] That
is, "God" (אלהים) represents the general concept "deity", "Yahweh"
(יהוה) represents "God" as an effective force in the world.[15] This
view provides a satisfactory understanding of the use of the two
designations with "angel" and "spirit". An "angel of God" is a divine messenger with no function specified; an "angel of Yahweh"
has a mission from God. A "spirit of God" is a divine spirit of any
sort; a "spirit of Yahweh" is one which inspires people to act in the
way desired by God. Saul's character was such that the spirit of
Yahweh, although originally with him, did not inspire him to act
as God wanted. The designations "God" and "Yahweh" do not designate different entities, but the different effects of the one entity
on the world.

15.3 Simple Designations: Oaths

15.3.1 The only clear case of preference for the use of "God"
(אלהים) to represent the God of Israel as agent is the oath formula
"Thus may God do..." (כה יעשה אלהים...). An oath of this sort calls
on God to punish the speaker (or addressee) in some unspecified
way if he does not perform some action which is (or is believed to

---

[14] Cf. the usage in 1S 4:4. The same values can be seen in Chronicles, although
the pattern there differs a little from that in Kings. Note the shift in 1 Chron 15:2:
"David said "No one should carry the ark of God (the object) but the levites,
because it was they that Yahweh chose to carry the ark of Yahweh (the potentially
dangerous symbol of God's power)". The designation "ark of God" is used only in
the corpus and in Chronicles; it is not used where the ark is mentioned in the Pentateuch or the Book of Joshua.
[15] Similar conclusions have been reached on other grounds, as in Rose, 1992:1006.

be) within his power. The intended action typically involves a radical change in the *status quo*, often including the death of another. This form of oath must, then, reflect intense feeling in the speaker.[16] The only use of the name of God in an oath of this sort in the corpus is "Thus may Yahweh do to Jonathan..." (כה יעשה יהוה ליהונתן, 1S 20:13) where Jonathan swears to help David escape King Saul, his father, should that become necessary. The unusual form of the oath (including the use of the speaker's own name, see §27.2.2) probably represents a stronger asseveration, as would be needed to convince David of the sincerity of Jonathan's undertaking to support David against his own father, and against what his father saw as his own interests.[17] The common use of "God" probably represents the prudent use of a general, distanced term when inviting divine action against oneself. Solomon, in swearing "Thus may God do...", is nevertheless said to "swear by Yahweh" (וישבע המלך שלמה ביהוה לאמר כה יעשה לי אלהים..., 1K 2:23).

15.3.2 The other common oath formula חי יהוה, translated "As Yahweh lives", uses the name "Yahweh" as a guarantee of the speaker's sincerity, but does not call for any action to be taken against speaker or addressee. The oath supports a statement of intended action harmful to another only where the statement includes justification for the action in "As Yahweh lives, if you had let them live, I would not be (determined on) killing you" (חי יהוה לו החיתם אותם לא הרגתי אתכם, Ju 8:19). The name is used in this formula in 27 cases, the title only in 2S 2:27. The precise intention of the speech there is uncertain. If the message is given the maximum ferocity,

---

[16] Death or destruction is involved in 1S 14:44, 25:22, 1K 2:23, 19:2, 20:10, 2K 6:31, other radical change in 2S 3:9, 19:14. The formula is also used by Eli to force Samuel to tell him the whole truth about the communication he received from God (1S 3:17, the only case where the oath calls on God to take action against the addressee), and by David in expressing his refusal to eat (2S 3:35).

[17] Ruth's use of the name of God "thus may Yahweh do" in Ruth 1:17 (the only example of the "thus may the deity do" formula outside the corpus) may be intended to demonstrate to Naomi the completeness of her assimilation to her husband's family and culture, (as suggested in Joüon, 1953, and Sasson, 1979). If so, she is effectively swearing by "the true God" (rather than some other being who might be designated as 'god'), and so using the strongest possible form of oath, reflecting the strength of her emotion and commitment.

the speaker swears that, if the addressee had not proposed a truce, his troops would have been pursued by those of the speaker until morning.[18] This is simply a threat designed to dissuade the addressee from further conflict at some future date. It is thus of little importance to the speaker personally, and it is possible that this lack of importance is reflected by the use of "God" rather than "Yahweh" in the formula supporting it.[19]

15.4 Simple Designations: Other Verbal Structures

15.4.1 The tendency to use "God" to make more general or distanced reference to the deity as agent can be seen elsewhere. The text states that "Yahweh gave wisdom to Solomon" in 1K 5:26, where there is a specific reference to the promise made in 1K 3:12-14. Where the statement is general, it is stated that "God" put wisdom in Solomon's heart (1K 5:9), and this is presented as the view of "all the land" in 1K 10:24. In some cases, "God" (אלהים) appears to represent the aspect of the deity which actually deals with humans. Manoah prays to "Yahweh"; "God" hears (Ju 13:8-9). Samson calls to "Yahweh"; "God" provides water (Ju 15:18-19). "Yahweh" is angered by Uzzah; "God" strikes him down (2S 6:7). "Yahweh" appears to Solomon; "God" invites him to ask for a gift (1K 3:5). However, it is "Yahweh" who provides counsel when "God" is asked (Ju 20:18, cf. Ju 18:5-6). Such use of both simple designations may be intended to present the equivalent of a compound designation in a way similar to the use of two designations in parallel hemistichs in a poetic couplet.[20] If this is the intention, however, it is surprising that the usage is so restricted.

---

[18]   This interpretation is supported in Driver, 1913. Fokkelman, 1990:59-60, 369, appears more likely to be right in arguing that it means "If you had not proposed a tournament this morning... there would have been no reason for a fight", but some questions about the language remain unanswered.

[19]   An oath of this type supporting an asseveration in the form of a past untrue condition is also found in 1S 25:34. Here the context shows that the speech is of considerable importance to the speaker, see §15.5.4, and this importance is reflected by the use, in the formula, of a compound designation including the name of God.

[20]   It is noteworthy, however, that the poetic parallel to "Yahweh" is not just "God", but "our God", or "my God" (1S 2:2, 2S 22:7).

15.4.2 Where the designation represents the patient, "God" is sometimes used where a general practice is involved, "Yahweh" where
the reference is to a specific occasion. In 1S 9:9, the narrator speaks
of typical wording used when a person was going "to seek God"
(לדרש האלהים). Someone seeking information on a particular occasion is said to "seek Yahweh" (לדרש את יהוה, 1K 22:8, 2K 3:11, 8:8,
22:13, 18). Similar contrast occurs between "the place where David
used to bow (ישתחוה) to God" (2S 15:32) and specific occasions of
"bowing to Yahweh" (1S 1:19, 28, 15:31). In 2S 21:14, "God accepted prayer" (ויעתר) is not related to a particular event. In 2S 24:25,
the same verb is used with "Yahweh" in connection with the halt-
ing of the plague. In other cases the use of "God" may be seen as
suggesting a weaker commitment than the use of "Yahweh". In Ju
20:18, the question "who will go up first for us" is put to "God" by
the rest of Israel about to attack Benjamin, evidently on their own
initiative. The same question is put to "Yahweh" in Ju 1:1 by the
"b. Israel", already under orders to settle the land. In Ju 21:2, the
council of Israel sits before "God", unsure how to deal with the unfortunate results of their attack on Benjamin, whereas in Ju 20:26,
they sit before "Yahweh" earnestly deploring the slaughter, and asking "Yahweh" if they really should continue the war. Similarly Gideon speaks to "God" where his commitment to his task needs support (אמר, Ju 6:36, 39). This is not the case with those who speak
to "Yahweh" (אמר, Ju 10:15, 2S 24:10, 17).

15.4.3 Where the designation is used in quoted speech, the use of
"God" is often connected with Saul. Thus Samuel tells Saul that
"God" is with him (1S 10:7), not "Yahweh" (cf. Ju 6:12, 1S 20:13,
etc.). Other examples of use related to Saul occur in 1S 9:27, 14:36,
45, 22:13, 15, 23:7, 28:15, and cf. the use of "spirit of God" in connection with Saul, as described in §15.2.2. Other cases of the use of
"God" in speech can be seen as the prudent avoidance of the actual
use of the name where the situation does not require it. The Danite
spies request the priest to "ask of God" about the success of their
journey (שאל נא באלהים, Ju 18:5). The professional confidently replies that it is "before Yahweh" (נכח יהוה, Ju 18:6). Abishai tells David that "God" has delivered his enemy, King Saul, into his power
(1S 26:8). Other examples occur in Ju 8:3, 10:10, 1S 10:19, 17:26, 36,
2S 14:14, 16, 1K 1:47, 2K 19:4. It is possible that this suggestion,

and the others made above, should be used to interpret the other cases of the use of "God" as a simple designation as having connotations different from the use of "Yahweh", but it could scarcely be argued that the making of such a distinction is clearly valid in all cases. There appears to be a tendency to use the two terms with different values, and this is quite marked in some cases. It is quite possible, however, that there was also a considerable area of use in which any difference between the two was unimportant. This could well reflect the fact that the narrator rarely needed to present different aspects of the deity in his narrative.[21]

15.5 Compound Designations: Yahweh God of Israel

15.5.1 The narrator's use of compound designations for the God of Israel resembles his use of them for prominent characters like David, who participate so regularly in the narrative that the weight of a compound designation is not needed to alert the reader to the importance of their appearance in any particular scene (see §4.13.1). Compounds make up only a small proportion of the total number of designations for God. They are sometimes used where God is first mentioned in a new context, but it is probable that their use is always intended to draw attention to some particular feature of the context. Thus "Saul said to Yahweh God of Israel..." (ויאמר שאול אל יהוה אלהי ישראל, 1S 14:41) begins a new context, but the main reason for its use is probably to draw attention to Saul's culpable rashness. His words set in motion the process which must end (as the reader knows) in the condemnation of Jonathan for contravening an oath of Saul's of which he had not been informed.

15.5.2 In any case, it is clear that the main function of compound designations of God is to draw attention to some feature of the

---

[21] It does not seem to me that the rabbinic view that "God" represents the deity as a just judge, while "Yahweh" represents him as merciful (Midrash *Shemoth Rabba* 3:6), is the most obvious interpretation of the usage of the corpus. It does seem that in the case of the king, however, the use of the title represents the official role, while the use of the name presents him as a human (and humane) individual. If the equivalent were true of the designation of God, the rabbinic view would be a satisfactory description of it. In any case, the usage of the corpus cannot be taken as representative of that of the Bible as a whole.

context in which they are used.[22] Thus a compound designation often closely follows a simple one, as in the typical use of a compound designation to highlight the more significant clause after an introductory one in 1K 11:9 "Yahweh became angry at Solomon because his heart turned away from Yahweh God of Israel, who had appeared to him twice" (ויתאנף יהוה בשלמה כי נטה לבבו מעם יהוה אלהי ישראל הנראה אליו פעמים). The designation "Yahweh God of Israel" is also used to draw attention to delinquency or wrongdoing where the perpetrator is a king of Israel (1K 15:30, 16:13, 26, 33, 22:54, 2K 10:31). In "He trusted in Yahweh God of Israel" (ביהוה אלהי ישראל בטח, 2K 18:5), the designation highlights King Hezekiah's reliance on God. The designation "Yahweh his God" might be expected here (see §15.6.1), but the more general designation may be used to indicate that the objects removed from the temple by Hezekiah (according to the previous verse) played no part in the (true) worship of Yahweh God of Israel.

15.5.3 The designation "Yahweh God of Israel" is often used to introduce important communications from God, as that conveyed by Deborah to Barak "Has not Yahweh God of Israel commanded, 'Go...'" (הלא צוה יהוה אלהי ישראל לך..., Ju 4:6). Many of the examples occur in the introductory formula "Thus says Yahweh God of Israel..." (כה אמר יהוה אלהי ישראל...), although the simple designation "Thus says Yahweh..." (כה אמר יהוה...) is more commonly used.[23] Communications introduced with the formula using the simple designation are generally of restricted relevance, as the command to Rehoboam not to attack the northern kingdom (1K 12:24), although some, as the promise to David so introduced in 2S 7:8, have a wider significance. The compound designation is usually used

---

[22] The title "Yahweh God of Israel" distinguishes the God of Israel from foreign gods in Ju 11:21. Other uses, not discussed below, occur in 1K 8:17, 20, 14:13, 2K 14:25.

[23] "Thus says Yahweh God of Israel" Ju 6:8, 1S 10:18, 2S 12:7, 1K 11:31, 14:7, 17:14, 2K 9:6, 19:20, 21:12, 22:15, 18. "Thus says Yahweh" 1S 2:27, 2S 7:5, 8, 12:11, 1K 12:24, 13:2, 21, 20:13, 14, 28, 42, 21:19, 19, 22:11, 2K 1:4, 6, 16, 2:21, 3:16, 17, 4:43, 7:1, 9:3, 12, 19:6, 32, 20:1, 22:16. The view that the compound designation introduces more important speech is consistent with the view that the same is true of a simple designation in contrast to a pronoun (see §4.3), a contrast parallel to that between compound and simple designations (see §4.13.4).

where the communication is of national importance, as that in Ju 6:8, introducing the recapitulation of God's association with Israel, and his subsequent denunciation of them. The different values can be illustrated by the fact that a compound designation is used to open the denunciation of David, God's servant, the ideal king (2S 12:7), while a simple designation is used to begin the denunciation of Ahab (no unimportant figure, even if despicable) for a similar crime (1K 21:19). The simple designation may also be used for a secondary introduction to a speech, repeating one using a compound designation, as in 2K 22:15-16.[24] Similarly, the formula of attribution "saying of Yahweh" (נאם יהוה), with the name alone, is subordinate to some formula introducing speech (1S 2:30, 2K 19:33), or is used where an earlier communication by God is recalled (2K 9:26). Where the compound designation "Yahweh God of Israel" is used (1S 2:30), the formula highlights the beginning of a new section of speech, introduced by "for this reason" (לכן).

15.5.4 The compound designation "Yahweh God of Israel" also contrasts with the name in other formulae. David swears "As Yahweh God of Israel lives" (חי יהוה אלהי ישראל, 1S 25:34) to express the idea that, had Abigail not intervened, he would have slaughtered her husband and the males of his household. The avoidance of this bloodshed is presented as part of the motivation for his thanks to God (1S 25:32, see §15.5.5) and to Abigail. The compound designation is also used in this formula by Elijah to support a prediction of events beyond his control, which lead up to his confrontation with the priests of Baal on Mount Carmel (1K 17:1). The words "Yahweh God of Israel" in 1S 20:12 are used as if in this formula.[25] They introduce a statement of what the speaker would ordinarily do if Saul were well-disposed toward David. This leads to a more emphatic oath introduced by "Thus may Yahweh do to Jonathan"

---

[24] Also in 2S 12:11, introducing the announcement that David's family life will be disrupted, following the strong denunciation of his killing of Uriah. Where a simple designation is used both at the beginning of a speech and within it, the first use accompanies introductory material, the second, the significant communication: the promise that David will found a dynasty (2S 7:5, 8), the threat of death (1K 21:19), or the promise that water will be provided (2K 3:16-17). Cf. §4.12.2.

[25] The initial "as... lives" (חי) may have been lost through error or ellipsis. Driver, 1913, suggests a different idiom with the same perlocutionary intention.

(see §15.3.1), which supports a promise to warn David and aid his escape if Saul is hostile to him. The form of oath introduced by "as God lives" is thus shown to be less prominent than the other, as argued above. The situations in which the oath is used in 1S 25:34, 1K 17:1, (and presumably 1S 20:12), suggest that the use of a compound designation provides the most emphatic wording of this form of oath.

15.5.5 The compound designation "Yahweh God of Israel" follows "blessed is" (ברוך) in the thanksgiving formula used by David in 1S 25:32 to express his gratitude to God for sending Abigail to prevent him from shedding blood unnecessarily, and by David in 1K 1:48, and by Solomon in 1K 8:15, in thanking God for keeping his promise to continue the Davidic dynasty.[26] The name Yahweh is used alone in this position where David thanks God for giving him justice by killing Nabal (1S 25:39), by Hiram thanking God for placing Solomon on David's throne (1K 5:21), and by Solomon in thanking God for maintaining his promise to Moses to give Israel rest (1K 8:56). This last can be considered introductory to Solomon's speech, which is mainly concerned with the future. Moreover it, like the other two cases in which the simple designation is used, does not concern the speaker personally, or is not such an important concern to him, as the examples in which the compound designation is used. There is, of course, room for argument about individual examples, but it seems clear from a general overview that the narrator or a speaker uses a compound designation of God in place of a simple one to show that the related wording is particularly important to him, or particularly worthy of the attention of the reader or addressee.

15.6 Other Compound Designations

15.6.1 In a designation of God composed of name and title, the word "God" is sometimes followed by a pronoun, or by a nominal other than "Israel", indicating some individual or group which has (or should have) a close relationship to God. A compound designa-

---

[26] For "Blessed is Yahweh" (ברוך יהוה) as a formula of thanks, see Lande, 1949: 106-108.

tion using a pronoun in this way is often used by the narrator in describing wrongful action, as in "The b. Israel did not remember Yahweh their God" (ולא זכרו בני ישראל את יהוה אלהיהם, Ju 8:34). It may be similarly used by a speaker charging the addressee with such action, as "You have not kept the commandment of Yahweh your God" (לא שמרת את מצות יהוה אלהיך, 1S 13:13).[27] In such cases, the pronoun draws attention to the relationship that should exist, and so, by contrast, highlights the delinquency. A compound designation of this sort may also be used in describing reliance on the relationship, or action consistent with it, or in exhorting an addressee to act in this way, as in "David strengthened himself in Yahweh his God" (ויתחזק דוד ביהוה אלהיו, 1S 30:6), "You will keep the charge of Yahweh your God" (ושמרת את משמרת יהוה אלהיך, 1K 2:3).[28] In such cases the use of the pronoun suggests that the relationship motivated, or should motivate, the action. A designation of this sort, which includes a pronoun, may also be used in recognizing, or in giving thanks for, benefits received on account of the relationship, in expressing a wish for such benefits, in indicating the possibility that they might be forthcoming, and so on.[29] A first person pronoun, expressing the devotion of the speaker or his community, is included in designations of this sort used as vocatives in address to God (see §15.7.4).

15.6.2 The use of a second person singular pronoun in a designation of this sort is easily understood where the addressee is charged with action inconsistent with the relationship, or is exhorted to act in conformity with it. In some situations, however, an English speaker

---

[27] Third person in narration: Ju 3:7, 8:34, 1K 11:4, 15:3, 4, 2K 16:2, 17:7, 9, 14, 16, 19, 18:12; in speech: 1S 12:9, 1K 9:9. Second person Ju 6:10, 1S 12:12, 13:13.

[28] Third person in narration: 1S 30:6; in speech: 1K 5:17, 2K 5:11. Second person: Ju 6:26, 2S 14:11, 1K 2:3, 2K 17:39, 23:21. First person plural: 1K 8:61, 2K 18:22. The first person singular is used to highlight action by the speaker in accordance with the relationship in 2S 24:24, 1K 5:19.

[29] First or second person recognizing, or giving thanks for, benefits: Ju 11:24, 2S 18:28, 1K 5:18, 10:9; wishing: 2S 14:17, 24:23, 1K 8:57, 59, and, with third person address, 1K 1:36; related usage: 1S 12:14, 25:29, 2S 24:3. The unique use of the first person plural in narration in 1K 8:65 (where third person is expected) was perhaps intended by the narrator to actualize this uniquely important event for the reader (see §8.1.5).

is likely to feel that the use of the second person implies "your God but not mine", as where the addressee is exhorted to appeal to God on behalf of the speaker in "Pray on behalf of your servants to Yahweh your God and let us not die" (התפלל בעד עבדיך אל יהוה אלהיך ואל נמות, 1S 12:19; other examples occur in 1K 13:6, 2K 19:4). Usage of this sort appears to be an expression of humility (as is suggested by the use, in the example quoted, of the deferential "your servants"). The use of the second person suggests that the addressee's relationship with God is such that any request from him is sure to succeed, or at least more likely to do so than a request from the speaker.[30] This view is supported by the contrasting use of the first person in "Do not turn silent on us, and not call on Yahweh our God that he save us from the Philistines" (אל תחרש ממנו מזעק אל יהוה אלהינו וישענו מיד פלשתים, 1S 7:8). Here, the speakers (the people) have just renewed their relationship with God under the direction of the addressee (Samuel), and so can rely on this relationship to ensure God's concern for them when Samuel prays. In 1S 12:19, the same group is conscious of delinquency which has not been expiated; they cannot rely on their relationship with God as a persuasive force. They must rely on that of Samuel, whose ability to persuade God to do as he asks has just been dramatically demonstrated to them.

15.6.3 The second person is used in a similar way by Saul addressing Samuel in 1S 15:15, 21, 30. The implication here seems to be that Saul has acted, or wants to act, in a way pleasing to "Yahweh your God", so that Samuel should be pleased because of his close relationship with God, and accept Saul's assertion, or grant his request. The oath formula "As Yahweh your God lives" (חי יהוה אלהיך, 1K 17:12, 18:10) similarly recognizes Elijah's close relationship with God, and so adapts the oath formula so as to present the asseveration in terms most persuasive to him. In "You swore by Yahweh your God" (אתה נשבעת ביהוה אלהיך, 1K 1:17), Bathsheba reminds David of the relationship which should ensure that he car-

---

[30]   This is no doubt related to the idea that God may act "for the sake of" particularly devoted servants, such as David (as in 2K 20:6).

ry out his promise.[31] In these cases, too, then, the relationship between the addressee and God is alluded to because of its relevance
to the situation. It is not intended to define the relationship between God and the speaker.

15.6.4 It is reasonable to say that the use of "Israel" in the compound designation "Yahweh God of Israel" similarly evokes the relationship between God and the community because of its relevance
to the situation in which the designation is used. Certainly this is
the case where some other nominal is used in the same situation.
Elisha calls out "Where is Yahweh God of Elijah" (איה יהוה אלהי
אליהו, 2K 2:14) where he makes his first attempt to use the power
which (in 2K 2:9) he requested through Elijah. In 2K 20:5 "Yahweh
God of David your father" is given as the source of a communication in which God promises help "for the sake of David my servant" (ולמען דוד עבדי, 2K 20:6). Elijah calls on "Yahweh God of
Abraham, Isaac, and Israel" (יהוה אלהי אברהם יצחק וישראל, 1K 18:36),
appealing to the association with the patriarchal ancestors of the
community to persuade God to demonstrate his power and resume
his rightful position in the esteem of their descendants.[32] In the
designation "Yahweh God of their fathers" (אבותם, Ju 2:12), or "of
his fathers" (אבתיו, 2K 21:22), the more general reference to the ancestors of the community, is used to draw attention to delinquency
in much the same way as is the pronoun in "Yahweh their/his
God", but presents this in terms of the historical relationship with
God, not just of that of those to whom the pronouns refer.

15.6.5 The designation "Yahweh of hosts" (יהוה צבאות) appears to
be associated with several important themes in the Bible as a whole,
but its origin, the development of its use, and the particular ideas it

---

[31]   King David, in referring to this oath, states that he swore by "Yahweh God of
Israel" (1K 1:30), viewing God's concern for the succession as an aspect of his relationship to Israel, not to himself alone.
[32]   The name "Israel" (rather than "Jacob") is no doubt intended to evoke both its
referents: the patriarch, and the community formed by his descendants. Cf. also
Exod 32:3.

was intended to evoke, remain unknown.[33] Since it is longer than a simple designation, and unusual, it was presumably used to attract the reader's attention in the same way as are other compound designations. In most of the situations in which the designation "Yahweh of hosts" is used in the corpus, it is reasonable to understand it as a more complete and evocative form of the name than "Yahweh" alone, used where God's concern for Israel, or for the speaker, is crucial. Thus it designates the God to whom Hannah, in bitter distress, prays for a child (1S 1:11), who orders Saul to destroy Amalek (1S 15:2), on whom David relies in his contest with Goliath (1S 17:45), and it is used in the designation of the ark at two critical junctures (1S 4:4, 2S 6:2, see §15.2.3n). The statement that Elkanah went periodically to worship "Yahweh of hosts" (1S 1:3) may have been intended to alert the reader that an event of the highest importance for Israel (the birth of Samuel) is about to be described. The form "Yahweh God of hosts", also used where the relationship with God is of highest importance (2S 5:10, 1K 19:10, 14), conflicts with the suggestion that "Yahweh of hosts" is a longer equivalent of the name "Yahweh", but might possibly be a further development from the shorter designation (originally suggested in Cross, 1973:69). In short, then, it can be said that designations of God in which the word "hosts" (צבאות) is used function like (other) compound designations, but that the reason why this designation, rather than another, is chosen in any particular situation is uncertain.

15.7 Address

15.7.1 Use by the narrator is not separated from spoken usage in the above discussion, so that the rarer designations can be treated in

---

[33] The name "Yahweh of hosts" (יהוה צבאות) occurs in the corpus in 1S 1:3, 11, 15:2, 2S 6:18, 7:8, 26, 1K 18:15, 2K 3:14, 19:31 (qere); also, with the addition "who dwells (between) the cherubim" (ישב הכרובים) 1S 4:4, 2S 6:2, with the additions "God of Israel" (אלהי ישראל), and "God of the ranks of Israel" (אלהי מערכות ישראל) 2S 7:27, 1S 17:45. The use of the latter addition could be said to show that "the lord of hosts" alone was not understood as identifying a militaristic aspect of Yahweh. The name may originally have been connected with the ark, and the shrine at Shiloh where it was once kept, but there is no reason to believe that the narrator intended to evoke this association whenever he used the name. A survey of these questions, with bibliography, in provided by Seow, 1992, Sherlock, 1993: 117-123.

the light of as much information as possible. The narrator and his characters are devotees of the same God, and so, in general, use designations in the same way. Differences between the use of designations of God in narration and their use in speech seem unimportant, but more attention needs to be given to the variety of designations used in address to God.

15.7.2 The designation of God most often used in address is the name "Yahweh". This is used either as the first (and only) vocative in a request, or to introduce a new section (not necessarily a request) in a longer speech in which the first vocative is a compound.[34] The phrase "(My) lord Yahweh" (אדני יהוה), which depicts the speaker's relationship with God as a master-servant relationship (see §2.3.7), is used as a vocative where the speech is of particular concern to the speaker. It is the only vocative in Gideon's lament that he has seen an angel (Ju 6:22. A request for help is implied, see §24.2.6). It is the first vocative in Samson's prayer for strength to avenge himself on the Philistines (Ju 16:28), and first in David's long prayer in 2S 7:18-29. David uses the same vocative repeatedly in the first section of that prayer, thanking God for the promise that he will found a dynasty, and offering praise (2S 7:18, 19, 19, 20, 22), and in his terminal request for God's blessing (2S 7:28, 29). Other vocatives are used in the intervening material, which concerns the people in general, or David's progeny, rather than David personally. "(My) lord Yahweh" (אדני יהוה) is also used as a vocative where Solomon closes his long prayer with a request for God's attention to the prayers of the king and his people (1K 8:53).

15.7.3 "(My) lord", introduced by a particle (בי אדני), is used as a vocative by Gideon in questioning his call (Ju 6:15) and by Manoah in requesting the return of the messenger who announced that his wife would have a child (Ju 13:8). These speeches could be understood as questioning or opposing the will of the addressee, a situa-

---

[34] The name is the only vocative in the speech in 1S 3:9, 2S 15:31, 24:10, 1K 19:4, 2K 6:17, 20, 20:3. The case in 2S 23:17 is to be added as the text stands, but more probably the idiom using the preposition מן before the designation, found in 1S 24:7, 26:11, 1K 21:3, was intended here.

tion in which deference is typically shown where speaker and addressee are human, and the latter is superior (see §20.4). The view
that the particle in question (בִּי) followed by a form of "lord" (אָדוֹן)
indicates particular deference is supported by the parallels in speech
between humans (§25.2.5-6). The title is used alone only as a secondary term of address after a more specific one, in the form "God"
(הָאֱלֹהִים) in Ju 16:28, and in the form "God of Israel" (אֱלֹהֵי יִשְׂרָאֵל)
in 1K 8:26.

15.7.4 Designations involving both name and title are used where
the concerns of the speech extend well beyond the personal.
"Yahweh God of Israel" (יהוה אֱלֹהֵי יִשְׂרָאֵל) is used as a vocative in
Ju 21:3, introducing a question concerned with the future of the
nation. David uses it in 1S 23:10, 11, in a question as to how he
should act for the good of his men and himself, God's chosen ruler.
It introduces Solomon's long prayer for God's support for king and
people (1K 8:23), and (with a reference to the cherubim) Hezekiah's
prayer that God save Israel from Sennacherib (2K 19:15). It is used
(within a longer prayer) in requesting that God keep the promise to
maintain the Davidic dynasty in 1K 8:25, as is the shorter form
"Yahweh God" (יהוה אֱלֹהִים) in 2S 7:25. The form "Yahweh of
Hosts, God of Israel" (יהוה צְבָאוֹת אֱלֹהֵי יִשְׂרָאֵל) is used by David in
2S 7:27, in the peroration of his prayer, to introduce reference to
God's promise that he will found a dynasty. It is followed by "(my)
Lord Yahweh" (אֲדֹנָי יהוה, 2S 7:28) introducing his final plea for
God's blessing and maintenance of the promise. The form "Yahweh
my God" (יהוה אֱלֹהַי), using the first person pronoun to remind the
addressee of the speaker's devotion (see §15.6.1) is used by Solomon
to introduce his request for wisdom to rule his people (1K 3:7), and
in asking that his prayer for the people be heard (1K 8:28). It is also
used by Elijah in his complaint about God's treatment of his host-
ess in 1K 17:20, and in the following request that her son be revived, that is, in making a personal appeal on a topic which does
not concern himself alone. King Hezekiah uses "Yahweh our God"
(יהוה אֱלֹהֵינוּ), evoking God's relationship to the community, in the
same way in 2K 19:19, in a prayer in which he himself is not mentioned.

15.7.5 "Yahweh of hosts" is used as a vocative by Hannah in her prayer for a child (1S 1:11), and, with the addition "God of Israel" by David, in expressing thanks as part of the introduction to his final request for God's blessing on his dynasty (2S 7:27). As elsewhere, the particular significance of the term "hosts" is obscure. The other examples suggest that, when God is addressed, the form of designation used as a vocative is chosen to suit the contents of the speech, and, in some cases, to show the attitude of the speaker. Similar care in the choice and use of terms of address is shown in speech between humans (see §25).

15.8 Conclusion

15.8.1 It is reasonable to argue that compound designations of God, including designations using the word "hosts" (צבאות), are used to draw attention to, and so give prominence to, the clause in which they are used, as are compound designations generally. They are not used to draw attention to appearance in a new context, as compound designations of humans often are. This is presumably because mention of God is so significant for the narrative, and so frequent in it, that there is only need to highlight particularly significant examples, not to the renewal of such mention after a lapse (see §4.13.1). The designation "(My) lord Yahweh" and "Yahweh my God", used in address, both appeal to a personal relationship with God. It is reasonable to argue that they are used distinctly, the first where the concern of the speech is mainly personal, the second where it is not, but the available evidence is too meagre to establish this. It appears that the title "God" is used as a simple designation with connotations different from those of the name in some situations, but this is not clear for all cases.

15.8.2 The use of "(my) lord" (אדני), alone, or in combination with the name "Yahweh", shows that the two were used distinctly as terms of address. It seems clear that, a part of the motivation for the use of "(my) lord" in this way was the desire to use the first person pronoun incorporated in the form to recall the speaker's close relationship to God. This may also be true where the term is used in spoken reference (1K 2:26, 2K 19:23). It is unlikely to be the case where "(my) lord" is used by the narrator, since the examples (1K 3:10, 15, 2K 7:6), do not suggest any reason for self reference of this sort. Compare his use of the first person plural pronoun in "Yahweh our God" in 1K 8:65, which can be seen as relating any reader immediately to this unique celebration of the festival. It seems likely, then, that the use of "(my) lord" (אֲדֹנָי) originated as a term of address, but gradually widened until it became the preferred simple designation of God in all situations. The uses of the term in narration presumably reflect that development. Similar shifts in the usual ways of designating God could account for the use of "hosts". It is easy to believe that this term was valued for its ancient associations, and so was retained, even though it played no part in the active usage of the narrator's time, and so had no specific value. The same may be true for some cases of the use of "God" as a simple designation. Apart from these exceptional cases, a small proportion of the total, it seems to me reasonable to argue that the designations of God in the corpus result from deliberate and meaningful choice, as do those of humans.

15.8.3 In general, then, one can say, for other characters as for rulers, that a more specific designation draws greater attention, and so gives greater prominence to the context of its use. The addition of "hosts" to designations of God can be seen in this light. Like the addition of epithets elsewhere, it increases the specificity of the designation concerned, and so highlights it. Conversely, "God" (אלהים) is less specific than "Yahweh", and so makes a more distanced reference when used as a simple designation, consistent with the values suggested above for those cases where the two seem to be used distinctly. Similarly, relationship terms, or social category terms, provide designations for humans less specific than a name. Such more distanced reference is used where the character in question is not thematic, or where prominence is not required for other reasons. The designation of unnamed characters reflects the same general principles which govern the designation of others. They are typically represented by a designation reflecting their role in the context, and so by the most specific designation available, corresponding to the name used as the common designation of a named character.

IV THE LOGIC OF CONCORD

Concord with Collective Nouns

16.1 Introduction

16.1.1 The term "collective" is used here in the limited sense of a noun which may have singular or plural coreferents, and which denotes (a group of) humans. Since such nouns typically do not designate individual humans, they could be considered outside the scope of this study. They are included because the variation in number in coreferents of collectives provides important support for the general interpretation of the way such variation is used in the language. The choice of number in coreferents of collectives is not determined grammatically, by the singular form of the noun, since plural coreferents are common (see §3.3). It is widely assumed that the use of the plural indicates that the narrator was thinking of the referent of the collective as a collection of individuals. However, it cannot be shown that the use of the plural is characteristic where the collective is represented as performing actions of particular kinds, as would be expected if this were the case. There is, however, a correlation between the choice of number and the function of the clause in question in its context. If the clause presents an important feature of the intended communication, the verb is plural. The pattern shown is too consistent to be regarded as the result of chance. The choice of number in the coreferents of collectives is expressive.

16.1.2 The conditioning of the choice of number in the coreferents of collectives was described at length in Revell 1993b. The singular must be regarded as default usage where the collective is subject of a verb, and in some other situations. The contrasting use of the plural marks the communication as immediate, in that the material presented is important to the purposes of the narrator, or central to the concerns of the speaker. As a result, the use of the singular shows that the material is "non-immediate": not unusually important or central. This usage is illustrated here by description of the choice of number in *waw* consecutive imperfect verbs with collective subjects.[1] Such verbs mark their clauses as "foreground" in terms of the grammatical structure used to present the narrative (see Longacre, 1989:81). The choice of number in the verb is able to indicate their value in the narrative more precisely. The verb is singular in 80 cases, plural in 63.

16.2 *Waw* Consecutive Imperfects with Collective Subject

16.2.1 The verb is singular Where a *waw* consecutive imperfect with a collective subject is singular, the clause is often introductory. It presents an action preliminary to more significant events presented in subsequent clauses, as in "The people of the land took (s) Jehoahaz... and anointed (p) him and made (p) him king" (ויקח עם הארץ את יהואחז... וימשחו אתו וימליכו אתו..., 2K 23:30). Other cases occur in Ju 7:23, 24, 1S 4:1, 4, etc. The same introductory function can be seen where the nominal subject is repeated in the following clause, as "All the people feared (s) the Lord and Samuel very much, and all the people said (p) to Samuel... (ויירא כל העם מאד את יהוה ואת שמואל ויאמרו כל העם אל שמואל..., 1S 12:18-19). Also, where the second clause has a nominal subject different from that of the first, but apparently with the same referent, as in "All the people heard (s) the news "Zimri has conspired... and all Israel made (p) Omri king..." (וישמע העם... לאמר קשר זמרי... וימלכו כל ישראל את עמרי), 1K 16:16).[2] Verbs of speech or perception have a similar introductory use where what is said or perceived is presented as motivation for following action, as "The people said (s) to Saul 'Shall Jonathan die...' and the people ransomed (p) Jonathan." (ויאמר העם אל שאול היונתן ימות... ויפדו העם את יונתן, 1S 14:45); "All Israel saw (s) that the king had not listened to them, and the people responded (p) to the

---

[1]   Revell 1993b uses different material to illustrate the usage. Judges chapters 1, 11:13-22, and 20, in which there is an unusual tendency to treat collectives as singular, are excluded from the present survey. The preference for the singular in these passages is not confined to coreferents of collectives, but extends to the use of the singular designations of tribes etc. where plural designations are available (see Revell 1993b, §9.4). This preference for the singular is presumed to reflect the detached attitude to the presentation of history taken in these passages, as argued there.

[2]   Another case occurs in 1K 12:16. A similar phenomenon occurs where the plural phrase "b. Israel" (בני ישראל) is used with the same referent as a collective, as in Ju 6:6.

king…" (…וישבו העם), ‏1K 12:16‏, ‏וירא כל ישראל כי לא שמע המלך אליהם
cf. 1K 16:16 quoted above). Other verbs of speaking are similarly
singular where the speech has a similar motivating function, or has
little significance for the following narrative, in 1S 10:11, 17:25, 27,
2S 18:3, 19:43, 44. In all, about half of the examples of a singular
waw consecutive imperfect with a collective subject occur in introductory clauses of these sorts.

16.2.2 In such cases the clause with a collective subject and singular
verb presents material which is "non-immediate": "background" in
terms of the events of the narrative, as opposed to the structures
used to present them.[3] The same is true for the remaining uses of
a *waw* consecutive imperfect in the singular with a collective subject. The subject is typically not the focus of the narrator's attention in the context, as in "Israel was thrown back (s) before the
Philistines" (וינגף ישראל לפני פלשתים, ‏1S 4:2‏). The preceding and
following verbs here have as subject "the Philistines", the thematic
actor in the context. Other examples occur in Ju 8:28, 1S 3:20, 13:8,
2S 19:40, 1K 20:20, 2K 11:20, 14:12, etc. The incident presented is
sometimes not even connected with the action described in the preceding and following clauses, as "A Philistine garrison advanced (s)
to the pass at Michmash" (ויצא מצב פלשתים אל מעבר מכמש, ‏1S 13:23‏).
The preceding verse deals with the lack of weapons in Israel; the
following begins the story of an exploit of Jonathan's. Other examples occur in 2S 19:9, 2K 1:1, 8:22). A clause with a singular verb
may be used to present descriptive detail, as "The people saw (s),
and behold sackcloth…" (…וירא העם והנה השק), ‏2K 6:30‏). Other examples occur in Ju 4:10, 1S 14:28, 2S 19:4. A singular verb is used
in a variety of other situations where the clause adds incidental detail. A verb with a collective subject is also singular where the agent
has an insignificant role in the ongoing narrative, as in "The Kenite
moved out (s) from Amalek" (ויסר קיני מתוך עמלק, ‏1S 15:6‏); the Ke-
nites are not mentioned again in the chapter. A clause which termi-
nates a section of narrative is similarly likely to be singular, as "All
the people went away (s), each to his house" (וילך כל העם איש לביתו,
2S 6:19). Other examples occur in 2S 19:9, 1K 12:16, 2K 23:3. Simi-

---

[3]   On the relation of the use of collective or plural designations to immediacy,
see Revell, 1993b, §2, §3.

lar usage is found in accounts of those fallen in battle (ויפל, Ju 4:16, 12:6, 1S 4:10, 2S 11:17); in statements that foreign nations have been subdued (Ju 3:30, 2S 8:2, 6, 14), and even where a momentous event previously chronicled is recalled in the course of treatment of a different aspect of the situation in 2K 25:21.

16.2.3 *The verb is plural* Where a *waw* consecutive imperfect with a collective subject is plural, the subject of the clause typically has a significant relationship with what precedes, that is, it is the focus of the narrator's attention, or at least an important participant in the context. The verb of a clause following an introductory clause is typically plural, as in the examples given in §16.2.1; others occur in Ju 2:4, 11:11, 1S 13:20, 2S 18:7, 1K 12:16, 2K 3:22, 7:17, 20, 25:5. The verb is also typically plural where the subject is shown as responding to speech or action, as "Samuel said to the people 'Go...' and all the people went (p)..." (ויאמר שמואל אל העם לכו... וילכו כל העם), 1S 11:14-15); "Joab blew the trumpet, and all the people stopped (p)" (ויתקע יואב בשופר ויעמדו כל העם, 2S 2:28); "They (Moab) came to the camp of Israel and Israel rose up (p)..." (ויבאו אל מחנה ישראל... ויקמו ישראל, 2K 3:24).[4] The plural is occasionally used to present an isolated incident which is of particular importance in its context, as "Israel rebelled (p) against the house of David" (ויפשעו ישראל בבית דוד עד היום הזה, 1K 12:19). This incident is clearly more significant in the narrative than those presented with the same verb in the singular in 2K 1:1, 8:22.[5] The plural can similarly be accepted as marking the significance of the event, that is, as marking the clause as immediate, where a verb introduces speech or perception which is important for the events described in the context, as in "All Israel heard (p) ... (...וישמעו כל ישראל, 1K 3:28). Here the verb introduces the people's perception of Solomon's wisdom, showing

---

[4]   Other examples occur in Ju 9:49, 15:10, 16:24, 18:11, 1S 4:4, 10:24, 11:4, 15, 12:19, 13:4, 14:34, 40, 45, 17:30, 25:1, 13, 28:3, 31:12, 2S 2:28, 10:17, 1K 3:28, 12:5, 14:18, 18:30, 2K 3:24.

[5]   Other examples occur in 1S 10:26, 22:2; also 1S 7:2, assuming that the verb וינהו indicates wholehearted return to God, as is consistent with most translations, whether they are based on the received Hebrew (where the verb is of uncertain meaning) or on the corresponding Greek, as McCarter, 1980:141 "turned after".

that the promise made by God in 1K 3:12 has been fulfilled. Other examples occur in Ju 8:1, 22, 10:18, 15:10.

16.2.4 It cannot be argued that the situations in which the verb is plural are always clearly distinct from those in which it is singular. The general pattern of use is quite clear, however, and is usually visible even in cases of apparent conflict. Thus, where the verb "was thrown back" (וינגף) is used in the singular in 1S 4:2, it describes a reverse which motivated Israel's decision to bring the ark into their camp, but plays no other part in the narrative (see §16.2.2). In 2S 18:7, where the same verb is used in the plural, the reverse is of much greater significance. It results immediately in the death of Absalom, and eventually in the restoration of David to his throne. Similarly, "Joab blew the trumpet, and the people returned (s)... (ויתקע יואב בשופר וישב העם, 2S 18:16), where the second verb is singular, occurs where the narrative is focussed on the fate of Absalom and its repercussions. The fact that the fighting is stopped is here of little consequence. In 2S 2:28 (quoted in §16.2.3), where the reaction to a trumpet signal is presented by plural verbs with a collective subject, the cessation of hostilities is central to the narrative (as argued in Revell, 1993b, §5.6). Similarly, the statement that Aram feared (p) to help the b. Ammon any more (2S 10:19) is of greater importance than most terminal statements, since this defeat allows David to remain in Jerusalem, and so to encounter Bathsheba. There are, of course, a few cases in which it is difficult to suggest any reason for the choice of a plural verb as in Ju 9:55, 2S 3:32, 34, 2K 11:18.

16.3 Clauses with Participial Predicates

16.3.1 *The predicate is adjectival* Similar arguments can be made about the choice of number in clauses in which the subject is collective, and the predicate is headed by a participle or adjective. These present "background" in terms of the grammatical structure, but their content may be of considerable significance for the narrative (cf. the function of the "detached participial clause" in English, described in Thompson, 1983). The singular is used in a clause of this sort where the predicate is adjectival, as "My clan is the poorest" (אלפי הדל, Ju 6:15). Other examples occur in Ju 7:4, 2S 17:29. The plural does not occur in this category.

16.3.2 *The clause presents a perception* Where the clause presents the perception of a character, the predicate is singular where the person who makes the perception is shown as reacting to it, so the narrator treats only one person as involved; as "He looked and the people was coming out (s) of the city and he attacked them and struck them down" (וירא והנה העם יצא מן העיר ויקם עליהם ויכם, Ju 9:43). Other examples occur in 2K 6:15, 11:14. The predicate is plural where the perception affects others in "The lookout lifted his eyes and looked and a large people were travelling (p) ... and Jonadab said to the king..." (וישא הנער הצפה את עיניו וירא והנה עם רב הלכים... ויאמר יונדב אל המלך..., 2S 13:34). Here the phenomenon perceived does not simply motivate action, it takes a place among the events of the narrative, evoking a comment from someone other than the person who perceived it.

16.3.3 *The clause is introductory* Where the clause presents introductory background, a singular predicate can be interpreted as representing a state of affairs, as "The tribe of Dan was seeking (s) a territory to settle" (שבט הדני מבקש לו נחלה לשבת, Ju 18:1). This provides a setting; the following narrative begins with a plural designation of the same group, "The b. Dan sent (p) ..." (וישלחו בני דן..., Ju 18:2). A singular predicate is also used in this way in introductory material, where the following clause has a different subject, in Ju 21:15, 2S 23:13, 1K 22:19 (the last example occurs in a narrative spoken by a character). Where a plural predicate is used in a situation which could be described as introductory, the subject of the participial clause is antecedent of the pronominal subject of a following *waw* consecutive imperfect, as in "Beth-shemesh were harvesting (p) ... and they looked up... (ובית שמש קצרים... וישאו את עיניהם..., 1S 6:13). Another example occurs in 2S 19:42. Such usage can be seen as signalling that the event so introduced is significant.

16.3.4 *Other situations* Most of the remaining clauses with participial predicate present ancillary detail within the narrative. The predicate is nearly always plural. A singular predicate can again be seen as presenting a state of affairs; the subject of the clause typically plays no part in the narrative in the context. Thus in 1K 8:14, "The whole congregation of Israel was standing (s)" (וכל קהל ישראל עמד) pictures the congregation as part of the scene at the ceremony; the actions of the congregation are not described in the immediate context; the narrator concentrates on the king.[6] In 1S 17:3, "Israel were standing (p) on the hill on one hand" (וישׂראל עמדים אל ההר מזה) represents one of two opposing forces. Their reaction (1S 17:11, 24) to the challenge issued by the representative of the other force (Goliath) is important in the narrative as a contrast to David's actions. In addition to cases of this sort in narrative, a plural predicate is usual where the clause occurs as part of the intended communication in direct speech (as opposed to its background use in the spoken narrative in 1K 22:19). Thus the predicate is plural in "For there are (p) Aram camped" (כי שׁם ארם נחתים, 2K 6:9). Other examples occur in 1S 29:1, 2S 3:1.

16.3.5 As in other cases, the distinction between the situations in which singular and plural are characteristically used is not clear cut, but the value of the plural in marking immediacy in the narrative is usually evident. In 1S 26:5, before he sets out to reach Saul, David sees that "The people were camped (p) around him (Saul)..." (והעם חנים סביבתיו). This adds suspense to the presentation of his dangerous undertaking (on the hazards implied, see §13.3.5). The danger is mentioned again in v. 7, and David's return unharmed is shown to be due to God's care (v. 12), In Ju 16:9, 12, "The ambush was sitting (s) for her ..." (...והארב ישׁב לה) the clause is related to Delilah's intentions (hence "for her", i.e. "She had an ambush sitting") rather than to Samson's danger. Samson is not shown to be aware of the ambush, so this danger (which is only mentioned once in connection with each of two separate events) has a much less significant part in the story than that faced by David.

16.4 Coreferents of Collective Subjects

A pronoun coreferent with a collective subject is typically plural where the head of the predicate is plural. A singular pronoun used in this situation has distributive value, as "All that generation were gathered (p) to his (s) fathers", i.e. "each to his fathers" (וגם כל

---

[6]   Other examples with singular predicates occur in Ju 16:9, 12, 20:33; also 2S 15:12. This last example contrasts with the use of the plural in 2S 3:1, but there the fortunes of the House of Saul are treated in what follows (from 1S 3:6, after a digression).

הדור ההוא נאספו אל אבותיו, Ju 2:10).[7] Where the head of a predicate
is singular, a pronoun coreferent with the collective subject in that
clause, or in a clause subordinate to it, is usually singular, as in "If
only the people had today eaten (s) of the spoil of its (s) enemies
which it (s) found" (לוא אכל אכל היום העם משלל איביו אשר מצא...,
1S 14:30. A plural coreferent is sometimes used in a subordinate
clause. Probably such cases are to be taken as contrasting with the
expected use of the singular, and so as indication of immediacy, as
in Ju 20:39, where "For they said (p) ..." (כי אמרו...) presents the
thinking which brought disaster on Benjamin (see Revell, 1993b,
§7.3). Coreferent pronouns in clauses other than that in which the
collective stands (or those subordinate to it) are typically plural.
This includes pronouns in direct speech coreferent with a collective
in the narrative introduction.

16.5 Conclusion

16.5.1 It can, then, be said that, where a collective noun acts as subject, the choice of number in the head of the predicate adds a further dimension to the grammatical marking of "foreground" and
"background" by indicating the relative significance of the events
presented by the clause in the narrative context, independent of
their presentation "on" or "off" the "narrative line". In speech, the
concerns of the speaker provide the equivalent of a narrative line.
This superficial description obviously overlooks a variety of examples which can be interpreted as conflicting with it. However, I believe that the description is sufficiently firmly based on formal features that the standard pattern must be held to be clear, and that
the interpretation of that pattern offered is at least more probable
than the alternative view that such a high proportion of consistency
in usage results from chance. The basic contribution of this survey
of number in the coreferents of collectives is to demonstrate that
where circumstances permit, the choice of number is used expressively; it reflects the attitude of the speaker or narrator to the structure in question. The choice of the plural marks the clause in question as immediate — central to the purpose of the communication

---

[7]   Other examples are listed in Revell 1993b, §§7.2, 8.5; cf. Levi, 1987:34-37.

being made. The choice of the singular marks it as non-immediate — having no unusual importance.

16.5.2 The correlation between number and immediacy most common with collectives differs from that common with other nominals, such as compounds, where plural is the most common choice in most situations (since a compound necessarily designates more than one person), so that the choice of singular is expressive. This underlines the point that expressive meaning is not conveyed by some particular feature, but by a contrast with expected usage (see §1.5.2). In the same way, the choice of plural coreferents for collectives is marked, and so expressive, where the collective is subject of a *waw* consecutive imperfect, but the choice of singular is marked and expressive in a clause with a participial predicate used to present ancillary detail within a narrative, since the usual choice there is plural. Beyond these general principles, the information derived from the study of coreferents of collectives makes a valuable contribution to the understanding of the phenomenon here called "immediacy". It provides specific examples which can be related to the use of other features studied here, such as the marking of introductory clauses as non-immediate or of particular incidental clause as immediate (see §28.5.1), and so helps to build up a detailed description of what was felt as immediate in narrative or speech.

Concord with Compound Nominals

17.1 Introduction

Where a compound nominal which has a singular component acts as subject, the verb (or other head of the predicate) may be singular or plural. There is a general correlation between the choice of number and the position of the subject relative to the verb. A verb which precedes its subject is usually singular; a verb which follows is usually plural. However, the evidence in the corpus does not show that this factor, either alone or in association with other grammatical factors, actually determines the choice of number. The position of a compound subject relative to its verb is determined by the same factors as govern the positions of subjects of other sorts: the need to mark the clause as (grammatically) foreground, or to highlight the subject. The choice of number in a verb with a compound subject is determined by the need to mark the singular component as focus of attention (typically as thematic actor), or the lack of such need, as described in Revell, 1993, which covers all examples in the corpus.

17.2 Number in a Verb with a Compound Subject

17.2.1 A singular component typically stands first in a compound nominal denoting humans which contains one or more such components. This initial component is the "principal" of the compound, it designates the leader or superior among those represented by the compound (Revell, 1993, §5-6). The choice of a singular verb recognizes the status of the singular component (already marked by the structure of the compound) as principal, as representing the most important actor in the context (see Revell, 1993, §9-11). In "Samson and his father and mother went (s)" (וירד שמשון ואביו ואמו, Ju 14:5), Samson, the hero of the story, is thematic actor, as is Jonathan in "Which Jonathan and his armour-bearer struck (s)" (אשר הכה יונתן ונשא כליו, 1S 14:14). In "the one whom the Lord and this people and every man of Israel chose (s)" (אשר בחר יהוה והעם הזה וכל איש ישראל, 2S 16:18), the Lord is obviously the most important actor.

In "Joab and Abishai his brother pursued (s) after Sheba b. Bichri"
(ויואב ואבשי אחיו רדף אחרי שבע בן בכרי, 2S 20:10), the clause effects
a transition from a passage describing the way Joab dealt with a
rival to one describing how the army was won over to him so he
was able to deal with Sheba. The use of the singular verb continues
the narrator's focus on Joab. The argument that the verb shows
concord specifically with the principal can be strengthened by the
observation (overlooked in Revell, 1993) that, where the initial
component of the compound is feminine singular, a singular verb is
also feminine, as in "Deborah and Barak b. Abinoam sang..." (ותשר
דבורה וברק בן אבינעם..., Ju 5:1. Other examples occur in 1K 10:13,
17:15 (qere), 2K 8:2, and (in speech) 2K 4:7. A full discussion of the
phenomenon is provided in Ratner, 1990.

17.2.2 Where a clause has a compound subject with a plural verb,
the status of the singular component of the compound as principal
is ignored. Such a clause may be used where the compound subject
does not include the thematic actor in the context. In Ju 8:12, "Zebah and Zalmunna fled (p)" (וינוסו זבח וצלמנע) is used in a context
which deals with Gideon's actions. In 2S 2:24, "Joab and Abishai
pursued (p) Abner" (וירדפו יואב ואבישי אחרי אבנר) occurs where
Abner is the focus of attention. In 1K 1:45, "Zadok the priest and
Nathan the prophet anointed (p) him" (וימשחו אתו צדוק הכהן ונתן
הנביא) occurs in a speech reporting the recent transfer of kingship
from David to Solomon. The individual actors are not important in
this context, as they are in the narrator's description of the events
as they occurred (cf. 1K 1:34, 38, 39). The plural verb precedes the
subject in the cases just described. Similar examples occur where the
verb follows the subject, in 1K 1:8, 2K 12:22, 19:37, etc.

17.2.3 A compound subject may also have a plural verb where the
clause ends a unit, so the status of the principal is not relevant what
follows. In 1K 8:63 "The king and all the people of Israel inaugurated (p) the temple" (ויחנכו את בית יהוה המלך וכל בני ישראל) termin-
ates the description of the main ceremony before other details are

recounted.[1] In 2K 3:12 "The king of Israel and Jehoshaphat and the king of Edom came down (p) to him" (וירדו אליו מלך ישראל ויהושפט ומלך אדום) ends a description of the actions of the kings, and moves to those of Elisha. The the verb precedes the subject in these cases. Similar examples occur where the verb follows the subject in 1S 24:23, 2S 3:30, 13:36, etc.

17.2.4 A compound subject may have a plural verb where the characters represented by the compound share equal responsibility for the action. In "The holy gifts which Jehoshaphat, Jehoram, and Ahaziah, his fathers... had dedicated (p)" (הקדשים אשר הקדישו יהושפט ויהורם ואחזיהו אבתיו..., 2K 12:19) no one of the three kings is thematic actor. In the case of "They confronted each other (p), he and Amaziah" (ויתראו פנים הוא ואמציהו, 2K 14:11), the context deals with both equally. In 1S 22:13, "Why did you league (p) against me, you and b. Yishai" (למה קשרתם עלי אתה ובן ישי), the use of the plural shows the two conspirators as equally involved. The verb precedes the subject in the above examples. Similar ones occur where the verb follows the subject, as in 1S 14:40, 31:7, 2S 19:30, etc.

17.2.5 Where a singular verb precedes the subject, or a plural verb follows it, the choice of number is unmarked, and its significance, considered alone, cannot be great. However, the choice of number does confirm, and so add to, the significance of other features. A singular verb preceding a compound subject confirms the status of the singular component as principal, as marked by the typical structure of a compound. A plural verb following a compound subject confirms that the subject does not play a part in the main line of the following narrative, as is suggested by the structure of the clause. Where a singular verb follows the subject, or a plural verb precedes it, the choice of number has clear independent significance, as can be seen in the examples above. In a few cases the same sub-

---

[1]   The V–O–S order of the Hebrew is an example of the use of unusual structures in terminal situations, seen in the use of chiastic structures, or other variations in word order, at the end of envelope structures (as in 2K 5:18, 19:32-3) or other literary units (as in 1S 24:3), see Mirsky, 1977. The order in 1K 8:63 also draws attention to the compound through the use of "end focus", as is also done for the subject (the new judge) in Ju 12:8, 11, 13.

ject is used with both numbers in different clauses, giving a clear idea of the way the contrasting value was used, as described in Revell, 1993, §18-20.

17.3 Coreferents of a Compound in Following Clauses

17.3.1 Pronouns in following clauses coreferent with a compound subject are usually plural; in fact this is so common that it is sometimes presented as the norm.[2] Compounds which do not act as subject are likewise typically treated as plural, so that it is safe to say that plural is the standard or "unmarked" number for coreferents of a compound nominal. The commonness of singular verbs with compound subject (some 85% of the total in the corpus) reflects the strong tendency of the narrator or speaker to concentrate on the thematic actor in any situation. This concentration on the thematic actor is sometimes continued by the use of singular coreferents in following clauses, as "She went, she and her companions, and she wept..." (...ותלך היא ורעותיה ותבך, Ju 11:38); "David and his men went (s) to Keilah, and he fought... he drove away... he defeated..." (...וילך דוד ואנשיו קעילה וילחם... וינהג... ויך), qere 1S 23:5); "Jehu and Jonadab b. Rechab came (s) to the temple of Baal, and he said..." (...ויבא יהוא ויהונדב בן רכב בית הבעל ויאמר), 2K 10:23). Similar examples occur in Ju 12:2, 1S 18:27, 2S 16:14, 2K 5:15, 8:2.

17.3.2 As these examples show, actions presented in this way with singular coreferent pronouns may be performed by the thematic actor alone (as is probable in 2K 10:23), or by the whole group (as is certain in 1S 23:5, probable in Ju 11:38). The choice of singular is not determined by the number of actors, but by the significance of the action in the context in terms of the narrator's treatment of the thematic actor. The choice of singular thus marks the clause as significant in the narrative, as immediate. This significance is usually directly related to the place in the narrative of the individual represented by the singular pronoun, but this is not necessarily the case. The singular is occasionally used in this way even where the part played by the principal of the compound (as distinct from the adjunct) is irrelevant. Thus in Ju 8:21 "Zebah and Zalmunna said (s)

---

[2]   GKC §146h. Levi, 1987:52-3, sensibly qualifies this view.

..." (ויאמר זבח וצלמנע...) the compound has a singular verb where the action (speech) motivates the following events in the narrative. The contrasting use of the plural in Ju 8:12 "Zebah and Zalmunna fled (p) " (וינוסו זבח וצלמנע...), shows the typical situation. Here the information is merely introductory to the description of their capture by Gideon, the thematic character, which could have been satisfactorily presented without the information that they fled.

17.3.3 In the first and second person, the relation between the use of singular coreferents and significance in the context — immediacy — is equally clear. Where the first person singular pronoun is used as a component of a compound, it is always the first component, and following coreferents are typically singular, as in Ju 12:2-3: "I had a serious quarrel, I and my people, with the Bene Ammon, and I called... but you did not help me... and I saw,... I placed... and I went against the Bene Ammon" (אשי ריב הייתי אני ועמי ובני עמון מאד) (ואזעק... ולא הושעתם אתי... ואראה... ואשימה... ואעברה...). The second person singular pronoun is always the first component of the compound unless the first person is included in it, and following coreferents are typically singular, as in 2S 9:10: "You (s) will work the land for him, you and your sons and your servants, and you (s) will deliver (the produce)... (ועבדת לו את האדמה אתה ובניך ועבדיך והבאת).[3] A plural verb may be used to show that principal and adjunct participated equally in the action, while following designations treat them separately, as in "the word which we spoke, I and you" (הדבר אשר דברנו אני ואתה, 1S 20:23; "Why did you conspire against me, you and b. Jesse?" (למה קשרתם עלי אתה ובן ישי), 1S 22:13). First person plural coreferents occur where the compound is not subject, in 1K 17:12 (where the speaker and her son are equally involved in the action), and in 2K 22:13 (where the speaker presents himself as a

---

[3]   Examples with plural coreferents are noted in §19.2.3n. The fact that, with compound subjects, the lower number (of 1st, 2nd, or 3rd person) always prevails in verb agreement is given as a universal in Moravcsik, 1988:101. Other examples occur with the first person in Ju 20:4-6, 1K 1:21, with the second in Ju 7:10-11, 8:22, 2K 8:1. A singular pronoun in this situation may refer to the speaker alone, but some clearly do not, as in the two examples quoted. The singular first person verb has a plural complement in 1K 1:21, so that both the immediacy for the speaker, and the equal participation of her son (represented by the other component of the compound) in the action are marked.

member of the community). The predominance of the singular merely reflects the fact a speaker typically regards his own actions as of prime concern, and those of the addressee as of greater concern than those of others.

17.4 Other Cases where the Narrative Concerns a Group

17.4.1 A singular coreferent may be used with the same function, the marking of immediacy, where any group is described. In Ju 4:7, the narrator uses a singular coreferent to maintain focus on an individual even where the compound in which he is named is not subject: "I will drag towards you... Sisera... and his chariotry and his multitude, and I will give him into your hand" (את...אליך ומשכתי סיסרא... ואת רכבו ואת המונו ונתתיהו בידך). Sisera is the enemy commander in chief, whose defeat and death is the main event described in the chapter. The same phenomenon may occur where no formal compound is used, as in "Gehazi went on before them (Elisha and the Shunammite)... and he returned to meet him (Elisha, the thematic actor)" (...לקראתו וישב ...לפניהם עבר ונחזי, 2K 4:31). A similar example of the use of a singular pronoun to focus on an individual occurs in "'Send towards them...' He went... towards him... The lookout announced 'The messenger has come up to them...'" (וישלח 2K 9:17 ,לקראתם... וילך... לקראתו... ויגד הצפה לאמר בא המלאך עד הם 18-). Here the plural pronouns reflects the viewpoint of the king and his lookout, who are aware only that a group of people (2K 9:17) is approaching.[4] The singular pronoun "him" reflects the viewpoint of the narrator, and represents Jehu, who is thematic actor in the context.[5]

17.4.2 This sort of variation in number can thus be used to focus on the thematic actor in any situation in which he is involved with others. The most striking example of this in the corpus occurs in Judges chapter 19, which presents an event, the rape and murder of

---

[4]   The collective is treated as plural because it is of immediate importance to the speakers, see §16.5.
[5]   Gender is involved in this maintenance of focus in the same way in 2S 4:4 and 2K 4:37, where the woman in question is the principal actor, so the use of pronouns takes no account of the child with her. The case is the same in Gen 21:14, quoted in Ratner, 1990:242.

a woman, which will give rise to the war described in the following chapter. The thematic character is a levite, husband of the woman (see §14.2.1). His actions form the central chain of events in the chapter, to which the actions of others are related. Actions presented by singular verbs, of which he is the subject, but often not the only actor, present those events which form this central chain. Plural verbs, of which the subject is a group composed of the levite and his wife and/or his servant (who are travelling with him), and the party's current host, present the less important actions in which the levite is involved.[6]

17.4.3 In verses 4-10, the levite and his wife and servant are staying with his wife's father. In verse 4, the levite accepts his father-in-law's invitation to stay ("he stayed", וישב). Plural verbs describe events up to the rising of the party next morning ("they ate, drank, spent the night, rose early", ...וישכימו ...וילינו וישתו ויאכלו, v.4-5). At this point, the levite sets out to go ("he got up", ויקם, v.5). His father-in-law invites him to refresh himself, and this is described in the plural ("They sat, ate, drank", וישתו ...ויאכלו וישבו, v. 6).[7] Despite another invitation to stay, the levite decides to go ("he got up... to go" ללכת ...ויקם, v. 7), but, under further pressure, he spends the night again ("He returned and spent the night", וילן וישב, v. 7). In the morning, he again sets out to go ("He rose... to go", וישכם... ללכת, v. 8), but again accepts an invitation to refresh himself ("They ate", ויאכלו, v.8). Finally, he sets out again ("he got up... to go", ללכת ...ויקם, v.9) The verb here is again singular but it has a compound nominal as its subject, naming the whole travelling party "He and his wife and his servant". His father-in-law again attempts to delay him, but this time he persists ("He was unwilling... and he got up and went and arrived...", ...ויבא וילך ויקם ...אבה ולא, v.10). The singular verbs thus show the levite as anxious to leave, but repeatedly putting it off to please his father-in-law. Under the strain of the competing priorities, he finally leaves at a time so late that travelling is dangerous.

---

[6]   It is not always clear which of the four possible characters are represented by the subject of the plural verbs, and, for present purposes, not relevant.

[7]   The father-in-law's speech shows variation in number in the second person similar to that in the narrative, with the same function. See §19.2.3.

17.4.4 In verses 11-14, after a discussion of where to spend the night, the group travels on, and turns in to Gibeah at sunset ("They travelled on, went... turned aside, ויעברו וילכו... ויסורו, v. 14-15). The plural verbs show that this is preliminary to the next significant action, entering the square to sit in expectation of an offer of hospitality, which is presented with singular verbs ("He came and sat", ויבא וישב, v. 15. There is no nominal subject). The group is eventually invited in.[8] Their initial enjoyment of the hospitality is described with plural verbs ("They washed... ate, drank, were enjoying themselves", וירחצו... ויאכלו וישתו המה מיטיבים את לבם, v. 21-22), but the house is attacked. The levite's response to this, which precipitates the tragedy which is the peak of the narrative, is naturally presented in the singular, as he is the only actor. This is not true for the action presented with singular verbs in v.15, however. There, as with the singular verbs in verses 4-10, the singular is chosen to focus on the levite as principal of the group. The reason that the verbs in question are singled out for such focus is that they present the significant chain of events in the narrative, and the choice of singular where plural could be used draws attention to this fact.[9]

17.5. Other Uses of Number

17.5.1 *Unspecified or indefinite subjects* Where the performer of an action is not identified, the action may be presented in any of three ways. Most commonly the third person plural is used, implying action by a group, "they". The context of such usage generally provides some idea of the group in question: the community in "they gave" (ויתנו, Ju 1:20), priests or their assistants in "they used" (ישרתו, 2K 25:14), but this is not always the case, as with "they informed" (ויגידו, 1K 2:39). There are some 130 examples in the corpus. Third person singular appears to be used in the same way, but this is

---

[8]   The host uses only second person singular in address, v. 17, 20. Number in the first person is characteristically varied in the levite's reply, v.18-19, see §18.2.3.

[9]   It is no doubt also true, as argued in Revell 1993, §26, that the singular reflects the authority of the levite acting as leader, while the plural is used for actions in which his involvement is not important, but the less specific description of meaning given here seems to me superior.

common only with forms of אמר "say" and קרא "call".[10] There are some 30 examples in which a singular verb could have an unspecified subject, but in about a third of these there is a possible antecedent in the context, as with ויקרא in Ju 15:17, קרא in Ju 15:19. In the other examples the verb does seem to be used indefinitely, the singular implying a single actor, as "someone called" (ויקרא, Ju 6:32), as "someone said" (ואמר, 1S 23:22, 24:11). The passive is used in a similar way only with the verb "to inform", as in "It was told to Abimelek, i.e. Abimelek was informed" (ויגד לאבימלך, Ju 9:25, 47). In these cases Abimelek has not involved himself in the affairs of those about whom he is informed. Where the plural is used in "They informed Abimelek" (ויגידו לאבימלך, Ju 9:42), he has. This seems to be the general basis of the choice of the passive in the 15 cases in which it is used in this way.[11] The three different ways of presenting an unspecified subject certainly do not carry clearly distinct meaning, but it is reasonable to suggest that they carry different implications. There is no reason to suppose that they could not coexist in a single form of the language. The existence of these variant possibilities at least does not conflict with the view that the language of the corpus can reasonably be treated as self-consistent to the same extent as is that of present-day authors.

17.5.2 *Distributives* The distributive structure provides a well-known example of the use of plural and singular pronouns with the same referent. Typically, a third person plural verb with a plural or collective subject is followed by "a man" (איש) and a coreferent singular pronoun, indicating individual action by each member of the group represented by the subject, as "The b. Israel went, each to his territory" (וילכו בני ישראל איש לנחלתו, Ju 2:6). The verb may be singular with a collective subject (1S 10:11, 2S 2:27, 6:19), or even a compound subject (1K 5:5, 2K 9:21). It is usually third person, but may be second (Ju 8:24, 21:21, 1S 14:34), or first (Ju 16:5, 21:22). A

---

[10]   The only other root possibly used more than once in this way is דבר "speak", in 1S 3:17, 1K 13:22, where the context implies God as subject, as is also the case with קרא "call" in 1S 3:9.

[11]   In a similar example in Lachish 3:13-14 the verb הגד could be passive, "Your servant was informed", conforming to the above suggestion, or singular active, "someone informed your servant".

nominal may also be treated in this way where it is not subject, as "David brought up his men... each with his family" (העלה ...ואנשיו דוד איש וביתו, 2S 2:3). Other examples occur in Ju 7:8, 2S 6:19, 1K 20:24.

17.5.3 The above description shows that the distributive structure is used with considerable flexibility. It seems clear that this extends to the omission of איש "each", as was noted in connection with collectives in §16.4. Other possible examples are "The city elders came with alacrity to meet him and said (s) 'Do you come in peace'" (ויחרדו זקני העיר לקראתו ויאמר שלום בואך), 1S 16:4); "Jehu came back out to his fellow officers who asked (s) him 'Is everything all right?'" (ויהוא יצא אל עבדי אדניו ויאמר לו השלום), 2K 9:11. These singular verbs could be understood as representing an unspecified subject, "someone said", although this seems unlikely where the group from which the speaker comes has been named.[12] Both cases could also be treated as examples of the distributive structure. This would not necessarily imply that each member of the group greeted Samuel, or enquired of Jehu. The distributive may be used to indicate general action among members of a group, particularly with the verb אמר "say", as "They said, each to his fellow, 'Who did this thing?'" (ויאמרו איש אל רעהו מי עשה הדבר הזה), Ju 6:29). In the same verse, the same verb, ויאמרו "They said", is used with no distributive structure to present the answer to this question. In both cases, the verb indicates speech by the group as a whole. The addition of the distributive structure to the first can hardly be taken as a literal description. Its effect is to draw attention to the fact that the question was an immediate concern for the members of the group. By this argument, the translation of the singular verbs in 1S 16:4 and 2K 9:11 as (distributive) plurals is correct for the text as it stands.

17.5.4 A similar usage seems to occur in Ju 2:18, where the anaphoric item is not a pronoun, but a noun with the definite article:

---

[12]   Both verbs are often emended to plural, with strong textual support, but that might result from a change in earlier readings to conform with the later usage of Hebrew or Greek. Both are also listed in the masorah as *sevirin*, cases in which a different reading is often suggested, but is contrary to the tradition. If "one of them" were intended, it could be expressed, as it is in 1S 16:18, 2K 6:3.

"When Yahweh raised up judges for them, Yahweh was with the
judge" (וכי הקים יהוה להם שפטים והיה יהוה עם השפט). While "the
judge" can be interpreted to mean "the judge at any particular
time", the effective meaning is "those judges (one after the other)",
or "each judge". Such usage presents the statement as applying to
each member of the group, and so heightens its impact through
specification. This is, then, another example of the use of a singular
coreferent with a plural antecedent to mark immediacy, equivalent
to what is suggested in §§18, 19, in explanation of number shift in
first and second persons. The marking of immediacy can, in fact, be
said to be a component of the meaning of any distributive structure.
A statement like "They rode, each on his mule" (וירכבו איש על
פרדו, 2S 13:29) can reasonably be taken as a literal statement that
each individual rode his own animal, but "They rode their mules"
is not likely to give a different picture. The specification (or "individuation") provided by the distributive structure sharpens the picture, and so heightens the impact of the clause. It makes it more
immediate.[13] The meaning of the distributive structure, then, can
be seen as having a specific component: action by each member of
a group, and a general component: the clause is immediate. Both are
always present, but one or the other is likely predominate in any
given context.

17.6 Conclusion

Variations between singular and plural in third person pronouns
which are not coreferent with collectives can almost all be account-
ed for in accordance with the above survey. The singular is chosen
to maintain focus on a particular actor, (typically the thematic actor
in a passage). In passages in which there is no thematic actor, a pronoun which has a plural antecedent may be used in the singular
with distributive value. Usage of this sort may indicate that the
action in question was performed by each individual represented by
the antecedent; alternatively, its main purpose may be to heighten
the impact of the clause, to present it as immediate. It is quite evi-

---

[13] See also §18.4. In the terms of Hopper and Thompson, (1980:253, 256-9),
greater individuation of the object increases the transitivity of the clause. On the
relationship of transitivity to foregrounding, see pp. 280-194 there. Greater transitivity is similarly related to immediacy, see Revell 1993b §2, 3.

dent from this description that number in biblical Hebrew pronouns does not relate to physical number in the way that the conventional labels "singular" and "plural" would seem to suggest.
Variation in number with function similar to that in the third person surveyed above, is also used in the first and second persons, as
described in the following sections.

Variation in Number
in the First Person Pronoun

18.1 Introduction

18.1.1 The relation between grammatical number and actual number in the first person pronoun is even less firm than in the third. A first person singular pronoun is sometimes used in a speech delivered by more than one speaker, and the plural is often used by a single speaker. The first person plural pronoun may cover the following groupings: speaker + addressee, speaker + addressee + other(s), speaker + other(s). (See Henderson, 1985). For the present discussion (as often) only two groupings need be recognized: "Inclusive" — groupings which include the addressee with the speaker, and "Exclusive" — groupings which do not.[1] The significance of these groupings for the expressive use of the first person plural can be seen from examples in English. An exclusive pronoun can be used by a single speaker (1) to avoid personal responsibility, as "We weren't looking" (cf. §18.2.2); (2) to use the greater authority of the group to back his words, as "We don't do that here". An inclusive first person plural can be used (3) to avoid appearing to censure the addressee, as "We should have turned right at the light" (cf. §18.2.7); (4) to encourage by a display of solidarity, as "We will win when we work willingly" (cf. §18.2.8). A speaker using (2) or (4) is likely to be status marked. A speaker using (1) or (3) is likely to be of lower status than the addressee, in which case he can be said to use self-effacement to show deference. Such forms are also used where the speaker is of equal or higher status. A speaker who is not subordinate to the addressee is said to use self-effacement to show politeness. The relative status of speaker and addressee is similarly significant for the interpretation of the use of the first person plural pronoun in the corpus.

---

[1]   The context usually shows clearly whether a pronoun is inclusive or exclusive, but some cases are ambiguous, as that in 2K 7:13.

18.1.2 The use of the first person singular by a group of speakers is relatively uncommon. This occurs in English in solemn communal declarations, as in "The sponsors shall respond 'I will'". The use of the singular by more than one speaker in the corpus similarly reflects the importance of the speech to the individual speakers (and so to the group as a whole), but it is not restricted to the undertaking of personal obligations (cf. §18.3). This use of the first person singular by several speakers can be related to the use of a third person singular coreferent with the subject of a plural verb to give a distributive value (see §§16.4, 17.5.3). The use of the singular to mark the importance of the speech to the speaker where the plural is appropriate is consistent in function with the use of singular pronouns to focus on a thematic character who is presented as principal of a compound (see §§17.2.1, 17.3.1-2). It conflicts with the use of a singular pronoun coreferent with a collective subject, which marks its clause as non-immediate (see §16.5.2) for the reasons given there. The very limited information on first person pronouns with a collective antecedent in the corpus suggests that their use was consistent with that typical for first person pronouns generally, not with that typical for third person coreferents of collectives. It is possible, however, that either pattern was available, and the determination of the meaning of the use of the pronoun was left to the reader or hearer to interpret, as is usual with expressive usage.

18.2 Speech Introduced by a Singular Verb

18.2.1 Where a verb introducing speech is singular, a coreferent first person pronoun within the speech is not uncommonly plural. This may be simply indexical; the speaker indicates that he acts as a member of a group. However, a first person plural pronoun of this sort may have singular coreferents, either first person, or the deferential third person "your servant", so it is reasonable to suppose that in some cases the main function of the choice of the less specific plural is to show self-effacement, non-immediacy. The extent to which the choice of the first person plural carries expressive connotations, and the nature of those connotations, varies with the relative status of speaker and addressee, and with the value of the pronoun as exclusive or inclusive.

18.2.2 *Exclusive Pronoun — Status-marked Addressee* Where the addressee is status marked, and is not included by the first person plural pronoun, the speaker may use the plural deferentially, as a form
of distancing or self-effacement. Rather than presenting himself as
an individual, the speaker presents himself as a member of a group,
and thereby avoids personal responsibility for what he says. The
angel greets Gideon with "Yahweh is with you" (יהוה עמך, Ju 6:12),
using a singular pronoun. Gideon's reply uses the plural: "So Yahweh is with us. Why then has all this happened to us?" (ויש יהוה
עמנו ולמה מצאתנו כל זאת, Ju 6:13). He thus shifts the focus of the
conversation away from his personal situation. Manoah similarly
uses a self-effacing plural in Ju 13:8, 15; (he never does use the first
person singular). David uses the first person plural in 2S 7:22, in a
speech which opens emotionally with the first person singular, but
otherwise uses only the deferential "your servant" or the personal
name for self-reference (2S 7:18-29). In 2S 13:24, Absalom refers to
himself as "your servant" in inviting the king to his celebration, but
shifts to the first person plural in 2S 13:26 in requesting the king to
allow his brother to come. An unnamed servant, and Nathan the
prophet each use "our master" (אדננו), not "my master", for reference when giving advice to the master's wife (1S 25:14, 17, 1K 1:11).
There is nothing surprising in the speaker's presenting himself as a
member of a group in this way, but it is significant that the plural
pronoun rather than the singular is chosen in precisely these situations where a certain level of deference is desirable. It seems clear
from the examples that the use of the first person pronoun stands
between the use of the first person singular and the use of a deferential nominal on a scale ranging from self-assertion to deference.

18.2.3 Such expressive use of the plural may alternate with the use
of the singular, as occurs in "We are travelling from Bethlehem in
Judah to the remote hills of Ephraim. I am from there, but I went
to Bethlehem in Judah, and I am going to the house of Yahweh,
and no man will take me into (his) house. There is straw and fodder for our donkeys, and there is food and wine for me, for your
maidservant, and for the lad with your servants" (עברים אנחנו מבית
לחם יהודה עד ירכתי הר אפרים משם אנכי ואלך עד בית לחם יהודה ואת
בית יהוה אני הלך ואין איש מאסף אתי הביתה גם תבן גם מספוא יש

לחמורינו וגם לחם ויין יש לי ולאמתך ולנער עם עבדיך, Ju 19:18-19).[2] This is a response to a question addressed in the masculine singular "Where are you going and where are you coming from?" (אנה תלך ומאין תבוא, Ju 19:17). The singular is used in those clauses which could be considered as the speaker's personal answer to this. The singular is also used for the complaint that no-one has shown hospitality, which does not affect the speaker alone. The first person plural is used for the introductory clause, and for the statement about fodder. Such use of the plural is quite natural. In the introductory clause, however, it contrasts with the singular of the question to which it responds, as in the case of Gideon's reply. This can reasonably be seen as self-effacing, as a form of politeness. The speaker's statement that he needs no fodder could be offensive, as impugning the hospitality of a prospective host. Here, too, the use of the plural can be regarded as polite, intended to show that no offence is meant. Since these plural pronouns are used, the contrasting use of the singular itself becomes expressive, marking the clause in which it occurs as of concern to the speaker personally, as immediate. The same is shown by the use of the singular in "I know" (ידעתי), where first person pronouns are otherwise plural in 2S 19:7, 2K 4:9-10. The first person plural is used expressively in the way described above in 1S 15:15, 25:7-8, 14-17, 30:14, 2S 11:23, 24:14, 1K 1:11 (see §6.9.2), 2K 19:19.

18.2.4 *Exclusive Pronoun — Non-status Addressee* An exclusive pronoun may be used to an addressee who is not status-marked simply because the speech requires reference to the group rather than to the speaker who represents it, as where Goliath shifts from the singular to the plural in 1S 17:9, 10, and where David does the same in 1S 17:46-47. The same is true where Jephthah uses the first person plural in his survey of the background of the quarrel of Israel with the Bene Ammon: "All which Yahweh our God has cleared before us, that will we possess" (ואת כל אשר הוריש יהוה אלהינו מפנינו אותו נירש, Ju 11:24). In Ju 11:27, Jephthah uses the first person singular to present the essential message of his speech: "I have not sinned

---

[2] On the use of number in the third person verbs in this chapter, see §17.4.2-4. "To house of Yahweh" is a traditional English representation of the Hebrew words, but their meaning is uncertain.

against you" (ואנכי לא חטאתי לך). The sinning is not Jephthah's personal act; he is still speaking as a representative of the community. The contrast is expressive. It could be said that in the first speech he thinks of himself as a member of the community, in the second as its leader, but, as is the case with the notional value of collectives treated as singular or plural, this view would not fit many of the cases in which the first person plural is used by a single speaker. The general pattern of use of first person pronouns supports the view that the use of the singular in such cases marks the clauses as central to the interests of the speaker, as immediate, in contrast to the use of the plural. King David uses the exclusive first person plural to a non-status addressee in "No, my son, let us not all come" (אל בני אל נא נלך כלנו, 2S 13:25). Here the use of the plural, rather than the singular "Let me not come/I don't want to come" can be seen as self-effacing, intended, with the "benevolent" vocative "my son" (see §25.3.3) to soften the effect of the refusal. In 1K 5:20, King Solomon's use of the plural in "there is not among us" (אין בנו) includes himself among his subjects as unskilled, showing self-effacing politeness to King Hiram, of whom he is making a request.

18.2.5 The singular and plural forms of the first person appear to be used in the same way where the subject of a singular verb introducing speech is not an individual. The coreferent of a collective is typically plural if it does not stand in a clause of which the collective is subject (see §16.4). The use of the plural in Ju 20:8-10, 1S 11:12, 2S 18:3, 19:10-11, where a singular verb introduces speech by members of a group about their own actions, is unmarked. In 2S 19:44 the speech of the men of Israel, consisting of a claim: "I have ten shares in the king..." (...עשר ידות לי במלך) followed by hostile criticism in interrogative form: "Why do you slight me...?" (ומדוע ...הקלתני) is clearly self-assertive and emotional. The consistent use of singular pronouns, marked usage where the speaker is represented by a collective (see §16.4), indicates this strong feeling. This speech is a response to that of the men of Judah in 2S 19:43, which also begins with a claim presented with first person singular pronouns. The following question "Have we indeed been fed by the king...?" (...האכול אכלנו מן המלך) uses the first person plural to present what is effectively a negative statement supporting the claim. That is, it provides background to the claim. Its non-immediate function is marked by the use of the plural (for similar use of other features, see §23.7). In Ju 11:17 Israel is represented as sending the message "Please let me pass through... (אעברה נא), and in Ju 11:19 "Please let us pass through... as far as my place" (נעברה נא...עד מקומי). The main effect of the use of the plural in Ju 11:19 is to highlight the contrast of the following singular pronoun. The expression of emotion through this use of the singular is certainly appropriate for this significant addition to the second request.[3] The use of the singular in Ju 7:2 "My own hand has saved me" (ידי הושיעה לי) is also self-assertive. This is questionable in Ju 1:3, where the use of the singular may simply reflect the tendency shown in Judges chapter one to treat collectives as singular (see §16.1.2.n).[4]

18.2.6 As with a collective, a coreferent of a compound subject in a following clause is usually plural, even where the compound is subject of a singular verb, so cases where a first person plural in speech is coreferent with the compound subject of the singular introductory verb (as in Ju 8:21, 2K 18:26) represent default usage. A singular verb relates to the principal of the compound, but does not show that the principal is the only actor (see §17.2.1). Consequently in "His father and mother said to him 'Is there not among the daughters of your brothers and among all my people a woman...'" (ויאמר לו אביו ואמו האין בבנות אחיך ובכל עמי..., Ju 14:3) the first person pronoun represents both speakers, and the choice of the singular reflects their personal concern, as in the other cases discussed. The difference in number in cases of this sort represents a psychological difference in the referent, not a physical difference.

18.2.7 *Inclusive Pronoun — Status-marked Addressee* Where a speaker who is not status-marked uses an inclusive first person plural pro-

---

[3] Similar contrast, in which the singular can reasonably be interpreted as expressing urgency or emotion, occurs in requests of the same sort in Num 20:19, 21:22, where the speaker is designated by a plural or a collective. The singular alone is used in Deut 2:27-28, where Moses speaks as leader.

[4] Where a collective is most commonly treated as singular, as is a collective subject overall, treatment as plural carries expressive meaning. Where it is most commonly treated as plural, as are coreferents of a collective in a clause other than that in which it stands, singular can be used to carry expressive meaning. That is, the meaning is not carried by the form itself, but by the contrasting choice. See §1.5.2.

noun, the intention may sometimes be to avoid the use of the
second person. In 1K 22:7, the king of Judah asks the king of Israel
"Is there not here a prophet of the Lord any more? Let us ask him"
(האין פה נביא ליהוה עוד ונדרשה מאותו). The subject of the proposed
enquiry is to be the expedition which the two kings have under-
taken. This expedition was instigated by the king of Israel (1K
22:4), and he asks the questions of the available prophets in 1K
22:6, 15. However, the recognition of this by the use of the second
person "You should ask him" would be potentially offensive. It has
the air of a command, and places on the addressee the sole responsibility for not going to the best sources of information. The polite
use of the first person plural avoids these problems. Other cases in
which it is reasonable to suggest that the use of the first person plural is similarly intended to avoid placing responsibility directly on
the addressee occur in 1S 9:6, 2S 17:11-13, 2K 3:11, 6:15. There are
ten other examples in which a non-status speaker uses an exclusive
pronoun.

18.2.8 *Inclusive Pronoun — Non-status Addressee* A status-marked
speaker often uses an inclusive first person plural pronoun. I have
noted 23 examples in all, over one third of the sixty examples of a
first person plural pronoun introduced by a singular verb with a
singular subject. In most cases this appears to express nothing more
than a comradely solidarity between a leader and his subordinates,
as in King Saul's suggestion to his troops in "Saul said 'Let us go
down after the Philistines by night...'" (ויאמר שאול נרדה אחרי
פלשתים לילה, 1S 14:36). It is, then, another case where a speaker
presents his relationship with the addressee as close in an effort to
persuade. The use of the plural in such situations is standard, unmarked, but it, too, may be used in expressive contrast. In 1K 12:9,
King Rehoboam shows solidarity of this sort where he puts to "the
youngsters who had grown up with him" the question "What do
you advise that we reply...?" (מה אתם נועצים ונשיב דבר...). This contrasts with the question put to "the elders who used to serve his father, Solomon": "How do you advise replying...?" (איך אתם נועצים
להשיב..., 1K 12:6). The use of the inclusive "we" in the one case but
not in the other indicates the king's predilections (also indicated by
the use of "youngsters", ילדים, see §2.2.3) and foreshadows his decision, suggesting that his favouring of inexperienced advisers is the

means by which God is to bring about the division of the kingdom which he intends (1K 11:31).

18.2.9 A similarly contrasting use of the plural with a further dimension to its value occurs in 1K 22:15. Here the use of the plural in the king's question to the prophet Micaiah "Shall we go...?" (הנלך) contrasts with the use of the singular in the same question put to other prophets in 1K 22:6 "Shall I go...?" (האלך). The first person plural used to Micaiah can be interpreted as inclusive, and so as showing politeness in the form of condescension, the voluntarily abandoning of the marks of rank.[5] If so, the usage is ironic. The king hates the prophet (1K 22:8), and his use of the prophet's personal name as a vocative to introduce the question appears to be a way of showing scorn (see §25.4.2).

18.3 Speech Introduced by a Plural Verb

18.3.1 Where a verb introducing speech is plural, first person pronouns in the speech which are coreferent with the subject are regularly plural. However, singular pronouns are occasionally used to present expressive contrast. Use of the singular shows that the information presented is of particular importance to the individual speakers, and so to the group as a whole. A first person pronoun in a deferential or honorific term designating the addressee is typically singular even in speech introduced by a plural verb: "My Lord" (אדני, 2S 15:15, 1K 1:2, 2K 2:19), "My father" (אבי, 2K 5:13).[6] The first person plural is used in direct address in "Our God", אלהינו, in 2K 19:19, where the speaker is appealing on behalf of his community. It is used in third person address in "our master" (אדננו, 1S 16:16), where servants give their master unasked advice. In both cases the speakers use the plural, submerging themselves in the anonymity of the group, to show humility and deference through self-effacement (see §18.2.2). The use of the singular in such cases re-

---

[5] This is unlikely to be the case in the similar situation in 2S 17:6, but the plural there shows no contrast with a singular. Absalom also uses the plural in asking for advice in 2S 16:20.

[6] The use of the first person singular is also typical in forms of this sort used in spoken reference, but the plural may be used where the relationship is not restricted to the speaker, as in "our father" Ju 11:2, "our master" 1S 25:14, 1K 1:11 etc.

flects the fact that the relationship expressed by the pronoun is immediate for the individual speakers, central to their interests.

18.3.2 The first person singular is used in the same way, reflecting the personal concern of the speaker, in speech introduced by a plural verb in "The Ekronites cried out (p) 'They have sent round to me the ark of the God of Israel to kill me and my people'" (ויזעקו העקרונים לאמר הסבו אלי את ארון אלהי ישראל להמיתני ואת עמי, 1S 5:10). It is certainly reasonable to see the first person singular as self-assertive, expressing emotion, regardless of the number of speakers. The same is true in the similar passage in 1S 5:11, in Ju 20:23, 28, and in "The fugitives of Ephraim said (p) 'Let me cross'" (יאמרו פליטי אפרים אעברה, Ju 12:5).[7] The introductory verb of speaking has a collective subject in "Every evil man responded (s)... and they said 'Because they did not go with me, we will not give them any of the spoil...'" (ויען כל איש רע... ויאמרו יען אשר לא הלכו עמי לא נתן להם מהשלל, 1S 30:22). The singular pronoun marks the introductory clause as of personal concern to the speakers. This is achieved through its contrast with the plural in the following clause, which represents standard usage where a collective is subject of a plural verb introducing speech (as in Ju 8:1, 22, 15:10, etc.).

18.4 Conclusion

Much of the variation in number described here has analogues in modern spoken languages close enough that it is easily acceptable to modern scholars. The use of the plural for self-effacement (as in §§ 18.2.2, 18.3.1) is an obvious example. In a few cases, the shift is so unexpected as to be disturbing. However, the usage in these cases is susceptible of explanations also valid for the usage in the others. A decision that the usage is acceptable in one case but not in another could only be arbitrary. On a more general level, it can be noted that the phenomenon of shift in number in first person pronouns can be shown to correlate with that in third person pronouns. In examples like those in Ju 12:5 and 1S 30:22, quoted in §18.3.2, the use of the singular pronoun after the plural verb in the first person

---

[7]   The contrast in number in the first person pronouns in 2S 21:4 would be difficult to interpret this way, but the singular occurs only in the *ketiv*, and could have arisen through scribal error.

is easily interpreted as distributive, just as in the third person (see §17.5.3). "The fugitives of Ephraim (each) said 'Let me cross'" is a suitable equivalent to "The fugitives of Ephraim said (p) 'Let me (personally) cross'", considering the relationship between the unmarked plural and the plural marked as distributive noted in §17.5.3 -4. That is, the increase in specification or "individuation" provided by the singular, reflecting emotion or urgency, marks the clause as immediate, just as it does in cases in which the term "distributive" is more commonly used.

Variation in Number
in the Second Person Pronoun

19.1 Introduction

In the more familiar European languages, the second person pronoun is that most characteristically used with expressive value. In Hebrew, variation in number with expressive function is less common in the second person than in the first, and the function itself (no doubt partly for that reason) is less easy to define. This difference in usage from that of the first person is strikingly shown in the matter of coreferents of deferential nominals, where the third person is much more regularly used in reference to the addressee than in reference to the speaker (see §20.2). The same phenomenon is reflected in the relatively small number of passages which require comment in this chapter. Despite the paucity of information, however, it can be shown that, although an individual is usually addressed in the singular, he may be addressed in the plural to avoid making him the obvious target of the speech. This is one way in which deference can be shown to a superior. Conversely, a group, although typically addressed in the plural, may be addressed with singular pronouns to heighten the impact of the speech on the individual members. This is one way of marking speech as urgent. The use of singular and plural is not divorced from the idea of number, but the relationship can not always be expressed literally in terms of one: more than one. The logic of the use differs from that of English, in part because, as with the coreferents of compounds, the singular is used to mark immediacy, the plural for distancing.

19.2 The Addressee is Presented as an Individual

19.2.1 Second person pronouns are typically singular where the addressee is represented by a singular noun or pronoun in the introduction to a speech, or in a speech which responds to speech by an individual. However, plural pronouns may be used, and both numbers may be used with the same antecedent. Variation of this sort can usually be explained as reflecting the speaker's view of the addressee as an individual (singular) or a group (plural), but, as in the case of other similar variation, the assumption that grammatical number literally corresponds to physical number in this way is sometimes absurd. The suggestion that the unexpected use of number has expressive value is often more attractive. The use of a plural pronoun to refer to a single addressee can be a means of avoiding direct reference to the addressee. As with other forms of distancing, this may mark the clause in which it stands as deferential, or as non-immediate. There seems no doubt that the desire to present such expressive content often motivates the choice of plural pronouns where singular is expected, but there is no formal difference between this expressive usage, and the use of the plural to refer to a group. The value of the plural, then, is determined by the context.

19.2.2 Both singular and plural pronouns are coreferent with a singular addressee in "The b. Dan said to him 'Do not make your (s) voice heard among us lest vicious men fall on you (p) and you (s) remove your life and the life of your (s) household'" (ויאמרו אליו בני דן אל תשמע קולך עמנו פן יפגעו בכם אנשים מרי נפש ואספתה נפשך ונפש ביתך, Ju 18:25). The addressee is leader of a group pursuing the Danites to recover stolen property. The speech is a response to his complaint (Ju 18:24), and so is addressed to him individually. The use of the plural is easily taken as indicating that an attack will not fall on the addressee alone, but on the whole party, while the following reversion to the singular places the responsibility for the resulting loss of life on the addressee alone. The essential message "Keep quiet if you value your life" would be the same if the clause containing the plural second person pronoun were omitted. That is, the singular second person pronouns are used in the significant clauses. There is, then, in this case, a relation between the use of the second person singular and the significance or immediacy of the clause in which it is used.

19.2.3 Other cases show the same relationship. The singular verb "sustain yourself" (סעד) in Ju 19:5, 8, presents the speaker's essential request. The following plural can be interpreted as referring to the group led by the addressee, or as marking the idea presented in the clause as of secondary importance, in "and afterwards you can go"

(ואחר תלכו, Ju 19:5), or as a result or consequence in "and delay (your departure)" (והתמהמהו, Ju 19:8). The parallel variation in the third person verbs in the passage strongly suggests that the latter, the marking of the verbs as non-immediate, is indeed the primary function of the use of the plural, whether or not the former index-ical function is associated with it (see §17.4.3). In "Go (s) and strike down (s) Amalek, and treat as *ḥerem* (p) all that is his. You (s) will not pity him, but kill (s) man and woman, infant and suckling, cat-tle and sheep, camel and donkey" (לך והכיתה את עמלק והחרמתם את כל אשר לו ולא תחמל עליו והמתה מאיש עד אשה..., 1S 15:3) the plural can be seen as adding secondary detail to the initial command. The singular verbs highlight the main requirement, the annihilation of Amalek. The use of the plural following a singular can be similarly explained in 1S 26:16, 2S 24:2 (and in 1S 9:19-20, 10:2 discussed in §19.3.2). In "I will put... into your (s) hand and you (p) will know ..." (ונתתי... בידך וידעתם..., 1K 20:28) the plural verb can also be re-garded as presenting consequences of the previous action, but this contrasts with the use of the singular in the parallel in 1K 20:13. Possibly the plural in verse 28 should be seen as including the Ara-maeans, whose talk is given as motivating God's speech. The plural also has clear numerical referent in Ju 11:26 (where it includes pre-vious generations with the addressee, who is referred to in the sin-gular in the preceding and following verses), and in 1K 9:6 (where it shifts the focus from the individual responsibility of the king to the possible actions of the whole community). A similar shift from second person singular to plural is motivated by the use of nominals in the course of address in 1S 17:45-47, 29:10, 2S 15:27-29, 34-36.[1]

19.2.4 Where the addressee is designated as singular, the initial co-referent is plural in "Yahweh said to Gideon, 'by the three hundred men who lapped will I save you (p) and I will put Midian into your (s) hand'" (ויאמר יהוה אל גדעון בשלש מאות האיש המלקקים אושיע אתכם ונתתי את מדין בידך, Ju 7:7). Here too the shift can be related to

---

[1] Plural coreferents also occur where the pronoun acts as a component of a com-pound within the speech in Ju 14:15, 2S 19:30, also 1S 22:13, where a singular pro-noun, referring only to the addressee, follows. However, following the usage stand-ard with compounds, coreferents in this situation are more usually singular (Ju 7:10-11, 8:22, 9:32-3, 1S 22:16, 28:1, 2S 9:10, 19:15, 2K 4:7, 8:1, 14:10).

number: God will save the whole community, and Gideon, as leader, will direct the victory.[2] Here too, however, the singular is used in the more significant clause. The speech can be interpreted as "I will (not only) save you, (but even) give you control of Midian." In 1S 2:29, the initial plural verb addressed to Eli by a man of God presents the misdeeds of the family, the following singular presents the specific charge against Eli, its head, which is obviously more immediate in the context.[3] The same shift occurs for the same reason in 1K 18:18. In a final example, the use of the plural in "spend the night" (לינו) addressed to the levite in Ju 19:9 is possibly intended to create a contrast to add to the impact of the use of the same verb in the singular in the following plea, but it may be correct to see dittography here, as do many critics (see Brockington, 1973, ad loc.).

19.2.5 In a number of cases, a single addressee is addressed only in the plural. The addressee is non-status in "He called his lad, his servitor, and said 'Please get (p) this (woman) away from me...'" (ויקרא את נערו משרתו ויאמר שלחו נא את זאת מעלי..., 2S 13:17). Such speech can easily be seen as directed to the group of which the single addressee is a member: servants as in the example (also 2K 6:13, 10:8) or others (as 2S 11:20-21, 20:21, 1K 1:45, 2K 18:22, 19:29), much as in cases where no addressee is indicated (see §19.4). Such usage simply shows that there is no need to single out the addressee as an individual. The reason for this, that he is not important enough to warrant it, or that the situation requires politeness in the form of a distanced reference (see §19.2.6) must be determined from the context.

19.2.6 Where a plural coreferent is used for a single status-marked addressee, it can similarly be understood as directed to the group he

---

[2]   The pronoun in "give into your hand" is singular where an individual is addressed, except (despite the fact that the addressee is typically treated as singular in the context) in Exod 23:31, where the speech concerns the distant future.

[3]   The second person singular is used before this in "Your father's house", but it is probable that this represents convention, not choice. "Home" or "family" is usually seen as having a single head, as in "Eli blessed Elkanah and his wife... and they went to his (Elkanah's) place" (והלכו למקמו, 1S 2:20).

represents. Since he is the speaker's superior, however, this usage
cannot indicate lack of importance. The avoidance of direct address
in this situation is most easily taken as the use of a non-specific reference for distancing, to show deference. The plural is used in the
presentation of an urgent suggestion in "They said to David 'Get
going (p) and cross (p) the river at once'" (ויאמרו אל דוד קומו ועברו
מהרה את המים, 2S 17:21). Other examples of plural imperatives used
in this way occur in 1S 11:12, 1K 3:26, 26.[4] Such usage allows the
speaker to use an imperative form to mark urgency, and yet to
avoid giving a direct order to a superior. Politeness is also intended,
where a more distanced, third person request form is used in "He
said to the king of Moab 'Let my father and mother go to you (p)'"
(...ויאמר אל מלך מואב יצא נא אבי ואמי אתכם, 1S 22:3). The use of the
plural here reduces the directness of the request by suggesting that
the persons mentioned will not be specifically the associates of the
addressee. The plural used by a ruler to a subordinate of high rank
in 2S 11:15, 16:20, may also be regarded as polite, as intended to
avoid the appearance of placing responsibility on the addressee
alone. Address in the plural to a non-status individual may have a
similar function where the addressee is expected to pass on the
command to others (certainly the case in 2S 20:21, possibly so in 2S
13:17, 2K 6:13, 10:8), or was not responsible for the events discussed, as in 2S 11:20-21.[5] In other cases the plural is presumably an
essential to the content of the message, indicating the group of
which the addressee is a member.

---

[4]   The phenomenon also occurs outside the corpus, as in "The people disputed
with Moses, and said to him 'Give (p) us...'" (...וירב העם עם משה ויאמרו תנו לנו,
Exod 17:2. There is strong textual support for the reading "Give (s)" (תנה), but this
would be the expected usage in later Hebrew or in Greek, and so is of uncertain
value. The plural verbs "pursue" (רדפו) and "overtake" (תשיגום) in Jos 5:2 present
another possible example. No addressee is mentioned, but the speech responds to
one by the king. Meier (1992:123n1) suggests that the plural shows that the speech
is directed to the messengers implied by the statement that the king "sent" (וישלח,
Jos 2:3), but no messengers are mentioned, so this is at least questionable.

[5]   It is noted in Brown and Levinson, 1987:198, that the use of plural second person forms to indicate polite address to an individual is found in many languages.
The use of "polite" forms by a status-marked speaker (where they are not required)
can be seen as expressing benevolence or loving concern.

19.3 The Addressee is not Presented as an Individual

19.3.1 Where the addressee is presented as plural, coreferent pronouns are typically plural. Singular coreferents occur, in the examples in the corpus, only in alternation with plural.[6] Where a singular coreferent is used, it is usually not the first, as in "Go up (p), for tomorrow I will put him into your (s) hand" (עלו כי מחר אתננו בידך, Ju 20:28). The use of the singular in the second clause marks it as the more immediate, as in the examples in §19.2.[7] The situation is similar to that of the shift of plural to singular in Ju 11:19 described in §§18.2.5. There, an addition is made to the second of two similar speeches made in similar circumstances, and the number in it is shifted to mark it as immediate. The shift of number can be interpreted in the same way in "I appealed to you (p) but you (p) did not help... and I saw that you (s) did not help... why have you (p) come...?" (ואזעק אתכם ולא הושעתם... ואראה כי אינך מושיע... למה עליתם..., Ju 12:2-3). The singular second person pronoun heightens the impact of the clause on the addressee, marking it as a serious personal concern of the speaker. A further example occurs in 2K 11:15. The order to bring out Athaliah is given in the unmarked plural; the following order, to kill anyone who follows (to rescue) her, is singular, to focus attention on this important precaution.[8]

---

[6]   There is an apparent exception in Ju 11:13, but the speech here is directed to Jephthah. The stated addressee, his messengers, simply act as the channel of communication.

[7]   The question to which this responds, though put by the b. Yisrael (plural), is put in the first person singular to mark urgency (see §18.3.2). The similar question in Ju 20:23 (using singular pronouns, but introduced by a plural verb of speech) is answered simply by "Go up (p) against him" (עלו אליו), so there is thus no particular reason to think that the imbedded clauses in Ju 20:27-8, concerning the ark and the priest, are concerned in the shift in number in the latter verse. It would be possible to argue that the singular pronouns, both first and second person, represent the leader of the b. Yisrael, but no such leader is mentioned in this chapter.

[8]   If not emended, המת, which presents this second order, is usually explained as an infinitive absolute, as in Cogan and Tadmor, 1988:130. GKC §113z, cited in support, lists two other cases of an imperative and an infinitive absolute in sequence. That in Isa 37:30 is a *ketiv* form (the *qere* is a plural imperative, as occurs in the parallel in 2K 19:29) so its value is uncertain. That in Amos 4:5 is pi'el, and so, like המת, is used both as singular imperative and as infinitive absolute. The only cases listed there in which an infinitive absolute clearly does follow a modal form are those in Est 2:3, 6:9, where the preceding jussive has an unspecified plural

The shift of number in the second person pronouns in 2K 1:3-4 is usually understood as representing a shift from the messengers to the king as addressee.

19.3.2 The first of several second person pronouns coreferent with a plural designating the addressee is singular in "They answered them and said 'Yes (the seer is here). (He is) ahead of you (s). Hurry (s) now... When you (p) enter the city you (p) will find him... Now go up (p)... You (p) will find him'" (ותענינה אותם ותאמרנה יש הנה) לפניך מהר עתה... כבאכם העיר כן תמצאון אתו... ועתה עלו... תמצאון אתו, 1S 9:12-13). The question to which this speech responds has a plural introductory verb "They said", so it is reasonable to take the singular pronouns as highlighting the affirmative response and the recommendation to hurry, and so marking immediacy.[9] There are two other cases of such variation in which the referent of the second person pronouns, Saul and his servant, is the same as in 1S 9:12-13: "Go up (s) before me... You (p) will eat with me today (...עלה לפני ואכלתם עמי היום, 1S 9:19) and "The donkeys which you (s) went to seek are found, and your (s) father has left the matter of the donkeys, and is worried about you (p), (נמצאו האתנות אשר הלכת לבקש והנה נטש אביך את דברי האתנות ודאג לכם, 1S 10:2). The addressee is Saul in both cases, and in both the speech continues with material important to him, also using singular pronouns. It can reasonably be argued that the plural is used, in both cases, to remind the reader

---

subject. (In the cases in Deut 14:21 and Jos 9:20, the verb is not modal as to position, and is neutral in form.) Joüon, 1991, §123x, lists only the examples in Isa 37:30 and Amos 4:5, as cases of an infinitive construct following an imperative, both queried. The evidence for expressive shift in number as a feature of the biblical language is considerably stronger than the evidence for an infinitive absolute in sequence with an imperative.

[9] As often, there is a widely accepted emendation based on the Greek translation (see McCarter, 1980:169). However the argument that "Hurry" (מהר) is illogical in the Hebrew (Driver, 1913, after Wellhausen) assumes that the girls have detailed knowledge of Samuel's movements. They seem simply to be urging haste because Samuel will be inaccessible when he goes to the high place. The argument that the last two letters of this word (מהר) are derived from an original "The seer" (הראה) is also unconvincing, as the natural place for that would be in the first clause, responding to the question "Is the seer here?"

that Saul is not alone, but is used in an unimportant clause, leaving the singular to mark the others as more significant.[10]

19.3.3 Another case occurs in "The Rab shakeh said to them 'Is it to your (s) master and to you (s) that my master has sent me? Is it not to the men sitting... with you (p)?'" (ויאמר אליהם רב שקה העל אדניך ואליך שלחני אדני... הלא על האנשים הישבים... עמכם, 2K 18:27).[11] The initial question addressed to the three officials uses singular second person pronouns to heighten its impact. The plural is used in the second question, where the contribution to the message made by the pronoun in "with you" is insignificant. In Ju 18:9, the singular קומה might be seen as distributive in intention "Get up, each of you", heightening the command (see §17.5.3-4), but the textual support for a plural reading is strong.

19.3.4 Where the addressee is designated by a collective, coreferent second person pronouns are typically plural, as in "Samuel said to the people, 'Do not fear (p) ...'" (ויאמר שמואל אל העם אל תיראו..., 1S 12:20). Commands are given with plural verbs in this situation in twenty one cases in all. Singular coreferents may be used. In 2S 19:44, singular pronouns are used to refer to speaker and addressee, the men of Israel and Judah, both designated by a collective. The use of singular first person pronouns in similar situations can be seen as as marking immediacy, through its distributive nature, in reflection of the speaker's emotion (see §§18.2.5, 18.4). The use of the second person singular coreferent with a collective or a plural antecedent also has a distributive nature. In "To your (s) tents, O Israel" (לאהליך ישראל, 1K 12:16), the singular is clearly distributive (possibly through ellipsis); "each" is expressed by איש in the parallel in 2 Chron 10:16, and the third person use of the same expression in

---

[10] The importance of eating may, of course, be variously evaluated, but there is no reason to believe the invitation to eat more important than the rest of Samuel's message. The Greek uses the singular here, but not in representing "about you (p)" (לכם, 1S 10:2). Variation in number also occurs where Saul's uncle addresses the pair on their return. See §19.3.5.

[11] The plural designation "to them" is often omitted here (with Isa 36:12), but the antecedent of the singular second person pronouns is then the compound nominal in the preceding verse, in which case the use of a singular coreferent is no less unusual. See §§17.3, 19.3.4.

2S 20:1. The same could be said for the second person pronouns in "Enough of your (p) going up to Jerusalem. Here are your (s) Gods O Israel, who brought you (s) up..." (רב לכם מעלות ירשולם הנה אלהיך ישראל אשר העלוך..., 1K 12:28). The shift to the singular heightens the impact of this reference to the Exodus through the specification characteristic of its distributive nature: "...the God of (each of) you, who brought (each of) you up...".

19.3.5 In "Saul said to the Kenite 'Go (p), turn away (p), leave (p) (the) Amalekite lest I remove you (s) with him, and you acted (s) kindly..."'(ויאמר שאול אל הקיני לכו סרו רדו מתוך עמלקי פן אספך עמו ואתה עשיתה חסד..., 1S 15:6) the use of the plural is standard. The singular is used in a subordinate clause which threatens the addressee with personal danger, as in the example in Ju 18:25 discussed in §19.2.2. Presumably the use of the singular adds to the impact of the threat in both cases. The continued use of the singular in the following clause, appealing to a former good relationship between speaker and addressee, is more surprising. It is possibly intended to enhance the impact of an appeal in personal terms, but should perhaps be considered anomalous. The use of the singular in Ju 1:3 is probably to be attributed to the unusual tendency to treat collectives as singular shown in that chapter.

19.3.6 Where the addressee is designated by a compound nominal with an initial singular component, coreferent second person pronouns are typically plural, as in "Saul's uncle said to him and to his servant 'Where did you (p) go?'" (ויאמר דוד שאול אליו ואל נערו אן הלכתם, 1S 10:14). There are ten other cases. The reply to this speech, which uses first person plural pronouns, is followed by the uncle's request "Tell (s) me, please, what Samuel said to you (p)" (הגידה נא לי מה אמר לכם שמואל, 1S 10:15). The singular "Tell me" could be regarded as directed to Saul as spokesman, or possibly as marking the uncle's curiosity as urgent. The only other case of a singular second person pronoun coreferent with a compound which occurs in the corpus occurs in 1S 2:20, where the use of the singular is required by the content of the speech.[12]

---

[12]   The phenomenon occurs outside the corpus, e.g. in Isa 36:12 (see §19.3.3n), and in Exod 10:17 (note the use of third person singular subjects in v.18).

19.4 No Addressee is Indicated

A second person plural pronoun is often used where no addressee is named. Where the clause introducing the speech names a group as speaker, the use of the second person without antecedent typically indicates that the members of the group are addressing each other (as in 1S 4:9, 17:25). Where the speaker is an individual, it can be assumed that the speech is addressed to servants, or to other bystanders, whose nature is indicated only by the context in which the speech is made, as in "Samuel said 'Assemble (p) all Israel in Mizpah'" (ויאמר שמואל קבצו את כל ישראל המצפתה, 1S 7:5).[13] This usage is, in some ways, equivalent to the indefinite use of the third person plural (§17.5.1). A second person plural without antecedent may be (or appear to be) coreferent with an unspecified third person, as in 1K 20:18, 2K 7:14, 17:27. As is the case with third person unspecified subjects, a singular second person without antecedent is occasionally used with much the same value as the plural. Examples occur in 2S 17:5, 1K 22:26, 2K 9:17, 21, and also Ju 3:19, if הס is an imperative. This compares with some 45 cases of the "indefinite" use of the second person plural.[14]

19.5 Conclusion: the Logic of Concord in Number

19.5.1 The evidence for the expressive use of variation in number in second person pronouns is not particularly strong, and much of it is conventionally expunged by emendation, with some versional support. Such support could well reflect a shift from an earlier usage to that of a later Hebrew copyist, or that familiar to the Greek translator.[15] The idea that the Hebrew represents a mindless con-

---

[13] Other examples occur in Ju 16:25, 1S 14:29, 42, 2S 20:16, 1K 1:28, 18:34, 20:18, 2K 4:41, 7:14, 9:27, 17:27, 18:28.

[14] The initial verb in 2K 3:15 is included among these, on the assumption that the verse division correctly separates this from the previous clause, addressed by the same speaker to the king of Israel. The initial plural imperative "take" (קחו) in 2K 4:41 is addressed to "the men" who spoke in 2K 4:40. The following singular imperatives are presumably addressed to a servant ("his servitor" משרתו, is mentioned in 2K 4:43).

[15] The fact that variants in Qumran biblical texts may reflect the usage of the time when they were copied was shown by Kutscher in 1959 (see Kutscher, 1974: 3). Greek translators similarly sometimes interpreted the biblical language in the light of Semitic usage familiar in their day, see Tov, 1981:125-6.

flation in which usage was never harmonized is not more probable (see §28.4). The variation in number in second person pronouns is not unique. It has parallels both in first and in third person. These parallels provide powerful support for the assumption that variation in number was intentional in origin, and had expressive value. Translators, and, no doubt, copyists, failed to understand the usage in later times, when it was no longer a feature of their own language.

19.5.2 A singular pronoun coreferent with a plural antecedent represents non-standard usage, and so is marked. The singular is distributive in nature; it refers to individuals, rather than to members of a group, and so is more specific than the plural. This is consistent with the use of nominal designations described above; those used where the designation is highlighted, and its context marked as immediate, are typically both marked and more specific. However, the two qualities have different functions. Markedness (as the term is used here) relates to the value of the term used. The unmarked used of the first person singular pronoun has the value "I" (the speaker). Its value as the marked form of the first person plural is "I and my companions".[16] A first person plural pronoun coreferent with a singular antecedent, equally marked, has a similar value. However, it does not show that the context is immediate, but the opposite; it distances speaker from addressee, and shows deference. This correlates with its low specificity in comparison to the singular pronoun. It is reasonable to argue, then, that the chief function of variation in specificity is the marking of immediacy and its opposite. The apparently conflicting use of number with collectives is consistent with this view. A singular pronoun representing a collective is less specific than a plural because it recognizes only a body, not the members who form it. Consequently, the use of the plural marks immediacy. However, a plural with a collective antecedent is, in its turn, less specific than a distributive singular, for the reasons valid elsewhere. Thus number can be used to represent three levels of specificity, from low to high: collective singular, plural, and distri-

---

[16]   It has long been recognized that the first person plural pronoun commonly has different values of a similar sort, which are evident only from the context of its use (see §18.1.1).

butive or actual singular. The use of one term (as the singular here) to represent either extreme of a scale, the other (as the plural) to represent the mean between them, seems not uncommon in cases of binary contrast (see §28.2.2).

V   DEFERENCE AND DISTANCE

Deferential Speech: Introduction

20.1 Definition

Where an addressee is superior in status to the speaker, the difference in status is often recognized by the use of "deferential forms" in the speech. Several features may be used to mark a speech as deferential, the most common being the use of deferential nominals and third person pronouns to designate the members of the dyad. The speaker is designated as "your servant" (עבדך, אמתך, שפחתך) and the addressee as "my lord" (אדני), or by the title "king" (המלך) or "man of God (איש האלהים).[1] Such third person reference avoids the appearance of intimacy produced by the use of first and second person forms, obviating the assumption that the speaker and addressee are equal. It suggests that the two are not participating in the same dyad, and so distances speaker from addressee. A third person may also be referred to as "your servant" in speech to a superior (see §13.4.3). The intention is often to recommend the person so named to the favourable notice of the addressee. In this case the speech usually includes other deferential features. However, such usage may be the only expression of the speaker's deference (as in 1S 17:58, 2S 11:21, 24), or may represent a convenient form of reference, as where the plural "your servants" is used in 2S 13:24, 2K 22:9. The deferential nominals used for third person address to a superior are also used as terms of address, with second person coreferents. In the discussion of deferential speech, they are called "deferential vocatives" in this use. The use of these vocatives is discussed in §25.2.

---

[1] The feminine equivalent of "my lord", (גברתי, see 2K 5:3), is not attested in this usage. Other titles would no doubt be shown also to be relevant, if our evidence were more extensive. "My lord the captain" (אדני השר) is used in deferential third person address in Meṣad Ḥashavyahu 1.

20.2 Concord with Deferential Nominals

As a general rule, a deferential nominal representing speaker or addressee is treated as third person within the clause in which it is used, but first or second person coreferents are used outside that clause. However, there is considerable difference in the treatment of speaker and addressee. Where a deferential nominal is subject, its verb is always third person.[2] Other pronouns coreferent with a deferential nominal representing the speaker, and used in the same clause, are third person in 1S 17:34, 2S 7:25, 27, 1K 8:28, 52. First person coreferents occur in 1S 22:15, 2S 14:16, 15:8, 1K 3:7, 18:9, 12.[3] Where the nominal represents the addressee, a second person coreferent is used in "your God" (1S 25:29, 2S 14:11). There is no comparable use with a third person coreferent; probably the second person was always used to express this relationship. Second person is also used in "your servant" in 2S 13:24, and as *qere* in 2S 14:22.[4] The expected "his servant(s)" occurs in nine cases.[5] Third person coreferents occur in twelve other cases. A coreferent which stands in a clause subordinate to another which contains the deferential nominal (or in a main clause with the deferential term in a subordinate) is first or second person as required in 28 of 32 cases, 88%, also Lachish 4:3, Meṣad Ḥashavyahu 9. A third person coreferent is used

[2] A deferential nominal may be used in apposition to a free first person subject pronoun, as in 1S 25:25. In poetry, a nominal is used as subject of a first person verb in Ju 5:7. A nominal in apposition to the subject of a second person verb, though called "subject" for convenience in some contexts (see §§21.3.1n, 25.1.2), is treated in a separate category, as a "free term of address" or "vocative" (see §25).
[3] The deferential nominal is subject in two of the five clauses in which third person coreferents are used, in two of the six in which the first person is used. The figures do not include the use of the first person in "My lord" (אדני), which is never changed (see §18.3.1). Where the pronoun represents the speaker, "My father" (אבי) is used in 1S 22:15, 1K 3:7, "his father" (אביו) in 1S 17:34.
[4] Various sources read or reflect "his servant" in 2S 13:24 (with a different preposition, cf. McCarter, 1984:330); the Hebrew second person might be due to attraction to the preceding "to your servant". Second person also occurs in Lachish 3:6, if the usual restoration is correct.
[5] 1S 22:15, 26:18, 19, 2S 9:11, 13:24, 14:15, 16, 22 (*ketiv*), 24:21; also Lachish 2:5, Meṣad Ḥashavyahu 2. The deferential nominal representing the addressee is subject in all the clauses considered except that in 1S 25:29.

in 2S 6:20, 17:16, 1K 8:30, 2K 8:13.[6] A coreferent of a deferential nominal in a following clause coordinate with that in which the nominal stands is almost always first or second person. Third person occurs in 1S 17:32, 1K 1:2.[7]

20.3 The Social Context of Deferential Speech

Deferential language is used where the speaker has the status of "servant" in relation to the addressee. That is, the addressee is not only of higher status than the speaker (as schematized in §2.5.2), but also the two are superior and subordinate in a formal relationship. Such a relationship imposes obligations on both members (see §2.3.7). A supplicant typically uses deferential language, assuming the subordinate role in a master-servant relationship, whatever the original social status (as, for instance, does Ben Hadad, the King of Aram, in 1K 20:32). Apart from such pleas, deferential forms are not usual where a formal social relationship does not exist (as with the Witch of Endor, in 1S 28:9, see §7.2.2). However they may be used out of politeness, to render speech more acceptable to a stranger (as by Jael addressing the foreigner, Sisera, in Ju 4:18, or the levite addressing a stranger in Ju 19:19). Where a relationship is described by kinship terms, deferential language is normally not used.[8]

20.4 Genres of Speech which Require Deferential Usage

20.4.1 Certain genres of speech, such as a request or contradiction, require particular care in presentation, as they may adversely affect the relationship between speaker and addressee. Even where there

---

[6] Third person is used for speaker and addressee in two cases each. "He chases" (ירדף, 1S 26:20) should possibly be added, but the subject may be unspecified.

[7] Once representing the speaker, once the addressee. Note also the use of coordinate third person verbs before the deferential nominal subject in "May my lord the king take and offer..." (...יקח ויעל אדני המלך, 2S 24:22).

[8] Kinship and deferential terms are combined in self-designation where a claim of servant status is expressed with the expectation (or hope) of friendly relationship in 2K 16:7 (cf. also 1S 25:8). Extra-biblical parallels are noted in Cogan and Tadmor, 1988:187. It appears that the titles "master" and "father" might similarly be used together, see §2.3.7. However, such cases are unusual. David's use of master-servant terminology in reply to Saul's use of kinship terms in 1S 26:17, 22, reflects his intention to break with Saul, see §23.8.2.

is no significant status difference, speech in such genres is often characterized by the use of polite forms. That is, the speaker often adopts some strategy to minimize the possibility that the speech will displease the addressee, as described Brown and Levinson, 1987: 68-71. Where the addressee is superior to the speaker (status marked), the potential for such damage is greater, so that added effort must be made to avoid it. This is undoubtedly the major factor motivating the use of deferential terms. In the corpus, deferential reference is characteristic of speech which is likely to offend a status-marked addressee because it criticizes his past actions, or appears likely to impose an obligation on him, or restrict his freedom of action in some other way.

20.4.2 The categories used below in the description of the deferential speech of the corpus fit under the four main headings of the analysis of "face-threatening acts" schematized in Brown and Levinson 1987:65-68 as follows:[9]

1. Acts which threaten the addressee's negative face want, or autonomy, by requiring action, or imposing an obligation which requires action. This would include all requests (see §§21, 23.4), including the subcategory "offer of a gift" (see §§21.3.4, 23.4.6).

2. Acts which threaten the addressee's positive face want, or positive self image. This would include clauses presenting criticism or opposition (see §§22, 23.5).

3. Acts which threaten the speaker's negative face want by indicating acceptance of an obligation to the addressee. This would include expressions of thanks (see §§21.2.2, 22.2.2, 23.7.3), and of praise (see §23.3). It would also include statements of fealty (see §23.2).

---

[9]   A speech is likely to have some implications for both members of a dyad (as noted, e.g. in Brown and Levinson, 1987:68), so that some speeches would fit well under more than one heading. The assignment of the categories offered here is affected by the way the speaker and addressee are referred to, and by an assessment of their relationship in terms of the linguistic structures used. The purpose is only to indicate that the relevant features of the corpus can be seen as motivated in the same way as is living usage, although views of the sort presented by Brown and Levinson do seem the best way of explaining the use of polite forms, see Braun, 1988:54-57.

4. Acts which threaten the speaker's positive face want. This would include protests of innocence (see §22.2.4), or statements of excuse, self-justification, or confession (§23.7.5).

20.4.3 Group 1 includes the greatest number of communications using deferential language. Personal pronouns are often used in a standard request form – they are usual for the addressee. However, where there is reason to fear that the request may offend the addressee both speaker and addressee are typically referred to deferentially. A deferential nominal is also used to refer to a speaker who will be benefited if a request for action by the addressee is granted. Group 1 also shows the greatest range of structures used to present the communication, ranging from the use of first or second person modals in the standard request form, through indicative clauses and third person modal clauses to the passive or impersonal structures used where a negative response will be particularly damaging to the speaker. Where a standard request form is avoided by the use of passive or impersonal structures, reference to speaker and addressee is sometimes also avoided. In group 2, third person reference to both speaker and addressee is usual where an action or a known intention or attitude of the addressee is clearly criticized or opposed. Where the speaker's emotions are aroused, however, as in expressions of astonishment (see §23.5), the use of first and second person pronouns is usual, at least in the clauses carrying the essential communication. In group 3, third person reference to speaker or addressee as subject is usual where the action referred is past, or benefits the speaker. Otherwise first or second person is used. In group 4, first person is usual, no doubt reflecting, in part, the strong feeling aroused in the speaker by the situation to which the speech refers.

20.4.4 This shows, then, that the use of deferential forms is usual in group (1) where the threat to the addressee's autonomy is (likely to be) unacceptable; in group (2) where his positive self image is (apparently) attacked; and in group (3) where an existing obligation is acknowledged by the speaker, who thereby makes himself a dependent, for whose wellbeing the addressee is (to some extent) responsible. The relationship of the use of deferential terms to the psychological needs which the strategies of "politeness" are designed to satisfy is thus quite clear. The use of deferential forms in the corpus, then, is sufficiently similar to patterns of usage found in spoken languages that it can readily be accepted as a self consistent system.

20.5 Deferential and Personal Reference: Expressive Contrast

20.5.1 In direct speech in general, the use of first and second person pronouns is unmarked, that of deferential forms marked. Where the deferential use of third person is appropriate, first and second person pronouns may be used, but their use in this situation is non-standard, marked, and so carries particular meaning. In general, such use shows that the speaker is closely concerned with the speech, and feels that the speech requires urgent attention, either because it conveys important information, or because the speaker's emotions are involved.[10] Where this is done, deferential forms are likely to be used in subordinate or other less important clauses. The use of personal pronouns to represent speaker and addressee thus marks the clauses of a speech as central to the interests of the speaker, as immediate; the use of deferential nominals marks them as peripheral, as non-immediate. The contrast of deferential forms with first or second person pronouns is thus used to express both deference and immediacy, the opposing poles of the system of expressive usage noted in §3.4.

20.5.2 A few examples of the use of deferential forms and personal pronouns in similar contexts can illustrate the value of the contrast. Joab's speech to King David is highly deferential in 2S 14:22, where he thanks the king for a favour in which he had little personal interest, and in 2S 24:3 where he opposes orders, but is, again, scarcely personally interested in the outcome. It is probable that deference was unnecessary in 2S 12:27-28, where Joab requests the king to

---

[10]   The use of personal pronouns where deferential forms are appropriate would be a form of the "bald-on-record usage" of Brown and Levinson, 1987:95-101. This is typically used where the speaker wants to perform a "face-threatening act" (speak words which may offend the addressee) with maximum efficiency *more than* he wants to satisfy the addressee's face (prevent his being offended) even to any degree. As is shown there, even usage of this sort may be mitigated in various ways, as, in Hebrew, by the use of "please" (נָא) with an imperative (second person) addressed to a superior. "Bald-on-record" forms are also used to a superior where the speech is expected to be pleasing.

lead the capture of Rabbath Ammon, since he is presumably following, not opposing the king's wishes (see §21.3.2). Deferential forms
would normally be used where the acts of a superior are criticized
(see §22.3), but Joab does not use them in 2S 3:24-25, where he
reproaches the king for entertaining the murderer of his brother, or
in 2S 19:6-8, where he reproaches the king for valuing his rebellious
son above his supporters. In the first case, Joab's emotions are clearly involved. In the second, the situation requires urgent action (the
fruits of victory are likely to be lost, see 2S 19:3-4), and Joab's language shows the strength of his feeling. The language of the plea of
a woman for her son in different situations can also be compared.
In 2S 14:4-9 the Tekoite (whose plea is fictitious) uses many deferential forms. In 1K 3:17-20, the harlot (whose son's life is at risk)
uses only one. There can be no doubt that the speech of the latter
is intended to show heightened emotion. The use of first person
pronouns where deferential forms are expected reflects the speaker's
strong personal concern. The unexpected use of second person pronouns, which is less common (see §20.2), shows that the speaker is
not treating the addressee as superior. This may reflect rejection
(non-subjects similarly do not use a title in reference to a king, see
§6.9.1). It may reflect the importance of the speech for the speaker,
in which case the use of the most direct form of communication
indicates urgency, or an effort to give the speech greater persuasive
force by the evocation of a personal relationship with the addressee.

20.5.3 Personal pronouns are sometimes used in parallel with deferential nominals where the main consideration may be seen as one of
style. Whether this is correct or not, their contrasting values can always be appreciated. The most striking example of such "artistic"
use of the conventions of deferential speech occurs in 2S 19:20.

(A) Let not my Lord impute to me wrongdoing
    (B) And do not remember that your servant did wrong
    (C) On the day when my Lord the king left Jerusalem
(D) By the king's paying attention (to it)

אל יחשׁב לי אדני עון
ואל תזכר את אשׁר העוה עבדך
ביום אשׁר יצא אדני המלך מירושׁלם
לשׂום המלך אל לבו

A and B present parallel forms of request. The use, in A, of "to me" with a first person pronoun, which is unusual in a negative request, is balanced by the use of "your servant" in B, which is expected in a negative request (see §21.3.3). The distancing use of the third person to represent the addressee is similarly balanced by the use of the second, expressing urgency (see §21.3.2). Immediacy and deference are thus both neatly presented. The use of "my lord" in A (appealing to personal relationship, see §25.2.1) is balanced by the use of the title "the king" alone in D, so that the two together contain the standard address form "my lord the king", (which is also used in C). This underlines the fact that A and D, which enclose the communication, contain its essential message, a plea that the king ignore the speaker's admitted wrongdoing.[11] The interplay of personal pronouns and deferential forms presents the speaker's appeal with emotion and urgency as well as deference, while displaying sophisticated use of language which may have been calculated to enhance the impact of the plea, supposing that wit was valued in King David's court as it was in many others. The use of first or second person pronouns in parallel with deferential nominals is not uncommon elsewhere (as in 1S 24:15, 25:26, 31, 2S 18:32, 19:36, 42, 1K 1:27). Again, the purpose is no doubt to include both personal and deferential elements in a speech.

20.6 The Description of Deferential Usage

The classification of speech in genres for the description of deferential usage is, of course, ultimately subjective, depending on an interpretation of the speaker's intention. It is also true, however, that a number of objective indicators can be followed. In an effort to make the most of these, the discussion below takes as its starting point the clause-types: modal, interrogative, declarative, found to condition the designation of kings (see §6.4.1-4). All uses of deferential nominals in the corpus are surveyed in an attempt to explain the motivation for the use of deferential speech in individual examples. "Deferential reference", the use of nominals with third person

---

[11]   For other forms of poetic parallelism in the use of designations, see §6.9.1. A further feature of the ingenuity with which this speech is composed is the fact that the three references to the king follow the usual pattern for the terms used, see §6.8.1-5.

coreferents in place of first or second person, is distinguished from the use of a "deferential vocative", the use of a title recognizing the addressee's status in a situation in which the addressee is treated as second person. Cases in which a subordinate addresses a superior without using deferential forms are also surveyed, to provide the best possible context in which to assess the use of deferential reference.[12] Usage in pre-exilic epigraphic materials shows patterns similar to those of the corpus, and some parallels are quoted (as has been done in §§20.1n, 20.2).[13] The discussion is based on clauses in which the subject represents the speaker or the addressee. The initial discussion is limited to human dyads. Address to God differs in some features from address to a human superior, and is consequently treated separately in §24.

---

[12] I have aimed to include all certain examples. Where speaker and addressee each outrank the other in one hierarchy, as king and man of God, they are considered as equals, and their speech is only included if it shows some feature of particular interest, as that of Bathsheba to her son, King Solomon, in 1K 2:21 (see §21.4.1).
[13] There are differences – e.g. deferential terms are more freely used in the Lachish letters than is usual in the corpus – but inadequate knowledge of the context of the epigraphic materials prevents any serious assessment of their usage.

Deferential Speech: Modal Clauses

21.1 Introduction

The verb forms termed "modal" here are imperative forms, or imperfect forms (whether "neutral" in form, or marked as "cohortative" or "jussive"), which begin a clause, or are used in association with אל or נא, as described in Revell, 1989:13-17. A second person modal is used to ask the addressee to act. A first person modal presents an action which the speaker hopes or intends to perform. Where the addressee is superior to the speaker, the action indicated by a first person modal requires the authorization of the addressee, and sometimes also some action to enable the speaker to act as intended. In this situation, then, a first person modal also presents a form of request. A third person modal with subject representing either addressee or speaker, may be used to avoid direct reference in asking the former to act, or to authorize action by the latter. A third person modal may also be used to ask the addressee to authorize action by a third party. Thus all modal forms used in deferential speech can be said to present a request to the addressee. As a general rule, the use of a third person subject representing speaker or addressee (whether or no a deferential nominal is used) reflects the fact that the speaker has reason to fear that the request will be refused, or at least is uncertain as to whether it will be received favourably.

21.2 The Subject Represents the Speaker

21.2.1 A modal form of which the speaker is subject is used to present an action which the speaker hopes or intends to undertake. The modal may be first or third person. The third person, expressing deferential self-effacement, is used where the request is contrary to the addressee's known wishes, and where the relationship of the speaker to the addressee is such that the request is likely to appear presumptuous. The first person is used in other situations. The third person is thus used to represent the speaker in situations in which the request may offend the addressee, and so be rejected.

Where the speaker is treated as first person, deferential reference to the addressee is not usual.

21.2.2 A third person modal form is used where the speaker asks for permission to speak (1S 25:24, 2S 14:12), to make an unsolicited suggestion relating to the king's weakness (1S 16:16), or to make a suggestion contrary to the king's expressed wish in "Please may your servant return and I will die in my city" (ישב נא עבדך ואמות בעירי, 2S 19:38).[1] A third person modal is also used by Hannah to express thanks to the priest Eli in "May your servant find favour in your eyes" (תמצא שפחתך חן בעיניך, 1S 1:18). This request recognizes Eli's expression of goodwill in the preceding verse as establishing a relationship equivalent to the master-servant relationship, which imposes obligations on both parties. Her choice of the third person shows that she is uncertain whether Eli will accept the relationship as she sees it. Ziba uses the first person to thank King David with the same formula "May I find favour in your eyes, my lord king" (אמצא חן בעיניך אדני המלך, 2S 16:4). The king has just made him an important landholder, an evidence of favour which shows that a satisfactory relationship is established, justifying his choice of the first person.[2] In the above cases in which the speaker is treated as third person, reference to the addressee within the speech includes a deferential nominal, but it is not necessarily used within the modal clause.

21.2.3 A first person modal is used to present a wish or intention of the speaker where (as in the case of Ziba in 2S 16:4) there is no reason to expect that the speech will offend the addressee. Where the addressee is only marginally affected by the intended action, or can be expected to benefit from it, neither speaker nor addressee is referred to deferentially, as in "Please let me kiss my father and moth-

---

[1] The second verb is modal by position. The initial request in 1K 1:2 should probably be treated as a further example of an unsolicited request, in a context similar to that in 1S 16:16. The subject is, on the face of it, impersonal, but the speakers will presumably be responsible for the search suggested.

[2] Joab uses the same formula in a declarative clause to offer thanks in 2S 14:22 (see §23.7.2). Clauses introduced by "blessed" (ברוך) can be regarded as offering thanks. They are declarative clauses in structure, though often translated as wishes (see §23.3).

er, and I will follow you" (אשקה נא לאבי ולאמי ואלכה אחריך, 1K
19:20), and "Please let us detain you, and prepare a kid for you"
(נעצרה נא אותך ונעשׂה לפניך גדי עזים, Ju 13:15; in this case the use of
the plural can be seen as deferential, see §18.2.2). Other examples
occur in 1S 9:6, 20:29, 26:8, 2S 16:9, 17:1, 18:19, 1K 11:21, 2K 6:1-2.
Cases also occur in 1K 20:25, 31, but here speaker and addressee are
Aramaeans, so the value of the examples is uncertain. The narrator
does not represent forms of deference in speech between foreigners
in a number of cases in which it would be expected, possibly from
lack of interest in their activities. In "Whatever happens, please let
me run" (ויהי מה ארצה נא, 2S 18:22), the speaker is repeating a request which has already been refused. It seems likely that here the
lack of deferential forms shows that the speaker's strong personal
feeling has overcome the wish to placate a superior usually shown
when opposing his expressed wish, as in 2S 19:38 (quoted above, see
also §21.3.3).

21.2.4 Where the first person is used, the addressee is referred to
deferentially in "Let me set out and go and collect to my lord the
king all Israel" (אקומה ואלכה ואקבצה אל אדני המלך את כל ישׂראל, 2S
3:21), where Abner's reference to "my lord the king" enhances his
picture of David's expanding sovereignty. That is, the usage is expressive rather than a conventional attempt to deflect the addressee's displeasure. The speaker is referred to deferentially in a preceding clause requesting some action by the addressee needed to enable
the speaker's intended act in 1S 12:19, 28:22, but not in 1K 20:25,
where speaker and addressee are foreigners, nor in 1S 30:15, where
there is no formal relationship between speaker and addressee.
There is likewise no deferential usage in 2K 7:13, where the preceding request is in indirect form, avoiding reference to action by the
addressee.[3] Deferential reference to the speaker occurs in a subordinate clause, following that with the first person modal, in "Please
let me go and pay my vow... For your servant made a vow..."
(אלכה נא ואשלם את נדרי... כי נדר נדר עבדך..., 2S 15:7-8). The unusual
deference presumably reflects the speaker's uncertainty as to how
this request to his father, the king, will be received. They have been

---

[3]   No deferential forms are used in 1S 27:5 either, but there, the speech begins
with "If I have found favour in your eyes", a formula showing deference.

on bad terms before (2S 14:24), and he may fear that his preparations for rebellion (2S 15:1-6) have become known.

21.3 The Subject Represents the Addressee

21.3.1 A request for action by the addressee is typically made with a second person modal form, that is, with an imperative.[4] This is the standard form for such requests, whatever the relative status of speaker and addressee. Direct reference to the addressee is sometimes avoided by the use of third person structures. The motivation for such usage appears to be fear that the request may offend the addressee (for reasons similar to those motivating third person reference to the speaker), or at least by uncertainty as to how the request will be received. The failure to use third person address where a request can be expected to cause displeasure shows that the speaker is not treating the addressee as a superior. This is obvious where a request form is used to present abuse, as in 2S 16:7, 2K 2:23. It is an equally reasonable suggestion where the speaker "forgets himself", or, more precisely, forgets his relationship to the addressee, in his desire to impress the need for action on him, as in Joab's exhortation to King David to show himself to the people, in 2S 19:8. In such cases, the use of second person modals with no mitigation reflects the speaker's feeling of urgency or other emotion. Where a third person structure is used, the subject may be a deferential nominal representing the addressee, or it may be a noun or pronoun representing neither speaker nor addressee. The verb may be active or passive. The choice of structure seems to be determined largely by the nature of the request. Where a request is made in the second person, deferential reference is usually made to the speaker if the granting of the request will benefit the speaker, that is, if the addressee's action can be interpreted as recognizing some responsi-

---

[4]   In the following discussion, the addressee is said to be "subject" of such forms. This is a matter of convenience, and not intended as a statement of theoretical significance, but see §25.1.2.

bility towards the speaker.[5] Otherwise the speaker is typically represented in the first person.

21.3.2 *Negative requests* Where a negative request is made, the addressee as subject is represented in the third person where a king is asked to abandon a known attitude to a past event or an existing fact, as in "Let not the king ascribe anything to his servant" (אל ישם המלך בעבדו דבר, 1S 22:15), referring to the charge of conspiracy made in verse 13. Other examples occur in 1S 19:4, 25:25, 2S 13:32-3, 1K 22:8. A further example occurs in "Let not my lord impute to me guilt" (אל יחשב לי אדני עון, 2S 19:20). Here the king's attitude has not been expressed, but hostility is to be expected, as the speaker is asking that wrongdoing to which he confesses be overlooked. A second person subject is used where the addressee is asked to abandon an intention or reaction which is only a possibility, as in "Don't spend the night in Arbot haMidbar" (אל תלן הלילה בערבות המדבר, 2S 17:16), and "Do not, my lord the man of God, do not deceive your servant" (אל אדני איש האלהים אל תכזב בשפחתך, 2K 4:16). Other examples occur in Ju 4:18, 1S 7:8, 1K 2:20, 20:8, 2K 18:26. Hannah's plea to the priest Eli (1S 1:16) is probably a further example, in that it is directed against his possible intention to classify her as a "scofflaw" (בת בליעל). If it is felt to refer to his suggestion that she is drunk, it could be argued that her emotion overcomes the need for deference (see §21.3.3). The use of a second person parallel to a third person negative request in 2S 19:20 is described in §20.5.3.

21.3.3 Where the addressee is treated as third person, deferential reference is also used for the speaker in the speech. This is also done in 1S 1:16 and 2K 4:16, where the addressee is treated as second person, but has shown hostility, or is being charged with possible intent to deceive, so that there is reason to believe that the speech may give offense. There is no deferential reference to the speaker in Ju 4:18, where the request "do not fear" (אל תירא) is intended to

---

[5] The request in the Meṣad Ḥashavyahu appeal (line 1-2, Weippert, 1990:459 clause I) also fits this description. It uses a third person modal with a deferential nominal representing the addressee as subject, and also refers to the speaker deferentially.

comfort the addressee, or in 1S 7:8, where the addressee is requested to continue to pray as he said he would (1S 7:5). The effect of the addressee's known views in determining usage is no doubt modified by the nature of the relationship between speaker and addressee, and the speaker's need (or the lack of it) to express urgency, as in the example in 2S 17:16, where the third person might have been used if the request were not urgent, or the speaker were not on good terms with the addressee. Clearly, however, third person reference to the addressee, and deferential reference to the speaker, is typically used where the speech is more likely to offend the addressee, second and first person where it is less so.

21.3.4 *The offer of a gift* A gift places the recipient under obligation to the giver. The offer of a gift is therefore a delicate matter for a subordinate, who may be seen as trying to gain control over the actions of his superior. Araunah uses a third person modal to offer a gift to King David in "Let my lord king take and offer whatever he wants" (יקח ויעל אדני המלך הטוב בעיניו, 2S 24:22). This contrasts with the use of the second person by Naaman to the prophet Elisha in "Please accept a gift from your servant" (קח נא ברכה מאת עבדך, 2K 5:15). Naaman's use of the imperative, implying or assuming equal status, shows presumption (see §21.4.2). He abandons his arrogance in his next speech, using a passive construction to make a new request (see §21.4.1). Araunah's use of the third person for the addressee to whom he is offering a gift is undoubtedly more appropriate, since it avoids the direct suggestion that acceptance of the gift will place the addressee under an obligation to him. Even so, the obligation entailed would be intolerable in this case, too, and the gift is rejected. Declarative clauses may also be used to offer gifts. Indeed, Araunah repeats his offer in 2S 24:23, in the form of a performative statement, which similarly distances the situation by the use of third person reference to both speaker and addressee, see §23.4.2.

21.3.5 *Third person requests in other situations* The addressee is the subject of a third person modal form in a few other cases. Some of these present a request which the addressee is incapable of granting, as "May the king live" (יחי המלך). These are classed as wishes, and are not considered as directed to the addressee (see §6.9.2). In

"Please let our lord speak" (יאמר נא אדננו, 1S 16:16) and "Please let the king remember..." (...יזכר נא המלך, 2S 14:11) a third person request form is used by servants, or by a plaintiff, in advising the king. Advice is typically presented with second person modal forms (e.g. 2S 16:21), with references to the speaker in the first person. Third person is presumably used here from fear that the advice, which concerns the king's personal affairs, and is unsolicited, will offend the king. The deferential reference to the speaker in 1S 16:16 reflects the same fear. A third person modal is also used in "Let my lord the king speak" (ידבר נא אדני המלך, 2S 14:18), to indicate that the speaker is ready for the significant question that the king has proposed asking her. There is no close parallel; the imperative "speak" in 1S 15:16 is used between equals. However, the speaker in 2S 14:18 is presenting a fictional plea, in which she asks the king to bend the law in her favour. She uses a high level of deference throughout her dialogue with the king, reflecting her uncertainty over her reception. Her use of the third person in 2S 14:18 is no doubt a representative example. David's use of a third person modal in requesting the king to listen (1S 26:19) is deliberate strategy. He intends to distance himself from the addressee (see §23.8.2). Absalom uses a third person modal to request King David, his father, to join the festivities at his sheep-shearing in 2S 13:24. Such deference might reflect the fact that such a request was unusual, or the fact that the speaker fears that his fratricidal intentions will be suspected.[6] A third person passive modal is used in "Let the king be informed..." (...יתבשר אדני המלך, 2S 18:31). The context clearly shows that the messenger has reason to fear that his news will be badly received, even though he represents it as good (see §23.6).

21.3.6 Where a request clause of which the addressee is subject includes a reference to the speaker, a deferential form is most commonly used (17 cases in all). In all such cases the addressee is asked to do something to benefit the speaker, as in "Listen to the words of your servant" (ושמע דברי אמתך, 1S 25:24), or to benefit someone else as a favour to the speaker, as in "Let not the king wrong his servant, David" (אל יחטא המלך בעבדו בדוד, 1S 19:4). Where the re-

---

[6] In 2K 6:3, a lesser prophet uses imperatives in inviting the Prophet Elisha to accompany a working party, where such concern was unnecessary.

quest presented by the modal form accords with the assumed wishes of the addressee, speaker and addressee are represented by first and second person (although the addressee's status may be recognized by a deferential vocative), as in "Whenever you desire to come, O king, come" (לכל אות נפשך המלך לרדת רד, 1S 23:20). Other examples occur in Ju 4:18, 1S 14:7.

21.3.7 The use of the first person pronoun where the third is expected represents self-assertion. The speaker abandons deferential self-reference in expressing his own urgent concern in the request presented, as where Joab exhorts King David to show himself to the people: "I swear that, if you don't go out... (...נשבעתי כי אינך יוצא, 2S 19:8, if the king abandons his position, Joab will lose his). Other examples occur in 1S 20:8, where David pleads with Jonathan (his superior, see §7.1.4n) not to turn him over to King Saul, and in 1K 12:4, 9, 10, where the northerners plead with King Rehoboam for a less oppressive regime. The use of the first person in the requests put by the people to Samuel in 1S 8:5, 6, 11:12 is probably also to be taken as expressing strong concern. Contrast their use of third person self reference (with an emotional first person pronoun in the reference to their death) in 1S 12:19 (see §15.6.2).[7] In 2S 19:20, the presentation of emotion (first person) and deference (third) is combined through stylistic variation (see §20.5.3). In 1S 20:29, David's used of the first person may be considered emotional, but more probably Jonathan, who quotes his words, has omitted expressive features, as is to be expected in quotation (see §23.2.2n, and cf. §21.3.6). In 1S 29:4, 1K 11:21, 22, the use of first person forms may reflect the fact that both speaker and addressee are foreigners (see §21.2.3).

21.4 The Subject Represents Neither Speaker Nor Addressee

21.4.1 A third person modal form may be used to request the addressee to authorize action by others. The proposed actor may be represented as subject of the clause, as in "Please let Tamar my sis-

---

[7]   The use of the first person pronoun in "[Please return] my garment" (השב נא] בגדי [את, Meṣad Ḥashavyahu 12 as restored in Weippert 1990:459, clause XV) can also reasonably be said to mark emotion reflecting the strong concern of the speaker (or here the writer) in the request being made.

ter come..." (...תבא נא תמר אחותי, 2S 13:5, 6). Other examples occur in 1S 22:3, 26:22, 2S 13:26, 2K 2:16. The subject may be unspecified, as in "Please let them take five of the horses..." (ויקחו נא חמשה מן הסוסים..., 2K 7:13). Direct reference to the involvement of speaker or addressee may also be avoided through metonymy, as in "Please let my soul live" (תחי נא נפשי, 1K 20:32) A similar example occurs in 2K 1:13-14, and another, requesting the addressee to suit his speech to his audience, in "Please let your word be like that of one of them" (1K 22:13). In "Let no man's heart fail..." (אל יפל לב אדם ..., 1S 17:32) the unspecified man (אדם) is possibly an oblique reference to the addressee, King Saul.[8] An unspecified subject is used to ask that the addressee present something to the speaker in "Let them give me... (יתנו לי, 1S 27:5). A passive structure is often used for a request of this sort, as in "Please let there be given to your servant..." (...יתן נא לעבדך, 2K 5:17). Similar examples occur in Ju 11:37, 2S 21:6, 1K 2:21, and 2K 2:9.

21.4.2 A second person modal (rather than a third person structure of the sort surveyed) is used where the speaker has no reason to expect that the request will pose a problem for the addressee. Examples in negative requests are given in §21.3.2. Affirmative examples occur where the speaker believes that the addressee is obligated to grant the request, as where David expects recognition of his care for Nabal's property in "Please give what you can..." (תנה נא את אשר תמצא ידך..., 1S 25:8), or is well enough disposed to grant it, as where a daughter appeals to her father in "Give me a blessing" (הבה לי ברכה, Ju 1:15). The second person is also used where the speaker is not subordinate to the addressee, as in "send and gather" (שלח קבץ, 1K 18:19, spoken to the king by the prophet Elijah). Where the use of the second person is avoided, the compliance of the addressee is not certain. Most such requests are clearly difficult to grant, as is specifically stated of that in 2K 2:9 (see verse 10). They require change of plans (1S 27:5), of opinion (2K 7:13), even possibly of the presentation of God's word (1K 22:13), or other unusual

---

[8] The show of deference represented by avoidance of direct reference to the addressee would be appropriate to the situation, see §23.4.2. The Greek shows the more specific "my lord" instead. However, אדם is unexpected in this use, and could have general reference, as "anybody".

concessions. In 2S 13:5, 6, 26, (and perhaps other cases), the speaker is concerned to conceal his motivation from the addressee. Where the passive is used, the speaker has had a previous request rebuffed (2K 5:17), or the request requires a concession which seems clearly hostile to the interests of the addressee (1K 2:21), or involves arbitrary executions (2S 21:6), or a delay which may be dangerous (Ju 11:37). It seems clear that avoidance of second person request forms is motivated by fear that the request will be refused, or at least by uncertainty as to how it will be received. The use of the third person distances the members of the dyad, and avoids any suggestion that the speaker intends to limit the addressee's freedom of action in any way, or to impose an obligation on him. The use of the passive goes as far as is possible in this avoidance, while still using a modal request form to express the urgency of the request.

21.4.3 An addressee who is not subject of a clause used to present a request is usually not referred to in that request.[9] Reference to the speaker in such clauses is usually first person. Third person is used in Naaman's request in 2K 5:17. The contrast with his use of the imperative to offer a gift (2K 5:15, see §21.3.4) shows clearly that he fears that this new request will be rebuffed, as was the former one. Third person is also used in the introduction to ben Hadad's request in 1K 20:32, where the context shows that the granting of such a request from a person in his position would be unusual.

21.5 Conclusion

The above survey of clauses using modal verbs shows that the designation of both speaker and addressee in such clauses is conditioned by the relative status of speaker and addressee, the content of the speech, the expected reaction of the addressee to it, and the speaker's attitude to the speech, and to the addressee. The use of first and second person pronouns is usual, even where the addressee is the superior. The speaker uses the third person for deferential

---

[9]   Second person reference is sometimes used where there is no formal relationship between speaker and addressee. The addressee is a "man of God" in 1K 22:13, 2K 1:13-14, a foreign king in 1S 22:3, where the plural in "with you" is most probably a deferential reference to the addressee (see §19.2.6), but could represent his community.

self-effacement, or for distanced reference to the addressee, where the speech may appear presumptuous, or may seem to impose an obligation on a superior addressee, as in the case of a gift, or to limit his freedom of action in some other way, as in the case of a negative request. That is, such distancing usage is resorted to where the speaker expects that his speech will be displeasing to a superior addressee, or fears that it may be. A speaker may use the second person in such a situation, abandoning deference, either to present his request as immediate, urgent, or because he does not recognize the addressee as a superior. The self-assertive use of the first person pronoun where a deferential form is expected also marks immediacy. It typically reflects the speaker's emotion, his strong concern for the request he is presenting.

Deferential Speech: Interrogative Clauses

22.1 Introduction

A clause introduced by an interrogative particle may simply present a question intended to elicit information. However, in Hebrew (as in other languages) an interrogative clause is often used for the forceful presentation of a statement: an affirmative statement where the question contains a negative, a negative statement where it does not. A rhetorical question of this sort which concerns the actions or intentions of a superior can be taken as presenting criticism or opposition, and so is likely to offend the addressee. The limited information available in the corpus suggests that deferential forms are used in such questions where the speaker is uncertain how the speech will be received, or where opposition is intended, but the speaker wishes to keep on good terms with the addressee. Deferential terms are not used where the purpose of the question is to obtain information (i.e. where opposition is not intended), or where the strength of the speaker's feeling overcomes his wish to mollify the addressee, or if he does not care if the addressee is offended.

22.2 The Subject Represents the Speaker

22.2.1 Where the speaker is the subject of a question in a deferential context, the third person is used where the question concerns an existing fact for which the addressee is responsible, or where the speaker intends to reject a proposal by the addressee. The first person is used where a question concerning a proposal made by the addressee is put to obtain information, and is not intended to indicate rejection, or where the speaker's strong emotion overcomes the need for deference. Presumably, the speaker uses the third person when there is reason to fear that the question may offend the addressee. The use of the first person shows that the speaker does not envisage this possibility, or is indifferent to it.

22.2.2 The interrogative typical for non-humans is used together with a deferential form representing the speaker in the formulaic

question "What is your servant that you have regarded a dead dog
like me?" (מה עבדך כי פנית אל הכלב המת אשר כמוני, 2S 9:8). The
speaker, who might have expected death at the hands of the addressee, King David (see 2S 19:29) here expresses thanks for the promise
of good treatment through a conventional protest that he does not
deserve it.[1] A similar question is used to express disbelief in a prediction made by the addressee in 2K 8:13. Taken literally, questions
of this sort suggest that the statement or action of the addressee was
wrong. The use of the third person is intended to show that this
opinion is not a threat to the addressee. In fact the speaker is giving
thanks for generous treatment (2S 9:8), or questioning a prediction
that he will have a brilliant future (2K 8:13). The form of speech
chosen is conventional rather than expressive. In both cases, however, the speaker represents a group which has recently been at war
with that represented by the addressee, and may well feel uncertain
about the nature of his relationship with the addressee. This uncertainty probably provides the motivation for the choice of such a deferential mode of speech.

22.2.3 Where the question concerns a proposal made by the addressee, first person reference to the speaker is usual, unless the proposal is to be rejected, in which case third person is used. In 2S 19:35-
36 Barzillai uses a series of questions to reject King David's invitation. The the actual rejection is presented in the last of these, "Why
should your servant be any more a burden to my lord the king?"
(ולמה יהיה עבדך עוד למשא אל אדני המלך, 2S 19:36), which uses the
third person. This can be seen as repeating the intent (though not
the words) of the initial question and answer in the first person
"How many are the days of the years of my life that I should go up
with the king to Jerusalem? Eighty years old (i.e. too old) am I
today." (כמה ימי שני חיי כי אעלה את המלך ירושלם בן שמנים שנה אנכי
היום, 2S 19:35-36). The two passages thus form an "envelope",
which contains three further questions on the theme "Could I benefit from what is suggested?" The first and third use the first person,
the second, the third person. The shift in this structure from predominant use of the first person to predominant use of the third —

---

[1]   Cf. Lachish 2:3-4, where the interrogative "who" (מי) is used, as also in 5:3-4,
6:2-3.

from personal to formal presentation — presents the speaker's opposition to the addressee's wishes with both urgency and deference.
Since the speaker does not wish to offend the addressee, deferential
terms predominate in the next verse, which culminates in a further
question in which the addressee is subject (quoted in §22.3.1.). A
third person question is similarly used in 1S 27:5 to indicate that a
state of affairs authorized by the addressee is inappropriate.

22.2.4 In 1S 18:18, David questions a proposal by King Saul using
the formula "Who am I?", with the interrogative typical for humans, and the first person pronoun, in "Who am I and what is my
family... that I should be son-in-law to the king?" (...מי אנכי ומי חיי
כי אהיה חתן למלך). David finally agrees to the proposal (1S 18:26),
so it appears that a question put in this form does not indicate firm
rejection. The speaker is represented in the first person where the
question is a protest of innocence, as "What have I done? and what
wrong is my responsibility?" (כי מה עשיתי ומה בידי רעה, 1S 26:18).
Other examples occur in 1S 20:1 (the speaker, David, is subordinate
to the addressee, Jonathan, see §7.1.4n), 1S 29:8, 1K 18:9. The question "Am I a dog's head..?" (...הראש כלב אנכי, 2S 3:8), which also
presents a protest that the speaker is being treated unjustly, can be
added to this group (see also §23.5). The Shunammite woman uses
first person questions protesting that she did what she could to protect her own interests when reproaching Elisha with the death of
her son in "Did I ask a son from my lord? Did I not say...?"
(...השאלתי... הלא אמרתי, 2K 4:28). The prophet's servant also uses
the first person in questioning his master's orders in "How can I
put this before a hundred men?" (מה אתן זה לפני מאה איש, 2K 4:43).
This question presumably expresses astonishment. The speaker's
emotion (surprise) overcomes his prudence, and he abandons deferential language. Emotion is also reflected in the other uses of the
first person mentioned: anguish in the cases of the Shunammite and
the protests of innocence, surprise in the questions used to reject an
honour offered by the king. A first person subject is also used
where the main purpose of the question is to obtain (or to present)
information in 1S 28:11, 2S 16:19, 2K 6:15, 8:9.

22.2.5 Where a question with the speaker as subject directly opposes
a suggestion made by the addressee, the addressee is referred to in

the third person (1S 18:18, and four cases in 2S 19:35-37). A second person pronoun is used in 1S 27:5, where David suggests to Achish King of Gath that David's residence in the capital, which he authorized, is inappropriate. A deferential term might be expected. David also fails to call Achish "my lord" (אדני) where it might have been expected in 1S 28:2 (see §23.2.2), so it is possible that the narrator deliberately avoided showing him admitting subservience in this way. However he does refer to himself as "your servant" (עבדך) in both passages, so David's use of the second person pronoun in 1S 27:5 is better seen as evoking the persuasive force of personal relationship (see §22.5). The use of the pronoun suggests that deference is unnecessary because his suggestion will coincide with the king's wishes. The Shunammite's reference to Elisha as "my lord" in her first question "Did I ask a son from my lord?" (השאלתי בן מאת אדני, 2K 4:28) tempers her emotional use of the first person. She does not wish to offend Elisha by appearing to reject what he intended as a reward for her kindness to him. Her purpose is to persuade him to help her. Her second question uses a second person reference in a quote.

22.3 The Subject Represents the Addressee

22.3.1 The use of third person to represent the addressee as subject of an interrogative clause has a basis similar to its use to represent the speaker. The addressee is represented by the third person where the question concerns an act completed or in process, as "Why is my lord crying?" (מדוע אדני בכה, 2K 8:12). Third person reference to the addressee is also used where the question concerns a known intention of the addressee, as the terminal question, confirming Barzillai's rejection of King David's invitation (described in §22.2.3) "Your servant will just cross the Jordan with the king. Why should my lord king reward me in this way?" (כמעט יעבר עבדך את הירדן את המלך ולמה יגמלני המלך הגמולה הזאת, 2S 19:37). Such examples occur in 1S 26:18, 2S 19:37, 24:3, 21, and (in parallel with second person) 1S 24:15.[2] The indirect question "Perhaps this event originated with my lord the king?" (אם מאת אדני המלך נהיה הדבר הזה,

---

[2]   Third person is also used in the distancing language of Michal's expression of scorn in 2S 6:20.

1K 1:27) also fits this pattern. Obadiah's use of a passive structure to remind Elijah of past events: "Was my lord not informed...? (הלא הגד לאדני..., 1K 18:13) is another example. The question in this last case suggests that the addressee has overlooked significant facts. The others imply various similar failures, save that in 2K 8:12, which the speaker may fear will be felt as charging the addressee with a weakness. The speaker thus has reason to fear in each case that the question will be offensive to the addressee, and this is no doubt the reason for the use of the third person.

22.3.2 Second person is used where what is questioned is an interpretation of the addressee's conduct or intentions, rather than a known fact or a stated purpose, as in "But why should you take me to your father?" (ועד אביך למה זה תביאני, 1S 20:8). The action in question has not been stated as the addressee's intention; it will result if he fails to do what the speaker is requesting. Other examples occur in 1S 24:10, 2S 14:13 (with a following parallel third person), and 2K 5:13. In the latter case, Naaman's servants oppose his reaction to the prophet's advice, but this reaction was given in question form, not stated as a definite intention. A question expressing astonishment at the addressee's conduct is also put in the second person in 2S 12:21.

22.3.3 There are several exceptions to the usage as described. Jonathan's question "Why should you wrong an innocent by killing David without cause?" (ולמה תחטא בדם נקי להמית את דוד חנם, 1S 19:5) refers to a proposal put forward by the addressee (his father, King Saul) in 1S 19:1. This question closes an "envelope structure" which is opened with a third person request "Let not the king wrong his servant, David" (אל יחטא המלך בעבדו בדוד, 1S 19:4). The second person question must thus be understood in its relationship with the deferential request (See §20.5.3). It shifts the plea from the formal to the personal level in much the same way as Barzillai's speech in 2S 19:35-37 shifts from personal to formal (see §22.2.3). The use of the second person, evoking the personal relationship, is presumably intended to make the appeal more persuasive (see §22.5). In 2S 3:24, where Joab criticizes King David for allowing the murderer of his brother to go free, the speaker's obvious emotion presumably overrides the need for deference. The same occurs in 1K 17:18, where a widow blames the supposed death of her son on Elijah, and in 1K 1:13, where Bathsheba points out to King David that it seems unlikely that her son Solomon will succeed him, as he had promised. In these two cases, however, the speakers temper the outburst of emotion by the use of deferential vocatives.[3] The second person is also used in a question concerning the addressee's identity in 1K 18:7, and in one concerning his state in 2S 13:4.[4] A deferential vocative is used in both, but the use of the third person is not expected as neither question is likely to offend the addressee.[5]

22.3.4 Where the addressee is treated as third person in these questions, the speaker is represented by a deferential nominal in 1S 26:18, 2S 24:21, and 1K 1:27. Barzillai uses the first person in his question in 2S 19:37 suggesting emotional recognition of the honour intended by the king (see §22.3.1). His use of deferential self-reference in the preceding statement avoids any appearance of impoliteness. In 1K 18:13, where a passive structure is used to mark great deference (see §22.3.1), the following use of the first person (which probably reflects the emotion typical in a speaker urging his own case, see §23.7.5), corresponds to the usage in requests in which the use of a subject representing the addressee is similarly avoided (see §21.4.3). Where the addressee is represented in the second person, the speaker is usually represented by the first person. A deferential

---

[3] In Ju 8:1, 12:1, interrogative clauses are used to criticize the actions of military leaders, but the speakers are not their subordinates, so deferential usage is not to be expected, and this is also true for speakers who have rejected subordinate status, as in 1K 12:16. The same is probably true for the Witch of Endor, who criticizes King Saul in 1S 28:9, 12. She is not his subject, but an outlaw, and so never refers to him as "My lord", although she does refer to herself as "Your servant" in her attempt to persuade him to eat (1S 28:21-22).

[4] Also in Ju 13:11, 17, but there, the speaker is not aware of the addressee's status.

[5] It may be felt that the question in 2S 13:4, "Why are you so haggard?" (מדוע אתה ככה דל), is quite as offensive as that in 2K 8:12, discussed in §22.3.1. In that case, however, the speaker is a foreign army officer and the addressee a powerful man of God. In 2S 13:4 although the use of the title "son of the king" probably does show that the addressee is of higher status than the speaker, the two are cousins. It may be that the difference in the use of deferential forms was motivated by the different relationship of the members of the two dyads, rather than by the difference in the content of the two questions.

nominal occurs only in "Did not you, my lord king, swear to your servant..." (...הלא אתה אדני המלך נשבעת לאמתך, 1K 1:13). The intention is presumably to avoid the appearance of presumption offensive to the addressee; the emotional appeal to personal relationship represented by the use of the second person is tempered by the use of deferential vocatives for the same reason.[6]

22.4 The Subject Represents Neither Speaker Nor Addressee

Where the subject of an interrogative clause does not represent either speaker or addressee, the purpose of the majority of questions is to obtain information, and deferential forms are not used. Where a rhetorical question takes this form, and criticism is intended, deferential reference is used to avoid offending the addressee in "Why does this dead dog curse my lord the king?" (למה יקלל הכלב המת הזה את אדני המלך, 2S 16:9). In "Why have they stolen you... and taken the king across..." (...מדוע גנבוך... ויעברו את המלך, 2S 19:42), the speakers' greater personal concern in the events is reflected by the use of the second person pronoun, but the appearance of presumption is avoided by deferential use of the title.[7] Both questions imply criticism such as "You should have prevented this"; deference is necessary to avoid the appearance of seeking to direct the king. A similar case in 1S 14:45 questions the expressed intention of the addressee, King Saul, who is not referred to. It can be assumed that the speakers did not expect to cause offence by enabling him to avoid killing his son. The official's question in 2K 7:2, 19, in effect "Even under the best conditions, how could this occur?" also fails to mention the addressee, the Prophet Elisha. This question implies that the prophet's word is false, and does so without the palliating show of deference used in 2K 8:13 (see §22.2.2). The question in 2K 7:2, 19, does cause offence; the summary punishment of the official recalls that of the officers in 2K 1:10, 12, who similarly fail to treat the Prophet Elijah with sufficient respect.

---

[6] In Ju 6:13, a first person plural pronoun is used by a single speaker in a question suggesting disbelief in the previous words of the addressee, an angel. The use of the plural is probably a form of deference, see §18.2.2. The failure to express greater deference no doubt reflects the fact (at least as represented by the masoretic vowelling) the speaker does not realize that the addressee is an angel.

[7] The similar case in 2S 19:22 is not presented as addressed to the king.

22.5 Conclusion

The use of deferential language in clauses introduced by interrogative particles has, then, the same basis as their use in requests. Where the speaker expects or fears that a question will displease a superior addressee, deferential forms are used in an effort to prevent this. Otherwise first and second person forms are used. Second person forms are used in a few questions where third person forms are expected (see §§22.2.5, 22.3.3). Where this occurs, the language is intended to persuade. In this context, it seems reasonable to interpret the use of the second person as intended to depict the relationship of speaker and addressee as close and personal. Such use attempts to evoke sympathy and fellow feeling, to render the addressee more susceptible to the speaker's effort to persuade (cf. §§23.5, 23.8, and the use of kinship terms in address described in §25.3). In requests, the unexpected use of the second person was seen as an expression of urgency, or as indicating rejection of subordinate status. In both cases, the use of the second person where the third is expected reflects the speaker's strong concern in the speech. The speaker abandons the distancing use of deferential forms in favour of the immediacy of person-to-person speech. The choice of second person rather than third naturally has different value in different contexts, just as does the choice of "thou" where "you" is expected according to the categorization in Wales 1983:116.

Deferential Speech: Declarative Clauses

23.1 Introduction

Clauses which have neither an introductory interrogative particle, nor a modal verb are called declarative. The examples of such clauses in which deferential forms are used in the corpus include members of two new genres: statements concerning master-servant relationship, here called statements of fealty, and statements of praise. In addition, declarative clauses can be used in place of other structures in the genres already discussed. In these examples, as in those already discussed, third person reference to speaker and addressee is used where the speaker is uncertain as to how his speech will be received, and so feels the need to display deference in order to avert any suggestion that it reflects hostile or presumptuous feelings. Consideration of the use of deferential forms in clauses which do not fit the categories described above shows that the use of deferential nominals (particularly those representing the speaker) is often restricted to clauses which do not carry the essence of a communication, but provide a framework for it, or background to it. The contrasting use of personal pronouns thus highlights the essential clauses of the communication. The occasional use of deferential reference to distance the speaker from the addressee is also noted.

23.2 Statements of Fealty

23.2.1 The term "statement of fealty" as used here denotes a declarative clause in which the speaker claims, or accepts, a master-servant relationship between himself and a status-marked addressee. Since a relationship of this sort is the most common motivation for the use of deferential speech, it is not surprising that statements that such a relationship exists typically use deferential terms for the speaker and also (but less consistently) for the addressee. However, a speaker claiming servant status in relation to the addressee does not use deferential terms. A servant identifying himself to, or responding to a summons from, a master also uses the first person except in a few cases in which particular circumstances call for a display of deference.

23.2.2 Third person reference to both speaker and addressee appears to be standard in statements confirming an existing master-servant relationship, as "As my lord the king said, so will your servant do" (כאשר דבר אדני המלך כן יעשה עבדך, 1K 2:38).[1] Other examples occur in 1S 16:16, 2S 9:11, 15:15, 21 (also Lachish 4:2-3). The same type of statement is suggested (though possibly not intended) by David's response to Achish King of Gath in 1S 28:2. This differs from the above examples in using second person reference for the addressee. This probably reflects David's important position and good relationship with Achish, which is confirmed by the latter's response. Abigail's response to the message that David intends to take her as wife can also be seen as a form of declaration of fealty: "Your servant is a serving girl (ready) to wash the feet of the servants of my lord" (הנה אמתך לשפחה לרחץ רגלי עבדי אדני, 1S 25:41). The relationship proposed by the addressee is accepted by the speaker, and so, like an existing relationship, is not under question. Since what is proposed is not a master-servant relationship, it seems probable that modesty provides the motivation for Abigail's highly deferential language. She uses third person reference to avoid showing emotion, saying, in effect, "I have no choice".[2]

23.2.3 Where a subordinate claims servant status in relation to the addressee, and this has not existed previously, the situation is different. First and second person pronouns are used in the speech sug-

---

[1]   No deferential terms are used where this is quoted by another speaker in 1K 2:42. Where speech is quoted, not presented by the original speaker, it is often shortened. One way in which this is done is by excising "synonymous words or phrases which add depth to the original speech, but convey no new information" (see Savran, 1988:30). This can include the abandonment of expressive features, as where Naboth's expression "the inheritance of my fathers" (נחלת אבתי, 1K 21:3) is replaced by "my vineyard" (כרמי) where Ahab repeats his speech in 1K 21:6. The same shortening has no doubt occurred in 1K 2:42.

[2]   The surprising language may indicate that Abgail is thinking of David as king. Her language in 1S 25:30 suggests that she is aware that he has been anointed. Bathsheba uses deferential language in her plea to King David in 1K 1:17-21. Otherwise spouses are shown conversing as equals (see §2.4.2n).

gested to Hushai for his approach to Absalom "Your servant, I, O king, will be... and now, I am your servant" (עבדך אני המלך אהיה...) ועתה ואני עבדך, 2S 15:34). Hushai's actual address to Absalom (2S 16:16, 18-19) opens with a wish "Long live the king", but avoids other direct reference to the addressee.[3] King Ahab's statement "I am yours, and all that belongs to me" (לך אני וכל אשר לי, 1K 20:4) uses the first person. The demand of Ben Hadad King of Aram to which he is responding mentions wives, children, and possessions, but not service, so the categorization of the statement is uncertain. Ahab's response to the second demand, "All that you sent to your servant at first I will do" (כל אשר שלחת אל עבדך בראשנה אעשה, 1K 20:9) has a first person subject, but uses deferential self reference in a subordinate clause. The confirmation of Ahab's willingness to submit to Ben Hadad's original demand is thus presented with immediacy, but with suitable deference. His emphatically worded refusal of fealty under the new terms in the next clause naturally uses the first person only "This thing I cannot do" (והדבר הזה לא אוכל לעשות). First and second person are used in a statement of fealty spoken by a group in Ju 11:10, 2K 10:5.

23.2.4 A speaker uses deferential self-reference in replying to a question from a superior intended to discover or confirm his identity in 2S 9:2, 6, where the addressee may be expected to be hostile, and in 2S 15:2, where speaker and addressee are evidently strangers. In 1S 17:58, in a similar situation, the speaker's statement of identification is not only deferential; it avoids direct self-reference: "(I am) son of your servant Jesse of Bethlehem" (בן עבדך ישי בית הלחמי). The first person is used by a speaker responding to a summons where he has no reason to doubt the goodwill of the addressee, as in the case of Samuel and the priest Eli in 1S 3:5, 6, 8, 16, or is beyond his power, as is the case of David and King Saul in 1S 26:17. In "Here am I,

---

[3] The use of "servant" as predicate or complement may preclude its use as subject, but this problem could have been obviated by the use of some other deferential nominal, as it is in Abigail's speech in 1S 25:41 (see §23.2.2). The use of the first person shows at least that the development of another nominal was not found necessary. Statements of this sort do, in fact, claim a privileged relationship (see §2.3.7), so that the use of the personal pronoun seems fitting. Cf. the use of a self-assertive form of the first person pronoun in claiming a position, noted in §26.3.1.

my lord" (הנני אדני, 1S 22:12), the priest Ahimelech combines the use of the first person with a deferential vocative (see §23.7.6). He is, presumably, conscious of no guilt, but the form of King Saul's command to listen, to which he is responding, certainly does not indicate goodwill (see §25.5.1). Ahimelech's use of the deferential vocative reflects unease about his reception. In these uses grouped under "fealty", then, the use of deferential terms can be seen as reflecting a feeling that it may be prudent to placate the addressee. First person forms are used where this is not felt to be necessary, or where emotion overcomes the need for deference.

23.3 Praise and Thanks

Third person reference to the addressee is used in some clauses which ascribe good qualities to the addressee, as "My lord is as wise as an angel..." (ואדני חכם כחכמת מלאך האלהים..., 2S 14:20). Other examples occur in 1S 25:28, 29, 2S 14:9, 19:28. In each of these cases, the speaker is in a difficult situation: pleading to save her homestead in 1 Samuel 25, her son (in a fictitious plea) in 2 Samuel 14, and pleading for his own life in 2S 19:28. The use of deferential forms no doubt reflects the speaker's fear that the plea will not be favourably received. Compare the use of the second person in expressing thanks in "You are a man of God, and the word of the Lord in your mouth is truth" (איש האלהים אתה ודבר אלהים בפיך אמת, 1K 17:24). Thanks to a superior is offered with the formula referring to "finding favour" with the addressee (מצא חן בעיני), with a modal verb (see §21.2.2) or an indicative (as in 2S 14:22, quoted in §23.7.2). A clause introduced by "blessed" (ברוך) may be used to thank an addressee who is not status marked (in which case he is represented as subject of the clause, as in Ju 17:2, 1S 15:13, 23:21, 25:33, 26:25, 2S 2:5, 1K 2:45, also Ruth 3:10). The same formula is used to "bless" or thank God for events favourable to the speaker (see §24.4n). In 1S 25:32 action by the addressee (the speaker's equal in status) is named as such an event in a "blessing" followed by others of which she is subject.

23.4 Requests

23.4.1 Declarative clauses can be recognized as presenting a request by the fact that they occur where a modal form is usual, or by the fact that they make a statement about future actions of the addressee which the speaker can not possibly expect to control. A declarative clause used in this way often refers to the indefinite future. It is not formally marked as a request, and so lacks the urgency indicated by the use of modal forms. A request may also be implied by the use of a clause which simply describes an unfortunate situation which the addressee could improve. This would appear to be the most humble and self-effacing form in which a request can be made, since the implication can be ignored without causing the embarrassment which the definite refusal of an explicit request would inflict on both members of the dyad.

23.4.2 *A Third Person Subject represents the Speaker* A third person declarative clause is used by the speaker, David, to volunteer a service in "Your servant will go and he will fight this Philistine" (עבדך ילך ונלחם עם הפלשתי הזה, 1S 17:32). This contrasts with the usual use of first person modal forms to express an intention expected to conform to the wishes of the addressee (see §21.2.3). The use of a second third person verb in 1S 17:32 is also unusual (see §20.2). David does not refer to the addressee, King Saul, in this passage (1S 17:32, 34-37) except through the pronoun in "your servant" (1S 17:32, 34, 36, and possibly by the non-specific term "man", see §21.4.1). The extreme deference shown by these various features is probably to be explained in part by the speaker's status, and in part by the situation. David, a "lad" (נער, see §2.2.6), and not a member of the army (cf. 1S 17:28), is taking up a challenge which King Saul and his troops have all refused. His deference deprecates a charge of presumption; it shows that this is not an attempt to place himself above them. A declarative clause, a performative statement with a third person subject representing the speaker, is used to offer a gift in "Araunah has given everything {O king} to the king" (הכל נתן ארונה המלך למלך, 2S 24:23).[4] The third person reference to both speaker and addressee distances them from each other and from the situation, obscuring the idea that accepting the gift will place the addressee under an obligation. A first person indicative is occasionally used to express an intention, as in 1S 9:8, where it responds to

---

[4] The word "O king" (המלך) was probably introduced through error, see §§ 25.7.3, 27.2.1. This clause follows, and complements, a modal request, with a third person subject representing the addressee.

an objection which the addressee presented to a plan proposed by the speaker.

23.4.3 *Requests in the Second Person* Declarative clauses which can reasonably be understood as requesting action by the addressee use second person forms. The verb may be imperfect, or perfect with *waw* consecutive. It may follow a modal request, as "Do not spend the night... You will indeed cross..." (אל תלן... וגם עבר תעבר , 2S 17:16), or it may not, as "You will remember your servant" (וזכרת את אמתך, 1S 25:31). Other examples occur in Ju 9:32-3, 11:8, 1S 20:5, 6, 8, 2S 18:3, 1K 11:22, 20:8, 25, 2K 19:4. In these cases the speaker is making statements about future actions of the addressee. Since the addressee is a superior, the speaker cannot ensure that these actions are carried out, so the statements must be regarded as conveying a wish or request. A preceding modal with the same subject, where it occurs, provides contextual support. The use of an indicative verb would appear to imply less urgency, and so greater deference, than the use of a modal form.[5] In 2S 17:16, this greater deference balances the unusual use of the second person in a negative request made to a superior (see §21.3.2). The use of the "infinitive absolute" supplies the indication of urgency required. It is also true that requests of this sort often apply to the indefinite future rather than to the immediate present, the sphere of reference of most modal requests. The use of the second person for the addressee is consistent with usage in requests using modal forms, see §21.3.1.

23.4.4 *Implied Requests* In 2K 2:19, "Look here, please, the site of the city is good, as my lord sees, but the water is bad..." (הנה נא מושב העיר טוב כאשר אדני ראה והמים רעים...) appears simply to be a statement describing unhealthy living conditions. However "Look

---

[5]   See Longacre, 1989:119-136, especially the schema on p. 121; Revell, 1989:21-29. The negative לא is ranked by Longacre with (clause-initial) indicatives, not with modals. This appears to fit the usage of the corpus, also (Revell, 1989:27), in contrast to its use in the Pentateuch to mark a strong prohibition. However, the point is debated. See Waltke and O'Connor, 1990:567 n6. It could well be argued that the opposition modal : indicative represents "urgent request for the near future" : "other request". The use of the indicative can then be interpreted (according to its context) as presenting a request that is either non-urgent, or not concerned with or restricted to the immediate future (see §28.2.2).

here, please" (הנה נא) typically introduces a statement made as the basis for a following request, as in 2K 2:16, 4:9, 5:15, 6:1. In 2K 2:19, the introductory statement alone is presented; the following request is implied. The same occurs in the request to speak in Gen 18:27, 31, both cases in which the purpose of the speaker (Abraham, trying to dissuade God from a proposed action) requires a great display of deference to avoid appearing presumptuous. In 2K 2:19, the speakers, the "men of the city" intend the speech as a request, but the prophet is under no obligation to help them, so they also need to avoid the appearance of presumption. Consequently, they phrase their request in such a way that it could be ignored without embarrassment to either party. The addressee, the Prophet Elisha, in fact reacts to the speech by dealing with the problem.[6] The speech of the debt-ridden woman in 2K 4:1, and the lament of the man who lost the borrowed axe in 2K 6:5, can similarly be taken as implied requests. Not only is a request form not used in these cases; there is no self reference by the speakers either, save indirectly, in 2K 4:1. This is, then, the most self-effacing form in which a request can be made. It thus expresses the greatest humility, and, by implication, the greatest respect for the addressee.

23.4.5 In the example in 2K 2:19, where the addressee has no certain relationship to the speakers, he is referred to deferentially. In 2K 6:5, where the speaker is related to the addressee as a servant (2K 6:3), a deferential vocative is used. In 2K 4:1, the speaker bases her appeal on the master-servant relationship between her dead husband and the addressee. She has a further claim on his assistance as a widow appealing on behalf of her children. She uses second person pronouns, invoking the persuasive force of personal relationship. Her use of the first person in referring to members of her family expresses her emotion and reflects the urgency of her case; the sale of her children as slaves is imminent. The same correlation between the forms of reference to speaker and addressee, their relationship, and the situation, can be seen in Ju 19:18-19, where speaker and addressee are equals and strangers. The addressee is obligated

---

[6]   I owe this insight (and much else in the treatment of modal and other requests) to Ahouva Shulman, who pointed out to me that נא is always used in connection with a request, even when not following a verb. See also Kaufman, 1991.

only by the custom of hospitality. The speaker runs no risk beyond the necessity of spending a night in the open. The speaker uses the first person in subjective position (using the plural to show deference, then the singular, reflecting emotion, see §18.2.3) and uses deferential terms for his party, or other members of it, in other positions. The addressee is not referred to except in the conventional use of the second person pronoun in these deferential terms.[7]

23.4.6 *The offer of a gift* The use of a performative statement, using third person reference to speaker and addressee, to avoid the suggestion that a superior will incur an obligation by accepting a gift from a subordinate, is described in §23.4.2. Where the speaker has real reason to fear that the addressee is not well-disposed, a passive or impersonal structure with indicative verbs may be used to present a request, including the offer of a gift (modal forms may also be used in this way, see §§21.3.5, 21.4.1). In "This gift, which your servant has brought to my lord, it will be given to the lads who follow my lord" (הברכה הזאת אשר הביא שפחתך לאדני ונתנה לנערים המתהלכים ברגלי אדני, 1S 25:27), the speaker, Abigail, is in a critical situation. If David, the addressee, is to abandon his expedition against her homestead, he must be persuaded to accept the gift she has brought. She uses a passive structure to avoid any suggestion that he is to incur an obligation by receiving the gift. She uses an indicative verb to avoid any hint of urgency. Her speech thus carries no suggestion of pressure to arouse suspicion or hostility in the addressee. Where Ziba replies to the king's question "What have you got there?" (מה אלה לך), he merely makes a statement "The donkeys are for the king's household to ride, the bread and fruit for the lads..." (החמורים לבית המלך לרכב ו{ל}הלחם והקיץ לאכל הנערים...), 2S 16:2). The importance to King David of the gift thus offered is shown by the size of the reward with which he discharges his obligation (2S 16:4). However, Ziba is servant to Mephibosheth, who could well become a figurehead for the uprising from which David is fleeing. He, too, has reason to avoid seeming to pressure the king

---

[7] The speech in 2K 5:4 should perhaps be included, but speaker and addressee are foreigners, and the lack of deferential usage may reflect the narrator's lack of interest in the details of their activities (see §21.3.7), as does his failure to represent the full speech.

to incur an obligation. Consequently, he uses a distanced form of expression, avoiding any reference to himself as offering, or King David as receiving, a gift. Vows, where the acceptance of the gift is not in question, are made with indicative verbs (see §24.7.2).

23.4.7 *The offer of a suggestion* Similar strategy may be used in offering a suggestion, to avoid any appearance that the speaker is directing the actions of the addressee. In 2S 17:8-13, Hushai gives his advice at the request of the usurper, Absalom. Despite the fact that his advice was asked for, he shifts to a passive structure where his advice involves Absalom: "I advise (that) all Israel will be gathered to you..." (... כי יעצתי האסף יאסף עליך כל ישראל, 2S 17:11). Hushai is known as a former supporter of the father against whom Absalom is rebelling. He no doubt guesses that he is being tested (2S 17:5), so he avoids the appearance of directing Absalom, showing great deference in order to lull suspicion.[8] He continues this strategy by using another third person reference in the following clause "and your presence will proceed to battle" (ופניך הלכים בקרב, 2S 17:11).[9] In "Even the whole he will take..." (...גם את הכל יקח, 2S 19:31), a third person indicative clause is used to offer a gift to a third party, an offer which will affect, and must be confirmed by, the addressee (King David). The following clause, giving the motivation for the request, has a third person reference to the king, reflecting the continued fear of the speaker (who has just been pardoned for not supporting him) that he is hostile.

23.5 Questions

In a few cases where words or actions evoke a negative response, this response is presented in a first person declarative clause, which must be understood in the context as a question, or an expression of astonishment. This occurs in "Today I first enquired of God for

---

[8]   Despite the enthusiastic reception of his advice in 2S 17:14, the two following verses show that he remains unsure that it will be taken.

[9]   "Your presence" (literally "your face") is also used in place of a second person pronoun in Exod 33:15, where the speaker's situation requires extreme deference, as does Hushai's here. Hushai may also use this term to avoid the expected title "king", which, for him, applies only to David. He is shown using the title, when speaking to Absalom, only in the non-specific "May the king live" (2S 16:16).

him? Damme!" (היום החלתי לשאול לו באלהים חלילה לי, 1S 22:15).
Another example, terminating in an oath formula, occurs in 2S
11:11. The speaker is strongly emotionally involved in both cases.
In 1S 22:15, he rejects a serious charge by the king, and is probably
indifferent to the king's reaction. In 2S 11:11, the speaker rejects the
king's suggestion, but would no doubt prefer to remain on good
terms. Third person reference to the speaker would be expected if
such opposition were expressed through an interrogative clause (see
§22.2.1). The use of the first person in these examples reflects the
speaker's emotion. Similar examples of a first person clause used to
reject suggestions occur in 1K 17:12, 2K 2:2, 4, 6, 4:30 (using an
oath formula), 1K 21:3 (using "Damme", חלילה, which appears to
represent the more emphatic rejection, as in 1S 22:15).[10] Both
"Damme" and an oath formula are used in 1S 14:45. A second person declarative clause which cannot be taken as a statement occurs
in "My lord king, you (must have) said..." (אדני המלך אתה אמרת...,
1K 1:24). The speech is intended to persuade; the evocation of personal relationship through the use of the second person pronoun is
intended to assist this (see §22.5). The speaker is, however, closely
concerned here also. If the king does not intervene to prevent
Adonijah from succeeding to the throne, he is in danger, as he has
supported a rival. His concern is shown in his emotional use of the
first and second person pronouns in the speech (tempered by the
derefential vocative), and prompts the display of deference and the
indirect format of the question with which the speech ends (1K
1:27).

23.6 Statement Clauses

The motivation for the use of deferential forms in unmarked clauses
which simply convey information is the same as in other clauses:
fear that the speech will offend an addressee whose goodwill the
speaker values, or at least uncertainty as to how the addressee will
receive the speech. Thus a speaker refers to himself deferentially in
2S 13:35, where the communication is, effectively, "I told you so",
in 2S 18:29, where it is "I don't know", and in 2K 5:25, where he

---

[10] First person is used after an oath formula to express opposition in Lachish 3:9-
12. The situation in Lachish 6:12-15 (where first person is not used) is not clear.

lies about his movements. The same strategy is used in 2K 4:2, where the speaker's answer appears likely to block the addressee's attempt to help her, and so is also likely to offend. Deferential reference to the addressee is made in a case of this sort in 2S 18:28, where the speaker presents news of the king's victory in the form of a blessing "Blessed is the Lord your God who delivered over the men who raised their hands against my lord the king" (ברוך יהוה אלהיך אשר סגר את האנשים אשר נשאו את ידם באדני המלך). The men in question were led by the king's son, who has been killed, despite the king's order that he be treated carefully (2S 18:5). The deferential usage of this speaker, and of the other messenger who brings the same news (see §21.3.5 on 2S 18:31), shows clearly that they fear that the king will be upset by the news. The speech of the Tekoite woman in 2S 14:19 includes deferential reference to herself and to the addressee, as well as a deferential vocative. The king is likely to be displeased by the speaker's admission that she has been deceiving him. Deferential reference to the king made in connection with requests to God (made in speech to the king) to prosper the reign of the son who is to succeed him (1K 1:36-7) possibly reflects the fear that the king will be annoyed by repeated reference to his supercession. Deferential vocatives are used in other declarative clauses in Ju 3:19, 1S 24:8, 26:17, 2K 1:9, 11, 4:40, 8:5, 9:5, 5. The main motivation for their use must sometimes be to attract the addressee's attention, (as in 2K 8:5, cf. 1S 24:8), but equally they are used where, as in that case, the speaker has reason to fear that his reception will not be friendly.

23.7 The Marking of Immediacy: First Person

23.7.1 The choice between pronouns and deferential forms can also be used to mark immediacy. The choice of a pronoun where a deferential term is expected shows that a modal or interrogative clause is immediate for the speaker (see §§21.5, 22.5). A similar effect can be achieved through the distribution of pronouns and deferential forms in declarative clauses. Where the speech provides scope for variation, the use of the third person representing the speaker tends to be restricted to non-subjective function, or to clauses which do not carry the intended communication, but provide a framework for it (as introductory or explanatory clauses), or add ancillary details to it (as relative or circumstantial clauses). The essential clauses of the speech are thus highlighted by the use of the first person pronoun. The position of deferential reference to the addressee may be varied in a similar way, but this is not so obvious. Where the situation requires the expression of deference, but standard usage (or the speaker's purpose) calls for the use of the second person, deference is typically shown by the use of vocatives.

23.7.2 A clear example of the correlation between the use of first person forms and the importance of the clause for the speaker's purposes occurs in David's response to Saul's rejection of his offer to fight Goliath. He begins with a third person self-reference "Your servant was a shepherd" (רעה היה עבדך, 1S 17:34). This clause is introductory (the perfect verb marks it as grammatical background). It provides the context in which the following narrative, which constitutes the basis for the message that David wishes to present, is to be understood. The narrative itself is given in the first person: "I used to go out after it (a predator) and I would strike it and I would rescue (its prey) from it. It attacked me. I would seize its hair and I would strike it and I would kill it." (ויצאתי אחריו והכתיו והצלתי מפיו ויקם עלי והחזקתי בזקנו והכתיו והמיתיו, 1S 17:35). This is recapitulated in the third person: "your servant struck" (הכה עבדך, 1S 17:36, note the perfect verb again). The intended message is then presented as a conclusion, using the first person: Yahweh who saved me (then)... he will save me from this Philistine" (יהוה אשר הצלני... הוא יצילני מיד הפלשתי הזה, 1S 17:37). The clauses in which the first person is used are those in which the speaker is most likely to be emotionally involved. They are also those essential to his argument. The two factors together account for the choice of first person here. The clauses in which the speaker is presented in the third person form the framework used to present the argument.[11]

---

[11]   The Meṣad Ḥashavyahu petition shows similar usage. The introductory clauses, which present the background to the complaint, refer to the complainant in the third person (Weippert, 1990:459, clauses I-VIII, also clause XI, which recapitulates the act complained about). The following clauses, which seek to vindicate the complainant, refer to him in the first person. The shift of person evidently occurs in clause X, where the act complained about has third person reference, followed by the first person used in a subordinate clause.

23.7.3 Further examples illustrating this feature of the distribution of deferential and first person forms are easily supplied. Ahab's speech in 1K 20:9, using the first person for the main verb, with deferential reference in a subordinate clause, is quoted in §23.2.3. In 1S 28:21-22, third person reference to the speaker is used in two introductory clauses "Your servant listened to your voice... now listen to your servant's voice...", but first person in the clauses they introduce "I put my life in danger, and I did listen..." and "Let me put a little food before you..." (הנה שמעה שפחתך בקולך ואשים נפשי בכפי ואשמע... ועתה שמע נא גם אתה בקול שפהתך ואשימה לפניך פת לחם ...).[12] In 2S 14:22, clauses using third person reference to the speaker frame one in which the first person is used in a speech of thanks: "Your servant now knows that I have found favour in your eyes, my lord king, since the king has followed the suggestion of his servant."(היום ידע עבדך כי מצאתי חן בעיניך אדני המלך אשר עשה המלך את דבר עבדך). The same pattern occurs in 1K 20:39-40, "Your servant went out... A man came and brought a man to me and said... Your servant was busy here and there..." (עבדך יצא... והנה איש סר ויבא אלי איש ויאמר... ויהי עבדך עשה...). In both cases, the use of the first person highlights the clause essential for the communication.

23.7.4 Where the speaker is usually referred to in the first person, deferential reference is not made through the subject of a main clause, but in less important situations. In the plea of the woman to King Solomon in 1K 3:17-21 the only deferential reference to the speaker is made in a circumstantial clause: "your servant was sleeping" (ואמתך ישנה, 1K 3:20). In Obadiah's plea to the prophet Elijah in 1K 18:9-14, third person reference is made to the speaker in 1K 18:9 as object, and in 1K 18:12 as subject of a circumstantial clause, but not otherwise. Other examples of deferential representation of the speaker in less important situations occur in 2S 14:15, 17 (in verbs introducing speech), and (in non-subjective functions) in Ju 19:19, 2S 14:6, 7, 18:29 (in a first person clause!) and 1K 1:17. There is also an interesting contrast in the report of Joab's messenger to

---

[12] In 1S 28:21, the clauses in this speech form an envelope structure which emphasizes the speaker's former compliance with the addressee's request. The English translation somewhat obscures the parallelism of the verbal roots שמע... שים... שמע... שים, wittily used to make the argument more telling.

King David. The relatively commendable action reported in 2S 11:23 is given in the first person. The third person is used for the report of casualties in 2S 11:24, which may be expected to anger the king.

23.7.5 The validity of this view of the use of first person subject pronouns in deferential situations is shown by their characteristic use in speeches presenting confession or self-excuse. In "Your serv-ant knows that I have sinned" (כי ידע עבדך כי אני חטאתי, 2S 19:21), the introductory verb is third person, that of the confession, first. First person confessions of sin against God, but spoken to a human, occur in 1S 12:19, 15:24, 2S 12:13.[13] First person is also used in statements that the speaker accepts the guilt for a past act (1S 25:24), or a potential one (2S 14:9). Use of the first person is also characteristic of clauses intended to excuse or justify the speaker's actions, as in 2S 19:27 (cf. the use of the first person in questions protesting innocence §22.2.4). Other examples occur in 1S 1:15-16, 24:11, 12, 26:23. A deferential nominal is used in one further exam-ple, but even there it stands in apposition to the first person; it does not replace it: "I, your servant did not see my lord's lads whom you sent" (ואני אמתך לא ראיתי את נערי אדני אשר שלחת, 1S 25:25).[14] The first person is also used by the Tekoite supplicant to present facts which justify her conduct in 2S 14:5, 19.[15] The use of the first per-son in these clauses marks the strong emotion in the speaker natural to confession, self-justification and similar genres. It also marks them as immediate in contrast to the deferential forms used in introductory clauses, as "Your servant knows..." (2S 19:21), or in other framework material, as "Let your servant speak..." (1S 25:24).

23.7.6 It is clear, then, that, where deferential forms are used, and the conventions of usage permit the use of first person pronouns as

---

[13]   In other examples the addressee is God (see §24.5), or is not a superior, as in 1S 26:21, 2K 18:14.

[14]   Nathan similarly uses a deferential term in apposition to the first person pro-noun, to combine the expression of emotion and deference in "And me, me your servant... he did not invite", ולי אני עבדך... לא קרא, 1K 1:26.

[15]   In the Meṣad Ḥashavyahu petition, first person pronouns are used in lines 10-11 (Weippert, 1990:459, clauses XII, XIII, and XIV) which present similar material.

well, the contrast between the two has expressive significance. The use of the first person pronoun is often reasonably explained as reflecting the urgency of the situation, or the speaker's emotional involvement for other reasons. Such motivating factors can all be covered by the statement that the use of the first person in a situation where the use of deferential forms is appropriate marks the clause as immediate. It is important to the speaker, central to his interest, of immediate concern to him. By contrast, the use of deferential forms marks the clause as relatively unimportant, as peripheral to the speaker's interests, as of distant concern. Where the speaker needs to use first person pronouns to express emotion, they are typically used as subject. Deferential forms are used in other functions. The importance of subjective function in this usage is consistent with the importance of that function shown throughout this study as particularly relevant to biblical Hebrew usage (see §5.4.2). In this, as in many minor details, deferential usage can be shown to be a part of a self-consistent system of expressive usage which pervades all areas of the language.

23.8 The Marking of Immediacy: Second Person

23.8.1 The second person pronoun is similarly used expressively in contexts in which deferential reference to the addressee would be appropriate. Its use can also be related to the expression of the speaker's strong concern, marking the clause as immediate. Deferential reference to the addressee is usual where the speaker feels that the speech is likely to be unfavourably received, and wishes to deprecate the hostility it may arouse. Second person reference is most often used to suggest that this is not the case — to attempt to predispose the addressee in the speaker's favour by representing their relationship as close and personal. However, the failure to use deferential reference to the addressee (as to the speaker), can also reflect indifference to the addressee's reception of the speech (see §21.5). The possibility that the former use will be mistaken for the latter can be avoided by the use of deferential vocatives. Such usage is illustrated in the pleas made to King David on the subject of the succession. Bathsheba's plea in 1K 1:17-21 is sharply critical of the king, and urges him to make a clear decision. Nathan's plea in 1K 1:24-27 is more circumspect (see §23.5). In consequence, Bathsheba uses three deferential vocatives to express her fealty to the King, whereas Nathan uses only one. Other cases of the use of deferential vocatives where the speaker is opposing a suggestion or possible intention of the addressee, or has other reason to fear that the addressee will not receive the speech favourably, occur in Ju 6:13, 1S 1:15, 25:24, 26, 2S 14:9, 19, 1K 1:13, 3:26, 17:18, 2K 1:9, 11, 13, 4:16, 6:12.

23.8.2 In contrast to the use of second person forms to present the speaker's association with the addressee as close and personal, third person reference to the addressee depicts speaker and addressee as distanced, not in personal contact. The usual intention of such usage is to placate the addressee. Third person reference to the addressee may also be motivated by the speaker's desire to distance himself, that is, to reject any close association with the addressee. David's use of deferential terminology in his speech to King Saul in 1S 26:17-25, contrasts sharply with his general use of the second person in 1S 24:10-16, a contrast which exemplifies the deterioration in their relationship.[16] Saul opens their dialogue with "Is that your voice, my son David?" (הקולך זה בני דוד, 1S 26:17). This use of a kinship term, expressing Saul's intention to effect a reconciliation, should evoke corresponding language, just as Saul responds to David's use of "my father" in 1S 24:12 with "my son" in 1S 24:17. David replies "(It is) my voice, my lord the king" (קולי אדני המלך) using a deferential form, a striking contrast. He goes on to assert that he is innocent and Saul in the wrong. This evokes a speech from Saul in which he abases himself, and admits wrong doing (1S 26:21), a speech also addressed to "My son David". In his reply, "Here is the king's spear" (הנה חנית המלך, 1S 26:22), David again uses deferential terminology (now in the third person) where a kinship term is expected. Fokkelman (1986:544) sees David's use of deferential terms as "correct, loyal, but without personal warmth", a view which is certainly valid. David's usage is more than this, however.

---

[16]   The second person is used only three times in twelve references to King Saul in chapter 26 (1S 26:19, 23, 24), none in subject position. In chapter 24, he uses the second person in 22 cases, six of which are in subject position. Among the five other references to King Saul, "my father" in 1S 24:12, appeals to their close relationship. Even the ironic use of the title "king of Israel" is balanced by a second person form used in parallel in 1S 24:15, but not in 1S 26:20.

As a reply to Saul's obvious desire for rapprochement, it represents a disdainful rebuff. David not only ignores Saul's attempt at conciliation, he uses deferential forms and the third person to distance himself, showing that there is no contact on a personal level between himself and Saul.

23.9 Conclusion

23.9.1 The material in this chapter supports the conclusions already reached above. Deferential forms, third person, low in specificity, are used for self-effacement and distancing where the speaker expects or fears that the speech will displease the addressee, in the hope of averting such displeasure. The use of the highly specific first and second person pronouns where deferential forms are expected marks immediacy, showing that the clause is of great concern to the speaker, a concern that is usually reasonably described in terms of urgency or some other emotion. This value of the use of these pronouns is also apparent in the distribution of pronouns and deferential forms in speeches in which both are used. Pronouns are typically used in the clauses essential to the communication, deferential forms in clauses which provide a framework for, or a background to them. A further example of this occurs in the speech of Jephthah's daughter "Let this thing be done for me: let me go for two months..." (יעשׂה לי הדבר הזה הרפה ממני שׁנים חדשׁים, Ju 11:37). A highly deferential form of request, with an impersonal passive verb (see §23.4.6) is used for introduction. Non-deferential, second person modal verbs are used to present the actual request. Again, the use of deferential forms correlates with non-immediacy, the use of non-deferential forms with immediacy. The clauses marked as framework or background in this way are of types similar to those marked as non-immediate in other ways (see §28.5).

23.9.2 The use of deferential forms described in §§21-23 can be related to usage described elsewhere in other important ways. The classification of clauses as modal, interrogative, or declarative found to be best for describing the use of deferential forms was found to be similarly significant in determining the choice between title and name (see §6.4). In both cases, the more distanced designation (the deferential term or title) is most commonly used in connection with modal clauses. In both cases it is clear that the structure of the clause is not the factor which determines the usage. The choice of designation is determined by the desired or expected perlocutionary effect, by what the speaker intends, expects or fears will be the effect of his speech on the addressee. Distancing designations are used in declarative clauses where they are intended or expected to carry the same sort of message as do modal clauses, or where they might be understood as doing so. This conclusion is important as showing that the same factors governing the choice of designation operate in different situations, confirming the view that the system of expressive usage is characteristic of the language as a whole, not of merely the use of particular features, such as pronouns.

Speech Directed to God

24.1 Introduction

Speech addressed to God shows many of the features of speech addressed to a human superior. The main difference is that the representation of the addressee as a third person subject, characteristically used in deferential communication with a human superior, does not occur in speech presented as directly addressed to God. The closest equivalent is an indirect request (a clause used to ask for action by God, but of which God is not the subject) or the designation of God by title in an oath formula or by name in the offer of a gift. The use of "your servant" representing the speaker as third person subject of a clause addressed to God is rare, and is restricted to background situations. The speaker may show deference by the use of an impersonal structure, or (in the case of a single speaker) by referring to himself by name, or with a first person plural pronoun. The following examples include cases of speech to an angel (מלאך), since this appears to be treated in the same way as speech addressed to God.

24.2 Requests

24.2.1 *Requests: The subject represents the speaker* A first person singular modal is used to indicate action intended by the speaker after some enabling action by the addressee has been requested, as "O lord Yahweh, please remember me and please strengthen me just this once, God, and I will avenge myself..." (אדני יהוה זכרני נא וחזקני ...נא אך הפעם הזה האלהים ואנקמה וחזקני, Ju 16:28). The initial request is also made by a second person modal form in 1S 12:10; in Ju 6:39, a third person modal is used with a metonymic subject which includes the second person pronoun (see §24.2.4). First person indicative forms following a second person modal are used in Ju 6:18 to give a deferential tone to the speaker's presentation of his own intentions (see §24.2.5). In Ju 13:15, where there is no initial request for an enabling act by the addressee, a first person plural modal is used by Manoah to offer hospitality to a stranger whom he sees as a "man of God", not as an angel (Ju 13:8, cf. 13:21). In 1K 22:22, a first person modal is used to describe an action by a spirit (רוח) volunteered at the request of God in answer to the question "How?"[1]

24.2.2 *Requests: The subject represents the addressee* Requests to God to act, or to authorize action by a third party, are made with the same range of structures as are requests to human superiors, with the exception that a nominal designating God is not used as a third person subject. A vocative is usually used with a request made to God in any form, either associated with the request clause itself, or with an ancillary clause which precedes or follows it. Where this is not the case the narrative introduction to the speech usually includes a designation of God, as "Gideon said to God..." (ויאמר גדעון אל האלהים..., Ju 6:36, 39).[2] God is not mentioned either in the introduction or as a vocative where the speech is a response in Ju 6:17, 1S 3:10, and also in 1S 10:19, where human speech is quoted by God.

24.2.3 *Requests with Second Person Modal Verbs* The most common form of request to God is made with a second person modal form. A request of this sort is used where the desired result will bring immediate benefit to the speaker, as in Ju 16:28 (see §24.2.1), or where it corresponds to the addressee's known wishes, as "Speak, Yahweh, for your servant is listening" (דבר יהוה כי שמע עבדך, 1S 3:9). In "Now, Yahweh, take my life" (עתה יהוה קח נפשי, 1K 19:4) the use of a second person modal probably reflects the speaker's emotion, but this example may be an exception. The speaker as subject is typically represented as first person. First person may also be used in other functions where the speaker's emotions are stirred, as in

---

[1]   Examples of volunteering action using first person verbs in 1K 22:21, 22, are difficult to compare, since the speaker is non-human, a "spirit" (רוח). "I shall trick him" (אני אפתנו, 1K 22:21), with indicative verb, responds to an appeal, and so is presumably not a request. In "I shall go out and be a deceitful spirit..." (אצא והייתי רוח שקר...), which answers the question "How?", and so is presumably a statement of intention, the initial verb is modal by position (but not in form).

[2]   Other examples occur in Ju 10:15, 11:30-31, 15:18, 1S 12:10, 2K 6:18. A vocative is used after an introduction of this sort where the first clause has a modal verb in Ju 13:8, 16:28, 1K 17:21, 20:3, (but not where this is the case in Ju 6:39, 2K 6:18).

1K 19:4, and where the request is for help in a difficult situation (Ju 10:15, 16:28, 1S 12:10, 1K 18:26, 37, 2K 20:3). In 2K 19:19, where the danger is evident but not immediate, the speaker, the king, uses the first person plural, probably a mark of humility less extreme than deferential self-reference (see §18.2.2). A deferential form representing the speaker is used as subject of a subordinate clause in 1S 23:11, where the danger is even less pressing. Such forms are also used in that way, or in non-subjective functions, where there is little reason for self-assertion, but much for deference (1S 3:9, 10, 23:11, 2S 7:25, 29, 24:10).[3]

24.2.4 *Requests with Third Person Modal Verbs* A third person modal verb is used in an indirect form of request where the action requested will benefit the speaker, and may be seen as presumptuous. In "May your wrath not burn... (...אל יחר אפך, Ju 6:39), Gideon's request for a second test might suggest distrust of the first. The prayer "O lord, let the man of God whom you sent come again to us" (בי אדוני איש האלהים אשר שלחת יבוא נא עוד אלינו, Ju 13:8) similarly requests a second chance. Elijah's request for the return of the boy's soul (נפש) in 1K 17:21 requests reversal of a past event. The other examples in 1K 8:26, 18:37, 2K 19:19, have consequences well beyond the addressee's interests as a private person: the maintenance of God's promise to David, or that the people generally should come to know God's power. The indirect request form reflects uncertainty as to how the request will be received. The case in Ju 13:8 shows the only example of reference to the speaker in this group. The use of the first person plural by the speaker (Manoah) is a form of deference, also reflecting uncertainty about the reception of his request (see §18.2.2).

24.2.5 *Requests with Indicative Verbs* A request made with a second person indicative form is usually ancillary to a request made with a modal, as in "If I have found favour in your eyes you will make me a sign... do not move from here until I come to you and I will

---

[3]   Requests addressed to God using second person modal forms occur in Ju 6:18 (negative, usage consistent with §21.3.2), 10:15, 16:28, 1S 3:9, 10, 12:10, 23:11, 2S 7:25, 29, 15:31, 24:10, 1K 8:25, 18:37, 19:4, 2K 6:17, 18, 20, 19:16, 16, 16, 19, 20:3 (also in the request to Baal in 1K 18:26).

bring my offering and place it before you" (אם נא מצאתי חן בעיניך
ועשית לי אות... אל נא תמש מזה עד באי אליך והצאתי את מנחתי והנחתי
לפניך, Ju 6:17-18). The initial indicative request introduces the essential request in the modal clause "Do not move..." which is made
with a second person modal. This, in turn, is followed by first person requests in the indicative, non-immediate usage which gives a
deferential tone to the speaker's presentation of his own intentions.
Another example of an introductory indicative request occurs in
"Today it will be known... (...היום יודע, 1K 18:36). The essential
request so introduced, "Answer me" (ענני, 1K 18:37), is followed by
further indicatives presenting requests consequent on that presented
by the modal. The same occurs with the second person requests in
1K 8:28-50 (dependent on the modal in 1K 8:26), and the third
person requests in Ju 6:39 ("there will be dew", יהיה טל), and 2S
7:26 (the house of your servant David will be established before
you", ובית עבדך דוד יהיה נכון לפניך). Indicatives are sometimes used
(with no preceding modal) to request action to benefit the speaker,
as in "Surely you will place a king over us" (כי מלך תשים עלינו, 1S
10:19). Solomon's request for wisdom (1K 3:9) is another example.
Similar usage in speech to humans suggests that this form of request
reflects a certain hesitancy; the speaker is not sure how his request
will be received. Reference to the speaker in these indicative requests is deferential where Solomon addresses God in 1K 3:9, 8:28-
50, where there is no particular urgency, first person where the request is somewhat more pressing (Ju 6:17, 1S 10:19, 1K 18:36).[4]

24.2.6 *Implied Requests* In "You enabled your servant to win this
great victory, and now I shall die... and fall..." (אתה נתת ביד עבדך את
התשועה הגדלה הזאת ועתה אמות... ונפלתי..., Ju 15:18), indicative verbs
are used to show that action by the addressee is required if a situation which he presumably does not desire is to be avoided. A request is thus implied, but not formally presented. Other examples

---

[4] Declarative clauses are sometimes used to express wishes (in the form of requests not shown as addressed to God), as in "Yahweh your God will bless you
(יהוה אלהיך ירצך, 2S 24:23). Another example occurs in 2S 14:17, where the verb
is indicative by position, though modal in form. The oath formula "Thus will God
do..." (...כה יעשה אלהים, see §15.3.1) also effectively presents a wish in this way.

occur in Ju 6:22, 36.[5] The use of this form of request probably indicates fear of refusal. The form is used by individuals who are (at the time) unimportant, in contrast to the indicative requests in 1S 10:19 (made by the people as a whole) and 1K 3:9 (made by the king).[6] The speaker is represented deferentially in Ju 15:18, by the first person in Ju 6:22, 36.

24.2.7 *The Offer of a Gift* A vow offering a gift to God is made in the form of a conditional sentence addressed to God, who is referred to in the second person in the protasis, by name in the apodosis, as "If you really do give... then whoever comes out... will belong to Yahweh, and I will offer him up" (אם נתון תתן... והיה היוצא... והיה ליהוה והעליתהו עולה, Ju 11:30-31). Another example occurs in 1S 1:11, where Hannah also uses the first person in the apodosis. She uses deferential self-reference in three clauses in the protasis, a first person pronoun in one. Jephthah is fighting the enemies of the people (and so of God), and can expect that his request for help will be well received. Hannah is asking for something previously denied her, and so arguably contrary to the addressee's intentions. Her use of deferential forms no doubt reflects a fear that her request will not be granted.[7] The reference to God, the addressee, by name in the apodosis presents him as third person, and so avoids the direct

---

[5] The protasis of conditional sentences used to present vows could be added (see §24.2.7). Elisha's question "Where is the Lord, God of Elijah" (2K 2:14) is probably also a request in intention, but is not presented as addressed to God.

[6] Samson uses the implied request in Ju 15:18, early in his career, where there is no evidence that his situation is really urgent. He uses a second person modal in Ju 16:28, where his prayer represents his last chance to achieve what he wants.

[7] A use of the first person similar to that found in these apodoses occurs in performative statements not presented as addressed to God, as Hannah's in 1S 1:28 "For my part, I devote him to God..." Another example occurs in Ju 17:3. See also the offer of a gift in 2S 24:23 (§23.4.2). A form of vow similar to those in Ju 11:30-31 and 1S 1:11 occurs in Num 21:2 (however there is no reference to God in the apodosis). A nominal is used in the protasis in 2S 15:8 (Yahweh) and in Gen 28:20 (God). In neither case does the introduction or the use of a vocative show that God is addressed. In 2S 15:8 the vow is being described, so indirect speech is to be expected (despite the introductory לאמר, see §1.6.1). In Gen 28:20, the apodosis promises that Yahweh will be the speaker's God, which may account for the unusual form of the protasis (this example also differs by using the second person in the third clause of the apodosis).

suggestion, that the use of the second person would make, that he will be put under an obligation by the speaker (as in human speech, see §§21.3.4, 23.4.2). Elijah's reference to God by name in "I have been very zealous for Yahweh, God of hosts" (קנא קנאתי ליהוה אלהי צבאות, 1K 19:10, 14) presumably has similar motivation.

24.3 Criticism and Opposition

24.3.1 *Direct questions* A question addressed to God which expresses criticism uses first and second person pronouns, but the addressee's status is also usually recognized by the use of a vocative (on the forms of vocative used, see §15.7). This occurs even in "Who am I, lord Yahweh, and who is my family, that you have brought me thus far?" (מי אנכי אדני יהוה ומי ביתי כי הביאתני עד הלם, 2S 7:18) where the criticism is purely conventional (cf. the use of the same formula to express humility to a human superior (§22.2.4). Other examples are "O my lord, how can I save Israel?" (בי אדני במה אושיע את ישראל, Ju 6:15),[8] "Yahweh my God, have you even harmed the widow I am staying with by killing her son?" (יהוה אלהי הגם על האלמנה אשר אני מתגורר עמה הרעותה להמית את בנה, 1K 17:20). No vocative is used in the question "How can I go?" (איך אלך, 1S 16:2). The speaker, Samuel, fears for his life, and abandons deference in expressing his emotion.[9] Questions asking for information or advice from God do not use deferential forms. First or second person pronouns are used if speaker or addressee is referred to, as in 1S 10:22, 14:37, 23:2, 30:8, 2S 2:1, 5:19. In "What more can David say to you?" (ומה יוסיף דוד עוד לדבר אליך, 2S 7:20), the speaker is represented by his personal name, probably expressing humility (see §27.2.1).

---

[8]   The speaker in Ju 6:15 might be asking for information (cf. Ahab's question in 1K 20:4), but the vocative is in a form used to mollify the addressee in important personal appeals (see §25.2.5-6). The same vocative is used in the same speaker's question in Ju 6:13, which clearly is critical, but there the addressee is taken to be a human superior. Since neither speaker nor addressee is referred to, deferential forms are not to be expected there (see §22.4), but the use of the first person plural does show humility.

[9]   The fact that God is addressed is indicated in this case only by the structure of the dialogue, consistent with the suggestion in Longacre, 1989:184 D4, that the presentation of an emotional outburst is one reason for failure to indicate the addressee.

24.3.2 *Indirect questions* A third person subject, with no reference to
the speaker or (beyond the vocative) to the addressee, is used to
criticize God's actions in "Why, O Yahweh, God of Israel, has this
happened in Israel?" (למה יהוה אלהי ישראל היתה זאת בישראל, Ju 21:3).
An example in which no vocative is used occurs is 2S 24:17, where
David admits his fault for which others are suffering, and asks
"what have they... done?"[10] Such indirect question forms presumably present a criticism of God's actions which is more deferential
because more distanced. It is reasonable to argue that these speakers
do not feel that their relationship to God is such as to justify appeal
to it as a persuasive force, an appeal which the use of pronouns
evoking the relationship would represent. Those who put critical
questions to God directly either have long had a close association
with him, as Samuel (1S 16:2), and Elijah (1K 17:20), or have been
chosen by him for a task, as Gideon (Ju 6:15), and so can expect a
sympathetic reception. It is reasonable to suggest that the indirect
structures used in Ju 21:3 and 2S 24:17 reflect humility arising from
a feeling of uncertainty or guilt.

24.4 Thanks and Praise

The remaining declarative clauses of which the addressee, God, is
subject can be assigned to these closely related categories. The term
praise is restricted to clauses which describe the addressee. Any reference to beneficial actions or intentions on behalf of the speaker or
his community is classified as thanks, even though the structure
may include statements of praise, as in 1K 8:23.[11] The speaker is
referred to in the third person in statements of thanks as defined.[12]
Examples occur in 2S 7:19-21, 27-29, 1K 3:7, 8:23. The first person

---

[10]   In Ju 21:3, the assembly of Israel, which uses a vocative with no pronoun, has
brought about disaster by action it thought required of it. In 2S 24:17, David, who
uses no vocative, is concerned with a disaster resulting from his own wilful action.
[11]   Blessings, introduced by "Blessed is Yahweh" (ברוך יהוה) can be regarded as
statements of thanks (see §23.3), but, like wishes, they are not presented as addressed to God. However, David's use of deferential self-reference in 1S 25:39 suggests
that this particular example was intended as address to God. Other examples occur
in 1S 25:32, 2S 18:28, 1K 1:48, 5:21, 8:15, 56.
[12]   Deferential reference is also made to "Your servant David my father" in 1K
3:6, 8:24. (The use of the first person is standard in the presentation of such close
personal relationship as "my father", see §18.3.1.)

is used in clauses subordinate to statements of praise in 1K 8:27, and in 2S 7:22, where the pronoun is plural, showing humility (see §18.2.2). There is no reference to the speaker in the example in 2K 19:15.

24.5 Confessions

The speaker uses first person pronouns in a confession addressed to God in "I have sinned greatly in what I did... I have been very foolish" (חטאתי מאד אשר עשיתי... כי נסכלתי מאד, 2S 24:10, cf. 24:17). Usage thus appears to be the same as in confessions with a human addressee, see §23.7.5). Examples spoken by a group occur in Ju 10:10, 15, 1S 7:6, 12:10.

24.6 Background

It was noted in §23.7 that, in address to a human superior, there is a tendency to restrict the use of deferential forms referring to the speaker to background situations. In address to God, they are little used outside in such situations. In "Yahweh God of Israel, your servant did indeed hear that Saul intends... to destroy the city on my account. Will the citizens of Keilah hand me over to him? Will Saul come as your servant heard? Yahweh God of Israel, please inform your servant" (יהוה אלהי ישראל שמע שמע עבדך כי מבקש שאול... לשחת לעיר בעבורי היסגרני בעלי קעילה בידו הירד שאול כאשר שמע עבדך יהוה אלהי ישראל הגד נא לעבדך, 1S 23:10-11), a deferential form is used in the terminal request, as is usual where the speaker uses a second person modal to express urgency, but is not in immediate danger (see §24.2.3). The other deferential forms occur in an introductory and a relative clause framing the essential clauses of the speech, the questions, in which first person is used (as is typical, see §24.5.1).[13] A deferential nominal designating the speaker is also used as subject in subordinate clauses in 2S 7:27, 1K 3:8, 8:29. The same basis for the use of the two forms of self-reference can be seen in David's speech of thanks, which (as is typical) is not shown as directed to God in "Blessed is the Lord who has upheld the case of my insult at Nabal's hand, and withheld his servant from wrong

---

[13]   Note, however, that the first person is also used in the introductory clause, in "on my account", referring to the speaker's personal danger.

(doing)" (ברוך יהוה אשר רב את ריב חרפתי מיד נבל ואת עבדו חשך מרעה,
1S 25:39). Here the first person balances the deferential form. However, the first person is used in referring to the significant action, marking it as immediate. The deferential form is used in referring to the beneficial result.

24.7 Conclusion

24.7.1 Speech addressed to God, then, shows much the same characteristics as speech addressed to humans, with the exception of the fact that a third person subject is not used to represent the addressee, and not often to represent the speaker. This is an interesting point, as it suggests that the master-servant relationship, and so the language addressed to kings, did not provide the model for speech addressed to God. Relations between God and humans were certainly described in terms of master-servant relationship, but parent-child relationship was also used (see §2.3.7n), and this more intimate equivalent may have provided the model for address to God. This would provide a reasonable explanation for the fact that deferential use of third person subjects is rare. Such distanced presentation was evidently foreign to so personal a relationship. If speech to parents was the original model, however, the usage has developed, in the stage represented in the corpus, to include the master-servant terminology, just as the same terminology may be used in speech to a father who is a king.

24.7.2 Speech to God, then, typically presents the concerns of the speaker as immediate, unlike deferential speech to humans. These concerns include the speaker's relationship with God, the addressee, which is represented in personal terms. In speech to a human superior, deferential nominals and third person reference are commonly used to distance speaker from addressee, and so show deference, where the speech might seem to criticize or oppose the addressee, or to place him under obligation or otherwise limit his autonomy, and so is likely to offend him. First and second person pronouns are used in such speech to show urgency or other emotion, and so present the speech as immediate. The extent to which they do this depends on the extent to which the deference is expected. Where the situation calls for deference, the high specificity of the pronominal designations (more specific than deferential nominal or third person) correlates with their status as marked. Where deference is not called for, deferential usage is marked, but its lower degree of specificity is used for distancing to show politeness, or, as in David's speech to King Saul in 1S 26:17-25, rejection (see §23.8.2). It seem evident that high specificity indicates immediacy, as noted in §19.5.2.

VI   THE INTERLOCUTORS

Vocatives

25.1 Introduction

25.1.1 A "vocative" or "free term of address" is a noun or noun phrase used to designate an addressee who is otherwise represented by second person pronouns. Most speech does not include a vocative, so the use of any term in this function is significant. The more obvious uses of vocatives are to attract the attention of the addressee, or to identify the intended addressee among a number of possibilities. However, vocatives may also serve to indicate the relationship between speaker and addressee, and to indicate the speaker's attitude to the speech. The word used as a vocative, and the position in the speech in which it is used, can be chosen to reflect the relative status of speaker and addressee, to show the speaker's view of their relationship as friendly, formal, or hostile, and to show whether the speech is intended as polite, urgent, brusque, etc. The choice of a vocative, and the placing of it, thus provides valuable information on the context of the speech, and helps to determine the expectations of the dyad concerned. It is this aspect of their use which is the main interest here.

25.1.2 Free personal pronouns are not considered to act as vocatives. There is no evidence of their use simply to attract attention, but they may be used with second person verb forms, including imperatives, and nominal vocatives may be used in apposition to them. A free pronoun referring to the addressee is most commonly used with an imperative where it enjoins the addressee to act in his or her turn, or to act rather than another. Thus, in the parable where the trees invite a succession of their number to rule them, a pronoun is used in the second, third, and fourth invitation: "You come and reign over us" (לכי את מלכי עלינו/לך אתה מלך עלינו, Ju 9:10, 12, 14), but not with the first: "Reign over us" (מלכה עלינו, Ju 9:8). Where a verb form other than an imperative is used to give instructions, a free subject pronoun may be used in the same way, as "For your part, you will count out..." (ואתה תמנה לך...‏, 1K 20:25).

The same may occur where an imperative and an indicative are used in sequence, as "You (are the one who must) be... and (consequently) you (are the one who must) bring..." (היה אתה... והבאת אתה...), Exod 18:19. There is, therefore, ample reason to regard the use of a free pronoun with an imperative as an aspect of the use of a free pronoun in apposition to the subject of a verb form, as is done in the discussion in Muraoka, 1985:47-59. For this reason a personal pronoun designating the addressee of an imperative has been referred to above as its "subject" for convenience.

25.2 The Use of Titles and "My Lord" as Vocatives

25.2.1 A speaker who uses a title as a term of address to a human thereby recognizes the superior status of the addressee. (Address to God is treated in §25.6.) This is clear with "king" (המלך), "man of God" (איש האלהים), and is, at least, a reasonable assumption with "prince" (בן המלך, 2S 13:4) and "captain" (השר, 2K 9:5, 5).[1] Deferential vocatives of this sort are typically used where there is no reason to think the speech will displease the addressee, or where the speaker wishes to use second person address to put his speech more forcefully or has some other reason for abandoning deference. Examples are noted in §§21.3.6, 22.3.3-4, 23.2.4, 23.4.5, 23.6, 25.8.1. Where deference is shown in this way, the title may be used alone. The term "my lord" (אדני) is often combined with a title where appeal to the personal relationship of the addressee to the speaker as master to servant is expected to influence him in the speaker's favour (see §§6.8.2, 13.4.1). The title is omitted, and "my lord" is used alone, to focus on the persuasive force of this relationship. "My lord" is also used alone to show deference where no suitable title is available for use as a term of address.

25.2.2 A vocative addressed to the king usually takes the form "my lord the king" (אדני המלך), thus including the appeal to personal relationship implicit in the use of "my lord" (see §6.8.1). This form is commonly used at the beginning of a speech to the king, particularly where the speaker requires the king's favour, as when present-

---

[1] On "prince", see §22.3.3. The Meṣad Ḥashavyahu plea is made to a superior addressed (in the third person) as "my lord the captain" (אדני השר, line 1).

ing a plea. It is used in this way in the wording suggested to Bathsheba by Nathan: Did not you, my lord the king, swear to your
servant..." (...הלא אתה אדני המלך נשבעת לאמתך, 1K 1:13). Other examples occur in 1S 24:9, 2S 14:9, 19, 19:27, 1K 1:24, 20:4, 2K 6:12,
26.[2] This form may also be used to begin speech with the king in
other situations, as in offering thanks by Joab (2S 14:22) and by
Ziba (2S 16:4), in proffering information by Elisha's servant Gehazi
(2K 8:5). In 1S 26:17, David uses "my lord the king" in the first
clause of his speech, as if about to present a plea, but instead de-
nounces Saul, so the usage may be considered ironic. "My lord the
king" is also used by Bathsheba within her plea to David (1K 1:18,
20). It seems likely that this reflects the strength of her anxiety for
herself and her son (see §25.8.5).

25.2.3 The form "O king" (המלך) is used as a vocative where the
speech benefits the addressee, as the announcement of a message (Ju
3:19), news that an objective is attainable (1S 23:20), or an offer of
service (2S 15:34). It thus appears to be used where the speech is expected to please the king, so that the appeal to relationship presented by the pronoun in "my lord" (אדני) is not required. "O king" is
also used where the failure to use "my lord" represents increased
deference (see §6.8.4), and so by Abner admitting ignorance in response to King Saul's enquiry (1S 17:55), and by the Tekoite in her
appeal for help (הושיעה המלך, 2S 14:4). Her purpose is to persuade
King David to undertake action he has so far rejected; her speech is
highly deferential throughout. The use of the more usual "my lord
the king" in the same appeal for help (הושיעה אדני המלך, 2K 6:2)
represents the lesser need for deference where the speaker is appealing for justice. The use of "my lord the king" is thus the default
term for address to the king. The marked form "O king" is used
where the claim of personal relationship represented by "my lord"
is abandoned because unnecessary, or, in the effort to show a deeper

---

[2]   In 1S 24:9-10, David begins his speech by protesting that rumours of his hostility to Saul are false, making a plea for just treatment.

level of deference, because appeal to master-servant relationship might appear presumptuous.[3]

25.2.4 A vocative addressed to a prophet is usually "Man of God" (איש האלהים). This occurs in a plea for mercy in 2K 1:13, and in other situations in 1K 17:18, 2K 1:9, 11, 4:40. Personal relationship is invoked by the use of "my lord" before the title in the plea of the Shunammite "Do not, my lord the man of God, do not deceive your servant" (אל אדני איש האלהים אל תכזב בשפחתך, 2K 4:16). In 1K 18:7, Obadiah, a senior official, addresses the prophet Elijah, whom the king has been hunting like a criminal, as "my lord Elijah" (אדני אליהו). The speaker is probably alarmed by the meeting even before Elijah makes a request of him which he feels endangers his life. The Shunammmite, too is frightened by the prophet's speech, as her attempt to reject his offer shows. The use of "my lord", adding an appeal to the personal relationship, presumably reflects the extent of the speakers' distress. It is, however, justified by close association in both cases. The prophet has often been the guest of the Shunammite (2K 4:8), and Obadiah's past association with Elijah is shown by the fact that he expects him to know of his earlier activities on behalf of the prophet's colleagues (1K 18:7).

25.2.5 Where a title could be used as a vocative, the use of "my Lord" (אדני) alone is marked. It refers only to the personal relationship, and so concentrates on the persuasive force of that factor, as do vocatives addressed to God which include a first person pronoun (see §§15.7.2, 15.7.4). This form is used where the speaker is in particular need of the addressee's help or favour. Bathsheba opens her appeal to King David in this way in 1K 1:17. A prophet is addressed as "my lord" where the speaker fears serious loss, or is in danger (2K 6:5, 15). The speaker is a close associate of the addressee in these cases, which may also have been a factor in the omission of the title. The priest Ahimelek addresses King Saul as "my lord" in responding to his summons (1S 22:12), probably an indication that he is apprehensive (see §25.8.4). The woman in pleading for the

---

[3]   The usage thus appears to be one of those in which the marked form represents either extreme in contrast to the mean, represented by the default form (see §28.2.2). On the use of "O king" in 2S 24:23, see §25.7.3.

restoration of her son in 1K 3:17, and for his life in 1K 3:26, uses "my lord" with a deferential prefix (בִּי אדנִי). This would appear to present the ultimate effort at persuasion (see §§15.7.3, 25.2.6).

25.2.6 In the other cases in which "my lord" alone is used as a term of address, the speaker wishes to show deference to an addressee who has no title suitable for use as a vocative. Sisera, addressed as "my lord" by Jael (Ju 4:18), has such a title, but not in her community. Priestly titles are not used as terms of address, so Eli is addressed as "my lord" by Hannah in 1S 1:15, 26. David is leader of a band of outlaws when Abigail addresses him as "my lord" (1S 25:24, 26). "My lord" is used with the deferential prefix (בִּי אדנִי) by Gideon to introduce speech contradicting an angel (Ju 6:13). Initially, he does not recognize his status, but presumably takes him as a "man of God" (as does Manoah in Ju 13:8), i.e. as God's human agent, and so able to wield superhuman power (see §12.6.2). Hannah's use of the same form of address (1S 1:26) is presumably intended to avoid the appearance of presumption in her claim that God has favoured her personally, and in her gift of her son to God's service.

25.3 The Use of Kinship Terms as Vocatives

25.3.1 A kinship term may be used in address where there is a blood relationship or where there is not. In either case, the use of a kinship term as a vocative implies that speaker and addressee have a close and friendly relationship, equivalent to the ideal form of the family relationship named (parent, child, or sibling). Where there is no blood relationship, a kinship term is typically used in address where the speaker is trying to persuade the addressee to some course of action. The use of these terms in address to natural kin often occurs in similar circumstances. This shows again that the evocation of personal relationship is expected to influence the addressee in favour of the speaker, recalling the use of the second person pronoun for this purpose in situations in which a deferential form is expected (see §22.5).

25.3.2 Where King Solomon addresses his mother as "my mother" (אמי, 1K 2:20), or a king addresses a prophet as "my father" (אבי, 2K 6:21, 13:14), speaker and addressee are each superior to the other in terms of a different hierarchy. Such usage is polite, or honorific. The function may be the same where the addressee is status-marked in relation to the speaker, as where the prophet Elijah is addressed as "my father" by his subordinate, Elisha (2K 2:12), and where Jephthah is addressed in the same way by his daughter (Ju 11:36). In the latter case, however, the vocative introduces a suggestion and a request, so the fact of the persuasive value of the term may have formed part of the motivation for its choice. Where "my father" is used by David addressing King Saul (1S 24:12), or by servants in addressing their master Naaman (2K 5:13), the term is certainly chosen mainly in the hope of persuading the addressee to act like a loving father: Saul should abandon the view that David is his enemy; Naaman should not be angry at subordinates who advise him against his intentions.[4]

25.3.3 Address as "my son" (בני) or "my daughter" (בתי) presumably expresses parental love and sympathy where Jepthah informs his daughter of his oath (Ju 11:35), and where David refuses Absalom's invitation (2S 13:25). Use of "my son" may have no other motivation than kindly feelings of a senior to a junior in the priest Eli's address to the messenger (1S 4:16), but the major factor motivating its use elsewhere where there is no natural relationship is its persuasive value, as in Joab's attempt to dissuade Ahimaaz in 2S 18:22, and in Joshua's attempt to persuade Achan to confess in Josh 7:19.

---

[4]   The vocative is often emended both in 1S 24:12 and in 2K 5:13, see McCarter, 1980:382, Cogan and Tadmor, 1988:65. In 1S 24:12, the combination ראה גם ראה is unusual but the use of גם with emphatic force, rather than denoting addition, is well attested. "Look, just look" is probably a reasonable equivalent. Cf. the use of the negative אל before and after a vocative to add emphasis to a negative request (Ju 19:23, 2S 13:12, 2K 4:16), and the repetition of the imperative itself where the request is affirmative (Ju 4:18). The fact that the vocative precedes the repeated items in 1S 24:12, rather than intervening between them, as in other cases, can be attributed to a desire to give the maximum prominence to the mollifying "my father". The servants' speech in 2K 5:13 can be read in a way suitable to the context either by assuming a relative clause with no introductory particle (see Waltke and O'Connor 1990, §19.6): "A great thing (which) the prophet asked you will you not do?" (for other clauses with a constituent placed before an interrogative particle, see 1S 20:8, 2S 24:3, 17), or by assuming a conditional clause without introductory particle (see Revell, 1991, p. 1288, §8.3). The use of a singular pronoun in "my father" is to be expected, see §18.3.1.

Its use in conjunction with the personal name by King Saul to David in 1S 24:17, 26:17, 21, 25, is obviously motivated by the king's desire to persuade David of his good intentions. The same combination is used by Eli to Samuel in 1S 3:16, leading up to his attempt to find out what God said to him. The persuasive value of the term is no doubt also a factor in Eli's use of it in his attempt to persuade his sons to reform (1S 2:24).

25.3.4 The terms "brother" (אח) and "sister" (אחות) are used among natural kin (2S 13:11, 12, 20), and metaphorically between individual equals (2S 20:9, 1K 9:13), or by one member of a group to the others (Ju 19:23, 1S 30:23). In Ju 19:23, 1S 30:23, 2S 13:12, the purpose of the speech is to dissuade an individual or group from some action. Words are the speaker's only recourse; a show of force is impossible. The kinship term is obviously used mainly for its persuasive value. In 2S 13:11, the speaker is attempting to win by request what he eventually takes by force, and in 2S 13:20 to quieten the laments of the victim. In these cases, too, the persuasive value of the term is important. Joab greets his rival Amasa as "my brother" before stabbing him (2S 20:9), presumably to put him off his guard by feigning friendship. King Hiram addresses King Solomon in the same way in 1K 9:13, presumably to soften the effect of his hostile question.

25.4 Personal Names as Vocatives

25.4.1 The characters in the narrative rarely use personal names in addressing each other.[5] It seems likely that such usage was normally restricted to family members and intimate associates. If so, the use of a personal name in address implies an intimate association, much as does a kinship term, but it carries somewhat different connotations. Used to equals, it probably reflects real intimacy. Close association is no doubt implied even where the name is used from necessity, in asking the question "Is that you, PN?" of an equal (2S 2:20), or, combined with "my lord", of a superior (1K 18:7, see §

---

[5]   The names of equals or inferiors are commonly used for reference, but even here restrictions are evident. In address to an equal, the name of a member of his family is typically avoided, or used with an appropriate relationship term (see § 13.4.2).

25.2.2). The latter is the only case in the corpus where the personal name is used in address to a superior. The addition of "my lord" presumably deprecates the addressee's possible feeling that the use of his name is presumptuous. The personal name may also imply intimacy when used to subordinates, but it is also used in the context of reprimand or sentence. Its use thus covers the natural range of address by parents to children. The typical use of personal names by God in address to humans suggests the language of parents as a possible model for that of God.

25.4.2 Elkanah addresses his wife Hannah by name in offering concern and sympathy (1S 1:8). The name is also used to issue a warning to a husband (Ju 16:9, 12, 14, 20) or to a friendly relative (2K 9:23). This probably reflects the normal patterns of address in such dyads, and so real intimacy.[6] Compare the use of a title by a junior warning a senior in 2K 4:40. The use of a personal name in address by a superior to a subordinate may be benevolent. The address of the Prophet Elijah to Elisha, his personal servant and successor, by name (2K 2:4) no doubt expresses benevolence in an attempt to persuade. This is also probably true of King David's address to his dependent, Mephibosheth in 2S 9:6, before offering him kindness, although his use of the name could be taken as necessary to the confirmation of identity. However, address to a subordinate by name can carry opposite implications. The king uses the personal name where the addressee is actually or potentially under sentence in 1S 14:44, 22:16, 2S 19:26. The address to the prophet Micaiah in 1K 22:15 can be included here, as he is punished for what he says in reply. The same is true of the Prophet Elisha's address to his servant Gehazi (2K 5:25). A speaker who fails to use the conventions of address customary between adults treats the addressee as without status as an adult in the society. The use of a form expressing familiarity where familiarity is not justified is a form of this phenomenon well known from other languages. The use of the personal name as a term of address to adults covers the range of address by parents to children, from expressions of love to sentence of punish-

---

[6]   Bathsheba's use of deferential terms in her address to King David in 1K 1:17-21 shows her addressing him as king, not as husband. Spouses typically converse as equals (see §2.4.2n).

ment. It is reasonable to see the use of a personal name as a vocative in presenting a reprimand or sentence as treating the addressee
as a child, and so as without status.[7]

25.4.3 The personal name is the only form of vocative which God
is shown in the corpus as using to humans. The examples show a
range of use similar to that by a human superior. The address to
Samuel in 1S 3:10 may be kindly or neutral. The question "What
are you doing here Elijah?" (מה לך פה אליהו, 1K 19:9, 13) appears
to carry overtones of reprimand. This suggests that speech by God
to humans is, at least in this respect, modelled on that of parents to
children, a view consistent with the suggestion that human address
to God was modelled on that of children to parents (see §24.7).

25.4.4 A few more surprising uses of the personal name can be interpreted in the light of the above discussion. David addresses Abner by name in 1S 26:14, and goes on to chide him as if he, David,
were the master. In fact, Abner is commander-in-chief to King Saul,
the master whom David has abandoned, and is now in charge of a
force attempting to recapture him. The intention of the use of the
name, treating Abner as a child or servant, is no doubt to insult
him. An important military officer is addressed by name by the
king in two cases. This may have been usual, but the considerable
evidence of the behaviour of King David to his officers provides no
support. Saul's use of the personal name in address to Abner in 1S
17:55 most probably represents typical usage between intimates;
they are cousins (1S 14:50). The use of the name by King Jehoram
in greeting Jehu, his officer, in 2K 9:22 could be seen as an attempt
to placate him by treating him as an intimate, or as intended to

---

[7]   A person under sentence is treated as a child in Josh 7:19, where Joshua addresses Achan as "my son". The term "lad" (נער) indicates someone subordinate
either through status or through age. "Boy" and "garçon" are used similarly. The
"familiar" form of the second person pronoun in French and early modern English
is also used for intimates, children, and subordinates. It is remarked in Brown and
Gilman (1960:274) that someone using the familiar form in anger to an adult outside these categories is treating the addressee "like a servant or child", and assuming
"the right to berate him" (a number of examples from literature follow). The
showing of disdain by the use of terms which treat the addressee as a child is also
mentioned in Parkinson, 1985:210.

"put him in his place" by treating him as a servant. Jehu's unexpected arrival, and the surprising events which led to the king's encounter with him have no doubt made the king uneasy.

25.5 Other Terms Used in Address to Humans

25.5.1 The use of a patronymic as a term of address recognizes only a member of a family, not an individual, and thus has the effect of distancing (see §13.2). The use of a patronymic by King Saul in addressing the priest Ahimelech in 1S 22:12 presumably indicates non-intimacy and so disdain. He is about to charge the priest with conspiracy. His use of the patronymic may suggest that he is already determined to condemn him to death, which he does with a typical hostile use of the personal name in 1S 22:16. The only other example of the use of a patronymic as a vocative is the prophet's address to the "wife of Jeroboam" in 1K 14:6. The failure to recognize her status as queen (even to the extent of naming her husband as king) marks the speaker as a non-subject, and carries at least overtones of disdain (see §13.2.2).

25.5.2 A few terms of address do not indicate the status, relationship, or name of the addressee, but denote some quality. They are used in "name calling" (see Parkinson, 1985:37-8). The purpose is to ascribe to addressee the quality named in the term of address. The one example which presents a positive quality "mighty man of valour" (גבור החיל) is used by the angel in his encouraging greeting to Gideon in Ju 6:12. The others embody various forms of insult, as King Ahab's greetings to the prophet Elijah: "troubler of Israel" (עכר ישראל, 1K 18:17), and "my enemy" (איבי, 1K 21:20). The other examples occur in 1S 20:30, 2S 16:7, 2K 2:23, 9:31.

25.5.3 The remaining nominals used as vocatives are names denoting a group used in address to that group. These may be used by a speaker who is a member of the group in exhorting the other members, as "Take courage and be men, Philistines" (התחזקו והיו לאנשים פלשתים, 1S 4:9) in the course of a speech made by "the Philistines", beginning in 4:7. Other examples occur in 2S 20:1, 2K 3:23. These terms are also used, by members of the group or outsiders, to attract attention, as "Listen to me, citizens of Shechem" (שמעו אלי בעלי שכם, Ju 9:7); other examples occur in 1S 14:38, 22:7, 1K 12:28,

22:28. Other examples are use to present an insult, a request, or a question expressing rejection (Ju 12:4, 20:7, 2S 16:10 = 19:23).

25.6 Terms Used in Address to God

The terms used in address to God have been discussed in detail in §15.7. God is most often addressed by name alone "Yahweh" (יהוה). This may be expanded by the use of "(my) lord" (אדני יהוה) to use the persuasive force of the personal relationship it refers to (10 cases). "(My) lord" alone is used with the deferential prefix (בי אדני) in Ju 6:15, 13:8. The title is used alone in the form "God" (האלהים) in Ju 16:28, or "God of Israel (אלהי ישראל) in 1K 8:26. Title and name are combined in "Yahweh God of Israel" (יהוה אלהי ישראל, 5 cases), and in "Yahweh God" (יהוה אלהים, 2S 7:25). The latter combination is also used with a first person pronoun, "Yahweh my/our God", to add the persuasive force of personal relationship to the speaker's words. Other terms of address used are "Yahweh of Hosts" (יהוה צבאות, 1S 1:11), "Yahweh of Hosts, God of Israel" (יהוה צבאות אלהי ישראל, 2S 7:27), and "Yahweh God of Abraham, Isaac, and Israel" (יהוה אלהי אברהם יצחק וישראל, 1K 18:36), which refers to the patriarchal ancestors of the community. As in the case of terms of address used for humans, there is a general correlation between the term of address chosen, and the content and circumstances of the speech, as described in §15.7. The only recorded vocative used to address a foreign God, "Baal" (הבעל, 1K 18:26), is, in origin, a title.

25.7 The Placing of Vocatives

25.7.1 In 1S 3:10, 16, 20:30, 24:9, 2S 9:6, an utterance consists only of a vocative. Elsewhere, vocatives are included with one or more clauses to form a longer speech. A vocative is a "free term of address"; clause structure is not affected by the presence or absence of a vocative, nor, where one is used, by its position in the clause. The vocative is placed as follows in relation to the clause with which it is associated.

1. Before the clause (50 cases, including vocatives following introductory "Alas", אהה, or "now", עתה).
2. After the first word or constituent in a clause of two or more constituents (19 cases).
3. After the clause (74 cases).

4. After the subject and the head of the predicate, but followed by one or more constituents (5 cases).

These figures suggest that position (3) is "default" or "unmarked" — the position used where no particular effect is desired.

25.7.2 The element which precedes a vocative standing in position (2) is an imperative verb form (1S 3:9, 2K 19:16, 16), the negative אל, beginning a negative request (Ju 19:23, 2S 13:12, 25), an interrogative particle (Ju 21:3), an asseverative word or phrase (1S 17:55, 2S 14:19, 2K 19:17), the subject of the clause (2S 7:24, 27, 29, also where combined with interrogative and negative particles, 1K 1:13), an extraposed pronoun (1K 1:20), or a preposition introducing a nominal or infinitival structure (1S 23:20, 25:24, 2S 14:9).[8] A vocative used in position (2) thus isolates a significant feature of the clause; it draws attention to, and so adds to the impact of, this feature. This is demonstrated by the fact that the feature so isolated may also be highlighted in other ways. In 1S 25:24, "On me, me, my lord, is the guilt" (בי אני אדני העון), the initial constituent is also highlighted by the repetition of the pronoun. In "On me, my lord king, is the guilt, and on my father's house" (עלי אדני המלך העון ועל בית אבי, 2S 14:9), the initial word is also highlighted by its separation from the remainder of the compound structure of which it forms a part. Where the clause consists of one word, a following vocative is assigned to position (3).[9]

---

[8]   Where a vocative follows the negative אל, the negative is repeated after the vocative, and followed by the verb. The case of a vocative following אל in 1S 2:24, where no verb is used, is assigned to position (3), since the text as it stands requires that the negative be understood to function as a clause. In the case in 1K 1:13, the vocative follows הלא אתה, a combination of interrogative particle, negative, and subject. This can be classed as "a single word or constituent", as the affirmative counterpart, האתה, would be.

[9]   In some such cases, the same word is repeated after the vocative, as in "Turn aside, my lord, turn aside to me" (סורה אדני סורה אלי, Ju 4:18). In others, the vocative is followed by a subordinate clause, as in "Come back, my son David, for I will not harm you" (שוב בני דוד כי לא ארע לך, 1S 26:21). It might be correct to assign such cases to position (2), on the ground that the vocative follows the first word in a semantic unit, but this seems equally justifiable in some other cases not formally distinct, so this was not done. The general description would not, in any case, have been significantly affected.

25.7.3 In position (4) the constituents preceding the vocative carry the essential message of the clause, as in "Why are you so haggard, prince, morning by morning?" (בבקר מדוע אתה ככה דל בן המלך בבקר, 2S 13:4). The vocative is followed by prepositional phrases also in Ju 12:4, 1K 8:23, 28, and by the verb "to be" in 2S 15:34, where its use is not required for the structure. It seems likely that the purpose of the placing of a vocative in position (4) is to isolate what follows in a form of "end focus", giving greater impact to its combination with what precedes the vocative. A further case in which this explanation could apply occurs in "Araunah has given everything {O king} to the king", (הכל נתן ארונה המלך למלך, 2S 24:23). However, the use of "O king" as a vocative here would produce a unique combination of second and third person reference to the addressee in the same clause. Considered as a vocative in position (4), "O king" in 2S 24:23 would be unique in that it does not follow the essential message, which would include the indirect object. The word most probably arises from error.[10] Its omission would leave a performative clause typical of those used to present gifts to a superior, even where second person has been used for the addressee in preceding clauses (as in Ju 11:30-31, 1S 1:11).

25.8 Position and Expressive Value

25.8.1 A vocative in position (1) or (2) designates an addressee who is superior to the speaker in 60 of 69 cases (87%). Where the vocative stands in position (3), the addressee is the speaker's superior in only 28 of 74 cases (38%). The use of a vocative in position (1) or (2) clearly correlates with the need for a display of politeness or deference. Position (3) is used where the relative status of the members of the dyad is such that there is no need for politeness or deference, or where the nature of the situation arouses feelings in a non-status speaker strong enough to overcome any such need.[11]

---

[10]   See §27.2.1. The versions generally show no equivalent, see McCarter, 1984: 508. However, in Fokkelman, 1990:329, the word is regarded as a vocative used in deliberate repetition of the title "king".

[11]   It is noted in Parkinson, 1985:32, that a vocative in Cairo Arabic typically occurs at the beginning or end of a clause, or "after the first word or phrase". Initial position is said to be particularly common where the clause is first in a speech, and the vocative is needed to attract the addressee's attention. Beyond this, possible correlation between position and the context or purpose of the clause is not discussed.

25.8.2 Where a vocative in position (1) or (2) is used to an addressee who is not superior to the speaker, the vocative is a kinship term, or a personal name. In position (2), such a vocative introduces a negative request in all cases. Where the vocative is in position (1) it may introduce a request, a question or a statement. In "Hannah, why do you cry?" (חנה למה תבכי, 1S 1:8) the question expresses loving concern. Sentiments of this nature can also reasonably be attributed to the speaker in the examples in Ju 11:35 (Jephthah laments to his daughter that his vow must affect her), 2S 13:20 (Absalom attempts to calm his sister after she has been raped), 2S 13:25 (King David refuses his son's invitation with a polite excuse), and 2K 2:4 (The Prophet Elijah tries to persuade Elisha, his servant and successor, to leave him). In "Do not, my brother, do not force me" (אל תעניני אחי אל, 2S 13:12), the speaker uses the persuasive force of a kinship term as a vocative in her attempt to prevent rape. In Ju 19:23, the host of the intended victim of a rape also uses a kinship term in the same structure in an effort to dissuade the aggressors. The initial vocative used in requesting a decision from the assembly in Ju 20:7 presumably treats the assembly as a superior, and so marks the speech as polite. Finally, in the king's address to the prophet Micaiah in 1K 22:15, the use of Micaiah's name as a vocative in initial position is presumably ironic, intended to add to the disdain shown by the use of the name (see §25.4.2). The king, after all, has no intention of taking Micaiah's advice, even though he appears to recognize its value.

25.8.3 It is reasonable to conclude, then, that the use of a vocative in positions (1) or (2), marks deference where the addressee is superior. Where the addressee is not status marked, such a vocative typically marks politeness, or its equivalent within a family, benevolence or loving concern. A kinship term is used in this position in Ju 19:23, 2S 13:12, in an attempt to evoke this "caring" attitude, and so forbearance, in a more powerful addressee who is threatening the speaker. The initial position of the vocative invites the addressee to focus his attention on it, thus highlighting the feelings it represents. In the case in 1K 22:15 (just described), where the personal name of a prophet is used as an initial vocative by a king in address which appears to be scornful, the use of "polite" position for the wrong function no doubt increases the impact of the intended rudeness,

just as does the use of a familiar form where familiarity is not justified (see §25.4.2).

25.8.4 A vocative designating a superior follows the clause in four
situations. [A] in "Save (me) O king" (הושיעה המלך, 2S 14:4) and in
other appeals in Ju 16:28, 2S 15:31, 1K 18:37, 2K 6:26, and in a
warning in 2K 4:40. (A terminal vocative is similarly used in warn-
ings to equals in Ju 16:9, 2K 9:23). [B] The same position is used in
"I have a confidential message for you, O king" (דבר סתר לי אליך
המלך, Ju 3:19), and similarly in the delivery of a message in 2K 9:5,
5, in response to address in 1S 1:15, 22:12, 26:17, 1K 20:4, 2K 6:12,
in invitation to take refuge (Ju 4:18), to speak (1S 3:9). [C] A terminal vocative is also used in an expression of thanks "May I find
favour in your eyes my lord king" (אמצא חן בעיניך אדני המלך, 2S
16:4, and, more humbly expressed, 2S 14:22), in a question expressing humility and gratitude (2S 7:18), rejection (2S 7:18), or surprise
(1K 18:7), and in insults (2S 16:7, 2K 2:23). [D] Vocatives placed
after the clause occur within, or at the end of, lengthy prayers in 2S
7:19, 19, 20, 22, 1K 8:53.

25.8.5 In group [A], the speaker's appeal is made, or warning given,
under urgent pressure of circumstances. The situation is also urgent
in group [B], but here the urgency is largely a matter of convention.
The communication is a response to, or otherwise to the benefit of,
the addressee, and should reach him without delay. In group [C],
the speaker can reasonably be said to be stirred by emotion, whether of gratitude, surprise, or indignation. It is reasonable to argue, of
the examples in these three groups, that the need for deference is
dominated by the strength of the speaker's feelings, which requires
the immediate presentation of the communication, whether these
feelings are evoked by pressure of circumstances, by desire to show
alacrity in the service of the addressee, or by other stimuli. The
vocative is placed last to give maximum prominence to the communication. The offering of insults could be described in the same
way, but it is also true that a speaker who insults a superior does
not recognize his status, so that a non-deferential placing of the
vocative is to be expected. The use of terminal vocatives within or
after prayers also presents the vocative as less important than the
clause with which it is associated. The prayers are marked as defer-

ential from the beginning. The terminal vocative (always "(my) lord
Yahweh" (אדני יהוה) reiterates a statement of relationship between
speaker and addressee, and so reinforces the claim of the former to
a sympathetic hearing.[12] A somewhat similar repetition of vocatives (using "my lord king", (אדני המלך) occurs in Bathsheba's plea
to king David (1K 1:18, 20), but there the vocatives are in position
(2).

25.9 Conclusion

The use of vocatives presents a self-consistent system, as do the other phenomena studied. The choice of a term for use as a vocative
can be seen to be generally consistent with the way some terms are
used for other functions. The choice is conditioned by the context
in which the term is to be used, important features of which are the
relative status of speaker and addressee, the purpose of the speech,
and the speaker's attitude to the situation. The position of the vocative in relation to the clause with which it is used is significant in
the same way as is the position of other constituents of a clauses. A
speaker places a vocative before the clause where it is intended that
the addressee should initially concentrate his attention on it, just as
the narrator uses initial position in a verbal clause to give prominence to a nominal constituent. This position is unmarked for address to a superior, marked for address to an inferior, where it indicates polite or kindly feeling. A vocative following the clause is, by
contrast, shown to be unimportant in relation to the clause itself.
This position is unmarked for address to an inferior, marked for address to a superior, where it indicates emotion or urgency. The fact
that the use of a vocative is irrelevant to the structure of the clause
allows a speaker to place a vocative in other positions, using it to
highlight other constituents of the clause.

---

[12]   Compare the reiteration of "says Yahweh" (נאם יהוה) or other reminders of the
authority behind the words of God in their presentation to humans.

The Free First Person Singular Pronoun

26.1. Introduction

26.1.1 The most striking case in which the Hebrew pronoun system requires a choice between alternative possibilities is that of the free first person singular pronoun. This appears in two forms, *ǎni* (אֲנִי) and *ʾānoki* (אָנֹכִי), which are, in terms of syntax, free variants. In terms of usage, however, they have distinct functions. This has been demonstrated in a study of the use of the two forms in the whole of early biblical prose in Revell, 1995. The present survey, is confined to the books of Judges, Samuel and Kings. It is, to some extent, a shortened form of the earlier study, but refines it, and shifts the focus somewhat. That article laid too much stress on the marking of difference in status. The contrast between *ǎni* and *ʾānoki* is used, as are other pronominal contrasts, to reflect differences in social status, emotional intensity, and personal concern, all of which can be subsumed under the heading "immediacy", as described in §3.4. The more common of the two forms of first person pronoun overall is *ǎni*. Nevertheless, in speech among humans, it is *ǎni* which marks immediacy, *ʾānoki* which shows that the structure in which is stands is not immediate.

26.1.2 *ǎni in speech by humans* In general, the use of *ǎni* by humans shows that the clause is "immediate", central to the interests of the speaker or addressee, foreground. In about half the examples, a speaker who uses *ǎni* is status-marked.[1] Superior rank ensures that the speaker's concerns must be of immediate interest to an addressee of lower status. Where *ǎni* is used by a non-status speaker, it typically reflects some form of emotion or strong feeling. This may originate in the fact that the speaker is putting forward a claim of some sort, or in the urgency of the situation, or in other factors. Such strong feeling for his own situation overrides respect for the

---

[1] In epigraphic materials, *ǎni* occurs only in Arad §88, where it is evidently subject of the verb "to reign" (מלכתי), consistent with this description.

addressee's status, and leads a non-status speaker to present his concerns to the addressee as "immediate". *ăni* may also be used by a non-status speaker to mark the pronoun, or the clause which contains it, as structurally significant in his speech. In this category, *ăni* is most commonly used to heighten a contrast or other shift in topic; it is one of several devices which can be used for this purpose, as the placing of a subject before the verb, or the use of a free pronominal subject in a verbal clause.

26.1.3 *ănoki in speech by humans* In contrast to such use of *ăni*, the use of *ănoki* shows that the clause is "non-immediate", peripheral to the concerns of speaker or addressee, background. *ănoki* is most often used by a speaker who is equal or subordinate to the addressee (although such speakers use *ăni* equally commonly, each 48 times).[2] A non-status speaker has no justification for presenting his speech as of immediate concern to others where there is no emotional pressure of the sort described. A status-marked speaker may use *ănoki* to renounce the status difference between speaker and addressee out of real feeling, or for rhetorical purposes. A status-marked speaker may also use *ănoki* to mark a clause as relatively unimportant, as background.

26.2 Status-marked Speakers

26.2.1 *Condescension* A status-marked human speaker typically uses *ăni*. (49 of 66 cases, 74%). This is the unmarked usage where the addressee is lower in status than the speaker. The use of *ănoki* by a status-marked speaker represents condescension in its positive sense: the voluntary abandonment of marks of status. In some cases, such usage forms part of the rhetoric of persuasion, as in "Stay with me, and be my father and priest, and I (*ănoki*) will give you..." (שבה עמדי והיה לי לאב ולכהן ואנכי אתן לך...‏, Ju 17:10). The speaker uses the free pronoun to highlight the shift in topic. By using *ănoki*, rather than *ăni*, he abandons the privileged position of employer, and presents himself as bargaining as an equal, even though the other party is only a "lad" (נער), not an established member of the

---

[2]   *ănoki* may occur in Hebrew epigraphic material in Lachish 6.8, (so Davies, 1991:3, but clearly most uncertain). It would refer to the writer, who is addressing a superior.

community like the speaker. Other examples of such condescension used to persuade occur in 2S 2:6, 13:28. The speaker may also use *ānoki* to indicate his own relative unimportance. This may be genuinely felt, as in 1S 23:17, where Jonathan's speech shows that he has accepted the fact that David, not he, will become king.[3] The same is true in 2S 15:28, where David evidently feels that Absalom, and not he, is in fact king (see §6.2.3). The unimportance shown by the use of *ānoki* may be rhetorical, as in "Today I (*ānoki*) am weak" (אנכי היום רך, 2S 3:39), where David excuses his inability to control the b. Zeruiah. The case in 2S 7:2 "I (*ānoki*) am living in a palace of cedar" (ואנכי יושב בבית ארזים), could be categorized in this way, as suggesting "I (unimportant though I am)...". In other cases, the abandoning of status language appears to express politeness, or its equivalent in a close relationship, benevolence and kindliness, as with Jephthah's use of *ānoki* in explaining his position to his daughter in Ju 11:35.

26.2.2 *Background* Status-marked speakers also use *ānoki* in clauses which do not present the main concern of the speech, but are introductory, or otherwise ancillary to the main concern. In "I (*ānoki*) just want to ask one thing of you..." (דבר אחד אנכי שאל מאתך, 2S 3:13, and similarly in 2S 14:18) David uses *ānoki* in a clause which introduces a request, but does not make it. *ānoki* is also used in relative clauses which add little to the content of the noun they modify, as in "Please run and find the arrows I shall shoot" (רץ מצא נא את החצים אשר אנכי מורה, 1S 20:36), where there is no evidence that other arrows are to be found. Other examples occur in 1S 2:23, 24, 21:3.[4] Where the default form, *ăni*, is used, the clause does not necessarily supply more significant information, but it is more central to the speaker's concerns, as in "That monument which I (*ăni*) see" (הציון הלז אשר אני ראה, 2K 23:17). Here the speaker is intent on destroying objects of heterodox origin, and suspects that the

---

[3]   The speaker, Jonathan, is status marked in relation to David. See §7.1.4n.

[4]   The text in 1S 2:23 is problematic. The narrative shows that Eli did not adequately discipline his sons. His use of *ānoki* in 1S 2:24, rather than *ăni* marking his status as parent, might be seen as reflecting a "benevolent" attitude to them (as in Jephthah's speech to his daughter in Ju 11:35, see §26.2.1) intended to add to the picture of Eli as a weak father.

monument he refers to is one. The speaker's chief concern in 1S 20:36 is David, who is to be given information through the shooting of arrows according to a pre-arranged code. The shooting is thus, for the speaker, a means, not an end; it is, in fact, rendered superfluous by his subsequent actions. *'ăni* is similarly used in other subordinate or introductory clauses which the speaker has no reason to mark as background in 1S 12:2, 2, 20:23, 2S 15:20, 2K 10:24.

26.3 Non-status Speakers

26.3.1 *Self-assertion* The use of *'ăni* by a non-status speaker draws attention to the use of the pronoun; it marks the clause in which is it used as particularly important to the speaker, and so deserving particular attention from the addressee. *'ăni* is thus used where the speaker is volunteering for (or requesting, or claiming) a position, as in "I (*'ăni*) will go down with you" (אני ארד עמך, 1S 26:6). Other examples occur in 2S 18:22, 1K 1:5, 22:21. *'ăni* is similarly used where the predicate of the clause presents a claim to consideration, as "I (*'ăni*) am your flesh and blood" (so your support of me will be mutually profitable), (עצמכם ובשרכם אני, Ju 9:2); a source of pride, as "I (*'ăni*) have been a Nazirite since birth" (נזיר אלהים אני מבטן אמי, Ju 16:17); evocation of a significant previous encounter, as "I (*'ăni*) am the woman who was standing with you here" (אני האשה הנצבת עמכה בזה, 1S 1:26). *'ăni* may even be used simply to admit identity significant in the context, as "I (*'ăni*) am" (אני), Joab's reply to the question "Are you Joab?" in 2S 20:17. This reply identifies him as the negotiator for one of two opposing forces. When he next speaks, indicating readiness to listen to his interlocutor, he has already been singled out as a key figure, so there is no need to draw attention to the pronoun in his reply. Consequently, he uses *'ānoki* in "I (*'ānoki*) am listening" (שמע אנכי, 2S 20:17), encouraging the woman negotiating for the other side to take the lead.

26.3.2 Other examples of the use of *'ăni* in marking self-assertion by non-status speakers occur in 1S 17:10, 2S 14:5, 15:34, 34, 34, 16:19, 19:44 (possibly with defective wording), 1K 13:18, 18:36, 2K 2:3, 5, 16:7. A demand for attention of this sort is typically put forward with some emotion, reflecting the speaker's personal interest. *'ăni* is also used where the speaker is strongly concerned in the speech for other reasons, that is, where the strong feelings of the speaker are more clearly the main motivation for its use. Abigail uses *ăni* where she accepts the blame for Nabal's insult to David, and excuses herself for not averting it: "On me, me (*ăni*), my Lord, be the guilt... I (*ăni*), your servant, did not see my Lord's servants whom you sent." (בי אני אדני העון... ואני אמתך לא ראיתי את נערי אדני אשר שלחת, 1S 25:24-25). The safety of her household and homestead depend on the success of her attempt to appease David's wrath. Her display of emotion reflects the strength of her concern.[5]

26.3.3 Where the clause ascribes to the speaker some characteristic or quality which is distasteful or shameful, or is a disqualification for some position, a non-status speaker uses *ănoki*, as "I (*ănoki*) am the least in my father's house" (ואנכי הצעיר בבית אבי, Ju 6:15). Similar ideas are expressed in 1S 9:21, 18:23. Other examples occur in 1S 1:15 (embittered), 22:22 (cause of death), 2S 11:5 (pregnant out of wedlock), 19:36 (too old), 1K 3:7 (young), 14:6 (bringer of bad news), 19:4 (not as good as he thought). *ănoki* is also used in the formulaic question 'Who am I?' indicating self-abasement (1S 18:18, 2S 7:18), and in the formula 'I am a dog', even where used, in question form, to argue that the speaker deserves better treatment (1S 17:43, 2S 3:8).

26.3.4 *Emphasis* In other cases the use of *ăni* by a non-status speaker seems to have no connotations beyond the desire to draw attention to the pronoun. It is used to highlight the actions of the speaker in contrast to those of others, as in "If he is able to do battle with me, and strikes me down... but if I (*ăni*) overcome him..." (אם יוכל להלחם אתי והכני... ואם אני אוכל לו..., 1S 17:9). Other examples occur in Ju 1:3, 8:23, 2S 12:28, 17:15, 1K 1:14, 21:7. *ăni* is similarly used to highlight a shift of the topic to the speaker's own situation, in Ju 12:2, 20:4, 1S 17:28. In other examples, the use of *ăni* seems simply to mark the clause in question as particularly significant. A messenger introduces himself to the priest Eli with *ăno-*

---

[5]   Other examples of the use of *ăni* by non-status speakers reflecting strong feeling occur in Ju 17:2, 19:18, 2S 11:11, 13:13, 19:21, 1K 1:21, 26, 3:17, 17:20, 18:12, 19:10, 14. The case in Ju 19:18 is included on the assumption that ואת בית יהוה indicates the goal of the levite's journey. The singular pronoun also reflects personal concern here, in contrast to the polite use of the plural (see §18.2.3).

ki, as is expected "I (*ānoki*) am the one who came from the battle" but uses *ăni* in pointing out that his news is fresh, and grave, "I (*ăni*) fled from the battle today" (אנכי הבא מן המערכה ואני מן המערכה נסתי היום, 1S 4:16). Similarly, lookouts use *ăni* in reporting significant developments in 2S 18:27, 2K 9:17. Samson's use of *ăni* in Ju 15:3 is presumably a further example.

26.3.5 Non-status speakers use *ānoki* where such highlighting is not required. It is used in clauses which are not central to the main concern of the speech, which provide "background" in various ways. Thus clauses which introduce a speech by providing a context against which what follows is to be understood most commonly show *ānoki*, "I (*ānoki*) am going to make one request of you" (שאלה אחת אנכי שאל מאתך, 1K 2:16). Other examples occur in Ju 7:17, 18, 1S 4:16, 9:19, 10:8, 2S 18:12, 1K 2:2, 20. The use of *ăni* in introductory clauses of this sort by the woman in 1K 3:17, and by Obadiah in 1K 18:12, reflects the strong emotion which is shown in their speech. *ānoki* is similarly used in clauses which add ancillary detail within a section of narrative, as in "I (*ānoki*) am from there" (משם אנכי, Ju 19:18). Other examples occur in Ju 8:5, 1S 18:23, 1K 14:6. Much of the use of *ānoki* by non-status speakers appears to be default usage, indicating that there is no reason to use *ăni* to mark the clause as immediate.[6]

26.3.6 Speech directed by humans to God forms a subdivision of this group in which *ānoki* is the default usage, as in "I (*ānoki*) am going to leave a fleece on the threshing floor" (הנה אנכי מציג את גזת הצמר בגרן, Ju 6:37). Cases in which God is mentioned as authority or motivating factor are treated in the same way, as "For my part (*ānoki*), far be it from me to sin against Yahweh..." (גם אנכי חלילה לי מחטא ליהוה, 1S 12:23). Other such cases associated with mention of God, or in direct speech to God, occur in Ju 6:15, 1S 1:28, 17:45, 2S 3:28, 7:18, 1K 3:7, 19:4. Some of these fit other categories of the use of *ānoki* (as 2S 7:18, 1K 3:7, mentioned in §26.3.3). Others are merely examples of the large group of uses of *ānoki* representing the unmarked, or default usage of non-status

---

[6] Default usage of this sort occurs in Ju 11:9, 27, 37, 17:9, 9, 1S 1:8, 15:14, 17:8, 20:5, 30:13, 2S 1:8, 13, 16, 2:20, 20:17, 19, 24:17, 17, 1K 2:18, 2K 4:13.

speakers. *'ăni* is used in address to God only by those closely associated with him: by Elijah in 1K 17:20, 19:10, 14, by a spirit in 1K
22:21, and (in early biblical prose outside the corpus) by Moses in
Exod 33:16, 16. The spirit is using the typical form for self-advance-
ment (§26.3.2). The usage in the other cases can reasonably be ascribed to pressure of emotion of some kind.

26.3.7 A good idea of the value of the contrast of *'ăni* and *'ānoki*
as used by non-status speakers can be seen by comparing their use
as free pronominal subject in the first of a pair of related verbal
clauses, a position in which the pronoun is highlighted (Muraoka,
1985:58-9). In "I (*'ānoki*) did not do you wrong, but you are wrong-
ing me" (ואנכי לא חטאתי לך ואתה עשׂה אתי רעה, Ju 11:27), the fact
that the free pronoun is used, and is placed before the verb, emphasizes the speaker as actor in the first of this pair of contrasting
clauses. The choice of *'ānoki*, however, shows that the speaker's
concern is not centred on this clause, and so directs attention to the
following clause, which presents the essential point of his speech.
The case is the same in 2S 24:17 (see §26.3.8). In "I (*'ăni*) — where
can I carry my shame?, and you will be as one of the wanton fools
in Israel" (ואני אנה אוליך את חרפתי ואתה תהיה כאחד הנבלים בישׂראל,
2S 13:13), the use of *'ăni* shows that the initial clause is the speaker's chief concern. The second is simply a supporting consideration.
The emphasis on the first person pronoun is, of course, increased
by its extraposed position, preceding the interrogative. By contrast,
the pronominal subject follows the verb in "I (*'ăni*) will not rule
over you; my son will not rule over you. Yahweh will rule over
you" (לא אמשׁל אני בכם ולא ימשׁל בני בכם יהוה ימשׁל בכם, Ju 8:23).
Despite the position of the subject, the use of *'ăni* shows that the
first clause is central to the speaker's purpose. It conveys his refusal,
the essence of the speech. The subject of the third clause is preposed, heightening the contrast, and drawing attention to the ideal
situation it presents. The second clause is in default format, without
prominence.

26.3.8 The fact that the use of *'ăni* primarily reflects immediacy,
and is only secondarily related to status, explains why there is no
positive correlation between the use of *'ānoki* and the use of deferential terms. *'ăni* is actually more common than *'ānoki* in the de-

ferential speech described above, (28 of 49 cases). It is the form of
free first person singular pronoun usual in clauses noted as reflecting strong emotion.[7] Where *ānoki* is used, strong feeling is not indicated, or the pronoun is used in a conventional way, as in Hannah's statement "I am an embittered woman" (אשה קשת רוח אנכי, 1S
1:15, cf. §26.3.). In "Look, I (*ānoki*) sinned, and I (*ānoki*) erred,
but these, the sheep, what did they do?" (הנה אנכי חטאתי ואנכי
העויתי ואלה הצאן מה עשו, 2S 24:17), *ăni* might be expected. It is
typically used to reflect the strong emotion usually shown in a confession (as 1S 25:24, 25, 2S 19:21, see §§23.7.5, 24.5). However,
David confessed in 2S 24:10. In 2S 24:17, he is not disclosing guilt,
but referring to a known fact. He presents this in an argument over
the fate of others. Their situation is his prime concern; he is not
personally involved. Consequently there is no need to draw attention to the first person pronoun by the use of *ăni*; he uses *ānoki*,
as is typical in human speech to God.

26.4 Speech Ascribed to God

26.4.1 *The use of* ānoki God is represented as using *ăni* only slightly more frequently than *ānoki* (11 of 20 cases, 55%). *ānoki* is used
where the speech concerns the addressee on a personal level, as in
"For my part (*ānoki*), I have heard" (וגם אנכי שמעתי, 2K 22:19, accepting the repentance of Josiah). Other examples occur in 1S 16:3,
24:5, and also in the speech of the angel to Gideon "I (*ānoki*) will
remain until you return" (אנכי אשב עד שובך, Ju 6:18). *ānoki* is also
used in speech by God in clauses which are "background" in that
they establish a context in which what follows is to be understood,
or are otherwise introductory to a speech, as "I (*ānoki*) shall do
something in Israel..." (אנכי עשה דבר בישראל..., 1S 3:11); "I (*ānoki*)
brought Israel up from Egypt..." (אנכי העליתי את ישראל ממצרים, 1S
10:18, and similarly Ju 6:8). Other examples occur in 2S 12:7, 7,
24:12.

26.4.2 *The use of* ăni ăni is usually used, in speech ascribed to
God, in clauses which do not refer to the addressee, as "I (*ăni*)

---

[7]   See 2S 11:11 in §23.5; 1K 18:12 cf. §23.7.4; 1S 25:24, 25, 2S 19:21 in §§23.7.5,
26.3.2; 1K 1:26, see §26.3.2 and 1K 17:20, see §§24.3.1, 26.3.6.

have rejected him" (ואני מאסתיו, 1S 16:1); "I (*ăni*) will be a father
to him" (אני אהיה לו לאב, 2S 7:14). Other examples occur in Ju
2:21, 1S 3:13, 2S 7:8 (spoken to Nathan, not to David), 2K 22:20.
The same is true in "You acted in secret, but I (*ăni*) will do this
thing before all Israel..." (כי אתה עשית בסתר ואני אעשה את הדבר הזה
נגד כל ישראל..., 2S 12:12), where the relevant clause does not mention the addressee, David, although it does closely concern him.
Here, *ăni* also functions to heighten the contrast with the preceding clause (see §26.3.4). In "Set out and go down to Keilah, for I
(*ăni* will give the Philistines into your hand" (קום רד קעילה כי אני
נתן את פלשתים בידך, 1S 23:4), *ăni* may be used simply to highlight
change of focus, although the wider study suggests that this is unusual in the speech of God. The similar clause in 1S 24:5 shows the
expected use of *'ānoki*.[8] *'ăni* is also used in clauses of self-identifi-
cation in which the name Yahweh (יהוה) is used, even where reference is made to the addressee, as in Ju 6:10, 1K 20:13, 28.

26.4.3 All examples in the corpus of free first person pronouns used
in speech ascribed to God are referred to in the above discussion.
'ăni is used 11 of 20 cases (55%). The use of *'ānoki* common where
God speaks to a human can be interpreted as the sort of condescension shown by a status-marked human who uses *'ānoki* as a form of
politeness (§26.2.1). The fact that such usage is rare with humans,
usual with God, may reflect the fact that God's status is never in
doubt, whereas human status may be questioned, and so is constantly asserted. It seems quite likely that, in this feature, the speech of
God may reflect that of human parents, who are unlikely (as usage
in other languages, as French and German, suggests) to use status
language to small children. *'ānoki* is also used in speech ascribed to
God, as in that of status-marked humans, to mark clauses as "background". *'ăni* is used where the use of *'ānoki* is not required for
the purposes described. Thus the use of *'ăni* and *'ānoki* in speech
by God can be explained as based on the same concepts as in speech
by humans.

---

[8]   The use of *'ānoki* in 1S 24:5 could possibly be due to the fact that God's word
is not presented as spoken here, but is quoted by others, see §23.2.2n.

The Designation of Speaker
or Addressee by Name or Title

27.1 Introduction

The present section is mainly concerned with the speaker's use of his own name or title in self-reference. The few cases in which a superior uses the personal name in third person address to a subordinate are also discussed. The personal name or title used in the third person in this way contrasts with the standard use of a first or second person pronoun to represent speaker or addressee in the same way as do the deferential nominals discussed above. The two are different forms of the same phenomenon, so that all cases of address by name or title to God, or to a human superior, have been discussed in §§21-25. Self-reference by name or title presents the public aspect of a speaker: his reputation with the addressee(s) if the personal name is used, his office if a title is used. The name is occasionally used where the speaker presents himself as a subordinate, and could have referred to himself as "your servant". In this situation the name presents a reference more personal than that of a deferential term, but less intimate than that of a pronoun. It thus serves to present an intermediate level of deference. A speaker who does not present himself as a subordinate appears to use this reference to his reputation or his office to provide a weightier, more impressive support for an important declaration than would the less specific reference provided by a pronoun. Third person address to a subordinate by name appears to be a form of distancing indicating rejection.

27.2 Self Designation by Name or Title: Speech of Humans

27.2.1 Where the speaker uses his own name in making a request or expressing thanks to God or to a human superior, it contrasts both with the first person pronoun and with the deferential "your servant" either of which could be used in such a context. In "Please give whatever you can to your servants and to your son, to David" (תנה נא את אשר תמצא ידך לעבדיך ולבנך לדוד, 1S 25:8), The fact that the messengers have previously been referred to as "the lads" (הנערים) highlights the use of "your servants". This term both marks the speech as deferential, and evokes personal relationship in an appeal for sympathy. The designation "Your son David" shows that "your servants" does not include David (as it otherwise could). It depicts speaker and addressee as subordinate and superior, but in a more intimate and kindly relationship than that of servant and master. It also avoids the self-assertion which the use of the first person pronoun would represent. In 2S 7:20, David's appeal to God "What more can David say to you" similarly suggests a close relationship, consistent with the statement (in 2S 7:14, in the promise for which David is offering thanks) that God's relationship with David's son Solomon will be like that of parent and child. This indication of close relationship is repeated with a fitting display of deference in "your servant David" (עבדך דוד, 2S 7:26). In "Araunah {the king} has given all to the king" (הכל נתן ארונה המלך למלך, 2S 24:23), Araunah uses his own name in a performative statement offering a gift to King David.[1] The use of third person reference to both speaker and addressee would provide distancing suitable to the offer of a gift to a superior (see §§23.4.2, 23.4.5). However, Araunah is not acting as a subordinate. He has rejected the king's suggestion and offered one of his own. He is bargaining as an equal. His use of his own name, instead of the deferential "your servant" (as in 2S 24:21) reflects this. In all these cases, then, the use of the personal name seems to carry a meaning intermediate between that of the personal pronoun and that of the deferential term.

27.2.2 Self reference by name occurs in oaths sworn by Jonathan (1S 20:13), David (1S 25:22), and Abner (2S 3:9).[2] Comparable cases

---

[1]   The word "the king" (המלך) was probably introduced through error. Araunah is otherwise referred to in a compound designation as "Araunah the Jebusite" (2S 24:16, 18; the spelling of his name is uncertain in both cases, the syntax of its use in the former). He cannot be king of Israel; if he were king of some other state, its name would be included in his title. It is thus highly unlikely that "the king" in his speech in 2S 24:23 is his title. On the equally unlikely possibility that it used a vocative, see §25.7.3.

[2]   In 1S 25:22, "the enemies of David" (איבי דוד), the word "enemies" is either a euphemism (see Anbar, 1979, followed in Fokkelman, 1986:735), or results from deliberate change in the original text (McCarter, 1980:394). Where the first person

without an oath formula occur in Ju 9:15 (the curse of the bram-
ble), 1K 2:45 (King Solomon declares himself blessed). A further example of the speaker's self-designation by name occurs in "Ahab
served Baal a little, but Jehu will serve him greatly" (אחאב עבד את
הבעל מעט יהוא יעבדנו הרבה, 2K 10:18). The use of the name in this
way carries implications such as "You know how Jehu acts, keeps
his word, etc." That is, the speaker presents his reputation, his public persona, as more significant in the context than a less specific
pronominal reference. A similar intention can reasonably be suggested for Samuel's use of his own name in 1S 12:11 — God sent
the well-known judge Samuel rather than the aged speaker. The effect of such usage is a heightened presentation of the speaker, an
emphatic equivalent of the first person pronoun. All three oaths referred to above support highly unusual undertakings, so that such
emphasis is appropriate to them.[3]

27.2.3 Self reference by title is used where the speaker's public
aspect, which is thus presented, is significant in the situation, while
his personal aspect, which is thus obscured, is not, as in "Why are
you going to be last to bring back the king to his house?... You are
my brothers. You are my flesh and blood. So why will you be last
to bring back the king?" (למה תהיו אחרנים להשיב את המלך אל ביתו...
אחי אתם עצמי ובשרי אתם ולמה תהיו אחרנים להשיב את המלך, 2S 19:12-
13). The first and last clauses of this typical envelope structure, referring to "the king", represent the action with which the speaker,
King David, is concerned, as viewed by his subjects, and so evoke
its political significance. The central clauses, referring to kinship
(presenting the same argument as is put forward by Abimelek in Ju
9:2), use the first person pronoun, evoking personal relationship to
which they refer. Personal pronoun and title are balanced against
each other much as are pronouns and deferential terms in 2S 19:20

---

pronoun is used in an oath formula of this sort in the corpus, the speaker is a king
(2S 3:35, 19:14, 1K 2:23, 20:10, 2K 6:31), but it is doubtful if this is relevant to the
interpretation of the use of the name. Jezebel uses neither name nor pronoun in
1K 19:2. Ruth uses the first person pronoun in Ruth 1:17.

[3]   Jonathan rejects his king and father in favour of David (see §27.4.2). Abner
similarly abandons family ties and his master in favour of David. David undertakes
the slaughter of innocents.

(see §20.5.3). In referring to "your master's servants" in 2S 20:6, 1K 1:33, rather than "my servants" the speaker similarly represents the addressee's viewpoint rather than his own in a conventional form of politeness.[4]

27.2.4 The personal name or title is naturally used in the standard introduction to a message to present the authority of the sender. In some cases the wording of the text suggests that the use of the name in this way is, in fact, part of the message, as in "Jephthah repeated his actions, and sent messengers to the king of the b. Ammon. He said to him "Thus says Jephthah..." (ויוסף עוד יפתח וישלח מלאכים אל מלך בני עמון ויאמר לו כה אמר יפתח..., Ju 11:14-15). The suggestion that the originator uses his own name in this way is even stronger where an introduction of this sort is used within a message to begin a new section, as in 2K 18:31. These are also cases in which (as the text stands), the name or title is used to present a public persona, since the private individual has no place in the context.[5]

27.3 Self-Designation by Name or Title: Speech Ascribed to God

27.3.1 The name of God is used in speech ascribed to God in much the same way as human speakers use their own names for self-reference, as in "Yahweh looks at the heart" (ויהוה יראה ללבב, 1S 16:7). Here, where God is agent, the use of the name can be understood as invoking the reputation as authority for the speech, as with the human usage described in §27.2.2. Similar cases occur in 2S 7:11, 11, 1K 17:14, and also in the passive structure with metonymic reference "This is easy in the eyes of Yahweh" (ונקל זאת בעיני יהוה, 2K 3:18). In "Go out and stand on the mountain before Yahweh" (צא ועמדת בהר לפני יהוה, 1K 19:11), where God is patient, the use of

---

[4]   See §13.4.3. In 1S 29:10 "Your master's servants" probably refers to the supporters David brought with him from Judah, as opposed to any troops from Ziklag which he may have under his command. Achish still regards David as Saul's "servant" (see 1S 29:3).

[5]   The use and function of the "messenger formula" used here is discussed in Meier 1992:277-291. The use of the singular verb "he said" in Ju 11:15 is perfectly acceptable in Hebrew (see §17.4). The versions and Hebrew MSS which use a plural verb may have been affected by the usage of the target language or the linguistic environment, but certainty is impossible.

the name suggests that the formal aspects of the situation are being presented, as in the human usage described in §27.2.3, and as where the title "king" is used in reflection of the agent's viewpoint (see §§ 5.4.1, 6.2.2). A similar case occurs in 1S 10:19. The expressions "The way of Yahweh" (דרך יהוה, Ju 2:22) and "An altar to Yahweh your God" (מזבח ליהוה אלהיך, Ju 6:26) could also be seen as invoking the authority of the name, but they are more probably examples of fixed phrases, used in spite of their third person viewpoint, as where "the house of Yahweh" (בית יהוה) is used to indicate the temple instead of "My house" (2K 20:5). Other examples of this sort of usage occur in 2S 12:9, 2K 9:6, 7, 22:18.

27.3.2 A nominal is occasionally used in parallel with the first person pronoun in the speech of God as in 2K 22:19:
"Because your heart was softened
    and you humbled yourself before Yahweh
        when you heard what I said...
and you tore your clothes
    and you wept before me
        I also have heard..."

יען רך לבבך
ותכנע מפני יהוה
בשמעך אשר דברתי...
ותקרע את בגדיך
ותבכה לפני
וגם אנכי שמעתי...

The patterning of the words can scarcely be accidental. The use of the name Yahweh can reasonably be seen as an integral part of the pattern, similar to the use of deferential terms in parallel with pronouns in 2S 19:20 (see §20.5.3). God as agent is represented by the first person. God as patient is represented by the name where the action is described in formal terms "you humbled yourself", but by the first person pronoun (reflecting God's parent-like concern, see §§24.7, 26.4.3) where the action "you wept" (as child before father) suggests genuine emotion.

27.3.3 In earlier writings, it is often uncertain whether spoken words should be ascribed to God or to the human presenting them (see Meier, 1992:289, 314). In at least one case, the use of "my lord" (אדני) in 2K 19:23, the designation used in a speech of God delivered by an intermediary is one that appears unsuitable for self-reference (see §15.8.2). On the other hand, there is no suggestion of an intermediary in the cases of the uses of God's name quoted in § 27.3.1, save in 2K 20:5. The examples in 1S 16:7 and 1K 19:11 occur in speech to Samuel and Elijah, who themselves often act as intermediaries, transmitting God's word to the people, so there is no reason to suppose that God would be thought to require one in speaking to them. It must be accepted, then, that the name of God was used in speech ascribed to God in much the same way as humans used their own names in their speech, providing a further means of adding expressive content. The extent of the usage is not clear, either for humans or for God, because of the possibility of confusion between the words of the originator of a message, and those of an intermediary who transmitted it. A full study of such usage in speech ascribed to God would extend to almost every book in the Bible. The main value of this survey of the small amount of material in the corpus is to indicate the potential interest and value of such a study.

27.4 Designation of Addressee by Name or Title

27.4.1 Most examples of the use of a nominal by a human speaker in third person reference to the addressee have already been treated in the discussion of deferential speech. Like the other uses of names and titles discussed here, the standard deferential terminology presents the public or institutional aspect of the person named, not the private, personal aspect. Deferential terms, and the few other nominals discussed in that section, are used only to an addressee who is of higher status than the speaker, or is treated as of higher status for the speaker's purposes, as in the presentation of a plea. A name is used by a human speaker in third person reference to an addressee who is, in fact, a subordinate in only one scene in the corpus. It is suggested below that this shows politeness, or possibly the speaker thinks of the addressee as his superior. God uses a name in third person reference to a human addressee in three cases in announcing punishment. This contrasts with the second person address usually used, and so presumably indicates distancing and rejection.

27.4.2 The only examples of the third person designation of a non-status addressee by name in human usage occur in the speech of

Jonathan to David. Jonathan expects to find, as a result of a conference with the king, that there is "Good(will) to David" (טוב אל דוד,
1S 20:12) for the immediate future, and he looks forward to a more
distant time "When God destroys the enemies of David" (בהכרת
יהוה את איבי דוד, 1S 20:15). Second person pronouns are used in
similar contexts in 1S 20:13, but the air of formality induced by the
use of David's name in the previous verse is maintained in 1S 20:13
by Jonathan's use of his own name in his oath (§27.2.2). Jonathan
undertakes, in this speech, to side with David against Saul, his father and king (see §15.3.1). The unusual usage is no doubt intended
to ensure that this extraordinary undertaking carries conviction.
The reason for Jonathan's behaviour is no doubt his belief in David's future greatness, whether this stems from knowledge that he
has been anointed to succeed Saul, or merely from appreciation of
his abilities.[6] His use of David's name can be understood as similar
to a speaker's use of his own name in an oath. It represents the individual specifically, providing a more formal and impressive reference than would a pronoun (see §27.2.2). It also avoids the sense of
intimacy and personal interest which the use of the second person
pronoun would convey (cf. §27.2.1). Jonathan's usage here, expresses politeness, foreshadowing his explicit acceptance of David as
his future ruler in 1S 23:17, and, in the wider context, provides one
of the first hints that David will attain the throne for which he has
been anointed.

27.4.3 God uses the name of a human he is addressing in third person reference only in announcing the punishment of wicked rulers:
Jeroboam (1K 14:10-11) Baasha (1K 16:3-4), and Ahab (with Jezebel
included) in 1K 21:21-24. In each case the sentence is preceded by a
statement of the reason for the punishment in which the king is addressed in the second person. The three passage use similar wording,
often formulaic. Reference by name in these cases, using the third
person, suggests distancing. The king is placed outside the sphere of
normal relations which is represented by the use of the name in the
vocative (parent-like, see §25.4.3), with second person pronouns

---

[6]   There is no evidence that it was widely known that David had been anointed,
but Samuel's action, though concealed from Saul, was public. Abigail's words in 1S
25:28-31 suggest that she knew about it.

used for reference. The sentence on Ahab is remarkable for the use of the second person in two of the four cases in which Jeroboam is referred to by name (one of the two in which this occurs in the passage on Baasha, which omits some of the material used in the others).[7] Even if it is correct to regard the sentence on Ahab as "redactional supplement" based on the other passages (see Montgomery and Gehman 1951:332), this use of the second person can reasonably be regarded as significant. The use of the name is usual in the situation. The contrasting use of the pronoun, abandoning the distancing use of nominals, is presumably to be seen as representing heightened feeling (as it does where a pronoun replaces a deferential nominal) and so a more impassioned condemnation, (see §22.5).

27.5 Conclusion

Nominal reference to speaker or addressee in the cases discussed in this chapter is, then, made on the same basis as such reference using deferential terminology. Any difference derives from the content of the nominals used, the stereotype they represent (see §28.2.1). The value of the use beyond this content derives from the context of the usage, and the contrast of the term used with the others typical of that context, just as with deferential terms. The use of non-deferential nominals for self-reference by humans is rare, and the specific intention in each case consequently somewhat uncertain, but there is no reason to doubt that the use is a genuine feature of the language of the corpus, and functioned in the way described. This suggests the potential value of a comprehensive study of the much more numerous examples of similar usage in speech ascribed to God. The difference in the care with which the words of God are kept distinct from those of a human speaker who delivers them by earlier and by later prophets noted in Meier, 1992:314, may, in fact reflect a diminishing of the use of nominal self-reference in later periods. Considerable difference in expressive usage between pre-exilic and post-exilic writers is to be expected.

---

[7]   In the clauses "I am bringing misfortune on you, and I will burn after you" (הנני מבי<א> אליך רעה ובערתי אחריך, 1K 21:21). The passage on Ahab also presents the material in a somewhat different order from that of the other two. The sentence is interrupted by the charge that the addressee has provoked God (1K 21:22), which precedes the sentence in the other two cases (1K 14:9, 16:2), and by the comment on Jezebel (1K 21:23).

VII CONCLUSION

Summary and Conclusion

28.1 Introduction

The assumption with which this study originated — that the designation of individuals in the corpus reflects a self-consistent system — appears to be fully justified. It has been found possible to offer an explanation consistent with the principles which the study shows to be basic to the usage for almost every one of the multitudinous examples surveyed. Cases in which the explanation could only be advanced with hesitation, and those in which no satisfactory explanation seemed possible, form a remarkably small proportion of the total. In this aspect of its usage, at least, the corpus can be regarded as homogeneous. The study shows, moreover, that the way in which individuals are designated is not simply a trivial matter of sociolinguistic convention. It has considerable significance as a way in which the speaker or narrator conveys his feelings about the matters presented, and attempts to influence the addressee or the reader. It has already been suggested above (as in §23.9.1) that the different phenomena described can often be seen as filling the same function, implying that there is a general system which governs their use, but this is obscured by the way the study is organized. This final chapter is used to point out a number of significant phenomena which deserve more general notice than has been provided above, and to suggest the main implications of the study.

28.2 The Use of Epithets

28.2.1 The basis for the use of an epithet is its lexical content. The title "king" is typically used where the person designated is being treated as a king, or is acting in a notably kingly manner (see §6.2.5). Other epithets can be seen to be used in the same way, and this seems particularly clear in the case of relationship terms. The use of the term usually indicates that the action described conforms to the ideal of the relationship represented by the term (see §§ 13.4.2, 14.2.2, and cf. §14.2.4). Failure to use the term where expected suggests lack of such conformity (see §§6.8.4, 14.2.2). Conformity with the ideal seems to extend to the result of the action. It appears that the use of an epithet is generally avoided where an action, which would have been successful if the stereotype represented by that epithet were ideally maintained, does not succeed (see §§ 8.1.3, 13.3.4n; §10.2.3 is possibly also relevant). Most commonly, then, an epithet is used where the person designated is acting, or is being treated, in accordance with the stereotype represented by the epithet. Literary critics generally follow this view, which, after all, is merely common sense. It is of some value, however, to have the conditions of the use of each epithet described in some detail, so that a clearer idea of the stereotype it represents can be attained. The conditions under which its use might be expected but does not occur are of particular interest. They not only improve knowledge of the stereotype; they also act as a key to the recognition of usage that is marked.

28.2.2 In addition to action consistent with the stereotype it represents, an epithet may also be used to highlight action inconsistent with that stereotype. This claim might seem nothing more than an attempt to justify all details of the usage of the text as it stands. However, the use of the same term to represent what appear to be opposite ends of a scale is familiar from other systems of designation. The default usage in such cases can be seen as representing the mean between two extremes. The opposition name : title is used to indicate that the king is acting in a standard way, or in some other way. "Other" may represent either extreme of non-standard action: exceptionally kingly or notably unkingly. Other examples of such use of binary contrast are noted in §§23.4.3n, 25.2.3, and more could be suggested, for instance the use of a personal name in expressing benevolence or its opposite.[1] The deliberate misuse of

---

[1]   Certain terms of address are used in Cairo Arabic as terms of respect where appropriate, but also as terms of endearment to children, as vehicles of sarcasm to friends, and almost as terms of abuse to the "wrong" addressee (see Parkinson, 1985:119). The use of opprobrious terms is similarly multivalent (see Parkinson, 1985:201), as is the "familiar" form of the second person pronoun in early modern English (see Wales, 1983:116). Opprobrious terms are used as endearments in a variety of languages (Braun, 1988:254; English examples could be added). Wales (1983: 116) points out that the appearance of conflict in meaning can be removed by calling such usage "non-polite" in opposition to a corresponding "polite" form. As usual, the context indicates the speaker's intention in using the non-polite form, here the expression either of intimacy or of contempt.

words to show irony, found in biblical Hebrew as in other languages (see §1.4.3), has a similar basis. The fact that such usage is
marked may be indicated, in spoken language, by particular prosodic features. In written language, however, and sometimes in
spoken, the only key to ironic intent is knowledge that the words
are inappropriate in their context, as conflicting either with common convention or with the speaker's known views. The context,
including this knowledge, is similarly the only key to the motivation of the irony, or to what it is intended to communicate.

28.2.3 The same is true of inappropriate or marked uses of epithets
which do not come under the heading of irony. Where a king is
patient, the title is typically used where the agent is his subject, but
not where the agent does not treat the patient as his king. However, assassins are typically said to attack "the king". Presumably
this is intended to impress on the reader the status of their victim,
and so to intensify the feelings of pity and horror evoked by the
act. (§8.1.2, other cases of usage of this sort are suggested in §§
7.1.2n, 13.4.6 on 1S 26:15). The value of the use of a term which reflects the relationship of one individual with another is inevitably
complex. In 2S 13:10, where Tamar is said to take food to Amnon
"her brother", she is treating him as a brother, but he is not acting
like one. The use of the epithet "brother" reminds the reader of the
relationship, and so adds to the impact of the dramatic irony created by the reader's knowledge that the man Tamar is treating with
sisterly kindness is in fact planning to entrap her. The epithet itself
simply represents the stereotype indicated by its lexical value, just
as the forms of second person pronoun in French represent the concept "addressee". In both cases, the intended value of any use is determined by the context in which the term is used, in accordance
with the values shared by the speaker or narrator and his intended
audience. The motivation and value of expressive usage is unlikely
always to be clear to an outsider, even if culturally relatively close
to this intended audience. Where the cultural difference is great, as
with modern scholars and the bible, uncertainty is inevitably common. We can only be sure of what a usage means to us. We can
only approach the meaning for the intended audience through the
sort of charting of the parameters within which an epithet is used,

and demonstration of its place within the relevant semantic field, which is attempted in this study.

28.3 Word Order

28.3.1 Variation in the order in which epithets are used in a designation has been mentioned sporadically above with the implication that it is significant. It is generally recognized that the order of the constituents in the clause in biblical Hebrew carries meaning, although the nature of that meaning may be debated. In the case of phrases, variation, if noticed, is likely to be attributed to error, or to the vagaries of a form of language characterized by redundancy.[2] Errors have presumably occurred, but the recognition of them requires a faith in our knowledge of biblical usage, which the above discussion suggests is not justified. The language does, no doubt, show redundant features, but close attention to the way words are used (as in the case of the forms of the first person pronoun) shows redundancy to be less common than is generally thought. One word may be used in place of another as a matter of style, but, if "total synonymy" does not exist, as seems to be the case, then stylistic variation will affect meaning. Patterns created with words, as in chiastic pairs, envelope structures, or the intricate patterns discussed in §§20.5.3, 27.3.2, are no doubt to be admired for themselves, but they are not used simply to elicit that admiration. They are used because they convey the thought expressed with greater impact than do simpler forms, through the harmonious combination of feelings usually contrasted, such as strong personal emotion and deference, or through the prominence given to particular items by repetition, or by position in the clause.[3] The discussion below assumes that different arrangements of the same elements are used

---

[2]　Such variation was noted as significant in Peretz, 1968:131. Literary critics also often recognize the significance of such variation, but many details of biblical usage remain inadequately explored.

[3]　As in "My servant Jacob and Israel my chosen" (עבדי יעקב וישראל בחירי, Isa 45:4), noted as an example of artistic influence on word order in Peretz, 1968:131. Here Israel, the name given greater prominence by the word order is the more evocative, representing both the patriarch, and the community formed by his servants (cf. its use in 1K 18:36, mentioned in §15.6.4).

to carry different meanings, but does not argue that this is the only reason for their use.

28.3.2 The placing of a vocative in a clause may be considered as a parallel to the placing of an epithet in a nominal designation, since the position is not, in either case, affected by syntactic relationship. A vocative is placed before a clause to make it the initial focus of the addressee's attention, or after the first word to highlight that word, while still providing considerable prominence for the vocative. A vocative is placed after a clause where it is desirable that the addressee concentrate on the clause, or where the vocative is less important for other reasons. It is placed between the core of the clause and following constituents to enhance the impact of those constituents as additions to the basic clause (see §25.8). Interjections, like vocatives, are not considered part of the structure of a clause. Those which express strong emotion, as expressions of despair (אוֹי, אֲהָהּ), are placed before the clause. נְאֻם יהוה, which merely reiterates authentication of a speech already introduced as originating from God, typically follows a clause, or stands within it. In the latter position, it adds to the impact of the following constituents, much as does a vocative which follows the core of a clause.[4] The language thus uses position relative to the other constituents of the clause in similar ways with different features, regardless of their intrinsic meaning.

28.3.3 It was demonstrated in §§13.3.7, 13.4.1, 13.4.4-5, that the position of a relationship term in a noun-phrase used as a designation carries meaning. In narration, a relationship term typically follows the name and any other epithets. In speech, however, it quite often precedes them where the relationship term is deferential, and the addressee is superior to the speaker. Kinship terms are also used in this position when they are used for purposes of persuasion, or

---

[4]   A simple break in the clause, marked by a pausal form may have the same effect, see Revell, 1980:171-5. The same is true of the accentuation. In Gen 22:10, "Abraham put out his hand and took the knife | to slaughter his son" the main verse division is not positioned so as to mark the main syntactical division, but so as to separate the description of Abraham's action from that of his purpose, thus highlighting the latter, with its horrifying implications.

where the speaker has other reasons to draw attention to the relationship. That is, as in a clause structure, an item is placed first in a phrase to make it the focus of the addressee's attention to that phrase. The narrator occasionally does place a relationship term before the name. This is so rare (four of sixty-seven examples) that any motivation suggested for it may reasonably be questioned. It may be recalled, however, that other examples of marked word order, such as the use of a preposed constituent in a verbal clause, are also more common in speech than in narration. There is no reason to doubt, then, that the narrator might also call attention to a relationship term by placing it before the name in a designation. Whether this was done intentionally, and the reason why such attention was required, in any particular instance, are, of course, matters for speculation. However, the argument that such variation in position is accidental, and carries no meaning, can not be sustained.

28.3.4 Where a designation is made up of name, patronymic and title, they typically occur in that order. However, where a designation of this sort is used for a priest or prophet, and the agent speaks to, sends to, or goes to the person designated in his capacity as priest or prophet, the title precedes the patronymic (1S 30:7, 2K 19:2, 22:14, see §§12.3.3, 12.8.3). Where the agent is not concerned with that capacity (as with King Saul and the priest Ahimelek in 1S 22:11), the title follows the patronymic. The same order is followed where the priest or prophet is not patient (1K 1:42, 11:29, 16:7, 2K 14:25, 20:1).[5] Where name, patronymic and title are used to designate a king, the title precedes the patronymic only in 2K 14:13. The king is here patient. The highlighting of the title can be seen as intended to emphasize the horror of the capture of the true king by a renegade, which might mean the end of the Davidic dynasty. Where these elements are used in the usual order, the designation of the king occurs in a synchronistic date formula, the king is actor,

---

[5]   The case of Deborah in Ju 4:4 may be considered not to be a "designation" and so ignored (see §12.8.3), or it may be considered an exceptional use of the marked order to draw attention to her function in the narrative, which is to present the commands of God to Barak.

the approach is by God, or the king is foreign.[6] Where some other title is used in a designation made up of name, patronymic and title used in that order, the person designated is agent (2K 18:18, 18, 37, 37) or the capacity named in the title is not in question (1K 2:32, 32, 2K 22:3). That is, the marked order is used where the person designated is patient, but this is not obligatory. It is done to highlight the purpose of the agent's activity, where there is reason to give prominence to the event recorded.

28.3.5 Where a designation consists of a name and an epithet, the name precedes the epithet except in the case of the relationship terms described above, and the title "the king". The initial position standard for "the king" (המלך) combined with a name contrasts not only with the position of the title of other offices, but also with the position of a king's title which includes the name of the state. It is also true that the narrator uses a designation of this sort chiefly for kings of the Davidic line, rarely for others (see §5.2.1). All this suggests that designations of the form "the King PN" may have originated as a marked usage. The position of "the king" in the community was unique; naming the office identifies its holder. The position was also of great importance, both in cultural and in practical terms. It is thus often more important to name the office than to identify its holder, and this is reflected in the initial position of the title. If this was the case, the marked usage eventually became the default, almost the exclusive usage.[7] During the exilic and Persian

---

[6]   In a synchronistic date formula: 1K 15:1, 2K 8:16, 16, 25, 25, 13:1, 14:1, 1, 17, 17, 23, 23, 15:1, 32, 32, 16:1, 18:1, 1, 9. In 1K 15:1, the title precedes the name, a unique arrangement the value of which is uncertain (see §10.3.3). The king is actor in 2K 8:29, 16:5. Where the agent is God, the king is designated in spoken reference (1K 12:23) so the standard order is expected. The foreign kings so designated function either as agent or as patient (1S 27:2, 2S 8:3, 12, 13:37, 1K 2:39, 15:18, 2K 20:12). Presumably as foreigners their status is unimportant.

[7]   The prevalence of preposed constituents, the common treatment of collectives as plural, and the abandonment of the longer form of first person pronoun, typical of later Hebrew, may well have resulted from ever-increasing attempts to add to the impact of speech by the use of marked forms, to the point at which such use became the norm. Similar reversals of usage have occurred elsewhere. "By the end of the 16C…, the status of *you* and *thou* was a direct reversal of that in the 13C" (when address to an individual as "you" was marked. Wales 1983:117).

periods, the community had no king, and so no reason to use the title. When it was revived for use by the Maccabaeans, the title "the king" was placed after the name, in the position standard for all other titles (see Talshir, 1991).

28.3.6 The corpus shows five examples of the use of the title "the king" following the name. In 2K 8:29, 9:15 (§10.3.3) the use of the title recognizes the encounter of the king of Israel with another king mentioned in the preceding verse (see §10.1.1). However, the action described, returning to recover from wounds, has nothing to do with kingship, and the title may have been deprived of its usual prominence for this reason. The same argument can be made for the reference to "David the King" in 2S 13:39 (§6.7), where (if the traditional interpretation of the obscure passage is correct), he is indulging in unkingly sentiment. In 1K 2:17, Adonijah's reference to "Solomon the King" suggests family usage (§8.3), as if the name were to be followed by "my brother" or "your son". This may be seen as a way of presenting his plea more persuasively, or merely as a reflection of the fact that Adonijah has only grudgingly recognized Solomon as king, and would be glad to ignore his status. In 1S 18:6, the women come out to meet "Saul the King" (§7.1.3). The usage surveyed shows that the title is typically given prominence where a king is approached by subjects. The form of this designation can be variously interpreted, but the suggestion that it is one of the means used by the narrator to point out Saul's unworthiness is not unlikely (see §7.1.2). There is no way of showing that the placing of the title in these five cases does represent the narrator's intention, but it is by no means impossible that it should.[8] The proper conclusion clearly is that variation in the order of the components of designations was used expressively. The origin of any particular example may be questioned, but the fact that it shows variant order cannot be regarded as, in itself, indication that it is intrusive.

---

[8]   The title in the form "the King PN" is occasionally used where the action might seem as quite as unkingly as in these five cases, as in 2S 3:31 (but perhaps the honouring of a hero was a kingly act), or 1K 12:18 (unless התאמץ implies kingly exertion to avoid disaster). As usual, certainty is unattainable.

28.4 Variation in Number

28.4.1 It is maintained above that variation in the grammatical number of the coreferents of a nominal is used expressively. Scholars accept such variation as deliberate where it can be related to physical facts, as with Levi's statement that singular coreferents may be used for a compound nominal to refer to the principal of the compound (Levi, 1987:53). Elsewhere, such variation is often either ignored as meaningless, as with the coreferents of collectives, or emended to produce consistency. The Greek translation is often cited in support of such emendation. It typically shows greater consistency than does the Hebrew, but the significance of this is uncertain, as such consistency is typical of the Greek language. The more important question is the origin of the variation in number in the Hebrew in passages where it is commonly emended, as in 1 Samuel 9-10. Most critics seem to rely on the idea that error was characteristic of Hebrew scribes. It is curious, however, that the proportion of error should be so high in some features, so low in others. Moreover, a shift in number would be a surprising error where consistency is characteristic both of the language of the scribe, and, as the view implies, that of his exemplar. It might be assumed that passages like 1 Samuel 9-10 existed in two forms, one consistently using singular pronouns and the other plural, which were conflated during the production of the received text. However, neither the received Hebrew, nor the Greek translation, provides evidence of a text free from variation in number. It is, in fact, scarcely credible that so much variation arising merely from conflation would have been allowed to survive in a linguistic environment which required consistency in number, through a long period in which the attitude towards the text did not inhibit correction of an exemplar. It seems much more likely that the variation in number in the received text represents ancient usage, modified, perhaps, to some extent in the course of transmission.

28.4.2 It is true, of course, that a proportion of the usage described in §§16-19 would be accepted by all as intentional. There is no doubt that variation in number sometimes is used meaningfully. As with other problems discussed above, the question is the extent to which the feature was used.[9] The Greek translation, though more consistent, shows the same sort of inconsistency as does the Hebrew. The Hebrew uses a plural among the singular second person pronouns in 1S 9:19, which McCarter (1980:169) censures as "inappropriate", preferring the reading of the Greek, which does not. In 1S 10:2, the Hebrew shows the same shift under similar conditions, and the Greek agrees with it. If this, too, is changed as "inappropriate", the Hebrew is being made to conform to patterns which cannot be shown to be relevant for it.[10] If the Hebrew is not changed (McCarter does not comment), then such inconsistency must be accepted as one of the characteristics of the language. In fact, variation in number in Hebrew is so common (under particular conditions) that it would be absurd to expunge it. Its occurrence in Judges 19, in all three persons under similar conditions and with (apparently) similar motivation justifies accepting all the forms of its discussed above as characteristic of biblical Hebrew (see §§17.4.2-4, 18.2.3, 19.2.3). This does not imply a claim that features of this sort have not been changed during the course of transmission of the text. The spelling of the text shows a proportion of unusual forms characteristic of the texts from Qumran, and it is reasonable to assume that other features have been changed during transmission in similar proportion. It does seem reasonable to argue, however, that earlier linguistic conventions are likely to be represented more accurately in Hebrew, of which they were once characteristic, than in Greek, to which they have always been foreign.[11]

---

[9] Thus the variation in the number of the first person pronoun (and its variation in relation to the number of the noun or pronoun designating the speaker in the introduction to the speeches) is not emended in Num 20:14-19, 21:22, Ju 11:17, 19, even in BHK.

[10] It should be remembered that many emendations of the sort discussed here go back to Welhausen and his generation, when it was generally assumed that language typically conformed to clear rules of standard usage. More recent observation finds that this is often not the case. A parallel in a less contentious area is provided by Baer's rules for the use of the *metheg* (formulated with the usual assumptions of scribal incompetence) as compared with the information provided by the careful descriptions of recent scholars.

[11] Linguistic change, beginning with that seen in "late biblical Hebrew", and social change, beginning with that resulting from the capture of Jerusalem in 587 B.C.E., must have had a considerable effect on the system of expressive usage described here. Writers represented at Qumran are unlikely always to have recogni-

28.4.3 The classification which determines concord is valid only within the domain of the structure concerned. Thus the significance of adjectival concord is limited to the noun phrase, and does not necessarily affect concord within a clause of which that phrase is subject, as is seen in "a great (s) people were travelling (p)" (עם רב הלכים, 2S 13:34, see Revell 1993b §6.6). Similarly, the classification which determines concord of the verb of a main clause with a nominal subject is typically valid for that clause, but does not necessarily affect the classification used in clauses subordinate to it, or in following main clauses. Practise varies somewhat, but these conventions clearly represent the principles basic to concord with collectives, or with nominals representing speaker and addressee, (see §§ 16.4, 17.3.1, 18.2.6, 20.2). The same principles no doubt underlie the various forms of variation in number described in §§17, 18, 19. In fact the governing principle in concord in biblical Hebrew is "notional", not grammatical, as has long been recognized. The fact that the "notions" which determine concord include both the physical facts of number, and the psychological facts of immediacy and its opposite, is no more unexpected than the similarly multivalent use of concord in number in the French second person pronoun, or of concord in gender in Arabic.

28.4.4 A theoretical basis for the variation in number can easily be suggested. One individual is typically represented by singular pronouns, more than one by the plural. Where more than one individual is concerned, they may be treated as a single entity, represented by a singular (collective) noun, and so treated as singular. Where the language concerns the group as an entity, and not the individuals who compose it, the singular is regularly used (see §3.3.4). However, one can only deal with a group in the abstract; in reality, one deals with some or all of its members. It is not surprising to find that a group is often treated as plural, even where represented by a singular noun. A group represented as plural may also be re-

---

zed such usage, or to reproduce it accurately. The vernacular and society known to the Greek translators would have been closer to those in which the Qumran manuscripts were produced than to those presented by the narrator. Their texts sometimes agreed with those of Qumran against MT. No doubt this extended to the inaccurate representation of expressive features.

ferred to by singular pronouns. These may represent the leader of the group (where a leader has been named and is thematic in the context), or they may have distributive value, representing each of the individual members of the group. A singular used in this way often does not indicate that only the leader is represented, or that every single member of the group is equally concerned. The singular used in this situation may function as a form of specification, indicating immediacy. The binary contrast in number is thus used with three values, each more immediate than the last: collective (or non-specific) singular, plural, and distributive (specific) singular (see §19.5.2).

28.4.5 An individual speaker typically uses the first person singular, but may use the plural, representing himself as a member of a group, as is the case in English. Where a group is said to speak, the plural is typically used. However, only individuals speak, groups do not, so it is not surprising that singular pronouns should also be used to represent a group as speaker. Where an individual speaks, the use of the first person plural is marked. For a status-marked speaker, this represents condescension, used to show politeness or comradely solidarity. Use by a non-status speaker indicates self-effacement, showing humility. Where a group is represented as speaking, the use of the singular is marked, showing self-assertion, and so immediacy.

28.4.6 An individual is typically addressed with singular pronouns. The plural is typically used where a group is addressed, even if it is represented by a singular noun. However, a group is not a sentient entity; speech is actually addressed to the individuals who form it. Consequently, singular pronouns may be used in this situation. Such use of the singular is marked. A singular pronoun used in this way can be said to be addressed either to an individual representing the group, or, distributively, to each individual member of the group. Where no individual representing the group is mentioned, and where the distributive nature of the reference is not explicitly indicated, such specification marks immediacy, as in the similar situation in the third person. An individual is occasionally addressed with plural pronouns. This marked form of address, distancing the speaker from the addressee, is a form of politeness where the addressee is a superior, and probably where he is a high-ranking subordinate, who can expect to be recognized as an individual. Such distanced address is more commonly directed to low-ranking subordinates, treating them as nonentities.

28.4.7 This view provides a generally satisfactory explanation of the use of number in narrative in early biblical Hebrew. It does not seem unreasonable to suggest, for instance, that the use of singular second person pronouns in Deut 4:19 indicates that the worship of astral bodies was a serious concern for the writer, while the use of the plural in Deut 4:16, in a clause to which that in 4:19 is parallel, shows that the making of images was a less immediate problem. There are certainly features for which an explanation based on this view does not seem satisfactory. For instance, the use of the second person singular in "You did not approach the land of the b. Ammon" (רק אל ארץ בני עמון לא קרבת, Deut 2:37) should highlight the statement, but there seems no reason for this. It is reasonable to suggest for the use of number, as for the text as a whole, that some modification of the narrator's original work has occurred. However, there is no strong reason to believe that the change has been great in the usage in narrative, even in the forms of the second person pronoun. Certainly any study restricted to the use of second person forms approaches only one facet of a larger question.

28.5 Immediacy and Distance

28.5.1 The marking of immediacy and its opposite has so frequently seemed the best explanation for the phenomena treated here that it has come to appear one of the major factors conditioning the usage of the corpus. The separate treatment of the various features discussed has somewhat obscured the extent to which the different features can be seen to be used in similar situations with the same function. A significant clause may be marked as "immediate", and material used to introduce or support it as "non-immediate" by the use of nominal designations (see §4.12, §7.1.2n on 1S 17:56, 28:13, §§12.2.2, 15.5.2) or by the variation in concord in number (see §§ 16.2, 16.3.3, 17.4, 18.2.5), or in concord in person (see §§23.7, 23.8, 23.9.1, 24.2.5, 26.3.4-5, 26.4.1). Choice between nominal designations, between nominal and pronominal, or between contrasting pronominal designations may similarly be used to mark a clause as immediate in terms of the narrative in other situations (see §§4.12.1, 4.13.2, 7.1.2, 15.5.2, 16.3.4-5, 17.3.2, 17.4, 18.3, 19.3, 23.7, 23.8). Relative position in the clause may be used in the same way (see §25.8). Typically, the use of a more specific designation shows that the clause is immediate.

28.5.2 Personal interest and emotion are features of immediacy according to the definition given in §3.4, so it is not surprising to find that these features, too, can be expressed by choice either between nominals or between pronominal designations. The choice of a relationship term rather than a title or a deferential nominal shows that a speaker is evoking his personal relationship with the addressee to add to the impact of his speech (see §§13.4.1, 22.5, 25.3). A speaker may use a non-specific term to present a distanced reference, whether to indicate disdain (using a patronym, §25.5) or to avoid showing emotion (as "lad" in 2S 12:16, see §14.3.3, or deferential terms in 1S 25:41, see §23.2.2). Choice of third person reference for speaker or addressee similarly shows distance, deference, suppression of emotion. Choice of first or second person claims a personal relationship, abandons deference, shows emotion (see §§20.5.1-2, 21.5, 22.5, 23.7, 23.8). Deference and emotion can be displayed together by using first or second person but plural number (§§18.2.2-3, 19.2.6), or by interspersing deferential nominals and third person reference with first or second person pronouns (as noted in §§ 20.5.3, 27.3.2, and *passim* in §§21, 22). The same can be achieved by using a compound nominal reflecting both deference and personal involvement, such as "my lord the king" (see §§6.8.2-4, 13.4). The features described in this study are not discrete features of grammar or nomenclature. They participate in an extensive system of expressive usage by which a speaker or narrator can indicate his attitude to the words presented. Choice is usually binary, so the attitudes presented are usually conveniently classified in binary terms, such as immediacy or distance, even though a more extensive set of terms could be used to reflect the range and versatility of the usage (see §3.4.2-3).

28.5.3 Although third person pronouns are non-specific, first and second person pronouns are highly specific in their reference to speaker and addressee (see §4.1.2, and Waltke and O'Connor, 1990, §13.1, where the term "definite" is used). The interrelation of the pairs specific: non-specific (or individuated, referential, or definite and their opposites), personal involvement: deference, and immediate: distanced is demonstrated for first and second person pronouns by the use of a singular pronoun, a plural pronoun, and third person (or nominal) reference, as increasingly distanced methods of representing speaker or addressee. Even greater distancing and deference can be shown by the use of metonymic or other indirect reference to a superior addressee; the most deferential clauses are those in which the subject represents neither speaker nor addressee (see §§21.4, 23.4.4-5). This correlates with the use of compound designations, the name, less specific nominal designations, and third person pronouns in a similar hierarchy marking descending order of immediacy in narrative. The marking of immediacy and distance in these ways can be seen to correlate with the relationship of specificity (or individuation, or definiteness) of the object to transitivity, and with the relationship of that of the subject to foregrounding or immediacy noted in Revell, 1993b, §§2-3. The importance of subjective function for the communication presented by the clause is further indicated by the fact that a clause in biblical Hebrew is typically presented from the point of view of the agent (see §5.4.1-2). This convention controls the choice of designation for other characters mentioned in the clause in narration (see e.g. §§6.2, 6.3) as it does in speech.[12]

28.5.4 Speech to or by God does not closely resemble that to or by status-marked humans in the features studied. Deferential features are more freely used in speech to status-marked humans than in speech to God. The use of the shorter form of the first person pronoun by God is more restricted than is the use by status marked humans (see §26.4.1). On one level, this could be seen as the result of the fact that humans react to flattery, and that God does not need to assert his status as a human speaker does, but no doubt this is not the only significance. The metaphoric equation of God and king is made in the corpus (e.g. Ju 8:23, 1S 12:12), but it is not presented in the designations used for God in the corpus, as it is, for

---

[12] For this reason, where no agent is named, the default designation is used, and so the name, despite the expectation that the title should be used to mark distance (see §§6.3.1, 7.2.2, 8.1).

instance, in those used in the Jewish liturgy. The title "lord" or "master" (אדון) is used for humans other than kings even in the corpus. The epigraphic evidence suggests that the frequency with which it does refer to a king in the corpus reflects the frequency with which kings appear there, not the fact that the society reflected rarely used "lord" to refer to others. Probably the use of this word in address to God (and subsequently as a general designation, see §15.8.2) originated in the language commonly used in presenting a plea to a father (or other male superior, see §2.3.7), not in forms of address specifically reserved for a king (as suggested, e.g. in Rose, 1992:1008). The patterns of usage in speech to or by God would seem to support this view (see §24.7, 26.4.3).

28.6 Other Implications

28.6.1 If the use of designations in the corpus is self-consistent, as this study suggests, it seems possible that this should be true of the "early biblical" form of Hebrew generally. From the viewpoint of an English speaker, particularly one versed in classical languages, biblical Hebrew appears to be characterized by a high degree both of polysemy and of synonymy or redundancy, and the text representing it to show generous measure of error. This appearance of redundancy or error often reflects the fact that a speaker or narrator could use various forms, choosing between them to reflect his attitude and intentions in a manner foreign to the usage of the languages most familiar to Europaean scholars. This study has been narrowly concerned with the designation of individuals, but choice between variant possibilities has been shown to be used to add to the impact of speech or narration in a wide variety of situations, and particularly to indicate the relative importance of the words or structures used. The major implication of this study would seem to be that such expressive choice must be considered as one of the possible conditioning factors where any form of linguistic variation is considered.

28.6.2 This claim can be tested by further investigation of variation in word order, a phenomenon of limited interest to this study (see §28.3), but common among the constituents of clauses. The material presented in Muraoka, 1991, is used for the investigation. That article is concerned to determine the "normal sequence" of the constituents of a verbless clause where one is nominal (N: a pronoun, noun, or noun phrase), and one adverbial (pN: usually a prepositional phrase, occasionally an adverb). Muraoka's conclusion is basically that the normal sequence is N – pN unless N is a pronoun. However, in narrative, and in speech quoted in it, clauses occur in a context, and this conditions the order of their constituents. The consideration of such conditioning is not central to Muraoka's purpose, the understanding of structure, so his attitude to it is somewhat casual.[13] For those who wish to understand the usage, systematic attention to the content of a clause and to the context of its use can add to Muraoka's basic conclusion without appreciable sacrifice of objectivity.[14]

28.6.3 The subject usually precedes the predicate in the clauses considered here, as in verbless clauses generally. It is reasonable to suggest that this reflects the fact that the word which represents the grammatical subject commonly also represents the topic or theme of the narrator or speaker, and that word order in biblical Hebrew, in verbless clauses at least, is governed by the theme first principle.[15] Thus, in the most common form of the clauses considered here, that in which the predicate is composed of a preposition followed

---

[13] "Focus" is mentioned as a conditioning factor in Muraoka, 1991:46 §4a, as are "contrast, identification, emphasis and the like" (p. 147 §4c). Oddly, anaphoric reference is mentioned only in §4c in connection with the first verbless clause in Ju 16:27, which, again oddly, is not included with the following clause among the circumstantial clauses in §5. It is also surprising that, in his conclusion, he appears to suggest that some special intonation pattern (not represented in the written text), was sometimes used to mark one constituent as prominent (Muraoka, 1991:151, cf. §4d, p. 148).

[14] The following discussion is based only on the early biblical Hebrew materials presented in Muraoka, 1991, those from Genesis and Judges. There are 63 examples. The nominal constituent stands first in nearly two thirds, more commonly in narration (18 of 27 clauses, 67%) than in speech (21 of 36 clauses, 58%).

[15] For a discussion of "theme" and how it is determined, see Tomlin, 1988:37-72. The relation between theme and grammatical subject is discussed on p. 71-2. Givón, 1983, uses "topic" much as Tomlin uses "theme". For the possibility that subject-initial order (and so presumably the theme first principle), is also basic to verbal clauses, see Jongeling, 1991. An extensive theoretical argument in support of this view has been successfully presented as a PhD thesis at Toronto by Vince de Caen, and is to be published by Peter Lang.

by a pronoun, where the order N – pN is used, it is typically reasonable to accept an initial nominal constituent as representing the
topic or theme. This initial nominal constituent:

a. — repeats a preposed element in "The hundred units of silver...
Look here, the silver (is) with me" (הנה הכסף אתי ...אלף ומאה הכסף),
Ju 17:2);

b. — is introduced by the presentative הנה (see Muraoka, 1991:149,
§6b) as in "Look here, Rebecca (is) before you; take (her) and go"
(הנה רבקה לפניך קח ולך), Gen 24:51, other examples occur in Gen
8:11, 20:15, also Ju 17:2, see a.);

c. — or by יש, with similar value, Ju 6:13;[16]

d. — is introduced by כי or באשר, marking it as the crucial factor
in an explanation, as in "because iron chariots (were) to them"
(כי רכב ברזל להם), Ju 1:19, and similarly 4:3, other examples occur
in Gen 25:28, 39:23, Ju 8:24);

e. — or by כי marking it as the phenomenon observed, Gen 39:3;

f. — or it is an item in a list, Gen 24:22;

g. — or is the first constituent of the first clause of a speech, as in
"Peace (is) to you" (שלום לך, Ju 19:20). Other examples occur in
Gen 20:15, 24:51 (both introduced by הנה), Gen 21:22, 25:23, 43:28,
Ju 3:19, 20, 6:12, 16:9, 12, 14, 20.

28.6.4 Where the order pN – N occurs, and pN is a preposition followed by a pronoun, the pronoun usually represents the theme of
the narrator or speaker in the context, while the nominal constituent does not. In this situation the theme first principle accounts
for the initial position of the adverbial predicate. In "to you (is) its
desire" (ואליך תשוקתו, Gen 4:7), the second person pronoun is coreferent with the subject of two preceding and one following clause in
this verse. Similarly, in "With him (was) a pair of donkeys" (ועמו
צמד החמורים, Ju 19:10), the third person pronoun represents "the
man", subject of the first four clauses in the verse. Other examples
occur in Gen 16:1, 33:1, Ju 3:16, 16:27, 19:18, 20:27.[17] In other ex-

---

[16]   The particle draws attention to the factual nature of a statement. It is here used
to give ironic impact to the protasis of an unmarked conditional clause.

[17]   The pronoun usually represents the subject of the preceding main clause. In Ju
3:16, it represents Ehud's sword, the object of the preceding clause, the form and
positioning of which is the concern of this verse. In Ju 19:18, the adverbial consti-

amples of the pN – N order, the nominal constituent represents the theme. In "Ours (is) the water" (לנו המים, Gen 26:20), the water is the topic about which the speaker is disputing. In "On me is your curse" (עלי קללתך, Gen 27:13, cf. 1S 25:24), the speech is a response to the previous speaker's statement that a proposed action would result in a curse. In both cases, the pronoun in the initial pN constituent expresses "self-assertion" of the sort highlighted by the use of the marked form of the first person pronoun (see §26.3.1-2). The constituent is placed first, to draw attention to this. In "because with you (am) I (now)" (כי אתך אנכי, Gen 26:24), the first person pronoun is thematic in the speech. The initial position of the adverbial constituent highlights the second person pronoun (the secondary theme of the speech) in "with you" in contrast to "Abraham" in the preceding clause "I (am or was) the God of Abraham". The highlighting of non-thematic material in this way marks it as "focus".[18]

28.6.5 The use of N – pN order, where pN – N might be expected, is explained in the same way. In "He (was) before them" (והוא לפניהם, Ju 3:27), "them" represents the subject of the preceding clause. "He" represents Ehud, subject of four preceding clauses, and of the clause following the one quoted, and is thus placed first, as representing the theme of the passage as whole. In "His concubine (was) with him" (ופילגשו עמו, Ju 19:10), the pronoun in both constituents represents the levite, subject of the first four verses in the clause, and so thematic. The order, however (contrasting with that of the previous clause), highlights the constituent which includes non-thematic material, marks it as focus, and so draws attention to the concubine, hinting at her importance in the ensuing narrative

---

tuent gives a significant part of the answer to a question. In Ju 20:27, the clause in question and the following one form a digression, the concern of which is the facilities for consulting God available at Bethel. The initial adverbial, which begins the digression, represents Bethel, which is mentioned in Ju 20:26.

[18] In this sense, "focus" denotes an item other than theme or topic which is highlighted. (The term "topicalized", sometimes used of such items, obscures the fact that the topic of the larger structure may also be represented in the clause). Such use of the term "focus" seems consistent with the general definition supplied in Crystal, 1991, and with the distinction between "focus" and "topic" made in Bandstra, 1982:77-78, but not with the definition offered in van der Merwe, 1990:45.

(see §3.4.3). In "Yahweh (was) with them" (ויהוה עמם, Ju 1:22) "them" represents the subject of the preceding clause, and of several succeeding clauses, and so the theme of the verse. The initial position of the nominal constituent marks it as focus; it draws attention to the intervention by God, which is commonly highlighted (see Muraoka, 1991:150, cf. §4.4.2). The situation is similar in "Manoah her husband was not with her" (Ju 13:9). In "400 men (are) with him" (וארבע מאות איש עמו, Gen 32:7), the pronoun "him" similarly represents Esau, the theme of the speech. The initial position of the nominal constituent marks it as focus, drawing attention to the number of those accompanying Esau, which suggests that his approach as hostile. The clause thus gives a warning, which is acted on in what follows.[19]

28.6.6 The order of the constituents in clauses in which the adverbial constituent contains a noun with a suffixed pronoun is similarly conditioned. In "To your husband (will be) your desire" (ואל אישך תשוקתך, Gen 3:16), the second person pronouns represent Eve, the theme of the speech. The initial position of the pN constituent marks it as focus, highlighting the shift of topic from Eve to her husband, subject of the following clause. In "Her pitcher (was) on her shoulder" (וכדה על שכמה, Gen 24:15, 45), "her" represents Rebecca, theme of the passage; the N – pN order correlates with the relevance of the pitcher for the ensuing narrative (cf. §28.6.5 on Ju 19:10). In "The peg (was) in his temple" (והיתד ברקתו, Ju 4:22), the peg used to kill Sisera is similarly placed in focus.

28.6.7 Similar considerations apply where the clause contains no pronouns. The more common order is N – pN; examples occur in Gen 1:2, 12:6, 41:29, Ju 4:17, 7:16, 14:8, 21:17. In each case, the nominal constituent may reasonably be said to represent the theme. The same is true of the adverbial constituent in "to Rebecca (was) a brother" (ולרבקה אח, Gen 24:29). Rebecca is subject of the two

---

[19]　In Gen 33:1, the same two constituents, ordered pN – N, are used in a clause describing Esau as seen by Jacob. Here the danger is already known, and Jacob's immediate reaction to it has been described. There is no need for such highlighting, and the order reflects the fact that Esau is the focus of Jacob's attention (see §28.6.4).

preceding clauses. In "On the roof about 3,000…" (ועל הגג כשלשת
אלפים..., Ju 16:27), the theme of location is also represented by the
initial constituent of the two preceding clauses "the house" and
"there". In "On all the ground (will be) dryness" (ועל כל הארץ חרב,
Ju 6:37), the position of the adverbial places it in focus, highlighting
its contrast with "on the fleece alone" in the preceding clause. The
same contrast is highlighted in a typical chiastic pair of verbal
clauses in Ju 6:39. In "From Yahweh it (was)" (מיהוה היא, Ju 14:4),
the initial position of the adverbial constituent places the significant
cause of a surprising event in focus (and highlights intervention by
God, as is usual). In "From Haran (are) we" (מחרן אנחנו, Gen 29:4),
the answer to a question is similarly placed in focus (cf. also §
28.6.3g).[20] Where a clause of this sort is introduced by an interrogative particle, the initial constituent typically represents the topic of
the question, and is placed first for that reason. In "Question: in
place of God (am) I" (התחת אלהים אנכי, Gen 30:2, similarly 50:19,
cf. 2K 5:7) the speaker asks "Am I in place of God or not?" not
"Am I in place of God or is someone else?". In "Question: peace (is)
to him" (השלום לו, Gen 29:6), he asks "Is he at peace or not", not
"Is he or someone else at peace.[21]

28.6.8 In verbless clauses with an adverbial predicate, then, word order is governed by the theme first principle. This usually gives rise
to the order N – pN. In descriptive clauses of the type known as
"circumstantial", it typically gives rise to the order pN – N where
the noun described is thematic in the context, and the nominal in
the pN constituent is coreferent with that noun. Where the theme
first order is reversed, the marked usage shows that the initial constituent is in focus. Such usage accounts for the small proportion of
examples of pN – N order in which the subject represents the
theme, and of N – pN order in which the nominal element in the

---

[20] See Revell, 1989b:6. In the case in 2S 9:4, mentioned there as an exception, the
adverbial in the question is an interrogative particle, and precedes the subject for
that reason. The subjective pronoun in the answer represents the theme of the conversation, and stands first for that reason.

[21] See the arguments on word order in such questions in Revell, 1989b:5. It could
be argued that an adverbial constituent which is an interrogative particle (Gen
29:4, 32:18, 18, Ju 6:13, 8:18) represents either topic or focus, and is placed in initial position for that reason.

predicate represents the theme. Focus of this sort is used to draw attention to a shift of topic or a contrast, or to mark urgency or emotion: the various factors included under the term "immediacy" as defined in §1.7.2. The same factors are aspects of "familiarity", described in Siewierska, 1988:61 as relevant to the conditioning of word order. These factors clearly have a role of considerable importance in the determination of word order in biblical Hebrew, and any discussion of it needs to be informed by a good understanding of them. Such understanding requires serious study of the whole gamut of the usage reflecting such factors in the language, and the development of suitably objective methods for describing and interpreting it.

28.7 Conclusion

This study, then, shows the value of close attention to, and careful assessment of, the factors reflecting the narrator's intention, among which the various sorts of designations of individuals are prominent. This is clearly of paramount importance to those studying the language. It is equally important for anyone attempting to understand the text. Scholars interested in the literary aspects of the text are used to using linguistic details as a guide to the narrator's intentions. It is to be hoped that this study can confirm and extend their appreciation of the value of such details. The study should, however, be of equal interest to those interested in historical analysis. Whatever the value of what has been said about the features discussed here, most cannot be shown to be abnormal in biblical Hebrew. Some of these are routinely cited as errors, or as evidence of the use of different sources. Such claims are not necessarily wrong, but, if the feature in question is not abnormal, it does not support such claims; other evidence is needed. It is quite often said that it is necessary to understand the text as it is before attempting to reconstruct some earlier form, but this idea is rarely keenly pursued. This study has attempted to do this for one facet of usage, and to demonstrate the value of such pursuit.

INDICES

Select Bibliography

ABDEL HALEEM, M.A.S. 1992 Grammatical Shift for Rhetorical Purposes: *iltifāt* and related features in the Qur'ān. *Bulletin of the School of Oriental and African Studies* 55:407-432.

ADLER, Max K. 1978 *Naming and Addressing: a sociolinguistic study.* Hamburg: Helmut Buske Verlag.

ALBRECHT, Karl 1895, 1896 Das Geschlecht der hebräischen Hauptwörter. *Zeitschrift für die alttestamentliche Wissenschaft* 15:313-25; 16:41-121.

AHARONI, Yohanan 1981 *Arad Inscriptions.* (In cooperation with Joseph Naveh, with contributions by A.F. Rainey, M. Aharoni, B. Lifshitz, M. Sharon and Z. Sofer.) Jerusalem: Israel Exploration Society.

ANBAR, M. 1979 Un euphémisme "biblique" dans une lettre de Mari. *Orientalia* 48:109-111.

ANDERSEN, Francis I. 1969 Israelite Kinship Terminology and Social Structure. *The Bible Translator* 20:29-39.

AVIGAD, Nahman 1986 *Hebrew Bullae from the Time of Jeremiah.* Jerusalem: Israel Exploration Society.

AVIGAD, Nahman 1987 The Contribution of Hebrew Seals to an Understanding of Israelite Religion and Society. In *Ancient Israelite Religion: Essays in Honor of Frank Moore Cross*, ed. Patrick D. Miller Jr., Paul D. Hanson, and S. Dean McBride. Pp.195-208. Philadelphia: Fortress Press.

BANDSTRA, Barry L. 1982 *The Syntax of Particle KY in Biblical Hebrew and Ugaritic.* PhD dissertation, Yale University. (Ann Arbor: University Microfilms International.)

BANDSTRA, Barry L. 1992 Word Order and Emphasis in Biblical Hebrew: Syntactic observations on Genesis 22 from a discourse perspective. In *Linguistics and Biblical Hebrew*, ed. Walter R. Bodine. Pp. 109-123. Winona Lake: Eisenbrauns.

BAR-EFRAT, Shimon 1989 *Narrative Art in the Bible.* (Journal for the Study of the Old Testament Supplement Series 70). Sheffield, Almond. Translated from the second Hebrew edition. Tel-Aviv: Sifrat Po'alim, 1984.

BARILKO, Hayyim 1982 פרשת נערים (The Matter of *nearim*). *Beth Mikra* 89-90: 101-108.

BARTHÉLEMY, Dominique 1980 La qualité du Texte Massorétique de Samuel. In *The Hebrew and Greek Texts of Samuel*, ed. E. Tov. Pp. 1-44. Jerusalem: Academon.

BARTHÉLEMY, Dominique 1982 *Critique textuelle de l'ancien testament.* (Orbis Biblicus et Orientalis 50/1). Fribourg: Éditions Universitaires.

BEN-ASHER, Mordechai 1978 The Gender of Nouns in Biblical Hebrew. *Semitics* 6:1-14.

BERLIN, Adele 1983 *Poetics and Interpretation of Biblical Narrative*. Sheffield: Almond.

BOLING, Robert G. 1975 *Judges: Introduction, Translation and Commentary*. (The Anchor Bible vol. 6A) New York: Doubleday.

BRAUN, Friederike 1988 *Terms of Address: problems of patterns and usage in various languages and cultures*. Contributions to the Sociology of Language 50. Berlin: Mouton de Gruyter.

BRETTLER, Mark 1989 *God is King: understanding an Israelite metaphor*. (Journal for the Study of the Old Testament Supplement Series 70). Sheffield: JSOT Press.

BRINKMAN, J.A. 1964 Merodach Baladan II. In *Studies Presented to A. Leo Oppenheim, June 7, 1964*. Pp. 6-53. Chicago: Oriental Institute of the University of Chicago.

BROCKINGTON, L.H. 1973 *The Hebrew Text of the Old Testament: The Readings Adopted by the Translators of the New English Bible*. Oxford University Press/ Cambridge University Press.

BROWN, Penelope, and Stephen C. LEVINSON 1987 *Politeness: Some universals in language usage*. (Studies in Interactional Sociolinguistics 4). Improved re-issue of the 1978 edition. Cambridge: Cambridge University Press.

BROWN, Roger and Albert GILMAN 1960 The Pronouns of Power and Solidarity. In *Style in Language*, ed. Thomas A. Sebeok. Pp. 253-76. Cambridge, Mass.: M.I.T. (Often reprinted).

CARLSON, R.A. 1993 David and the Ark in 2 Samuel 6. In *History and Traditions of Early Israel: Studies Presented to Eduard Nielsen*, edd. André Lemaire and Benedikt Otzen. (Supplements to Vetus Testamentum 50.) Pp. 17-23. Leiden: E. J. Brill.

CARTLEDGE, Tony W. 1992 *Vows in the Hebrew Bible and the Ancient Near East*. (Journal for the Study of the Old Testament Supplement Series 147.) Sheffield: JSOT Press.

CAZELLES, Henri 1967 Passages in the Singular within Discourse in the Plural of Dt 1-4. *Catholic Biblical Quarterly* 29:207-219.

CLANCY, Patricia M. 1980 Referential Choice in English and Japanese Narrative Discourse. In *The Pear Stories: Cognitive, Cultural, and Linguistic Aspects of Narrative Production*, ed. Wallace L. Chafe. (Advances in Discourse Processes III.) Pp. 127-202. Norwood: Ablex.

CLINES, D.J.A. 1972 X, X *ben* Y, *ben* Y: personal names. *Vetus Testamentum* 22:266-287.

COGAN, Mordechai and Hayim TADMOR 1988 *II Kings: A New Translation with Introduction and Commentary*. (Anchor Bible vol. 11). New York: Doubleday.

COHEN, Chaim (Harold Robert) 1979 Studies in Extra-biblical Hebrew Inscriptions I. The Semantic Range and Usage of the Terms אמה and שפחה. שנתון *(Shnaton, an Annual for Biblical and Ancient Near Eastern Studies)* 5-6:XXV-LIII.

COHN, Robert L. 1985 Literary Technique in the Jeroboam Narrative. *Zeitschrift für die alttestamentliche Wissenschaft* 97:23-35.

COHN, Robert L. 1985b Convention and Creativity in the Book of Kings: The Case of the Dying Monarch. *Catholic Biblical Quarterly* 47:603-616.

CROSS, Frank Moore 1973 *Canaanite Myth and Hebrew Epic: Essays in the History of the Religion of Israel.* Cambridge Mass.: Harvard University Press.

CRYSTAL, David 1991 *A Dictionary of Linguistics and Phonetics,* 3rd ed. Oxford: Blackwell.

DAVIES, G.I. 1991 *Ancient Hebrew Inscriptions: Corpus and Concordance.* Cambridge: Cambridge University Press.

DONNER, H. 1959 Art und Herkunft des Amtes der Königinmutter im Alten Testament. In *Festschrift Johannes Friedrich zum 65. Geburtstag gewidmet,* edd. R. von Kienle, A. Moortgat, H. Otten, E. von Schuler und W. Zaumseil. Pp. 105-145. Heidelberg: Carl Winter.

DRIVER, S.R. 1913 *Notes on the Hebrew Text and the Topography of the Books of Samuel.* 2nd ed. Oxford: Clarendon.

EID, Mushira 1983 On the Communicative Function of Subject Pronouns in Arabic. *Journal of Linguistics* 19:287-303.

FITZMYER, Joseph A. 1979 Aramaic Epistolography. In *A Wandering Aramean: Collected Aramaic Essays.* (SBL Monograph Series 25). Pp. 183-204. Missoula: Scholars Press.

FOKKELMAN, Jan P. 1981 *Narrative Art and Poetry in the Books of Samuel. I. King David.* Assen: van Gorcum.

FOKKELMAN, Jan P. 1986 *Narrative Art and Poetry in the Books of Samuel. II. The Crossing Fates.* Assen: van Gorcum.

FOKKELMAN, Jan P. 1990 *Narrative Art and Poetry in the Books of Samuel. III. Throne and City.* Assen: van Gorcum.

FOKKELMAN, Jan P. 1992 Structural Remarks on Judges 9 and 19. In *Sha'arei Talmon: Studies in the Bible, Qumran, and the Ancient Near East presented to Shemaryahu Talmon,* edd. M. Fishbane and E. Tov. Pp. 33-45. Winona Lake: Eisenbrauns.

FOKKELMAN, Jan P. 1993 *Narrative Art and Poetry in the Books of Samuel. IV. Vow and Desire.* Assen: van Gorcum.

FORNEL, Michel de 1987 Reference to Persons in Conversation. In *The Pragmatic Perspective: selected papers from the 1985 International Pragmatics Conference,* edd. Jef Verschueren and Marcella Bertuccelli-Papi. Pp. 131-40. Amsterdam: John Benjamins.

FOWLER, Jeaneane D. 1988 *Theophoric Personal Names in Ancient Hebrew: A Comparative Study.* (Journal for the Study of the Old Testament Supplement Series 49.) Sheffield: JSOT Press.

FOX, A. 1983 Topic Continuity in Biblical Narrative. In *Topic Continuity in Discourse: a Quantitative Cross-Language Study,* ed. T. Givón. Pp. 215-54. Amsterdam: John Benjamins.

GARSIEL, Moshe 1985 *The First Book of Samuel: A Literary Study of Comparative Structures, Analogies, and Parallels.* Ramat-Gan: Revivim Publishing House. Translated from the Hebrew edition of 1983.

GIVÓN, Talmy 1976 Topic, Pronoun, and Grammatical Agreement. In *Subject and Topic,* ed. Charles N. Li. Pp. 149-88. New York: Academic Press.

GIVÓN, Talmy 1983 Topic Continuity in Discourse: an introduction. In *Topic Continuity in Discourse: a Quantitative Cross-Language Study*, ed. T. Givón. Pp. 1-41. Amsterdam: John Benjamins.

GKC *Gesenius' Hebrew Grammar as edited and enlarged by the late E. Kautzsch*. 2nd English Edition revised... by A.E. Cowley. Oxford, Clarendon Press, 1910.

GOLDENBERG, Gideon 1991 On Direct Speech in the Hebrew Bible. In *Studies in Hebrew and Aramaic Syntax presented to Professor J. Hoftijzer on the occasion of his Sixty-fifth Birthday*, edd. K. Jongeling, H.L. Murre-van den Berg and L. van Rompay. Pp. 79-96. Leiden: E.J. Brill.

GREENBERG, Joseph H. 1980 Universals of Kinship Terminology: Their Nature and the Problem of their Explanation. In *On linguistic anthropology. Essays in honor of Harry Hoijer 1979*, ed. Jaques Maquet. Other realities, vol. 2. Pp. 9-32. Malibu: Undena Publications.

GREENSTEIN, Edward L. 1989 The Syntax of Saying 'yes' in Biblical Hebrew. *Journal of the Ancient Near Eastern Society*, 19:51-59.

GROSS, Walter 1981 Syntaktische Erscheinungen am Anfang althebräischer Erzählungen: Hintergrund und Vordergrund. *Congress Volume, Vienna 1980*, ed. J.A. Emerton. (Supplements to Vetus Testamentum 32.) Pp. 131-45. Leiden: E.J. Brill.

HARRAN, Menahem 1970 Biblical Studies: The Literary Applications of the Numerical Sequence X / X+1 and their Connections with Patterns of Parallelism. *Tarbiz* 39:109-136.

(סוגיות מקרא: דגם המספר המודרג לצורותיו אל הדפוסים הפורמאליים של התקבלותם. תרניץ תש״ל.)

HARRAN, Menahem 1972 The Graded Numerical Sequence and the Phenomenon of "Automatism" in Biblical Poetry. *Congress Volume, Uppsala 1971*. (Supplements to Vetus Testamentum 22.) Pp. 238-267. Leiden: E.J. Brill.

HENDERSON, T.S.T. 1985 Who are *we* anyway? A study of personal pronoun systems. *Linguistische Berichte* 98:300-309.

HOPPER, Paul J. 1990 The Emergence of the Category 'Proper Name' in Discourse. In *Redefining Linguistics*, edd. Hayley G. Davis and Talbot J. Taylor. Pp. 149-162. London: Routledge.

HOPPER, Paul J. and Sandra A. THOMPSON 1980 Transitivity in Grammar and Discourse. *Language* 56:251-99.

HURVITZ, Avi 1971 "Diachronic Chiasm" in Biblical Hebrew. In *Bible and Jewish History: Studies in Bible and Jewish History Dedicated to the Memory of Jacob Liver*, ed. Benjamin Uffenheimer. Pp. 248-255. Tel-Aviv: Tel Aviv University.

(כיאזמוס דיאכרוני בעברית המקראית. המקרא ותולדות ישראל: מחקרים במקרא ובספרות ימי בית שני לזכרו של יעקב ליוור. תל-אביב: אוניברסיטת תל־אביב. תשל״ב.)

JACKSON, Kent P. 1989 The Language of the Mesha Inscription. In *Studies in the Mesha Inscription and Moab*, ed. J. Andrew Dearman. (Archaeology and Biblical Studies 2.) Pp. 96-130. Atlanta: Scholars Press.

JACKSON, Kent P. and J. Andrew DEARMAN 1989 The Text of the Mesha Inscription. In *Studies in the Mesha Inscription and Moab*, ed. J. Andrew Dearman. (Archaeology and Biblical Studies 2.) Pp. 93-95. Atlanta: Scholars Press.

JONGELING, K. 1991 On the VSO Character of Classical Hebrew. In *Studies in Hebrew and Aramaic Syntax presented to Professor J. Hoftijzer on the occasion of his Sixty-fifth Birthday*, edd. K. Jongeling, H.L. Murre-van den Berg and L. van Rompay. Pp. 103-111. Leiden: E.J. Brill.

JOÜON, Paul 1953 *Ruth: commentaire philologique et exégétique*. (Reprinted 1986, original edition 1924.) Rome: Institut biblique pontifical.

JOÜON, Paul 1991 *A Grammar of Biblical Hebrew Translated and Revised by T. Muraoka*. Rome: Pontifical Biblical Institute.

KÁA, Mo 1976 The Logic of non-European Linguistic Categories. In *Universalism versus Relativism in Language and Thought*, ed. Rik Pinxten. (Contributions to the Sociology of Language 11.) Pp. 85-96. The Hague: Mouton.

KAUFMAN, Stephen A. 1991 An Emphatic Plea for Please. *Maarav* 7:195-8.

KHAN, Geoffrey A. 1984 Object Markers and Agreement Pronouns in Semitic Languages. *Bulletin of the School of Oriental and African Studies, University of London* 47:468-500.

KHAN, Geoffrey A. 1988 *Studies in Semitic Syntax*. (London Oriental Series vol. 38.) Oxford: Oxford University Press.

KHAN, Geoffrey A. 1991 Morphological Markers of Individuation in Semitic Languages and their Function in the Semitic Tense System. In *Proceedings of the Fifth International Hamito-Semitic Congress, 1987*, ed. Hans G. Mukarovsky. Vol 2 (Beiträge zur Afrikanistik Bd. 41) pp. 235-244. Wien: Afro-Pub.

KNAUF, Ernst Axel 1990 War "Biblisch-Hebräisch" eine Sprache? *Zeitschrift für Althebräistik* 3:11-23.

KUTSCHER, E.Y. 1974 *The Language and Linguistic Background of the Isaiah Scroll (I Q Isaᵃ)*. (Studies on the Texts of the Desert of Judah VI. Revised and enlarged form of the Hebrew edition of 1959.) Leiden: E.J. Brill.

LANDE, Irene 1949 *Formelhafte Wendungen der Umgangssprache im alten Testament*. Leiden: E.J. Brill.

LAYTON, Scott C. 1990 *Archaic Features of Canaanite Personal Names in the Hebrew Bible*. (Harvard Semitic Monographs 47.) Atlanta: Scholars Press.

LEHMANN, Manfred R. 1969 Biblical Oaths. *Zeitschrift für die alttestamentliche Wissenschaft* 81: 74-92.

LEMAIRE, André 1978 Le sceau CIS, 11,74, et sa signification historique. *Semitica* 28:11-14.

LEMAIRE, André 1979 Note sur le titre *BN HMLK* dans l'ancien Israël. *Semitica* 29:59-65.

LEMAIRE, André 1988 Récherches actuelles sur les sceaux nord-ouest sémitiques. *Vetus Testamentum* 38:220-230.

LEVI, Jaakov 1987 *Die Inkongruenz im biblischen Hebräisch*. Wiesbaden: Harrassowitz.

LIEBERSON, Stanley 1984 What's in a name? ... some sociolinguistic possibilities. *International Journal of the Sociology of Language* 45:77-87.

LINDHAGEN, Curt 1950 *The Servant Motif in the Old Testament: a preliminary study to the Ebed-Yahweh problem in Deutero-Isaiah*. Uppsala: Lundequistska Bokhandeln.

LODE, Lars 1984 Postverbal word order in Bibical Hebrew: Structure and function. *Semitics* 9:113-164.

LODE, Lars 1989 Postverbal word order in Bibical Hebrew: Structure and function. Part Two. *Semitics* 10:24-39.

LONG, Burke O. 1984 *I Kings with an Introduction to Historical Literature*. (Forms of Old Testament Literature 9.) Grand Rapids: Eerdmans.

LONGACRE, Robert E. 1989 *Joseph: A Story of Divine Providence*. Winona Lake: Eisenbrauns.

LYONS, John 1977 *Semantics*. 2 vols. Cambridge: Cambridge University Press.

MACDONALD, J. 1975 Some Distinctive Characteristics of Israelite Spoken Hebrew. *Bibliotheca orientalis* 32:162-175.

MACDONALD, J. 1976 The Status and Role of the Na'ar in Israelite Society. *Journal of Near Eastern Studies* 35:147-170.

MCCARTER, P. Kyle Jr. 1980 *I Samuel: A New Translation with Introduction, Notes and Commentary*. Anchor Bible vol. 8. New York: Doubleday.

MCCARTER, P. Kyle Jr. 1984 *II Samuel: A New Translation with Introduction, Notes and Commentary*. Anchor Bible vol. 9. New York: Doubleday.

MELAMED, Ezra Zion 1961 Break-Up of Stereotype Phrases as an Artistic Device in Biblical Poetry. In *Studies in the Bible*, ed. Chaim Rabin. (Scripta Hierosolymitana 8.) PP. 115-53. Jerusalem: Magnes.

MEIER, Samuel A. 1992 *Speaking of Speaking: the Marking of Direct Discourse in the Hebrew Bible*. (Supplements to Vetus Testamentum 46.) Leiden: E.J. Brill.

MILLARD, A.R. 1971 Baladan, the Father of Merodach-Baladan. *Tyndale Bulletin* 22:125-6.

MILLARD, A.R. 1976 Assyrian Royal Names in Biblical Hebrew. *Journal of Semitic Studies* 21:1-14.

MIRSKY, A. 1977 Stylistic Device for Conclusion in Hebrew. *Semitics* 5:9-23.

MITCHELL, T.C. 1969 The Meaning of the noun ḥtn in the Old Testament. *Vetus Testamentum* 19:93-112.

MONTGOMERY, James A. and Henry Synder GEHMAN 1951 *A Critical and Exegetical Commentary on the Book of Kings*. Edinburgh: T. and T. Clark.

MORAVCSIK, Edith A. 1988 Agreement and Markedness. In *Agreement in Natural Language: Approaches, Theories, Descriptions*, edd. Michael Barlow and Charles A. Ferguson. Pp. 89-106. Centre for Study of Language and Information, Stanford University.

MORESHET, Menahem 1967 The Predicate Preceding a Compound Subject in the Biblical Language. *Leshonenu* 31:251-260.
(הנשוא הקודם לשני נושאים בלשון המקרא. לשוננו ל״א.)

MÜHLHÄUSLER, Peter and Rom HARRÉ 1990 *Pronouns and People: The Linguistic Construction of Social and Personal Identity*. Oxford: Blackwell.

MURAOKA, Takamitsu 1985 *Emphatic Words and Structures in Biblical Hebrew*. Jerusalem: Magnes / Leiden: E.J. Brill.

MURAOKA, Takamitsu 1990 The Nominal Clause in Late Biblical Hebrew and Mishnaic Hebrew. *Language Studies* 4, ed. Moshe Bar-Asher. Pp. 219-52.

(הפסוק השמני בלשון המקרא המאוחרת ובלשון חז״ל. מחקרים בלשון ד׳)

MURAOKA, Takamitsu 1991 The Biblical Hebrew Nominal Clause with a Prepositional Phrase. In *Studies in Hebrew and Aramaic Syntax presented to Professor J. Hoftijzer on the occasion of his Sixty-fifth Birthday*, edd. K. Jongeling, H.L. Murre-van den Berg and L. van Rompay. Pp. 143-151. Leiden: E.J. Brill.

NAVEH, Joseph 1990 Nameless People. *Israel Exploration Journal* 40:108-23.

NELSON, Richard D. 1981 *The Double Redaction of the Deuteronomistic History.* (Journal for the Study of the Old Testament Supplement Series 18.) Sheffield: JSOT Press.

NOTH, Martin 1928 *Die israelitischen Personennamen im Rahmen der gemeinsemitischen Namengebung.* (Beiträge zur Wissenschaft vom alten Testament. Dritte Folge, 10.) Stuttgart: W. Kohlhammer.

PARKINSON, Dilworth B. 1985 *Constructing the Social Context of Communication: Terms of Address in Egyptian Arabic.* Contributions to the Sociology of Language 41. Berlin: Mouton de Gruyter.

PERETZ, Yiṣḥaq 1968 Juxtaposition of Proper Name and Title. In *Fourth World Congress of Jewish Studies. Papers. Vol. 2:129-133.* Jerusalem: World Union of Jewish Studies.

(צמידות של שם פרטי ותואר כבוד. דברי הקונגרס העולמי הרביעי למדעי היהדות. כרך ב׳. ירושלים: האיגוד העולמי למדעי היהדות.)

PISANO, Stephen S.J. 1984 *Additions or Omissions in the Books of Samuel.* (Orbis Biblicus et Orientalis 57.) Freiburg (Schweiz): Universitätsverlag.

POLZIN, R. 1985 The Speaking Person and His Voice in I Samuel. In *Congress Volume: Salamanca, 1983*, ed. J.A. Emerton. (Supplements to Vetus Testamentum 36). Pp. 218-229. Leiden: E.J. Brill.

PORTEN, Bezalel and Ada YARDENI 1986 *Textbook of Aramaic Documents from Ancient Egypt I: Letters.* Jerusalem: Hebrew University, Dept. of the History of the Jewish People.

PROVAN, Iain W. 1988 *Hezekiah and the Books of Kings.* (Beihefte zur Zeitschrift für die alttestamentliche Wissenschaft 172). Berlin: de Gruyter.

RAINEY, Anson F. 1981 Three Additional Texts. In Aharoni, 1981:122-127.

RATNER, Robert J. 1990 The "Feminine Takes Precedence" Syntagm and Job 19,15. *Zeitschrift für die alttestamentliche Wissenschaft* 102:238-51.

REGT, L.J. de 1993 Participant Reference in some Biblical Hebrew Texts. *Jaarbericht van het Vooraziatisch-Egyptisch Genootschap "Ex Oriente Lux"* 32 (1991-2):150-172.

REVELL, E.J. 1980 Pausal Forms in Biblical Hebrew: their Function, Origin and Significance. *Journal of Semitic Studies* 25:165-179.

REVELL, E.J. 1989 The System of the Verb in Standard Biblical Prose. *Hebrew Union College Annual* 60:1-37

REVELL, E.J. 1989b The Conditioning of Word Order in Verbless Clauses in Biblical Hebrew. *Journal of Semitic Studies* 34:1-24.

REVELL, E.J. 1991 Conditional Sentences in Biblical Hebrew Prose. *Semitic Studies in Honor of Wolf Leslau*, ed. Alan S. Kaye. Vol. II:1278 - 1290. Wiesbaden: Harrassowitz.

REVELL, E.J. 1993 Concord with Compound Subjects and Related Uses of Pronouns. *Vetus Testamentum* 43:69-87.

REVELL, E.J. 1993b Concord with Collectives in Biblical Narrative. Forthcoming in *Maarav* (expected Autumn 1993).

REVELL, E.J. 1994 Gentilics and Geography. Forthcoming in a Festschrift for Shelomo Morag. (Expected Autumn 1994)

REVELL, E.J. 1995 The Two Forms of the First Person Singular Pronoun in Biblical Hebrew: redundancy or expressive contrast? *Journal of Semitic Studies* 40:199-217.

ROSE, Martin 1992 The Names of God in the Old Testament, *Anchor Bible Dictionary* 4:1001-1011. New York: Doubleday.

ROSÉN, H.B. 1966 Quelques phénomènes d'absence et de présence de l'accord dans la structure de la phrase en hébreu. *Comptes rendus du Groupe Linguistique d'Études Chamito-Sémitiques* 10:78-84.

ROSÉN, H.B. 1984 אנכי et אני: Essai de grammaire, interprétation et traduction. In *East and West: Selected Writings in Linguistics by Haiim B. Rosén* (edited for the occasion of his sixtieth birthday by a group of friends and disciples). Part 2:262-81. Munich: Wilhelm Fink.

ROSEN, Lawrence 1989 Responsibility and Compensatory Justice in Arab Culture and Law. In *Semiotics, Self, and Society*, eds. Benjamin Lee and Greg Urban. Pp. 101-20. Berlin: Mouton de Gruyter.

SACKS, Harvey and Emanuel A. SCHLEGOFF 1979 Two Preferences in the Organization of References to Persons in Conversation and their Interaction. In *Everyday Language: Studies in Ethnomethodology*, ed. G. Psathas. Pp. 15-21. New York: Irvington.

SASSON, Jack M. 1979 *Ruth: A New Translation with a Philological Commentary and a Formalist-Folklorist Interpretation.* Baltimore: Johns Hopkins University Press.

SAVRAN, George W. 1988 *Telling and Retelling: Quotation in Biblical Narrative.* Bloomington: Indiana University Press.

SAVILLE-TROIKE, Muriel 1989 *The Ethnography of Communication: An Introduction.* Second Edition. Oxford: Basil Blackwell.

SCHIMMEL, Annemarie 1989 *Islamic Names.* Edinburgh: Edinburgh University Press.

SCHLEY, Donald G. 1990 The *šālīšîm*: Officers or Special Three-man Squads? *Vetus Testamentum* 40:321-326.

SEOW, C.L. 1992 Hosts, Lord of. *Anchor Bible Dictionary* 3:304-307. New York: Doubleday.

SHERLOCK, Charles 1993 *The God who Fights: The War Tradition in Holy Scripture.* (Rutherford Studies in Contemporary Theology 6.) Edinburgh: Rutherford House.

SIEWIERSKA, Anna 1988 *Word Order Rules.* London: Croom Helm.

SLONIM MAYER G. 1939 The Substitution of the Masculine for the Feminine Pronominal Suffixes to Express Reverence. *Jewish Quarterly Review* 29:397-403

SLONIM MAYER G. 1942 The Deliberate Substitution of the Masculine for the Feminine Pronominal Suffixes in the Hebrew Bible. *Jewish Quarterly Review* 32:139-158.

SLONIM MAYER G. 1944 Masculine Predicates with Feminine Subjects in the Hebrew Bible. *Journal of Biblical Literature* 63:297-302.

STAGER, Lawrence E. 1985 The Archaeology of the Family in Ancient Israel. *Bulletin of the American Schools of Oriental Research* 260:1-35.

STÄHLI, Hans-Peter 1978 *Knabe-Jüngling-Knecht: Untersuchungen zum Begriff* נער *im Alten Testament.* Beiträge zur biblischen Exegese und Theologie, Band 7. Frankfurt am Main: Peter Lang.

STERNBERG, Meir 1985 *The Poetics of Biblical Narrative: Ideological Literature and the Drama of Reading.* Bloomington: Indiana University Press, 1985.

TALMON, Shemaryahu 1978 The Presentation of Synchroneity and Simultaneity in Biblical Narrative. In *Studies in Hebrew Narrative Art Throughout the Ages,* ed. Joseph Heinemann and Shmuel Werses. (Scripta Hierosolymitana 27.) Pp. 9-26. Jerusalem: Magnes.

TALSHIR, David 1991 יהונתן המלך או המלך יהונתן (Jonathan the King or King Jonathan). *Leshonenu* 55:277-80.

TALSTRA, Eep 1991 Hebrew Syntax: Clause Type and Clause Hierarchy. In *Studies in Hebrew and Aramaic Syntax presented to Professor J. Hoftijzer on the occasion of his Sixty-fifth Birthday,* edd. K. Jongeling, H.L. Murre-van den Berg and L. van Rompay. Pp. 180-193. Leiden: E.J. Brill.

TALSTRA, Eep 1993 *Solomon's Prayer: Synchrony and Diachrony in the Composition of 1 Kings 8,14-61.* Kampen: Kok Pharos.

THOMPSON, Sandra A. 1983 Grammar and Discourse: The English Detached Participial Clause. In *Discourse Perspectives on Syntax,* ed. Flora Klein-Andreu. Pp. 43-65. New York: Academic Press.

TOMLIN, Russell S. 1986 *Basic Word Order: Functional Principles.* London: Croom Helm.

TOV, Emmanuel 1981 *The Text-Critical Use of the Septuagint in Biblical Research.* Jerusalem: Simor.

ULRICH, Eugene Charles Jr. 1978 *The Qumran Text of Samuel and Josephus.* (Harvard Semitic Monographs 19.) Missoula: Scholars Press.

VAN DER MERWE, C.H.J. 1990 *The Old Hebrew particle gam: A syntactic-semantic description of gam in Gn-2Kg.* (Arbeiten zu Text und Sprache im alten Testament 34). St. Ottilien: EOS.

VAN DER MERWE, C.H.J. 1991 The Function of Word Order in Old Hebrew - with special reference to cases where a syntagmeme precedes a verb in Joshua. *Journal of Northwest Semitic Languages* 17:129-144.

WALES, Kathleen M. 1983 *Thou* and *You* in Early Modern English: Brown and Gilman Re-appraised. *Studia Linguistica: A Journal of General Linguistics* 37:107-25.

WALTKE, Bruce K. and Michael P. O'CONNOR 1990 *An Introduction to Biblical Hebrew Syntax*. Winona Lake: Eisenbrauns.

WATSON, Wilfred G.E. 1984 *Classical Hebrew Poetry: a Guide to its Techniques*. (Journal for the Study of the Old Testament Supplement Series 26.) Sheffield: JSOT Press.

WEIPPERT, Manfred 1990 Die Petition eines Erntearbeiters aus Meṣad Ḥăšavyāhū und die Syntax althebräischer erzählender Prosa. In *Die Hebräische Bibel und ihre zweifache Nachgeschichte. Festschrift für Rolf Rendtorff zum 65. Geburtstag*, edd. Erhard Blum, Christian Macholz and Ekkehard W. Stegemann. Pp. 449-66. Neukirchen: Neukirchener Verlag.

WHITELAM, Keith W. 1992 King and Kingship. In *Anchor Bible Dictionary* 4:40-48. New York: Doubleday.

WÜRTHWEIN, Ernst 1977, 1984 *Die Bücher der Könige übersetzt und erklärt: 1 Kön. 1-16, 1 Kön. 17-2 Kön. 25*. (Das alte Testament Deutsch Teilband 11,1-2.) Göttingen: Vandenhoeck und Ruprecht.

Subject Index

Index to References to
Biblical and Epigraphic Sources